Register Now for On
to Your Book

M000189814

SPRINGER PUBLISHING COMPANY
CONNECT™

Your print purchase of *Clinical Mental Health Counseling* **includes online access to the contents of your book**—increasing accessibility, portability, and searchability!

Access today at:

http://connect.springerpub.com/content/book/978-0-8261-3108-9 or scan the QR code at the right with your smartphone and enter the access code below.

> 2AU6VE33

Scan here for quick access.

SPC

SPRINGER PUBLISHING COMPANY
View all our products at springerpub.com

Lisa Lopez Levers, PhD, LPCC-S, LPC, CRC, NCC, was the Rev. Francis Philben Endowed Chair in African Studies (2012–2017) and is a Professor of Counselor Education and Human Development in the Department of Educational Foundations and Leadership, School of Education, at Duquesne University. She recently has completed her 30th year of university teaching. Prior to entering the academy, she worked in community mental health for 15 years, counseling extensively with child, adolescent, and adult survivors of trauma as well as with individuals affected by alcohol and drug addictions. Professor Levers has published books, scholarly chapters in textbooks, and articles in peer-reviewed journals regarding issues of relevance to African culture, trauma and disaster, disability issues, and the counseling profession in general. She edited the widely used textbook, *Trauma Counseling: Theories and Interventions*; a second edition is underway. She has been awarded numerous grants and was a Fulbright Scholar at the University of Botswana (2003–2004). She has received a number of awards for her scholarship and service. Professor Levers first traveled to Africa in 1993. She has worked extensively throughout the southern, eastern, and central regions of Africa. Her current scholarly projects involve the HIV and AIDS pandemic in sub-Saharan Africa, especially cultural implications and psychosocial effects; indigenous knowledge; roles of indigenous healers and local authorities in constructing culturally appropriate interventions; the impact of trauma on childhood and adolescent development; adult sequelae associated with early childhood trauma; addictions; designing and developing culturally sensitive community-based services for vulnerable children and adults; psychosocial issues of disability; and building culturally relevant systems of training for helping professionals. She works with marginalized communities in developing culturally sensitive systems of care, creating better access to health/mental health services, designing responses to community trauma, and building community resilience. Her local projects involve trauma-informed community development and a recent county grant (*Neighborhood Resilience Project*, in the Hill District of Pittsburgh) to establish a first-responder service for gun-related violence.

Debra Hyatt-Burkhart, PhD, LPC, NCC, ACS, is an Associate Professor and Director of Program Practices of the Counselor Education and Supervision program at Duquesne University. She has taught at the graduate and undergraduate levels and has provided myriad trainings to community counseling agencies. Dr. Hyatt-Burkhart has published on issues related to positive approaches and responses to working with trauma, clinical supervision, marriage, family, and couples counseling and has presented internationally and nationally on these topics. She has an extensive background in community-based mental health practice, clinical supervision, and administration, with over 30 years of experience in the field.

CLINICAL MENTAL HEALTH COUNSELING
Practicing in Integrated Systems of Care

Lisa Lopez Levers, PhD, LPCC-S, LPC, CRC, NCC
Debra Hyatt-Burkhart, PhD, LPC, NCC, ACS

EDITORS

SPRINGER PUBLISHING COMPANY

Springer Publishing Company, LLC
11 West 42nd Street
New York, NY 10036
www.springerpub.com
http://connect.springerpub.com

Acquisitions Editor: Rhonda Dearborn
Compositor: Amnet Systems

ISBN: 978-0-8261-3107-2
ebook ISBN: 978-0-8261-3108-9
Instructor's Manual: 978-0-8261-3638-1
Instructor's PowerPoints: 978-0-8261-3639-8
DOI: 10.1891/9780826131089

Instructors Materials: Qualified instructors may request supplements by emailing textbook@springerpub.com.

19 20 21 22 / 5 4 3 2 1

The author and the publisher of this Work have made every effort to use sources believed to be reliable to provide information that is accurate and compatible with the standards generally accepted at the time of publication. The author and publisher shall not be liable for any special, consequential, or exemplary damages resulting, in whole or in part, from the readers' use of, or reliance on, the information contained in this book. The publisher has no responsibility for the persistence or accuracy of URLs for external or third-party Internet websites referred to in this publication and does not guarantee that any content on such websites is, or will remain, accurate or appropriate.

Library of Congress Cataloging-in-Publication Data

Names: Levers, Lisa Lopez, editor. | Hyatt-Burkhart, Debra, editor.
Title: Clinical mental health counseling : practicing in integrated systems
    of care / Lisa Lopez Levers, Debra Hyatt-Burkhart, editors.
Other titles: Clinical mental health counseling (Levers)
Description: New York, NY : Springer Publishing Company, LLC, [2020] |
    Includes bibliographical references and index.
Identifiers: LCCN 2019018714 (print) | LCCN 2019019226 (ebook) | ISBN
    9780826131089 (eBook) | ISBN 9780826131072 (print : alk. paper) | ISBN
    9780826136381 (instructors manual) | ISBN 9780826136398 (instructors
    powerpoints)
Subjects: | MESH: Counseling | Mental Health | Delivery of Health Care,
    Integrated
Classification: LCC RC466 (ebook) | LCC RC466 (print) | NLM WM 55 | DDC
    362.2/04256—dc23
LC record available at https://lccn.loc.gov/2019018714

Contact us to receive discount rates on bulk purchases.
We can also customize our books to meet your needs.
For more information please contact: sales@springerpub.com

Lisa Lopez Levers: https://orcid.org/0000-0002-7723-6893
Debra Hyatt-Burkhart: https://orcid.org/0000-0001-8414-8026

Printed in the United States of America.

CONTENTS

CONTRIBUTORS

Ngozi Jane-Frances Chima Adaralegba, MBBS
Department of Rehabilitation and Health Services
University of North Texas
Denton, Texas

Nancy Fair, PhD
Private Practice
Pittsburgh, Pennsylvania

Latoya Haynes-Thoby, PhD
Assistant Professor
University of Florida
University Park, Pennsylvania

Debra Hyatt-Burkhart, PhD, LPC, NCC, ACS
Associate Professor, Department of Counseling, Psychology, and Special Education
Duquesne University
Pittsburgh, Pennsylvania

Patrick Igbeka, MS
Department of Rehabilitation and Health Services
University of North Texas
Denton, Texas

Sara P. Johnston, PhD, CRC
Associate Professor
Drake University
Des Moines, Iowa

Rebekah Knight, PhD, PHR
Lecturer
University of North Texas
Denton, Texas

Lisa Lopez Levers, PhD, LPCC-S, LPC, CRC, NCC
Professor of Counseling and Human Development,
Department of Educational Foundations and Leadership
Duquesne University
Pittsburgh, Pennsylvania

Qiwei Li, MS
Department of Rehabilitation and Health Services
University of North Texas
Denton, Texas

Maidei Machina, MOTR/L (Hons)
Occupational Therapist
Department of Geriatric Medicine
Westmead Hospital
Sydney, Australia

Regina R. Moro, PhD
Associate Professor
Boise State University
Boise, Idaho

Elias Mpofu, PhD, DEd, CRC
Department of Rehabilitation
and Health Services
University of North Texas
Denton, Texas;
University of Johannesburg, Auckland
Campus, South Africa;
University of Sydney, Cumberland
Campus, Australia

Eric W. Owens, PhD, LPC, NCC, ACS
Associate Professor and Department
Chairperson, Department of
Counselor Education
West Chester University
West Chester, Pennsylvania

Ratanpriya Sharma, MSED
PhD Student
University of Miami
Miami, Florida

Rex Stockton, EdD
Chancellor's Professor
Indiana University
Bloomington, Indiana

Vilia M. Tarvydas, PhD, CRC
Professor Emerita
University of Iowa
Iowa City, Iowa

Boya Wang, BAppSC (Phty)(Hons)
Physical Therapist, Department of
Geriatric Medicine
Westmead Hospital
Sydney, Australia

Justin Watts, PhD, NCC, CRC
Assistant Professor, Department of
Rehabilitation Health Services
University of North Texas
Denton, Texas

**Carlos P. Zalaquett, PhD, MA,
Lic., LMHC**
Professor, Department of Educational
Psychology, Counseling, and Special
Education
The Pennsylvania State University
University Park, Pennsylvania

PREFACE

This graduate-level, introductory textbook provides instructors and students with a comprehensive overview of the profession of clinical mental health counseling (CMHC). Designed to cover the Council for the Accreditation of Counseling and Related Educational Programs (CACREP) 2016 Standards and to provide an inclusive overview of the work of professional counselors, this book offers an in-depth exploration of the professional knowledge, skills, current issues, and dynamic trends in professional counseling that are essential parts of the educational journey of emerging clinicians.

More than just an overview of topics that eventually will be covered in entire courses, this text is structured to address essential subjects that may not be given sufficient coverage in other classes. We have approached this text with an intent to provide readers with practical, applicable, real-world information upon which they can build throughout their programs of study and practice. Issues such as strength-based approaches, the various settings in which clinical mental health counselors may practice, record keeping and documentation, advocacy, professional roles, third-party payers and managed care, and self-care and professional development are vitally important to new counselors, and these subjects often are glanced over in an information-packed curriculum. In addition, we have covered the topics of crisis, disaster, and trauma, which constitute relatively new areas of emphasis within the CACREP Standards.

Conceptually, this book looks at the history, roles, functions, settings, and contemporary issues of counseling through the lens of human ecological and integrated systems-of-care approaches. Within the scope of a contemporary counseling ethos and its related practices, the importance of these perspectives cannot be emphasized enough. Unique to this particular textbook, and in juxtaposition to an ecological perspective of the individual, a focus on integrated systems of care in clinical mental health endeavors provides students with knowledge and skills that can help them to move seamlessly into the current world of work as clinical mental health counselors. Because one of the underlying structures of each chapter is to move the student from an understanding of theory to an emphasis on elements of practice, the book provides students with ample opportunities to integrate theoretical concepts with real-world examples, which vary across chapters, in the form of case illustrations, tips from the field, and relevant programming issues. All case illustrations are either fictitious or based on composites of likely client scenarios.

An important aim, for every chapter in the textbook, is that students can benefit from the wealth of experience provided by the qualified clinicians and academics who have authored the chapters. We further believe that certain professional issues resonate strongly with the preservice training of CMHCs, and these concerns have been woven into the topical areas of the various chapters throughout the textbook. Robust discussions of these essential factors have been integrated into the chapters, and we believe that if CMHC students are afforded an early introduction to such key strands of information, it can enhance their overall learning experience.

We have thought a lot about the "usability" of this textbook, especially as this relates to new graduate students who recently have matriculated into a master's program in CMHC and are taking an introductory foundations course. The points that we believe are important include the following: (a) relatively short chapters that strike a balance between being accessible and intellectually stimulating; (b) chapters that end with additional resources (also included in an instructors' manual) that pertain to the specific topical areas of the chapter; (c) a variety of profession-relevant topics that anticipate advanced coursework, but at the same time, allow the new student to construct a vision of how the various strands intersect in ways that matter to the work of the clinical mental health counselor; (d) chapters that are informed by contributing authors' practice and research in CMHC; and (e) content that is linked to the current landscape of integrated healthcare. Finally, instructors can find a supplementary instructor's manual with useful resources, discussion questions, activities, exercises, and test bank items, as well as key PowerPoint slides aimed at helping students with this integration of the material. *Qualified instructors may obtain access to supplements by emailing textbook@springerpub.com.*

ORGANIZATION OF THE TEXTBOOK

This textbook is comprised of five sections, spanning the following clusters of CMHC-relevant information: (a) Introduction to Professional Counseling and Clinical Mental Health Counseling, (b) Working with Clients, (c) Practice Issues, (d) Working within Systems, and (e) Client-Care and Self-Care Practices. A brief description of each chapter is provided below, along with the chapter-related CACREP Standards (a one-page table mapping the CACREP Standards that are covered in each chapter is located in the *Instructor's Manual*).

Section I: Introduction to Professional Counseling and Clinical Mental Health Counseling

1. **Introduction to Clinical Mental Health Counseling and the Underlying Dynamics of Practice**
   This chapter provides an introduction to Clinical Mental Health Counseling (CMHC). Important underlying dynamics of CMHC practice are identified and explored. The chapter offers a foundation for understanding the individual from a bioecological perspective, as well as for appreciating the delivery of mental

health services from more contemporary community-based and systems-of-care models. This chapter sets the stage for understanding important dynamics of CMHC practice that are relevant across all of the chapters in the textbook.

2. **Context for Understanding and Beginning the Practice of Clinical Mental Health Counseling**

This chapter provides a historical overview of the counseling profession and its developmental trajectory, emphasizing the origins of mental health treatment and the reemergence of counseling as a wellness-based approach. Discussion is provided concerning the push toward a pathogenic model of conceptualizing mental illness and the subsequent, current resurgence of a strength-based notion of care. A brief overview of the major theories of counseling is provided as a means for understanding the development of counseling as a unique and separate field from psychology, psychiatry, and social work. The chapter offers specific definitions of counseling and practice as a professional counselor; it identifies the specializations within the counseling field, the range of employment opportunities and the current labor market, and how counseling is integrated within a system-of-care approach. Basic information regarding counselor licensure, certification, and accreditation is provided. The following CACREP standards are addressed in this chapter:

CACREP 2016 2F1.a, 2F1.b, 2F1.c, 2F1.g, 2F1.h, 2F5.a, 5C1.a, 5C1.b
CACREP 2009 1.a

Section II: Working with Clients

3. **Allied and Clinical Mental Health Systems-of-Care and Strength-Based Approaches**

This chapter covers the concept of systems-of-care and the movement toward integrated treatment for individuals and families. The trend toward multidisciplinary, consumer-driven treatment is discussed, with an emphasis on how it promotes natural supports and casts a wide net to involve stakeholders. The chapter focuses on using strength-based, salutogenic concepts to improve consumer ownership and investment, which leads to greater efficacy of treatment. The following CACREP standards are addressed in this chapter:

CACREP 2F1.b, 2F1.c, 2F5.b

4. **Case Conceptualization, Assessment, and Diagnosis**

This chapter introduces the student to conceptualizing clients' presenting problems from a holistic, strength-based perspective. It explains the connections between the ability to conceptualize a case and the use of effective assessment strategies that eventually lead to clinicians becoming competent diagnosticians; within this context, the chapter also addresses dual diagnosis as both an area of clinical focus and a common tension. The chapter emphasizes the ability to assess client dangerousness, offering a basic description of how to determine when clients' aggressive behavior is escalating, when the potential for harmful behavior exists, and when the clinician should intervene. The information in this chapter is intended as a beginning point for newer counseling students to start thinking about these important clinical issues. This chapter anticipates a more advanced course on diagnosis, assessment, and treatment planning, preparing students to be ready to engage this material at a higher level in such courses. The chapter focuses on the skills necessary for developing basic case conceptualization skills. The following CACREP standards are addressed in this chapter:

CACREP 2F5.b, 2F5.g, 2F7.a, 2F7.b, 2F7.b, 2F7.c, 2F7.e, 2F7.j

5. **Crisis, Disaster, and Trauma Issues in Clinical Mental Health Counseling**
This chapter provides an overview of how clinical mental health counselors work with crisis, disaster, and trauma issues. A focus is placed on the pragmatic, neurobiological, and existential natures of crisis, disaster, and trauma along with the ways that these dynamics are implicated in numerous counseling scenarios. Basic crisis intervention skills are presented, disaster response is discussed, and the importance of understanding trauma is emphasized. The chapter anticipates that students will have an advanced course that covers these important topics more fully. The following CACREP standards are addressed in this chapter:

CACREP 2016 2F3.g, 2F5.m, 2F7.d, 5C2.f

Section III: Practice Issues

6. **Community-Based Mental Health Counseling, Recovery Models, and Multidisciplinary Collaboration**
This chapter covers counseling services that typically are offered in community, in-home, and private practice office settings. Issues that are addressed relate to consumer confidentiality, maintaining respectful relationships in a variety of settings or the consumer's home, counselor safety issues, and boundary issues. The chapter devotes attention to the often-problematic relationships between community-based providers who are working simultaneously with addictions and mental health issues. It focuses on working with providers from other systems, the difference between addictions provider regulations and MH regulations, how to communicate amid and navigate strict confidentiality regulations, and how to provide a recovery-based approach that bridges the gap. The chapter addresses some of the common stressors and problems found in interdisciplinary collaboration and offers suggestions for increasing success and cooperation among providers. Additional pertinent issues are addressed that concern releases of information, consumer-driven/consumer-friendly provider meetings, how to work with schools, and how to empower consumers to establish a network of support that includes their natural supports and providers alike. The following CACREP standards are addressed in this chapter:

CACREP 2016 2F1.b, 2FL.c, 2F1.i, 5C2.a, 5C2.c, 5C2.e, 5C2.l, 5C2.m, 5C3.d
CACREP 2009 2.a

7. **Record Keeping and Documentation**

   This chapter emphasizes the importance of appropriate record-keeping practices, policy issues, and related regulations. It includes a discussion of the Health Insurance Portability and Accountability Act (HIPAA), progress noting, treatment planning, and what happens when you and/or your records are subpoenaed. Connections between adequate record keeping and legal/ethical issues of the profession are illuminated. The following CACREP standards are addressed in this chapter:

   CACREP 2016 2F1.i, 5C2.l, 5C2.m, 5C3.c
   CACREP 2009 2.m

8. **Legal Issues, Ethics of Practice, and Counselor Behaviors**

   This chapter focuses on the legal and ethical issues salient to clinical mental health counselors. Specifically, the chapter addresses the latest American Counseling Association (ACA) ethical code, 2009 and 2016 CACREP standards, licensure and certification, mandated reporting, confidentiality, duty to warn, and scope of practice. The chapter also focuses on the responsibility of counselors to engage in ethically based practice. Covered topics include values clarification, bias assessment, boundary awareness and maintenance, mindfulness, and the importance of self-reflection. The following CACREP standards are addressed in this chapter:

   CACREP 2016 2F1.i, 5C2.l
   CACREP 2009 2.1

Section IV: Working within Systems

9. **Client Advocacy Access, Equity, and Resilience**

   This chapter discusses the strategic positionality of the counselor as an advocate for addressing social and institutional barriers that reduce client access, equity, and success. Methodologies for and approaches to client care and advocacy are identified, and the ways that they foster resilience and growth are emphasized. The chapter also addresses strategies to promote client understanding of and access to a variety of community-based resources. The following CACREP standards are addressed in this chapter:

   CACREP 2016 2F1.e, 2F2.h, 2F3.i, 2F5.k, 5C3.e

10. **Professional Roles and Functions in Clinical Mental Health Counseling**

    This chapter takes an in-depth look at a variety of functions, counseling and administrative roles, and tasks that may be required of counselors in clinical mental health settings. Pertinent issues include balancing consumer care with administrative duties, balancing employee well-being with productivity standards/financial concerns, ethical marketing and recruitment, and remaining current in the field while in nonclinical roles. The following CACREP standards are addressed in this chapter:

    CACREP 2016 1.b, 1.i
    CACREP 2009 2.a, 2.1

11. **Contexts of Cultural and Systemic Influence**

   This chapter addresses multicultural issues in the provision of CMHC. Specific topics include a discussion of diversity, culturally competent counselor traits, and barriers to and the strengths that can be found in working with diverse populations. The chapter further explores the connections between culturally competent care and the potential role for clinical mental health counselors in ascertaining the systemic need for new agency- and community-based programs. The student is introduced to basic tenets of designing and developing new programs aimed at meeting the clinical mental health needs of diverse and varied clients. The following CACREP standards are addressed in this chapter:

   CACREP 2016 2F1.b, 2F2.c, 2F2.e, 2F2.h, 5C2.j

12. **Advocacy, Third-Party Payers, and Managed Care**

   This chapter addresses the counselor's role as being an important advocate for the profession. Discussions offer information about professional counseling organizations, including membership benefits, activities, services, and ways these organizations promote the development of the profession, not just the counselor. The chapter also demystifies the issues of payment for counseling services, specifically third-party billing, managed care, medical assistance programs, and other issues therein. The importance of government legislation and public policy with respect to the profession also are addressed.

   CACREP 2016 1.f, 1.g,

   CACREP 2009 2.k, 2.m, 2.i

Section V: Client-Care and Self-Care Practices

13. **Clinical Supervision and Professional Development**

   This chapter provides a brief overview of models of clinical supervision. It also offers a brief discussion of best practices, common struggles, and a salutogenic- or wellness-based approach to supervision, emphasizing how the latter complements parallel treatment interventions with consumers. The chapter urges counselor trainees to develop continuing education and continued professional development as a part of their career-pathway planning. The discussion emphasizes the importance of remaining current, concerning clinical counseling issues, as an ethical issue that is inherent in being a professional. The following CACREP standards are addressed in this chapter:

   CACREP 2016 2F1.l, 2F1.m

14. **Counselor Self-Care and Personal Development**

   This chapter addresses issues related to counselor self-care and maintaining a healthy ability to continue with the work. The issues that are addressed include vicarious responses to trauma (both positive and negative), stress management, potential for burnout, and maintaining work/life balance. The following CACREP standards are addressed in this chapter:

   CACREP 2016 2F1.k, 2F1.1

   CACREP 2009

15. **New Frontiers for Clinical Mental Health Counselors**

    This final chapter summarizes pertinent issues discussed throughout the text. In addition, the chapter identifies new frontiers for counselor practice, such as new opportunities for counselors within the Veterans Administration and TRICARE system, in hospital settings, in hospice programs and assisted living environments, in school-based programs, and in college counseling centers. The chapter also addresses the influence of technology upon the counseling profession, discussing Internet-based services, such as virtual counseling and tele-counseling. The chapter provides a discussion of the ethical, legal, and practice concerns related to this developing branch of counseling.

We believe that the structure of this textbook offers a cogent pedagogical format for enabling new master's-level CMHC students to gain awareness and understanding of some of the most relevant aspects of practice in CMHC. We have designed the layout of the textbook so that information is presented in what we consider to be a developmentally appropriate trajectory for those students wishing to enter the profession and to begin their careers. The contemporary clinical landscape is perhaps more complex than ever before in the history of our CMHC profession. We therefore dare to hope that this textbook can contribute to igniting the earliest stage of CMHC preservice training in transformative ways that spark passion and authenticity for the important clinical work to be undertaken by the newest generation of CMHC students.

Lisa Lopez Levers
Debra Hyatt-Burkhart

SECTION I

INTRODUCTION TO PROFESSIONAL COUNSELING AND CLINICAL MENTAL HEALTH COUNSELING

INTRODUCTION TO CLINICAL MENTAL HEALTH COUNSELING AND THE UNDERLYING DYNAMICS OF PRACTICE

LISA LOPEZ LEVERS | DEBRA HYATT-BURKHART

This chapter provides an introduction to clinical mental health counseling (CMHC). Important underlying dynamics of CMHC practice are identified and explored. The chapter offers a foundation for understanding the individual from a bioecological perspective, as well as for appreciating the delivery of mental health services from more contemporary community-based and systems-of-care models. This chapter sets the stage for understanding important dynamics of CMHC practice that are relevant across all of the chapters in the textbook.

The following Council for Accreditation of Counseling and Related Educational Programs (CACREP) standards are addressed in this chapter:
CACREP 2016:
2F1.a, 2F1.b, 2F3.a, 2F3.f, 2F3.i, 2F5.a, 5C1.a, 5C1.b
CACREP 2009:
2G1.a, 2G3f, 2G3.h, 2G5.a, 2G5.d, 2G3.h, 2G5.a

LEARNING OBJECTIVES

After reviewing this chapter, the reader should be able to:

1. Develop an introductory awareness of the major constructs and dynamics pertaining to the practice of CMHC;

2. Identify the relevance of a bioecological perspective concerning individuals who seek CMHC services; and,

3. Explain the importance of community-based and systems-of-care models in the practice of CMHC.

A PRELIMINARY INTRODUCTION TO THE CMHC FIELD

The purpose of this chapter is to offer an overview of the profession of CMHC and to do so in a way that illuminates some of the relevant dynamics that underlie the practice of CMHC. Details about the counseling profession, and specifically CMHC, are provided in Chapter 2 of this textbook. In the current chapter, we present content that links the practice of CMHC with the importance of an ecological perspective of the individual and to the current landscape of integrated healthcare. Understanding this link is integral to understanding the context for the profession that is presented in Chapter 2; further, it is relevant to the clinical practice and professional issues that are discussed in every subsequent chapter in this book. The clinical landscape has changed dramatically since the early genesis of the counseling profession. The field has moved from the psychodynamic influences of the late 19th and early 20th century pioneers, to both behavioral and humanistic influences by the mid-20th century, to later systemic and more community-based approaches to care. We believe that it is important to orient the preservice training of clinical mental health counselors to an understanding of these important changes and trends and how these dynamics have taken root in practice and service provision.

We have framed these issues, in this first chapter, as advanced organizers to assist students in anticipating how these important matters interface with various aspects of their CMHC training. Discussions of these essential factors appear in the following sections of this introductory chapter: (a) Contemporary Counseling Ethos, (b) Human Ecology and Systems, (c) Professional and Therapeutic Tensions and Dynamics, and (d) Relevance of Understanding the Council for the Accreditation of Counseling and Related Educational Programs Standards. We believe that if new master's-level students are afforded an early introduction to these key strands of information, which have been integrated throughout the chapters of this textbook, it can enhance their overall learning experience. These discussions are followed by a brief integrative summary of the chapter, which echoes the overarching message that it is important for CMHCs to understand the big picture and the underlying dynamics and tensions of the CMHC field before drilling down to other basic and pertinent details about the profession.

CONTEMPORARY COUNSELING ETHOS

In its beginnings, the counseling profession stressed a client-centered, humanistic, biopsychosocial, and strength-based approach to working with people. Along the pathway toward the field of counseling developing a more robust professional identity, this trajectory was detoured, necessarily, toward a more problem-focused, medical/illness-based modality of treatment. We say "necessarily," because the playing field for counselors began to be defined more narrowly, beginning in the 1960s, as a result of licensure regulations in other psychosocial helping professions. This increasingly became the case, in the 1970s through the 1990s, due to the advent of managed care and third-party reimbursement requirements (managed care and third-party reimbursement are discussed in detail in Chapter 12 of this textbook). Eventually, if counselors wished to have parity with other helping professions, it was necessary to push for licensure, and the process required a stronger diagnostic and pathology-focused orientation in order to meet the demands of regulatory bodies and to fit within the established view of mental health treatment (counselor licensure is discussed in detail in Chapter 8 of this textbook, and professional advocacy issues are addressed in Chapter 12). This is not to suggest an either/ or approach, in terms of counseling being *either* wellness *or* psychopathology oriented, because we believe that it functions as both (the professional roles of clinical mental health counselors are discussed in detail in Chapter 10).

In various chapters of this textbook, we address the tensions that exist between the potential benefits and detriments of diagnosis. However, with the dawn of the 21st century, we see a strengthening movement to return to the roots of counseling as a collaborative, salutogenic, systems-sensitive endeavor, which is dynamic enough to account for the entire continuum of human experience. Whereas psychology focuses more on the individual, and social work focuses more on systems, we view professional counseling as a unique enterprise in that professional counselors often focus on the interface between the individual and his or her multiple environments, inclusive of social systems and culture. We believe that this is a strength of the counseling model that has not been highlighted enough. Following this organic aspect of our professional history, we endorse the movement toward returning to our more existentially oriented roots, with multiple emphases on authenticity in and the positionality of the counselor–client relationship in the here and now.

▓ HUMAN ECOLOGY AND SYSTEMS

We believe that an ecological perspective of the individual, along with a focus on the integrated systems of care in clinical mental health endeavors, provides clinical mental health counselors with knowledge and skills that can help them to work and innovate more dynamically in their practice as clinical mental health counselors. In the following subsections, we offer brief descriptions of the bioecological model of human development and integrated healthcare and behavioral healthcare models. These discussions directly connect with related topic-specific discussions in the subsequent chapters of this textbook.

Bioecological Model of Human Development

For many decades, counseling, psychological, and psychiatric services have focused almost exclusively on the individual. It was not until about the 1970s that professional attention shifted to the important reciprocal dynamics between the individual's personal scope-of-existence and broader-yet-interconnected environments. Bronfenbrenner (1979, 2004) first developed his human ecological systems theory in the 1960s, as he was assisting the federal government in the design of the *Head Start Program*. Later in his life, he added a temporal component to his theory and renamed it as the *Bioecological Model or Theory*.

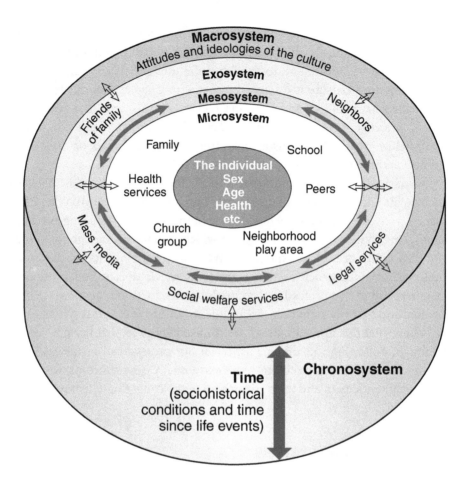

FIGURE 1.1 Bronfenbrenner's bioecological model of human development.

SOURCE: Santrock, J. W. (2011). *A topical approach to life-span development*. New York, NY: McGraw-Hill Education.

The bioecological model posits that every individual operates within multiple environments and that the individual is nested within a series of proximal (closer or nearby) as well as more distal (farther away or at a greater distance) social and cultural systems of influence. Bronfenbrenner (1979, 2004) identified the following levels of environmental influences on and in interaction with human development: the microsystem, the mesosystem, the exosystem, the macrosystem, and the chronosystem. As illustrated in Figure 1.1, each of these environmental levels has distinct influences on the developing person. Although Bronfenbrenner's initial research was oriented toward the developing child, as his theory evolved, especially with the addition of time as an important element, the model has been considered to be applicable across the lifespan.

The defining aspect of the microsystem encompasses the individual, inclusive of the particular individual's attributes, temperament, age, gender, and other personal characteristics. But the microsystem also comprises the environmental context that includes social systems and social spaces that are most proximal to the individual. These include social units such as family, school, workplace, peers, close friends, and some healthcare providers; the microsystem also includes proximal spaces such as places of worship, community centers, the nearby neighborhood, and play or work areas.

The mesosystem constitutes any person, social unit, or space that facilitates interaction between systems within the microsystem and also that facilitates interaction between the microsystem and the exosystem. This could include a teacher's conference between a child's parents and the school (both within the microsystem); it also could involve a primary healthcare physician (microsystem) referring a patient needing a procedure to a specialist (mesosystem), who then arranges for clinic or hospital care (exosystem) for the patient.

The exosystem includes social influencers who are a bit more distal, such as friends of the family, neighbors who live a few blocks away rather than next door, the mass media, and social or legal services with which the individual or family may be involved. The social units comprising the exosystem do not have as direct an influence on the individual as those in the microsystem, but these more distal influencers still can have a profound systemic effect on the person.

The macrosystem, which is most distal to the individual, encompasses attributes of the society. These include social attitudes, ideologies, and cultural norms of the particular society at large. It is this feature of the bioecological model that provides its cultural robustness or elasticity. Depending upon the culture in which the individual lives, the macrosystemic features may have differing impacts upon how the other systems influence the person, including at the microsystemic level.

Finally, the chronosystem comprises temporal influences upon the individual. This includes both personal time and sociohistorical time. In other words, the chronosystem represents both the lifespan of the individual, from birth to death, as well as the sociohistorical era in which the person lives. Examples that illustrate the latter would be the impact of the great American depression on people living in the United States during that time (beginning in 1929 and lasting approximately a decade), or the effects of the technological era on digital natives living during the current time—and the sociohistorical influences may be different among people living in a developed or modern context versus those living in a developing or traditional context.

Several constructs are important in gleaning a further appreciation of the elegance of this model. First is the notion of reciprocity. The bidirectional arrows shown in Figure 1.1 represent the reciprocal dynamic between the individual and the various systemic environments: The individual has an impact on his or her environment at the same time that the environment has an impact on the individual. Concomitant with the importance of an awareness of reciprocity is an understanding of risk factors and protective factors. The potential for risk factors exists across all of the biopsychosocial systems for every human being. Risk factors may be as pervasive as poverty or as singular as someone who is ill not having transportation to a doctor's appointment on a particular day. The potential also exists, in the same way, for protective factors across the person's multiple environments. Protective factors may include nurturing parents, reliable and supportive social contacts, or equitable access to education and healthcare. Issues pertaining to risk factors and protective factors may have a direct relationship with social justice issues, which also are relevant to the work of clinical mental health counselors. Some of the very groups of people experiencing a greater proportion of risk factors (e.g., poverty and community violence) also may experience the least environmental protective factors (e.g., access to education and access to adequate healthcare). The impact of such social inequities for individual clients and within their social networks are important considerations for clinical mental health counselors (matters of access, equity, culture, and systemic influences are discussed in detail in Chapters 9 and 11).

TIP FROM THE FIELD 1.1

UNDERSTANDING RISK AND PROTECTIVE FACTORS

If we think about the clients we serve, the importance of understanding risk and protective factors begins to come into sharper focus. If we are able to identify certain risk factors faced by clients, we may be able to find ways or resources for mitigating or even extinguishing these risk factors. Likewise, if we work with clients who have few or no existing protective factors, we can find ways to advocate for clients' needs to be met. Understanding these elements of the bioecological model leads to a brief discussion of another important aspect of the contemporary counseling ethos, especially to the practice of CMHC, that is, the importance of advocacy and social justice.

Advocacy and Social Justice

Client advocacy, especially relative to social justice, has gained increasing importance in the professional counseling field over the last several decades (Kiselica & Robinson, 2011; Lewis, Ratts, Paladino, & Toporek, 2011; Ratts & Hutchins, 2009; Toporek, 2011). These two systemic concerns are interwoven throughout various chapters in this textbook and involve advocating for clients, particularly vulnerable and marginalized clients, around the intersectionality of race/ethnicity, gender, ability, and class/income issues. An awareness of and sensitivity to these important cultural humility concerns (Hook, Davis, Owen, & DeBlaere, 2018) are paramount to the work of all helping professionals, including clinical mental health counselors.

Integrated Healthcare and Behavioral Healthcare Models

Integrative healthcare, the incorporation of behavioral health practices into medical services, including complementary and alternative medical (CAM) practices (e.g., acupuncture, tai chi, yoga, medicinal herbs, and mindfulness techniques), has been a focus of public health efforts for at least a decade (American Psychiatric Association [APA] & Academy of Psychosomatic Medicine [APM], 2016). Integrated healthcare is broadly viewed as a mechanism for improving individuals' experiences of care (Heath, Wise, & Reynolds, 2013). The President's New Freedom Commission on Mental Health (2008) final report highlighted the need for increased coordination among primary care physicians, mental health providers, and other stakeholders, such as schools and community organizations, in order to improve treatment outcomes for those experiencing mental health issues. As the field of professional counseling has continued to respond to this call for integrative services, we have seen the development of a number of approaches to achieving this goal.

Integration of services generally occurs in one of two ways. One way is that mental health services are integrated into physical health services. An example of this approach is that of a patient whose primary complaint to his or her physician is fatigue, sleeplessness, and an overall sense of depression. Most physicians in this case likely would order tests to check for physical/medical causes for the symptoms (e.g., thyroid functioning, blood counts); this has been the traditional allopathic or biomedical approach to providing care. In a more integrated approach, the physician also might delve into the patient's psychosocial systems, explore current problems, and offer a referral for counseling services related to the patient's life circumstances and stressors. The physician would then follow up with the patient, the counselor, and any other providers who have joined the treatment team to coordinate and monitor progress toward the goal of reducing symptoms and improving functioning. An alternative approach to care occurs essentially in reverse of what was just presented. An individual seeks services from a counselor because of the same presenting issues of depression. Here, the counselor would proceed with developing a treatment plan to help the client improve his or her functioning and would refer the client to a physician in order to rule out possible medical causes for the complaints. This integration of treatment, in whichever direction it originates, helps to reduce common issues, such as failure to treat comorbid physical and mental health conditions, lack of access to care due to stigma, and an overall underutilization of the mental health system (Butler et al., 2008).

CASE ILLUSTRATION 1.1

LISTENING TO THE CLIENT

Mrs. Smith was referred to the community mental health clinic upon discharge from a psychiatric unit. She was assigned to a licensed clinical mental health counselor, Isabella, who conducted a thorough intake evaluation. Although Mrs. Smith already carried a diagnosis of Schizophrenia, Isabella did not feel that Mrs. Smith fully met the Diagnostic and Statistical Manual of Mental Disorders (DSM) criteria for the disorder. In addition, Isabella, who had a specialty in psychiatric rehabilitation and a lot of experience working with severe psychiatric disorders, did not find Mrs. Smith's demeanor and behaviors to fit, qualitatively, with what Isabella had come to understand from previous clients' lived experiences of the disorder. At the end of the appointment, they rescheduled a counseling session for the following week, as well as an appointment to see the agency psychiatrist immediately following the counseling appointment. At that same time, Isabella asked Mrs. Smith to bring her prescription bottles with her to the next appointment, as she was unable to tell Isabella the names of her medications. Isabella was shocked the following week when Mrs. Smith brought her meds to the appointment in a shopping bag. Isabella waded through the many medications, writing their names into the client file so that the psychiatrist could see them, but also noting to herself that some of the meds were contraindicated with some of the other meds and that there was a high risk of potentiation of side effects between some of the prescriptions.

Alarmed, Isabella reported to the psychiatrist between Mrs. Smith's counseling session and her psychiatric-intake appointment. The psychiatrist shared Isabella's concern, and they agreed that Isabella would call Mrs. Smith's primary care physician (Isabella already had obtained signed consent from the client). When Isabella called the physician to inquire about whether he was aware of the number of medications that had been prescribed to the client, he was rude and demeaning and kept asking "What is your degree?" The physician abruptly terminated the conversation without providing the requested information. Although the physician had been abrasive, Isabella knew that it was in the client's best interest that she not take it personally, and she decided to pursue the most professional course of action. Isabella waited until Mrs. Smith was finished with the psychiatrist. She then asked Mrs. Smith to remain in Isabella's office, while Isabella consulted with the psychiatrist and explained to the psychiatrist what had transpired. The psychiatrist immediately went into action, ordering appropriate blood testing for Mrs. Smith and having her stop some of the psychotropic medications. Subsequently, based upon the results of the tests, the psychiatrist had Mrs. Smith stop all of her medications, with the exception of her mediation for diabetes. The psychiatrist and counselor continued to monitor Mrs. Smith, along with physicians to whom the psychiatrist had referred Mrs. Smith, and they watched her condition improve. Finally, one day some time later, when Mrs. Smith arrived for her counseling appointment, with tears in her eyes, she hugged Isabella in the waiting room and said "Thank you! You have given me my life back. I tried to tell them that I wasn't Schizophrenic, that I just needed my diabetes medication. But they wouldn't listen to me. They just put me in the hospital. But you listened to me, and now I'm me again. I have my life back."

The Affordable Healthcare Act of 2012 and subsequent Medicaid expansion efforts in many states allowed for the development of programs that reconceptualize the provision of services. Programs that incorporated community-based services, interdisciplinary treatment teams, in-home family services, and innovative technologies have been developed to bridge the gaps among all of the treatments needed for those who are experiencing mental health issues (Mechanic, 2012). Community-based treatments fill the need created by the closure of residential facilities and state psychiatric hospitals, upon which society previously relied, to assist those with mental health issues.

It is important to note that integrated care not only is happening between the realms of physical and mental health. School and mental health partnerships are increasing the number of children and adolescents who receive mental health services by reaching them within the school setting. These partnerships are helping to reach ethnic minority groups, those without transportation to traditional services, individuals who may be dissuaded by stigma, and those without financial resources (Acharya et al., 2017). Schools provide an avenue by which to reach millions of children each day. When the partnership is expanded to include physical health, case management services, and family interventions, among others, children have a greater chance to achieve lasting improvement than if they received stand-alone treatment outside of the school environment.

By combining case management/social work services with professional counseling interventions, medication management, physical health treatment, and social/community connection services, we can approach an individual's needs holistically, which bodes for better outcomes. When we consider the biopsychosocial nature of human existence, we also must consider that client issues do not occur exclusively in one domain. In order to facilitate lasting recovery, we must employ treatment interventions that span domains and provide a comprehensive view of the issues presented. This integrated approach to treatment is referenced across chapters of this textbook.

PROFESSIONAL AND THERAPEUTIC TENSIONS AND DYNAMICS

We believe that it is important for CMHC students to develop an understanding, as early in their training as possible, of some of the field-based tensions that they eventually will encounter. Therefore, each chapter in this textbook identifies professional and therapeutic tensions and dynamics associated with working with clients in the CMHC context. For example, in the chapter on self-care, the author addresses how empathy for one's clients presents the tension between a necessity for effectiveness in treatment and the possibility of vicarious traumatization. We believe that by looking at such clinical tensions or challenges in the early stages of training, counseling students can develop a greater awareness of and sensitivity to the kinds of dilemmas, and potential ethical dilemmas, that are sure to arise with clients at the time that the students begin their clinical fieldwork experiences. We further believe that exploring the construct of "clinical tensions" is highly relevant, as it offers insight into how counselors negotiate the often-taut spaces between, and maintain some semblance of balance within, the competing interests that often intricately affect the lived experiences of clients. We have identified relevant tensions, and these are discussed within the text of each chapter.

RELEVANCE OF UNDERSTANDING THE COUNCIL FOR THE ACCREDITATION OF COUNSELING AND RELATED EDUCATIONAL PROGRAMS STANDARDS

The CACREP (2016) is the major accrediting body for counselor education programs (CEPs). We believe that it is critical for entry-level students to understand the logic of the educational, professional, and ethical standards that they are expected to learn, master, and embrace. Therefore, each chapter in this textbook highlights content-relevant CACREP Standards, emphasizing both the 2009 and the 2016 Standards. Our logic in asking authors to address the CACREP standards that are related to the specific chapter is twofold. First, our intention is to offer as much support as possible, within the limitations of a textbook, to instructors in meeting the standards in this course. Second, we believe that it assists students to acquire the requisite competencies if they can understand what is being required of them in the process of becoming competent and ethical practitioners. We have identified both 2009 and 2016 standards because some programs may still be making the transition. Students and instructors alike can compare the two sets regarding each topic, viewing them as a tension or on a developmental continuum, identifying the similarities and differences, and from a certain perspective, understanding some of the nuanced ways in which the counseling profession has evolved. An additional emphasis is in assisting the students to understand how important it is for CEPs to adhere to the CACREP Standards.

CONCLUSION

This chapter has offered an introduction to some of the key elements that epitomize the CMHC profession and that serve as underlying dynamics in CMHC practice. In so doing, the chapter also has mapped out the most efficacious constructs involving the practice of CMHC and that appear across the subsequent chapters in this textbook. By focusing on a preliminary orientation to current CMHC concerns, trends, settings, and practice-based issues, the major aim of this chapter was to provide an impressionistic picture of contemporary clinical mental health counselor. In the pursuit of this goal, more broadly, this chapter, along with the other chapters of the textbook, frames a type of human ecology, social justice advocacy, and critical systems thinking that advocates for the practice and profession of CMHC.

We have endeavored to offer a big-picture perspective of CMHC issues in this chapter, in a way that enables clinical mental health counselors to connect the proverbial dots, as they emerge or appear, across the content areas that are clinically and professionally relevant to the practice of CMHC. We believe that it is important to understand the overarching themes as well as the underlying dynamics and tensions of the CMHC field before drilling down to other basic and pertinent details about the profession that are found in Chapter 2.

RESOURCES

Print

Lopez–Baez, S. I., & Paylo, M. J. (2009). Social justice advocacy: Community collaboration and systems advocacy. *Journal of Counseling & Development, 87,* 276–283.

Online

SAMHSA-HRSA Center for Integrated Health Solutions. (n.d.). *Behavioral health in primary care.* Retrieved from https://www.integration.samhsa.gov/integrated-care-models/behavioral-health-in-primary-care

SAMHSA-HRSA Center for Integrated Health Solutions. (n.d.). *Integrated care models.* Retrieved from https://www.integration.samhsa.gov/integrated-care-models

Videos

National Center for Primary Care, Morehouse School. (2008). *Health care best practice: Cherokee Health Systems: Disparities: Mental health: Electronic medical record.* Retrieved from https://www.youtube.com/watch?v=OtqMPhDH5TU&feature=channel_video_title

Purcell, S. (2018). *Direct primary care: Remaking the health care system.* TEDxFurmanU. Retrieved from https://www.youtube.com/watch?v=5gjCKurF_Zw

■ REFERENCES

Acharya, B., Maru, D., Schwarz, R., Citrin, D., Tenpa, J., Hirachan, S., … Kohrt, B. (2017). Partnerships in mental healthcare service delivery in low-resource settings: Developing an innovative network in rural Nepal. *Globalization and Health, 13* (1), 2. doi: 10.1186/s12992-016-0226-0

American Psychiatric Association & Academy of Psychosomatic Medicine. (2016, Spring). *Dissemination of integrated care within adult primary care settings: The collaborative care model.* Retrieved from https://www.psychiatry.org/psychiatrists/practice/professional-interests/integrated-care/get-trained/about-collaborative-care

Bronfenbrenner, U. (1979). *The ecology of human development.* Cambridge, MA: Harvard University Press.

Bronfenbrenner, U. (2004). *Making human beings human: Bioecological perspectives on human development.* Thousand Oaks, CA: Sage Publications.

Butler, M., Kane, R. L., McAlpine, D., Kathol, R. G., Fu, S. S., Hagedorn, H., & Wilt, T. J. (2008). Integration of mental health/substance abuse and primary care. *Evidence Report/Technology Assessment,* (173), 1–362.

Council for the Accreditation of Counseling and Related Educational Programs. (2016). *2016 CACREP standards.* Retrieved from http://www.cacrep.org/wp-content/uploads/2017/08/2016-Standards-with-citations.pdf

Heath, B., Wise, R. P., & Reynolds, K. (2013, March). *A review and proposed standard framework for levels of integrated healthcare.* Washington, D.C.: SAMHSA-HRSA Center for Integrated Health Solutions. Retrieved from https://www.integration.samhsa.gov/integrated-care-models/A_Standard_Framework_for_Levels_of_Integrated_Healthcare.pdf

Hook, J. N., Davis, D., Owen, J., & DeBlaere, C. (2018). Introduction: Beginning the journey of cultural humility. In J. N. Hook, D. Davis, J. Owen, & C. Deblaere (Eds.), *Cultural humility: Engaging diverse identities in therapy* (pp. 3–16). Washington, DC: American Psychological Association. Retrieved from http://www.apa.org/pubs/books/Cultural-Humility-Intro-Sample.pdf

Kiselica, M. S., & Robinson, M. (2001). Bringing advocacy counseling to life: The history, issues, and human dramas of social justice work in counseling. *Journal of Counseling & Development, 79,* 387–397. doi:10.1002/j.1556-6676.2001.tb01985.x

Lewis, J. A., Ratts, M. J., Paladino, D. A., & Toporek, R. L. (2011). Social justice counseling and advocacy: Developing new leadership roles and competencies. *Journal for Social Action in Counseling and Psychology: Special Issue on Social Justice Leadership, 3* (1), 5–16.

Mechanic, D. (2012). Seizing opportunities under the Affordable Care Act for transforming the mental and behavioral health system. *Health Affairs, 31* (2), 376–382. doi:10.1377/hlthaff.2011.0623

The President's New Freedom Commission on Mental Health. (2008). *Achieving the promise: Transforming mental health care in America.* Retrieved November 26, 2018, from https://govinfo.library.unt.edu/mentalhealthcommission/reports/FinalReport/downloads/FinalReport.pdf

Ratts, M. J., & Hutchins, A. M. (2009). ACA advocacy competencies: Social justice advocacy at the client/student level. *Journal of Counseling & Development, 87*, 269–275. doi:10.1002/j.1556-6678.2009.tb00106.x

Toporek, R. L. (2011). Social justice and counseling. In D. J. Christie (Ed.), *Encyclopedia of Peace Psychology* (pp. 1–5). Hoboken, NJ: Wiley-Blackwell.

CHAPTER 2

A CONTEXT FOR UNDERSTANDING AND BEGINNING THE PRACTICE OF CLINICAL MENTAL HEALTH COUNSELING

LISA LOPEZ LEVERS

This chapter provides an historical overview of the counseling profession and its developmental trajectory, emphasizing the origins of mental health treatment and the reemergence of counseling as a wellness-based approach. The chapter offers discussion concerning the push toward a pathogenic model of conceptualizing mental illness and the subsequent, current resurgence of a strength-based notion of care. A brief overview of the major theories of counseling is provided as a means for understanding the development of counseling as a unique and separate field from psychology, psychiatry, and social work. The chapter provides specific definitions of counseling and of practice as a professional counselor; it identifies the specializations within the counseling field, the range of employment opportunities and the current labor market, and how counseling is integrated within a system-of-care approach. Basic information regarding counselor licensure, certification, and accreditation is provided.

The following Council for Accreditation of Counseling and Related Educational Programs (CACREP) standards are addressed in this chapter:
  CACREP 2016:
    2F1.b, 2F1.c, 2F1.d, 2F1.e, 2F1.f, 2F1.g, 2F1.h, 2F5.a, 5C1.a, 5C1.b
  CACREP 2009:
    2G1.a, 2G1.f, 2G1.g, 2G3.d

LEARNING OBJECTIVES

After reviewing this chapter, the reader should be able to:

1. Understand the history and evolution of the counseling profession, including clinical mental health counseling (CMHC);

2. Define counseling and the scope-of-practice of professional counselors and clinical mental health counselors;

3. Identify relevant professional, accreditation, licensure, and certification bodies; and

4. Understand the range of employment opportunities for clinical mental health counselors and the field's position in the labor market.

INTRODUCTION: ORIGINS AND HISTORICAL CONTEXT OF THE COUNSELING PROFESSION

Since our earliest beginnings, the counseling field has made great strides as a helping profession. Professional counseling is an increasingly growing field; credentialed and licensed professional counselors provide various mental health and human development services in a myriad of service settings. Professional counselors have the opportunity to focus on a variety of clinical areas and provide services to a diversity of clients in varying contextual situations. Clinical and developmental areas of interest include, but are not limited to, the following skill sets: clinical mental health counseling (CMHC); clinical rehabilitation counseling (RC); vocational RC; multicultural counseling; trauma counseling; crisis intervention counseling; marriage, family, and couples counseling; pastoral counseling; wellness counseling; career counseling; school counseling; college/university counseling; student affairs counseling; gender-related counseling; gerontology counseling; addictions counseling; and forensic counseling.

It is important for beginning CMHC students to understand that their engagement in the CMHC specialty is one part of the larger professional counseling framework. For this reason, this chapter describes the historical background for the practice of professional counseling, with an emphasis on how the CMHC specialty arose from the broader counseling context. The subsections within this first part of the chapter briefly outline the historical context of professional counseling, emphasizing professionalism and our professional values, the clients with whom we work, and elements of professional counselor identity, including discussions of the professional counseling associations, divisions, and international honor society. Following these subsections, in this first part of the chapter, the remaining major sections of the chapter include the following topics: training and credentials of a professional counselor, the specialty of CMHC, and a conclusion to the chapter that frames future perspectives for the field.

Historical Context of the Counseling Profession

From its earliest origins in the beginning of the 20th century, the counseling profession has grown, evolved, and matured (Hodges, 2019; Leahy, Rak, & Zanskas, 2016; Levers, 2007). These origins are shared, in part, with the other disciplines of psychological and emotional helping practices that arose from the 19th and early 20th century theories of Freud, Jung, and Adler. However, Frank Parsons, Jesse B. Davis, and Clifford Beers actually are considered the pioneers of early counseling efforts (Leahy et al., 2016; Smith,

2012). Their work in the initial decades of the 20th century established the beginning of the vocational guidance movement (Parsons, 1909), began school guidance programs in public schools (Davis, 1914), and exposed the wretched conditions, at that time, in mental institutions (Beers, 1908).

The field has seen several paradigmatic transformations, from early psychodynamic theories (Adler, 1927; Freud, 1913; Jung, 1933), to a focus on Carl Rogers' person-centered therapy (Rogers, 1942, 1951). With some time overlap, the field then moved on to behavioral (e.g., Eysenck, 1952; Pavlov, 1926; Skinner, 1938; Wolpe, 1973) and cognitive therapies (e.g., Bandura, 1997; Beck, 1979; Ellis, 2011), which led to cognitive behavioral therapy (CBT) interventions (e.g., Butler, Fennell, & Hackmann, 2010; Dattilio & Freeman, 2007; Hofmann, 2011; Ingram & Siegle, 2010). More recently, professional focus has shifted to systemic and ecologically oriented approaches to counseling (e.g., Corsini & Wedding, 2008; Lynch & Levers, 2007; Sharf, 2016) as well as to body-energy healing, energy field, and other complementary and alternative medicine (CAM) perspectives (Nichols, 2015). An important part of the shifting professional counseling landscape has been a more recent emphasis on cultural competence, cultural humility, and social justice; while these dynamics are being embedded into existing and emerging approaches to professional counseling, a robust body of literature has continued to contribute to our understanding of their efficacy (e.g., Bemak & Chung, 2005; Hook, Davis, Owen, & DeBlaere, 2018; Kiselica & Robinson, 2001). Contemporary counseling practices also are being informed by cutting-edge neuroscience research and polyvagal theory (Porges, 2011) with an increasing trend toward integrative interventions (e.g., Levers, 2012) and integrated systems of care, as already suggested in Chapter 1 and detailed in Chapter 3 of this textbook.

While the above set of shifts presents a broad and dense continuum to absorb initially, most counselor education programs (CEPs) offer separate courses, in which CMHC students learn the various theories and techniques associated with the field. It is of significant importance to note, here, that the earliest developmental stages of the guidance and vocational movements of the early 20th century were marked uniquely by a paradigm of wellness rather than psychopathology (Myers, 1991). Although we have veered away from the wellness model, somewhat, at various junctures in our professional history, we never completely abandoned it. Therefore, counselors are positioned to promote, advocate for, and deliver the strength-based services that currently are reemerging as a part of the integrative therapeutic landscape (Myers & Sweeney, 2008). At the same time that professional counselors adopt strength-based and wellness approaches, professional counselors also are trained to assess mental disorders and to provide diagnostic services.

Birth of the Counseling Associations

A significant juncture in our professional counseling history was the 1952 birth of the American Personnel and Guidance Association (APGA). This organization offered the first professional framework, in the United States, that enabled counselors to begin to network with other members of the profession and differentiated counseling services from other helping services. The name of the organization was changed in 1983 to the American Association of Counseling and Development (AACD), and again in 1992 to the American Counseling Association (ACA). These name changes signified the evolution of the profession and coincided with the growing momentum of passing state-level counseling licensure laws across the country. The ACA has become "the world's largest association exclusively representing professional counselors in various practice settings" (ACA, 2018a, "About ACA," para. 1). The existence of a primary association of this magnitude has been important to the field, because it has provided the format through which professional counselors, collectively, have been able to coordinate systematic best practices for service delivery. It is through the organized efforts of the ACA and other professional counseling organizations that counselors have been empowered to advocate for the profession, thus continuing to attain higher levels of professionalism.

Emergence of Professional Counseling

While the word "counseling" first appeared in print in the early 1900s (Proctor, 1925; Proctor, Benefield, & Wrenn, 1931), it was not until fairly late in the 20th century that the terms "professional counseling" and "professional counselor" began to be used (Levers, 2007). The adoption of these unifying terms began to shape and designate a credentialed and licensed profession, and the definition of professional counseling has evolved over the decades. Leahy et al. (2016) have offered the following astute observation about the historical roots of the counseling profession:

> *Rather than the profession of counseling evolving first, followed by a logical sequence of specialization of practice (as evident in the medical and legal professions), the specialty areas actually emerged first in response to a variety of human needs and were only later conceptualized as belonging to the common professional home of counseling. This unusual sequence of professional emergence has had a direct impact on the institutions, regulatory bodies, and professional associations that represent the profession and the specialty areas of practice. (p. 3)*

Leahy et al.'s (2016) observation is useful in assisting us to understand the evolving trajectory of our professional identity development. We have made great strides in our professionalization efforts, especially in regard to accountability in providing evidence-based services to clients. As a result of the ACA's original *2020: A Vision for the Future of Counseling* meeting at ACA's 2010 annual convention, and as a product of an iterative and recursive process involving consensus making among 29 relevant counseling organizations (Kaplan, Tarvydas, & Gladding, 2014), the following definition of professional counseling was adopted by the profession: "Counseling is a professional relationship that empowers diverse individuals, families, and groups to accomplish mental health, wellness, education, and career goals" (ACA, 2018a, "What is counseling?," para. 1).

Counselor Professionalism and Values

The construct of professionalism has been discussed for a long time in the professional counseling literature, offering various insights about the issue (e.g., Francis & Dugger,

2014; Gale & Austin, 2003; Hanna & Bemak, 1997; Ivey & Ivey, 1998; Ivey & Van Hesteren, 1990; Levers, 2007; Myers, Sweeney, & White, 2002; Ritchie, 1990). The benchmarks of what constitutes a profession include having preservice training standards, professional associations, credentials like licensure laws and professional certifications that govern accepted practices, and a code of professional ethics. Most counseling professionals agree upon the following assumptions about professionalism: that individual counselors graduate from an accredited program (with an increasingly strong push toward mandated 60-semester-credit-hour programs [90 quarter hours]), that they hold membership in professional associations, that they acquire the necessary and appropriate credentials to practice ethically, and that they adhere to the profession's code of ethics (Levers, 2007). This last point, adherence to professional ethics, is perhaps the most important aspect of professionalism that a counselor encounters in daily practice (the importance of professional ethics is detailed in Chapter 8 of this textbook).

State licensure laws require licensed counselors to adhere to a professional code of ethics. The *ACA Code of Ethics* has codified the ethical standards for professional counselors. The Code most recently was reauthorized in 2014 and can be found online (ACA, 2014). The various specialty areas of counseling and their related professional associations also may have codes of ethics that are specific to the client care involved in the delivery of specialty services (e.g., Commission on Rehabilitation Counselor Certification, 2016). Any professional counselor who has a state license must adhere to the state-mandated licensure code, regardless of specialty or certification area. However, any counselor who holds a specialty certification, in addition to state licensure, also must honor the ethical code mandated by the certification. The ethical codes offer relevant professional guidance concerning the various aspects of the counseling process, the counseling relationship, and relationships with other professionals; ethical codes provide further insight concerning methods for resolving ethical issues. Not all codes followed in the counseling profession offer the same mandates; in the case of following multiple codes of counselor ethics, the most restrictive (i.e., most protective of clients) should be followed.

Cottone and Tarvydas (2016), Forester-Miller and Davis (1996), and Tarvydas and Johnston (2018) have offered excellent discussions of the foundational moral principles of codes of ethics; they also offer useful models for ethical decision-making. Professional counselors are able to maintain higher standards of professionalism when they have a better understanding of the underlying moral principles of ethical practice; in support of this, it is equally important to have a ready model for facing ethical dilemmas and determining the best courses of action (detailed in Chapter 8 of this textbook). In addition to ethical practice and the tenets of professionalism discussed earlier, professional counselors embody an attitude and ethos of caring. This attitude is demonstrated by shared professional values such as empathy, compassion, authenticity, trust, respect, empowerment, diversity, social justice, and advocacy for both clients and the profession. Beginning CMHC students are likely to be required to take an entire course, within their master's program, that focuses exclusively on professional ethics.

Counseling Professionals and Their Clients

Client populations span the life cycle, as well as the spectrum of human dilemmas, and may include, but are not limited to children, adults, elders, couples, families, groups, persons with disabilities (including physical, developmental, intellectual, cognitive, and psychiatric), persons who have been traumatized, diverse groups of people who have experienced historical trauma, persons in the LGBTQIA+ community, persons who are in crisis, persons with various types of addictions, and persons who are or have been incarcerated. Professional assistance may be offered to individuals, couples, families, or entire communities—communities in crisis, trauma-affected communities, and communities experiencing natural and human-made disasters. Professional counseling services also are rendered to other professionals, as in the case of providing clinical and administrative supervision as well as in CEPs, or as in the case of systems and organizations in need of consultation. Counseling settings may include community-based agencies, schools, institutions of higher education, nonprofit agencies, governmental organizations, nongovernmental organizations (NGOs, usually not-for-profit), hospitals, outpatient clinics, rehabilitation centers, nursing homes, respite-care facilities, prisons, and private practices. Increasingly more professional counselors also are working in international venues that incorporate a variety of counseling practices and skill sets (Levers, 2017).

Professional Counseling Identity

The field of counseling has had a long history of an evolving professional identity, from working as noncertified and unlicensed guidance counselors and vocational counselors in the 1940s and 1950s, to community-based paraprofessionals in the 1960s and 1970s. The first state counselor licensure law was passed in Virginia, in 1976, the same year that the American Mental Health Counselors Association (AMHCA) was formed (Weikel, 1985, updated 2010). Through the decades, extensive professional advocacy has resulted in licensure in all 50 states, the District of Colombia, Guam, and Puerto Rico (ACA, 2018d, "State professional counselor licensure boards," para. 1). The goal of such intensive licensure-related professional advocacy could not have been achieved without the diligent assistance of the professional associations and divisions. The remaining parts of this subsection illuminate how the development of professional counseling associations and divisions, as well as an international professional counseling honor society, have contributed to the further professionalization of the field of counseling.

Professional Counseling Associations and Divisions

Professional Counseling can be considered the "umbrella" term for the counseling profession. The predominant professional association for professional counselors is the ACA; however, numerous other professional affiliates also are available for membership within the ACA organization. The ACA houses 18 divisions within its organizational framework (ACA, 2018c), representing a plethora of professional counseling interests and practices, and ACA members may join whichever divisions are the most relevant to their professional and personal interests.

Until March 2019, the ACA had 19 divisions, which included the AMHCA as a division. However, according to a recent update (ACA, 2019; Goodman, 2019), the AMHCA has disaffiliated from the ACA as a division and is now an independent organization. The update asserts that, "Both organizations look forward to continued collaboration on issues that will benefit mental health counselors and the profession" (ACA, 2019, *ACA divisions*, para. 2). (The AMHCA's website may be accessed at www.amhca.org.)

The ACA, its current 18 divisions, and links to their respective websites are provided in Box 2.1, as many of these major organizations may be of interest to CMHCs for various reasons and at a variety of junctures in the career pathways of CMHCs (more information about the 18 divisions can be found at the ACA website).

BOX 2.1   THE DIVISIONS OF THE AMERICAN COUNSELING ASSOCIATION

- American Counseling Association (ACA)
  www.counseling.org
- Association for Adult Development and Aging (AADA)
  www.aadaweb.org
- Association for Assessment and Research in Counseling (AARC)
  http://aarc-counseling.org
- Association for Child and Adolescent Counseling (ACAC)
  http://acachild.org
- Association for Creativity in Counseling (ACC)
  www.creativecounselor.org
- American College Counseling Association (ACCA)
  www.collegecounseling.org
- Association for Counselor Education and Supervision (ACES)
  www.acesonline.net
- Association for Humanistic Counseling (AHC)
  http://afhc.camp9.org
- Association for Lesbian, Gay, Bisexual and Transgender Issues in Counseling (ALGBTIC)
  www.algbtic.org
- Association for Multicultural Counseling and Development (AMCD)
  https://multiculturalcounselingdevelopment.org
- American Rehabilitation Counseling Association (ARCA)
  www.arcaweb.org
- Association for Spiritual, Ethical, and Religious Values in Counseling (ASERVIC)
  www.aservic.org

- ▪ Association for Specialists in Group Work (ASGW)
  www.asgw.org
- ▪ Counselors for Social Justice (CSJ)
  https://counseling-csj.org
- ▪ International Association of Addictions and Offender Counselors (IAAOC)
  www.iaaoc.org
- ▪ International Association of Marriage and Family Counselors (IAMFC)
  www.iamfconline.org
- ▪ Military and Government Counseling Association (MGCA, formerly ACE)
  http://acegonline.org
- ▪ National Career Development Association (NCDA)
  https://ncda.org/aws/NCDA/pt/sp/home_page
- ▪ National Employment Counseling Association (NECA)
  www.employmentcounseling.org

In addition to its divisions, the ACA has regional- and state-level associations and divisions. There are four ACA regions, which include the Midwest Region, the North Atlantic Region, the Southern Region, and the Western Region (ACA, n.d.). ACA has 56 chartered branches, spanning the United States (each state is represented by state-level associations and divisions), Europe, and Latin America (ACA, n.d.). More information about state issues and activities is available on the websites of the individual state associations and divisions. Online information about divisions, regions, and branches can be found at the ACA-related URLs listed in the Resources section at the end of this chapter.

Additional professional organizations, outside the affiliation of the ACA, may be of special interest to some professional counselors. The American Psychological Association (APA), not affiliated with the ACA, has a division for counseling psychologists, known as Division 17. Some counseling psychologists maintain simultaneous membership in Division 17 and professional counseling associations. However, this pertains to counseling psychologists who have obtained the doctoral degree and are licensed as psychologists; master's-level counselors should maintain a clear sense of professional identity as professional counselors and understand that membership in APA has limitations for those who are not licensed psychologists. Some rehabilitation counselors may hold simultaneous membership in ACA divisions and two other organizations that also are not affiliated with the ACA, the National Rehabilitation Counseling Association (NRCA) and the National Rehabilitation Association (NRA). Some marriage and family counselors may hold simultaneous membership in ACA and the American Association for Marriage and Family Therapy (AAMFT), also not affiliated with the ACA;

however, membership in this organization may pose professional limitations for many counselors. Some counselor educators and researchers also belong to non-ACA affiliates such as the American Educational Research Association (AERA). Finally, the American School Counselor Association (ASCA) was once an affiliate of the ACA but now operates independently.

Of all of the divisions discussed here, the AMHCA is one of the most relevant divisions for clinical mental health counselors. Initiated in 1976, the AMHCA has a long history of promoting and advocating for counselors to be recognized as competent and professional clinical mental health providers (for a brief history of the early origins of the AMHCA, see Weikel, 1985, updated 2010). Key aspects of this history are discussed, briefly, later in this chapter.

Professional Counseling Honor Society

Chi Sigma Iota (CSI) offers an international honor society for qualified professional counselors. Membership in the society is based upon excellence in academic achievement in a counselor education program. The society supports a system of university-based local chapters and has members throughout the world. To become a member of CSI, a counseling student must be matriculated into a CEP and have completed one or more semesters of full-time graduate study, possess a Grade Point Average (GPA) of 3.5 or higher on a 4.0 scale, and be recognized by the CSI chapter as showing "promise for a capacity to represent the best about professional counseling through appropriate professional behavior, ethical judgment, emotional maturity, and attitudes conducive to working to advocate for wellness and human dignity for all" (CSI, 2018, "Eligibility," para. 1). More information can be found at CSI's website, listed in the Resources section at the end of this chapter.

▦ EDUCATIONAL REQUIREMENTS AND CREDENTIALS OF A PROFESSIONAL COUNSELOR

The master's degree is the entry-level degree for the counseling profession. Various master's degrees are offered, but the most typical degrees awarded are the master of education (M.Ed.), the master of arts (M.A.), and the master of science in education (M.S. Ed.). It is not surprising, then, that most licensure laws and professional certifications for counselors require at least a master's degree, preferably from an accredited university program. Most licensure laws require post-degree supervision in order to qualify for application. Some licensure laws require additional graduate courses that address specified clinical areas (e.g., the Licensed Professional Clinical Counselor credential under Ohio's licensure law, or Florida's requirement that the applicant has taken a course regarding human sexuality). It therefore is vital that counselors become familiar with the licensure laws in the states where they plan to practice.

Master's-level professional counselors sometimes gain field-based experience and then return to a university to acquire a doctoral degree (typically a Ph.D. or an Ed.D.);

counselors also may matriculate into a doctoral program, immediately after completion of the master's degree, depending upon the requirements of the specific CEP. Some counselors may return to a university, simply in order to advance their clinical and theoretical knowledge sets; others also may wish to teach in a university CEP or in another related program. Instructors of counselor education usually hold a doctorate in order to teach at a university. An important exception is when doctoral students teach or supervise master's students in their CEPs, under the supervision of their professors. A less frequent exception occurs when a counseling practitioner, with a master's degree and a lot of clinical experience, teaches at a university as an adjunct instructor.

Various credentialing organizations administer the preservice and educational practices that are associated with the training and preparation of professional counselors; therefore, differing credentials may qualify counselors to practice in a variety of settings. The following subsections offer further elaborations regarding professional counseling accreditation, licensure, certification, and related professional identity issues.

Professional Counseling Accreditation

Counselor education programs can be accredited in a number of ways. First, universities are accredited by regional accrediting bodies that include the Middle States, New England, North Central, Northwest, Southern, and Western Associations of Colleges and Schools (MSACS, NEACS, NCACS, NACS, SACS, and WACS, respectively). Because CEPs are a part of the larger university environment, programs must be attentive to these more macrosystem requirements. Second, CEPs usually are housed in a school or college of education within the university, so CEPs may be accredited, along with their schools or colleges, through the Council for the Accreditation of Educator Preparation (CAEP). In some cases, a CEP may be housed in a school or college of health sciences or related discipline; in such cases, the school or college is likely to have its own layer of other discipline-related accreditation. Third, if a CEP offers a school counseling program, the specific state's department of education accreditation is necessary. Finally, the accreditation processes that are of most relevant concern to counselors and counselor educators are those of the Council for Accreditation of Counseling and Related Educational Programs (CACREP). This last accrediting body governs both master's-level and doctoral programs, offering guidelines for rigorous professional curricula and providing standards for academic training. More information can be obtained from the CACREP website.

During the latter half of the 20th century, master's-level CEPs have tended to move from a more generic training model to one that has greater emphasis on preparing professional counselors to work within specialty areas, while still preserving a core counseling curriculum. Counselor education programs (CEPs) have been accredited by the Council for the Accreditation of Counseling and Related Educational Programs (CACREP), since its inception in 1981; CACREP is the accrediting body that ensures a high quality of preservice training for professional counselors. The *Council on Rehabilitation Education* (CORE) previously accredited rehabilitation counseling (RC) programs; rehabilitation counseling is the specialty area that focuses on the needs of people living with disabilities. However, upon the merger of CORE with CACREP, which officially took place on

July 1, 2017, CACREP now accredits RC programs (CACREP, 2018). CACREP formally recognizes and accredits the following master's-level specialty areas:

- Addiction counseling;
- Career counseling;
- Clinical mental health counseling;
- Clinical rehabilitation counseling;
- College counseling and student affairs;
- Marriage, couple, and family counseling;
- Rehabilitation counseling, and
- School counseling.

CACREP also accredits doctoral degrees in Counselor Education. The doctoral degree is granted either as a PhD or an EdD, depending upon the structure of the higher education institution, the curriculum of the program, and requirements for the degree.

According to Bobby (2013), CACREP has evolved over the decades. Its current focus is on accrediting specialty areas as separate programs within larger CEPs. Bobby (2013) asserted that this shift has assisted in the advocacy efforts that the counseling profession be seen as a single and unified profession, which is important to the professional counseling field. She further emphasized that CACREP has strived to view the relevance of the specialty areas as subordinate to the integrity of counseling as a singular profession.

Licensure

Licensure is a mandatory process for professional counselors who practice in states where counseling titles and/or practices have been written into state law. Licensure is a legal mandate, not a choice, if one intends to hold oneself out as a licensed practitioner in a particular state. As previously mentioned, counselor licensure now includes all 50 states, Washington, DC, and two U.S. territories. However, criteria vary, depending upon whether the law is a title-only or a practice law. This is an important distinction for counselors to understand. Licensure in some states only protects the title of the professional counselor, meaning that only a licensed professional counselor may use the licensed professional counselor (LPC) title (in a few states, the designated title is worded slightly different, but the principle is the same), and the title-only law protects only the title. In other words, other professionals may perform counseling activities, but only a licensed counselor may use the title. This is in contrast to the practice law, which protects the scope of professional counseling practice. Scope of practice includes the processes and applications of counseling—it is what we actually *do* with clients. So a practice law, which is considered stronger than a title law, means that only someone licensed as a counselor may engage in the scope of practice covered by the state's law. Even with this distinction, criteria vary vastly, from state to state. Therefore, it is incumbent upon the licensee to understand the mandates and restrictions of the law in the particular state in which the license is sought. The protection of consumers is the primary reason for enacting laws that regulate professional practices. A secondary reason, concerning mental health–related laws, regards the consumer's freedom of choice in selecting a service provider. These and related issues are covered more fully in Chapter 12 of this textbook.

In the most recent data retrieved, the ACA (2011) has reported that more than 120,000 professional counselors have been licensed throughout the country. The licensure laws typically require that the applicant has graduated from a master's or doctoral program in counseling or a closely related field, has a graduate degree that includes supervised practicum and internship experiences, has passed an examination, and has had a specified time (typically 2 to 3 years) of post-degree clinical experience under the supervision of a qualified practitioner (ACA, 2010).

State Licensure Boards

Every state with a professional licensure law has a state board that regulates the law and monitors the professionals who practice under the law. State licensure boards also determine the preservice educational requirements of the professionals to be licensed (Bergman, 2013); these governmental bodies institute the professional training standards, which, in many cases, are in alignment with CACREP standards, but not always. It is not unusual for professional counselors to be grouped with other helping or allied healthcare professionals within the mandate of the state board. For this reason, boards that exist across the different states have different names. Every clinical mental health counselor who wishes to be licensed needs to explore the parameters of the specific board in his or her state as well as the requirements of the board (ACA, 2016).

The American Association of State Counseling Boards (AASCB) is responsible for organization of and facilitation among the state licensure boards. Due to the variability that exists across licensure laws and to the lack of a formal portability arrangement, professional counselors who relocate to another state may experience difficulty in acquiring the new licensure. For this reason, the AASCB and other professional organizations have worked diligently on licensure portability and other credentialing issues, and the National Credentials Registry (NCR) was inaugurated (AASCB, 2005). More information about the progress that has been made in this area can be found on the website for the National Board for Certified Counselors (NBCC, 2018), which is listed in the Resources section, at the end of this chapter. More information about the licensure laws in individual states can be found by accessing the websites of ACA and NBCC as well as ACA's report on licensure requirements across the states (ACA, 2016).

Portability

The NBCC (2018) has argued that a national portability law is vital. Portability, in this context, means that a licensed counselor, theoretically, would be able to carry or transfer his or her license to another state or to acquire licensure in a new state without repeating the complete application process. Regarding professional counselor licensure, portability and reciprocity have the same meanings (ACA, 2018b). As mentioned above, the AASCB supports portability (AASCB, 2005); in fact, in 2017, representatives of the

AASCB, ACES (Association for Counselor Education and Supervision), AMHCA, and NBCC formed a Portability Task Force, with the mission of creating a portability process that would assist counselors. The ACA participated in the task force but did not endorse the emergent process. The ACA has framed portability and reciprocity as a crisis, due to little state-to-state consistency, stating the following on the Association website:

> The crisis in licensure portability occurred because state licensing boards developed their rules and regulations independently of each other. . . . There are currently over 45 counselor licensure titles, no two scopes of practice are the same, minimum graduate credit hours vary from none stated to 60, and supervision requirements vary from 500 to 4,500 hours. State counseling boards recognize that licensure portability is in crisis, as characterized by one licensing board Chair who stated in . . . [an] article that, "I see this [licensure portability] as the most important discussion point in the regulatory process for our profession." (ACA, 2018b, "What caused this crisis?," para. 1)

In their national examination of state licensure application processes and the potential for professional counselor licensure portability, Olson, Brown-Rice, and Gerodias (2018) found many discrepancies across states and recommended that the profession develop a central application review location. However, such a recommendation is accompanied by its own set of hurdles. The issue of license portability presents a tension with many challenges to our profession, not the least of which relates to the ramifications of reopening, for change, laws that already have been passed. This matter is going to require persistent professional advocacy, engagement in collaborative processes, and a high level of organization in order to resolve the dilemma.

Certification

Certification is a voluntary process that adds an additional professional credential beyond the license. The national certifications that are of most interest to professional counselors include the National Certified Counselor (NCC), the National Certified School Counselor (NCSC), and the Master Addictions Counselor (MAC), all endorsed by the National Board of Certified Counselors (NBCC); the Certified Rehabilitation Counselor (CRC), endorsed by the Council for the Certification of Rehabilitation Counselors (CCRC); the Certified Clinical Mental Health Counselor (CCMHC), endorsed by the Academy of Clinical Mental Health Counselors (ACMHC) and NBCC; and the Approved Clinical Supervisor credential, managed by the NBCC affiliate, the Center for Credentialing and Education. Individual states also may have additional state-specific requirements for the state-based certification of school counselors, addictions counselors, and those employed at various levels of the mental health service delivery system; such state regulations are independent of national certifications and state licensure requirements.

Certification usually is *not* encoded in the law and is volitional, in contrast to licensure, which has legal implications and is mandatory, if professionals wish to practice in a state in which state law regulates the particular professional title or scope of practice. A major exception to this relates to school counselors, who adhere to the ASCA's (2016) *Ethical Standards for School Counselors* but also must follow state-mandated, certification-related ethical practices, often derived from or recurring back to ACA and ASCA ethical standards. The issue of ethical standards is important, in the particular case of certified school counselors. Although all states require school counselors to hold *state* certifications (Bureau of Labor Statistics, 2018a), this is not the same as the voluntary *national* certification for school counselors. The certification process is determined by experts in the particular area of certification and is based on commonly held "best-practice" standards in the professional sphere of certification. To obtain a professional certification, the counselor must meet the requirements of the application process; such application requirements are established by individual certification governing bodies, and these vary across certification types.

Related Professional Identity Issues

Regardless of counseling specialization, populations to which services are delivered, or settings where counseling takes place, some fundamental expectations about professional identity are consistent across the counseling continuum (Levers, 2007). First, counselors live and practice in diverse contexts, and therefore aim to develop insightful multicultural and social justice perspectives; professional counselors need to be sensitive to issues of diversity, including but not limited to race, ethnicity, class, gender, ability, religion, sexual orientation, and related potential areas of client vulnerability. Second, counselors tend to practice from relatively holistic and systemic frameworks, viewing individual clients as whole persons, who have multiple and complex social and cultural interactions; professional counselors understand that client problems cannot be compartmentalized simply, and they attempt to engage clients in synergistic counseling relationships. Third, professional counselors broadly work from a strengths-based model; however, in parallel functions, professional counselors routinely assist clients with problem-solving and provide diagnoses as needed. During the core years of advocacy for state licensure and third-party reimbursement, there was a push toward a more pathogenic model of conceptualizing mental illness, but more recently, we have seen a subsequent, current resurgence of a salutogenic (Antonovsky, 1979) or strength-based perspective of care. Fourth, counselors are required to practice ethically and abide by any professional codes of ethics mandated within their scope of practice. Professional counselors are required to maintain confidentiality about clients; however, depending upon a specific state's legal code, a licensed professional counselor may or may not have privileged communication. Fifth, professional counseling is a self-reflexive practice, and effective counseling relies upon the ability of the professional counselor to engage in authentic self-reflection. Finally, professional counselors focus on interpersonal skill building with clients, thus demonstrating such profession-endorsed values as empathy, compassion, authenticity, trust, respect, therapeutic relationship building, empowerment, social justice, advocacy, and in-the-here-and-now processing.

Professional counselors use many of the same theories and techniques as those used by other helping professionals; these are discussed in the various chapters throughout this textbook, and the standard counselor education curriculum devotes an entire course, sometimes two, to theories and techniques. Philosophical and epistemological variations exist among different disciplines of helpers, so the ways in which professional counselors approach the helping process, or the onus upon which they focus, may differ paradigmatically from other helping professionals. A simple way of viewing these differences is offered in the following explication: The psychiatric approach is based on the biomedical model, and psychiatrists are medical doctors; the psychological approach tends to emphasize psychopathology and the individual; the sociological or social work approach tends to focus on systems and systemic dynamics; and the professional counseling paradigm tends to pay particular attention to how individual clients intersect with the relevant cultures, systems, and interpersonal relationships within their personal ecosystems. Counseling is a highly interdisciplinary profession (Levers, 2007; Smith, 2012), not only influenced by psychology and sociology, but also by disciplines like education, anthropology, philosophy, theology, other humanities, and the biological sciences. While many of the students who enter counseling master's programs have an undergraduate degree in psychology, others matriculate into counseling master's programs from a wide variety of undergraduate disciplines.

Having asserted such a "slippery slope" proposition (pathology vs. wellness), in order to make gross distinctions among some of the key mental health–related professions, it must be reemphasized that while professional counseling is a separate and unique profession, similar theories and practices are shared across all of the helping professions and among all of the helping professionals in assisting clients. Such comparisons have created some discord within the profession and across disciplines since the earliest professional licensure efforts (we had to present evidence to state legislatures that the practice of counseling is a discreet and unique practice, separate from the scopes of practice of other helping professionals). A full discourse on the professional identity of counselors, in relationship to the nuances of intra- and interprofessional similarities and differences, is beyond the scope of this brief introductory chapter, but the literature is replete with discussion of this issue (e.g., Anderson, Barenberg, & Tremblay, 2007; Bayne-Smith, Mizrahi, Korazim-Körösy, & Garcia, 2014; Bergman, 2013; Francis & Dugger, 2014; Gale & Austin, 2003; Hanna & Bemak, 1997; Ivey & Ivey, 1998; Lightfoot, Nienow, Moua, Colburn, & Petri, 2016; MacNaughton, Chreim, & Bourgeault, 2013; Myers et al., 2002; Skovholt, Rønnestad, & Jennings, 1997; Van Hesteren & Ivey, 1990). For purposes of the present discussion, it suffices to say that professional counseling identity is informed by client self-efficacy, pluralism, social justice, and multidisciplinary influences. The remainder of this chapter is organized around some of the more salient issues that pertain specifically to the CMHC specialty area.

▮ THE SPECIALTY OF CMHC

The American Mental Health Counseling Association (AMHCA) has developed and evolved over the decades, in sync with the larger counseling profession. Just as the earlier parts of this chapter focused on the context for, growth of, and elements related to professional counseling, this part of the chapter focuses on parallel issues concerning the specialty of CMHC and becoming a clinical mental health counselor. As the AMHCA was instrumental, first in the development of community mental health counseling, and more recently in the CMHC specialty area, relevant aspects of the AMHCA organization are discussed as well. The following subsections briefly identify the key aspects of CMHC history, the current labor market for clinical mental health counselors, the attributes of a competent and effective clinical mental health counselor, the importance of personal health and wellness, networking, and advocacy. More information about wellness and self-care appears in Chapter 14 of this textbook.

Key Aspects of CMHC History

The history of CMHC is linked integrally with the history of the AMHCA; to understand the development of the CMHC specialty, it is important to understand the historical context of the AMHCA. As stated earlier in this chapter, the AMHCA was inaugurated in 1976 (AMHCA, 2016), the same year in which the first counselor licensure law was passed in Virginia and prior to the launch of CACREP. An earlier iteration of the ACA, the APGA, was the major professional organization for counselors, but it did not have a division for community and agency counselors (Weikel, 1986, updated 2010).

In a parallel professional universe, universities had been training master's-level rehabilitation counselors for several decades. Funding was allocated by the federal government, as a part of the *Vocational Rehabilitation Act Amendment of 1954*, for university programs to train graduate-level practitioners to work with people with disabilities (Leahy, 2004; Leahy et al., 2016). By the early-to-mid-1970s, rehabilitation counselors already had moved to community settings, following their patients and clients with disabilities from hospitals and other institutional settings. I was trained as a rehabilitation counselor at that time, and my master's-level education focused as much on professional community activism as it did on vocational and disability issues. In a very real sense, those of us who became rehabilitation counselors in the mid-1970s also were engaging in the early community-based counseling movement, especially as some of us were beginning to focus on psychiatric disability as a clinical area. Another parallel aspect of this history is that the CORE, funded by federal money, was founded in 1974 and accredited its first rehabilitation counselor education (RCE) program in 1975 (Geist, 1984). This was a full 6 years prior to the establishment of CACREP in 1981 (CORE and CACREP merged in 2017, and RCE programs now are accredited by CACREP). At the same time, in the early-to-mid-1970s, the community mental health movement, initiated by the earlier Kennedy-era *Community Mental Health Act of 1963* (CMHA), began to take hold in communities across the United States (Cutler, Bevilacqua, & McFarland, 2003). Psychiatric patients, previously warehoused in archaic and often abusive institutions, began to be deinstitutionalized. During the growth of this 1970s-era community mental health movement, rehabilitation counselors and other master's-level counseling practitioners began to work in community mental health settings. Community-based counseling is discussed at greater length in Chapter 6 of this textbook.

To a large extent, master's-level counselors working in community mental health settings were practitioners in search of a professional home, circa 1976. A synergy already was building, with requests for the "representation and recognition of nonschool counselors in APGA" (Weikel, 1985, updated 2010, "A brief history," para. 2). A proposal for establishing a new division in APGA was initiated. According to Weikel (1985, updated 2010, "A brief history," para. 2), "The name American Mental Health Counselors Association was chosen that first day 'because we wanted to have counselors who worked in mental health settings identified and we wanted the name to have a good ring to it' (J. J. Messina, personal communication, November 14, 1983)." However, in response to an application for a new division, put forward by an enthusiastic group of counselors and counselor educators, the APGA Board passed a resolution for a moratorium on new divisions, and the proposal was not entertained. By that time, the mental health counseling group had established a strong steering committee, bylaws were written and approved, and the AMHCA was incorporated in late 1976 as an independent organization (Weikel, 1985, updated 2010). The AMHCA established its flagship journal, the *Journal of Mental Health Counseling*, in 1979 (Weikel, 1985, updated 2010).

By the time that CACREP began to accredit counseling programs in 1981, a plethora of master's-level counselors already were working in community mental health settings. With the 2009 iteration of the CACREP standards, existing community counseling programs and mental health counseling programs were required to change their designations to the then-new master's-level CMHC program (CACREP, 2014). In the meantime, CACREP established the master's-level clinical RC program (CACREP, 2018), which has some requirements that are parallel to the CMHC program. In CEPs that offer both specializations, some students graduate with both degrees, requiring only a limited number of extra courses. The recent disaffiliation of the AMHCA from the ACA will not have an impact on CACREP's accreditation of clinical mental health counseling programs.

Current Labor Market Trends for Clinical Mental Health Counselors

According to the *Occupational Outlook Handbook* (U.S. Department of Labor, Bureau of Labor Statistics, 2018b), "Employment of substance abuse, behavioral disorder, and mental health counselors is projected to grow 23 percent from 2016 to 2026, much faster than the average for all occupations" ("Job outlook," para. 1). Obviously, CMHC is a growing field, with solid job prospects; practitioners who want a career in counseling can maintain a fairly high confidence in job assurance. The *Occupational Outlook Handbook* (U.S. Department of Labor, Bureau of Labor Statistics, 2018b) further states that "The median annual wage for substance abuse, behavioral disorder, and mental health counselors was $43,300 in May 2017" ("Pay," para. 1). So, the pay may not be great. However, salaries for clinical mental health counselors vary; they differ based upon location (state-to-state and urban vs. rural), they depend upon the type of employing organization, and they differ depending on job function (case manager vs. supervisor or program director). Many clinical mental health counselors develop private practices. This can be tricky, in terms of salary, because there are so many variables, for example, the strength or weakness of licensure in a particular state, the acceptance of clinical mental health counselors by insurance panels, and so forth. These issues are described more fully in Chapter 12 of this textbook.

One of the reasons that projected job prospects are so good for clinical mental health counselors relates to the demand for services. The rate of employment growth is expected to be high, because "people continue to seek addiction and mental health counseling" (U.S. Department of Labor, Bureau of Labor Statistics, 2018b, "Job outlook," para. 1). In other words, an increasing number of people who have serious mental health problems are seeking help with their problems. Individuals who decide to attain the education and credentials to become a clinical mental health counselor also must consider personal disposition and attributes, so that they can ascertain whether they are good fits for the profession and for the clients who need services.

Attributes of a Competent and Effective Clinical Mental Health Counselor

For clinical mental health counselors to deliver truly competent and effective CMHC services, they need to acquire, develop, integrate, and synthesize many professional and personal attributes. Among these many characteristics, it is essential for the effective counselor to master at least baseline technical competencies. Ivey and Ivey (2003) have identified some of these competencies as attending to or being with the client, focusing, active listening, questioning and observation skills, reflecting feelings, confrontation skills, interviewing skills, operating from an ethical framework, influencing or motivating, and the ability to integrate skills. The efficacy of these technical competencies is enhanced by fidelity to the core values to which the profession commonly adheres; mentioned earlier in this chapter and worth repeating here, these include respect, understanding, warmth, genuineness, and client empowerment. Counselor efficacy also denotes a strong knowledge of theory and the ability to apply theories appropriately, as well as possessing multicultural and ethical competencies.

Efficacy in CMHC requires that the counselor learn and master client-relevant sets of techniques and skills. However, efficacy also requires the counselor to move beyond a singular "technology" of helping to a more tacit dimension of being with, listening to, and offering succor to clients (Fuchs, 2001; Polanyi, 1967). These less tangible skills include an ability to focus on client meaning-making and to facilitate the level of self-actualization or self-efficacy that the client desires or can tolerate within his or her context (Levers, 1997, 2007). Beyond the essential technical skills that are learned in courses, professional counselors need to learn and develop a more nuanced array of clinical responses, like sensitivity, recursion, timing, and maturity. There are no tried-and-true guidelines for this. In order to embrace this tacit dimension of counseling sufficiently, and this may be the most salient nontechnical characteristic of an effective clinical mental health counselor, the counselor needs to have the capacity for honest self-reflection and self-discovery (Levers, 2007). While some theorists attempt to particularize the counseling process as *either* "art" *or* "science," the most effective CMHC practice offers a balance among adequate and mature self-knowledge, a keen mastery of theory and technique, the ability to engage in an authentic relationship, and the knowledge of when to use which set of skills based on client needs.

Importance of Personal Health and Wellness

The professional work performed by clinical mental health counselors often leads to a sense of fulfillment and personal satisfaction. The flip side of this coin is that counseling also can be challenging for counselors and even result in undue distress. Clinical mental health counselors run the risk of eventual professional burnout when they do not take care of themselves. Self-care includes the counselor's lived experience on multiple levels: emotionally, cognitively, spiritually, existentially, psychologically, socially, and physiologically. Professional counselors usually counsel clients who are feeling vulnerable and may be experiencing differing degrees of crisis and trauma; such client states can have negative effects on the counselors, so it is important for counselors and supervisors to be vigilant about this issue (issues related to clinical supervision are discussed in Chapter 13 of this textbook).

TIP FROM THE FIELD 2.1
DEVELOPING A WELLNESS PLAN

Clinical mental health counselors need to develop a personal plan to maintain overall wellness. Such a wellness plan must include healthy outlets for stress. Without a wellness plan, it becomes too easy for counselors to "take on" clients' problems and begin to feel overwhelmed or even burned out. This, then, can constitute unchecked countertransference and potentially lead to therapeutic misadventures or unethical behaviors on the part of the counselor. By the way, countertransference is not necessarily negative; in CMHC, *counter*transference happens frequently, precisely because clients *transfer* personal content onto counselors. Where there is transferences, we find countertransference—it is a reciprocal human dynamic. However, the self-aware practitioner is able to understand and identify countertransference and then knows the importance of processing it with a clinical supervisor. Understanding the relevance of transference and countertransference can lead, in turn, to productive interactions with clients concerning the countertransference event. Usually, countertransference only becomes a potential clinical problem when it remains unrecognized or the clinician is in denial about it.

The *2014 ACA Code of Ethics*, in its "Introduction to Section C Professional Responsibility," states the following: "counselors engage in self-care activities to maintain and promote their own emotional, physical, mental, and spiritual well-being to best meet their professional responsibilities" (ACA, 2014, p. 8). Likewise, the CACREP standards (2016) encourage and support counselors' continued self-development and self-care activities, as do most counselor-preparation programs. The importance of counselors taking care of themselves cannot be overemphasized. Clinical work environments can be demanding and stressful; therefore, counselors must assure that they take proactive measures to maintain personal health and to develop appropriate and sufficient wellness plans (issues related to self-care are discussed in Chapter 14 of this textbook).

Professional Networking

Professional networking is a relevant dimension of the clinical mental health counselor's ability to maintain a functional work ethos. Networking can contribute to client advocacy, to professional growth, and to an increased understanding and awareness of field-based and systemic issues. CMHCs should seek opportunities to network with other organizations that serve clients, so that a rich source of referrals and resources can be maintained. CMHCs also should create opportunities to network with other professionals at seminars, workshops, conferences, and conventions to stay abreast of newly developing clinical concerns and to learn about current trends in the field. Finally, CMHCs should take advantage of opportunities to network through their professional associations and professional interest groups.

Advocacy

The issue of advocacy is significant for clinical mental health counselors working in the contemporary integrative healthcare and behavioral healthcare landscape. Advocacy functions within two adjoining arenas, that of client advocacy and that of professional advocacy. Because it is difficult to advocate adequately for clients if counselors have not advocated sufficiently for the profession, the two functions are profoundly interconnected. With the absence of either client advocacy or professional advocacy, clinical mental health counselors would operate from a weaker professional vantage point.

Client Advocacy

When vulnerable, marginalized, or disenfranchised individuals seek counseling, they often are not positioned to advocate for themselves. It is for this reason that clinical mental health counselors, concerned with issues of social justice, are called upon to take on advocacy roles with clients or consumers. While not all professional counselors are positioned equally to assume an advocacy role, many counselors are attracted to the field due to a strong sense of social justice, compassion, and the will to assist others in having better lives. However, while altruism is an admirable trait, it is important to maintain a professional balance between client advocacy and the possibility of violating boundary issues. Potential problems in this area can be averted by discussing such issues in clinical supervision.

The need for client advocacy has many faces. It may result from intended abuse or inadvertent neglect of client welfare, on the part of other individuals, families, or social institutions. A consumer need may be met, or a problem set may be remedied easily by drawing attention to social justice inequities or by raising awareness of particular unjust issues. Conversely, a societal issue, for which counselors need to advocate, may be difficult to fix, because systemic changes generally take time. The need may result from benign acceptance of personal or social disparities. It may be the product of larger cultural and social inequalities arising from issues related to race, ethnicity, class, gender, ability, religion, and sexual orientation (Levers, 2007). Wherever client advocacy is needed, professional counselors potentially can have a positive impact upon people's lives. For this reason, and as a direct part of the counseling relationship, counselors have a duty and responsibility to respect client dignity, preserve professional integrity, and maintain an ethical perspective while initiating and responding to client advocacy needs. Issues related to client advocacy are discussed in Chapter 9 of this textbook.

Professional Advocacy

Because professional counseling is focused on assisting clients, it may seem counterintuitive to raise the discussion of professional advocacy. However, the field of professional counseling continues to need a strong advocacy plan. Other helping professions have a longer history of licensure and credentialing than counseling, so the long struggle to attain legal recognition has been difficult (Bergman, 2013). The ACA, in harmony with other professional counseling organizations, has organized and inaugurated professional advocacy strategies that have had a strong initial effect on policy and legislation surrounding critical professional issues.

The need continues for professional advocacy that ensures a stronger and better coordinated professional service agenda (Gillig, 2003; Myers & Sweeney, 2004). Individual clinical mental health counselors have substantial opportunities to become involved with the work of professional advocacy committees at state, regional, and national levels. It is essential for clinical mental health counselors to keep abreast of current professional affairs that may have legal and professional ramifications for the profession. Not doing so could impair the profession's ability to continue to provide quality services to clients (issues related to professional advocacy are discussed in Chapter 12 of this textbook).

▦ CONCLUSION

This chapter provided an historical overview of the field of professional counseling along with details regarding the particular history of CMHC and the dimensions of CMHC that are important for clinical mental health counselors in training to consider. The chapter offered a contextual perspective of professional counseling, concomitant with a focus on the specialty area of CMHC, illuminating the intersection of AMHCA and CMHC history. Additional sections of the chapter discussed issues associated with professional counselor training, the credentials of professional counselors, and the specialty of CMHC.

Several discussions that were presented in this chapter assist in framing some of the future perspectives for the field. Both client and professional advocacy continue to be essential for clinical mental health counselors. The issue of license portability is paramount to all professional counselors, including clinical mental health counselors, at this juncture in our professional history. All licensed professional counselors must push all of our professional associations to advocate for the eventual reality of portability. Finally, it is urgent for clinical mental health counselors to understand integrative practices and to develop pathways for clinical mental health counselors to create and assume vital roles in integrative systems of care. Integrative practices mark the current landscape of therapeutic work, and involvement in integrative systems of care constitutes our professional future. Strategic thinking about, planning of, and doing advocacy, portability, and integrative practices has major implications for the future of the CMHC profession.

RESOURCES

Print and Digital

American Counseling Association. (2010). *Licensure requirements for Professional Counselors—2010*, a report by the ACA. Retrieved from https://www.counseling.org/docs/licensure/72903_excerpt_for_web.pdf

American Counseling Association. (2014). *2014 ACA code of ethics*. Retrieved from https://www.counseling.org/resources/aca-code-of-ethics.pdf

American Counseling Association. (2018). *About us*. Retrieved from https://www.counseling.org/about-us/about-aca

American Counseling Association. (2018). *Divisions*. Retrieved from https://www.counseling.org/about-us/divisions-regions-and-branches/divisions

American Counseling Association. (n.d.). *Knowledge center: Ethics*. Retrieved from https://www.counseling.org/docs/default-source/ethics/2014-aca-code-of-ethics.pdf?sfvrsn=fde89426_5

American Mental Health Counselors Association. (2018). *Home*. Retrieved from http://www.amhca.org/home

Chi Sigma Iota. Retrieved from http://www.csi-net.org

National Board for Certified Counselors. Retrieved from http://www.nbcc.org

Northwestern University. (2015). *Timeline: The history of counseling*. Retrieved from https://www.slideshare.net/CounselingNU/history-of-counseling-timeline

Wakefield, M. (2013). "Health licensing board report to Congress." Retrieved from www.hrsa.gov/ruralhealth/about/telehealth/licenserpt10.pdf

Videos

AIMS Center. (2018). *Daniel's story: An introduction to collaborative care*. University of Washington, Psychiatry and Behavioral Sciences, Division of Population Health. Retrieved from https://aims.uw.edu/daniels-story-introduction-collaborative-care

National Council for Behavioral Health. (2015). *What is integrated care?* Retrieved from https://www.youtube.com/watch?v=S-029Yf7AYM&feature=youtu.be

nserrano4ME. (2008). *Primary care behavioral health: MH care redesign*. Retrieved from https://www.youtube.com/watch?v=t0MsDjlTQfo&feature=channel_video_title

REFERENCES

Adler, A. (1927). *Understanding human nature*. Oxford: Greenberg.

American Association of State Counseling Boards. (2005). *AASCB national credential registry: Portability*. Retrieved from https://associationdatabase.com/aws/AASCB/asset_manager/get_file/37388

American Counseling Association. (2010). *Licensure requirements for professional counselors—2010*, a report by the ACA. Retrieved from https://www.counseling.org/docs/licensure/72903_excerpt_for_web.pdf

American Counseling Association. (2011). *Who are licensed professional counselors*. Retrieved from https://www.counseling.org/PublicPolicy/WhoAreLPCs.pdf

American Counseling Association. (2014). *2014 ACA code of ethics*. Retrieved from https://www.counseling.org/resources/aca-code-of-ethics.pdf

American Counseling Association. (2016). *Licensure requirements for professional counselors: A state-by-state report*. Report by the ACA Center for Counseling Practice, Policy and Research Retrieved from http://web.oru.edu/current_students/class_pages/grtheo/mmankins/CounselingLicensure/ORU%20Counseling%20Licensure%20Requirements%20Website%20Update%202-16-16/state%20licensure%20requirements%202016%20edition.pdf

American Counseling Association. (2018a). *About us*. Retrieved from https://www.counseling.org/about-us/about-aca

American Counseling Association. (2018b). *ACA licensure portability model FAQS*. Retrieved from https://www.counseling.org/knowledge-center/aca-licensure-portability-model-faqs

American Counseling Association. (2018c). *Divisions*. Retrieved from https://www.counseling.org/about-us/divisions-regions-and-branches/divisions

American Counseling Association. (2018d). *Licensure & certification—State professional counselor licensure boards*. Retrieved from https://www.counseling.org/knowledge-center/licensure-requirements/state-professional-counselor-licensure-boards

American Counseling Association. (2019). *ACA divisions*. Retrieved from https://www.counseling.org/about-us/divisions-regions-and-branches/divisions

American Counseling Association. (n.d.). *Divisions, regions, and branches*. Retrieved from https://www.counseling.org/about-us/divisions-regions-and-branches/divisions

American Mental Health Counselors Association. (2016). *AMHCA standards for the practice of clinical mental health counseling*. Retrieved from http://connections.amhca.org/HigherLogic/System/DownloadDocumentFile.ashx?DocumentFileKey=e6b635b0-654c-be8d-e18c-dbf75de23b8f

American School Counselor Association. (2016). *ASCA ethical standards for school counselors*. Retrieved from https://www.schoolcounselor.org/asca/media/asca/Ethics/EthicalStandards2016.pdf

Anderson, A., Barenberg, L., & Tremblay, P. R. (2007). Professional ethics in interdisciplinary collaboratives: Zeal, paternalism and mandated reporting. *Clinical Law Review, 13*, 659–718.

Antonovsky, A. (1979). *Health, stress and coping*. San Francisco, CA: Jossey-Bass Publishers.

Bandura, A. (Ed.). (1997). *Self-efficacy: The exercise of control*. New York, NY: Worth Publishers.

Bayne-Smith, M., Mizrahi, T., Korazim-Körösy, Y., & Garcia, M. (2014). Participation in interprofessional community collaboration. *Issues in Interdisciplinary Studies, 32*, 103–133.

Beck, A. T. (1979). *Cognitive therapy and the emotional disorders*. New York, NY: Plume.

Beers, C. (1908). *A mind that found itself*. New York, NY: Doubleday.

Bemak, F., & Chung, R. C.-Y. (2005). Advocacy as a critical role for urban school counselors: Working toward equity and social justice. *Professional School Counseling, 8*, 196–202.

Bergman, D. M. (2013). The role of government and lobbying in the creation of a health profession: The legal foundations of counseling. *Journal of Counseling & Development, 91*, 61–67. doi:10.1002/j.1556-6676.2013.00072.x

Bobby, C. L. (2013). The evolution of specialties in the CACREP standards: CACREP's role in unifying the profession. *Journal of Counseling & Development, 91*(1), 35–43. doi:10.1002/j.1556-6676.2013.00068.x

Bureau of Labor Statistics, U.S. Department of Labor. (2018a). *Occupational outlook handbook: School and career counselors*. Retrieved from https://www.bls.gov/ooh/community-and-social-service/school-and-career-counselors.htm

Bureau of Labor Statistics, U.S. Department of Labor. (2018b). *Occupational outlook handbook: Substance abuse, behavioral disorder, and mental health counselors*. Retrieved from https://www.bls.gov/ooh/community-and-social-service/substance-abuse-behavioral-disorder-and-mental-health-counselors.htm

Butler, G., Fennell, M., & Hackmann, A. (2010). *Cognitive-behavioral therapy for anxiety disorders: Mastering clinical challenges*. New York, NY: Guilford Press.

Chi Sigma Iota. (2018). *Membership*. Retrieved from https://www.csi-net.org/page/Membership

Commission on Rehabilitation Counselor Certification (CRCC). (2016). *Code of professional ethics for rehabilitation counselors*. Retrieved from https://www.michigan.gov/documents/wca/wca_vr_code_ethics_473348_7.pdf

Corsini, R. J., & Wedding, D. (Eds.). (2008). *Current psychotherapies* (8th ed.). Belmont, CA: Thomson Brooks/Cole.

Cottone, R. R., & Tarvydas, V. M. (2016). *Counseling ethics and decision making* (4th ed.). New York, NY: Springer Publishing Company.

Council for Accreditation of Counseling and Related Educational Programs. (2014). *An update on the transition to clinical mental health counseling*. Retrieved from https://www.cacrep.org/articles/an-update-on-the-transition-to-clinical-mental-health-counseling-2

Council for Accreditation of Counseling and Related Educational Programs. (2016). *2016 CACREP standards*. Retrieved from http://www.cacrep.org/wp-content/uploads/2018/05/2016-Standards-with-Glossary-5.3.2018.pdf

Council for Accreditation of Counseling and Related Educational Programs. (2018). *CACREP/CORE merger*. Retrieved from https://www.cacrep.org/news-and-events/cacrepcore-updates

Cutler, D. L., Bevilacqua, J., & McFarland, B. H. (2003). Four decades of community mental health: A symphony in four movements. *Community Mental Health Journal, 39*(5), 381–398. doi:10.1023/A:1025856718368

Dattilio, F. M., & Freeman, A. (Eds.). (2007). *Cognitive-behavioral strategies in crisis intervention* (3rd ed.). New York, NY: Guilford Press.

Davis, J. B. (1914). *Vocational and moral guidance*. Boston, MA: Ginn.

Ellis, A. (2011). *Rational emotive behavior therapy: Theories of psychotherapy* (3rd ed.). Washington, DC: American Psychological Association.

Eysenck, H. J. (1952). The effects of psychotherapy: An evaluation. *Journal of Consulting Psychology, 16*(5), 319–324.

Forester-Miller, H., & Davis, T. E. (1996). *Practitioner's guide to ethical decision making*. Retrieved from https://www.counseling.org/docs/default-source/ethics/practioner-39-s-guide-to-ethical-decision-making.pdf?sfvrsn=f9e5482c_10

Francis, P. C., & Dugger, S. M. (2014). Professionalism, ethics, and value-based conflicts in counseling: An introduction to the special section. *Journal of Counseling & Development, 92*(2), 131–134. doi:10.1002/j.1556-6676.2014.00138.x

Freud, S. (1913). *The interpretation of dreams* (A. A. Brill & J. Strachey, Trans.). London: Macmillan. (Original work published 1940)

Fuchs, T. (2001). The tacit dimension. *Philosophy, Psychiatry & Psychology, 8*(4), 323–326. doi:10.1353/ppp.2002.0018

Gale, A. U., & Austin, B. D. (2003). Professionalism's challenges to professional counselors' collective identity. *Journal of Counseling & Development, 81*(1), 3–10. doi:10.1002/j.1556-6678.2003.tb00219.x

Geist, C. F. (1984). The Council on Rehabilitation Education (CORE). *Journal of Education for Library and Information Science, 25*(2), 105–108. doi:10.2307/40323050

Gillig, S. E. (2003, Spring). Counselor advocacy tips. *Exemplar, 18*(1), 6.

Goodman, A. (2019). *AMHCA and ACA separate Associations*. Retrieved from https://www.amhca.org/blogs/howard-goodman/2019/04/26/amhca-and-aca-separate-associations

Hanna, F. J., & Bemak, F. (1997). The quest for identity in the counseling profession. *Counselor Education and Supervision, 36*(3), 194–206. doi:10.1002/j.1556-6978.1997.tb00386.x

Hodges, S. (2019). *101 careers in counseling*. New York, NY: Springer Publishing Company.

Hofmann, S. G. (2011). *An introduction to modern CBT: Psychological solutions to mental health problems*. Chichester: Wiley-Blackwell.

Hook, J. N., Davis, D., Owen, J., & DeBlaere, C. (2018). Introduction: Beginning the journey of cultural humility. In J. N. Hook, D. Davis, J. Owen, & C. Deblaere (Eds.), *Cultural humility: Engaging diverse identities in therapy* (pp. 3–16). Washington, DC: American Psychological Association. Retrieved from http://www.apa.org/pubs/books/Cultural-Humility-Intro-Sample.pdf

Ingram, R. E., & Siegle, G. J. (2010). Cognitive science and the conceptual foundations of cognitive-behavioral therapy: Viva la evolution! In K. S. Dobson (Ed.), *Handbook of cognitive-behavioral therapies* (3rd ed., pp. 74–93). New York, NY: Guilford Press.

Ivey, A. E., & Ivey, M. B. (1998). Reframing *DSM-IV*: Positive strategies from developmental counseling and therapy. *Journal of Counseling & Development, 76*(3), 334–350. doi:10.1002/j.1556-6676.1998.tb02550.x

Ivey, A. E., & Van Hesteren, F. (1990). Counseling and development: "No one can do it all, but it all needs to be done." *Journal of Counseling & Development, 68*(5), 534–536. doi:10.1002/j.1556-6676.1990.tb01406.x

Jung, C. G. (1933). *Modern man in search of a soul* (C. F. Baynes & W. S. Dell, Trans.). London: Kegan Paul, Trench, Trubner and Co.

Kaplan, D. M., Tarvydas, V. M., & Gladding, S. T. (2014). 2020: A vision for the future of counseling: The new consensus definition of counseling. *Journal of Counseling & Development, 92*(3), 366–372. doi:10.1002/j.1556-6676.2014.00164.x

Kiselica, M. S., & Robinson, M. (2001). Bringing advocacy counseling to life: The history, issues, and human dramas of social justice work in counseling. *Journal of Counseling & Development, 79*(4), 387–397. doi:10.1002/j.1556-6676.2001.tb01985.x

Leahy, M. J. (2004). Qualified providers of rehabilitation counseling services. In T. F. Riggar & D. R. Maki (Eds.), *The handbook of rehabilitation counseling* (pp. 142–158). New York, NY: Springer Publishing Company.

Leahy, M. J., Rak, E., & Zanskas, S. A. (2016). A brief history of counseling and specialty areas of practice. In I. Marini & M. Stebnicki (Eds.), *Professional counselors desk reference* (2nd ed., pp. 3–8). New York, NY: Springer Publishing Company.

Levers, L. L. (1997). Counseling as a recursive dynamic: Relationship and process, meaning-making and empowerment. In T. F. Riggar & D. R. Maki (Eds.), *Rehabilitation counseling: Profession and practice* (2nd ed., pp. 170–182). New York, NY: Springer Publishing Company.

Levers, L. L. (2007). On being a professional counselor. In J. Gregoire & C. Jungers (Eds.), *Counselor's companion: Handbook for professional helpers* (pp. 2–17). New York, NY: Earlbaum.

Levers, L. L. (2012). Conclusion: An integrative systemic approach to trauma. In L. L. Levers (Ed.), *Counseling survivors of trauma: Theories and interventions*. New York, NY: Springer Publishing Company.

Levers, L. L. (2017). Disability issues in a global context. In V. M. Tarvydas & M. Hartley (Eds.), *The professional practice of rehabilitation counseling* (pp. 173–200). New York, NY: Springer Publishing Company.

Lightfoot, E., Nienow, M., Moua, K-N. L., Colburn, G., & Petri, A. (2016). Insights on professional identification and licensure from community practice social workers. *Journal of Community Practice, 24*(2), 123–146. doi:10.1080/10705422.2016.1165328

Lynch, M. F., & Levers, L. L. (2007). Ecological-transactional and motivational perspectives in counseling. In J. Gregoire & C. Jungers (Eds.), *Counselor's companion: Handbook for professional helpers* (pp. 586–605). New York, NY: Earlbaum.

MacNaughton, K., Chreim, S., & Bourgeault, I. L. (2013). Role construction and boundaries in interprofessional primary health care teams: A qualitative study. *BMC Health Services Research*. Retrieved from https://bmchealthservres.biomedcentral.com/track/pdf/10.1186/1472-6963-13-486

Myers, J. E. (1991). Wellness as the paradigm for counseling and development: The possible future. *Counselor Education and Supervision, 30*(3), 183–193. doi:10.1002/j.1556-6978.1991.tb01199.x

Myers, J. E., & Sweeney, T. J. (2008). Wellness counseling: The evidence base for practice. *Journal of Counseling & Development, 86*(4), 482–493. doi:10.1002/j.1556-6678.2008.tb00536.x

Myers, J. E., Sweeney, T. J., & White, V. E. (2002). Advocacy for counseling and counselors: A professional imperative. *Journal of Counseling & Development, 80*(4), 394–402. doi:10.1002/j.1556-6678.2002.tb00205.x

National Board for Certified Counselors. (2018). *Portability proposal.* Retrieved from http://www.nbcc.org/Portability

Nichols, L. M. (2015). The use of mind-body practices in counseling: A grounded theory study. *Journal of Mental Health Counseling, 37*(1), 28–46. doi:10.17744/mehc.37.1.v432446211272p4r

Olson, S., Brown-Rice, K., & Gerodias, A. (2018). Professional counselor licensure portability: An examination of state license applications. *The Professional Counselor, 8*(1), 88–103. Retrieved from http://tpcjournal.nbcc.org/professional-counselor-licensure-portability-an-examination-of-state-license-applications

Parsons, F. (1909, Posthumously Published). *Choosing a vocation.* Boston, MA: Houghton Mifflin Company.

Pavlov, I. (1926). *Conditioned reflexes.* Oxford: Oxford University Press.

Polanyi, M. (1967). *The tacit dimension.* Garden City, NY: Anchor Books.

Porges, S. W. (2011). *The polyvagal theory: Neurophysiological foundations of emotions, attachment, communication, and self-regulation.* New York, NY: W. W. Norton & Company.

Proctor, W. M. (1925). *Educational and vocational guidance.* Boston, MA: Houghton Mifflin Company.

Proctor, W. M., Benefield, G. R., & Wrenn, C. G. (1931). *Workbook in vocations.* Boston, MA: Houghton Mifflin Company.

Ritchie, M. H. (1990). Counseling is not a profession—Yet. *Counselor Education and Supervision, 29*(4), 220–227. doi:10.1002/j.1556-6978.1990.tb01161.x

Rogers, C. (1942). *Counseling and psychotherapy: Newer concepts in practice.* Boston, MA; New York, NY: Houghton Mifflin Company.

Rogers, C. (1951). *Client-centered therapy: Its current practice, implications and theory.* London: Constable.

Sharf, R. S. (2016). *Theories of psychotherapy and counseling: Concepts and cases* (6th ed.). Boston, MA: Cengage.

Skinner, B. F. (1938). *The behavior of organisms.* New York, NY: Appleton-Century-Crofts, Inc.

Skovholt, T. M., Rønnestad, M. H., & Jennings, L. (1997). Searching for expertise in counseling, psychotherapy, and professional psychology. *Educational Psychology, 9*(4), 361–369. doi:10.1023/A:1024798723295

Smith, H. L. (2012). The historical development of community and clinical mental health counseling in the United States. *Turkish Psychological Counseling and Guidance Journal, 4*(37), 1–10.

Tarvydas, V. T., & Johnston, S. P. (2018). Ethics and ethics decision making. In V. M. Tarvydas & M. T. Hartley (Eds.), *The professional practice of rehabilitation counseling* (pp. 313–342). New York, NY: Springer Publishing Company.

Van Hesteren, F., & Ivey, A. E. (1990). Counseling and development: Toward a new identity for a profession in transition. *Journal of Counseling & Development, 68*(5), 524–528. doi:10.1002/j.1556-6676.1990.tb01403.x

Weikel, W. J. (1985, March; updated 2010, July). *A brief history of the American Mental Health Counselors Association.* Retrieved from http://www.amhca.org/Go.aspx?MicrositeGroupTypeRouteDesignKey=430fca37-b93a-492b-8d69-277eef72bd9b&NavigationKey=a159b7c4-8cca-42da-8016-291ce825bc87

Wolpe, J. (1973). *The practice of behavior therapy* (2nd ed.). Oxford: Pergamon Press.

SECTION II

WORKING WITH CLIENTS

CHAPTER 3

ALLIED AND CLINICAL MENTAL HEALTH SYSTEMS-OF-CARE AND STRENGTH-BASED APPROACHES

ELIAS MPOFU | MAIDEI MACHINA | BOYA WANG | REBEKAH KNIGHT

Allied and clinical mental health case management is a systems-of-care and strength-based model of care that transcends professional affiliations. Allied health professionals and mental health clinicians (hereafter allied and clinical mental health professionals) implementing systems-of-care and strength-based case management approaches work collaboratively within multidisciplinary teams (MDTs) to provide patient- or client-oriented care services to maintain, augment, and restore health and function. This case management provided by allied and clinical mental health professionals includes the design system-of-care-wide therapeutic interventions for supporting patients/clients in their healthcare management, inclusive of mental health. Systems-of-care and strength-based approaches are framed by addressing the full scope of the health needs of the patient or client across areas of activity and participation and capitalizing on the patient's or client's resources for health recovery while maintaining the efficient use of treatment care resources. The successful implementation of a systems-of-care and strength-based model of care by allied and clinical mental health case managers depends on the use of appropriate training and skills, as well as a case referral system that minimizes service discontinuities. Misalignment of systems-of-care to patient's or client's needs and marginalization of the patient or client assets for health recovery, including mental health functioning, would result in suboptimal patient or client health outcomes and would rely on using stand-alone rather than integrated healthcare services. This chapter presents a systems-of-care and a strength-based approach to allied health case management likely to result in superior mental health function and well-being for patients or clients, their families or significant others, and care providers.

The following Council for Accreditation of Counseling and Related Educational Programs (CACREP) standards are addressed in this chapter:
CACREP 2016:
 2F1.b, 2F1.c, 2F5.b, 5C3.d, 5C3.b, 5C3.e
CACREP 2009:
 2G1.b, 2G5.a

LEARNING OBJECTIVES

After reviewing this chapter, the reader should be able to:

1. Define allied and clinical mental health case management from a systems-of-care and strength-based approaches perspective.

2. Outline the evolution of allied and clinical mental health case management, highlighting the significance of the systems-of-care and strength-based oriented practices.

3. Discuss systems-of-care and strength-based role and functions of allied and mental health clinicians in the delivery of case management services in acute and community care settings.

4. Identify and discuss ethical issues in the use of systems-of-care and strength-based approaches to allied and clinical mental health case management.

5. Apply systems-of-care and strength-based case management approaches to case illustrations of patients or clients with complex (mental) healthcare needs.

6. Discuss the potential of and constraints to systems-of-care and strength-based approaches to allied and clinical mental health case management to address mental health function needs in patients or clients.

▨ INTRODUCTION

Allied and clinical mental health case managers seek to optimize healthcare coordination for the patient or client, ensuring comprehensive care provision, while reducing healthcare use and costs (Case Management Society of America [CMSA], 2010; Hudon, Chouinard, Lambert, Dufour, & Krieg, 2016; Robinson, 2010). Major players of allied health and clinical mental health include occupational therapists, physiotherapists, nurses, social workers, and clinical mental health counselors. Each of these professionals has unique care roles in providing a system-of-care that spans disciplines and complements expertise, and that focuses on augmenting patient or client health and functional strengths. For instance, occupational therapists typically focus on conducting comprehensive assessments and designing treatment plans that address the physical, cognitive, affective, social, financial, environmental, and spiritual components that influence a client's health and well-being (Willard et al., 2014). Physiotherapists focus on optimizing clients' active mobility, while social workers conduct comprehensive psychosocial assessments that explore the physical, psychological, and social aspects of the clients and their respective situations (Society for Social Work Leadership in Health, 2015). Clinical mental health counselors provide interventions designed to improve a client's mental health functioning. Clinical mental health counselors and nursing staff are critical to safe discharge planning and sustainable community living with chronic illness or disease. In addition to their discipline-specific responsibilities, all allied health professionals assist with generic case management tasks that include, but are not limited to, monitoring symtoms, providing supportive counseling, organizing family conferences, referring clients to in-hospital and external services, and assisting with discharge planning (Lloyd, King, & Ryan, 2007; Smith, 2011).

Allied and clinical mental healthcare professionals work with federal agencies, healthcare policy makers, and healthcare providers, working collaboratively to provide high quality and efficient client-centered healthcare services while ensuring health system sustainability. Sustainable health services are likely only when mental healthcare needs are addressed together with any presenting physical healthcare needs. Chronic illness and disease often are accompanied by mental health challenges that need to be addressed in order to achieve sustained recovery (see Chapter 6).

The Association of Schools of Allied Health Professionals (2018) defines allied health case management as "the segment of the healthcare field that delivers services involving the identification, evaluation, and prevention of diseases and disorders; dietary and nutrition services; and rehabilitation and health systems management" (p. 1). This involves the mental healthcare that is primary or secondary to other health conditions. Similarly, the CMSA (2010) defines case management as "a collaborative process of assessment planning, facilitation, care coordination, evaluation, and advocacy for options and services to meet an individuals' and family's comprehensive health needs through communication and available resources to promote quality cost-effective outcomes" (p. 6). These service qualities are optimal when mental health needs are addressed as a part of comprehensive healthcare provision.

Current health policies emphasize the need for systems-of-care and strength-based services to provide integrated and coordinated care for patients with chronic diseases, such as asthma, diabetes, heart disease, stroke and vascular disease, osteoarthritis, rheumatoid arthritis, osteoporosis, and cancer. Case management services are pertinent for people with chronic conditions who often require long-term care that crosses conventional care service boundaries, but such clients or patients typically have experienced, fragmented, and poorly coordinated care management.

There is a growing body of evidence that suggests that a positive correlation exists between the implementation of a systems-of-care and strength-based case management approach to the delivery of healthcare services and improved health outcomes for clients with chronic diseases (Burke et al., 2016; Gabbay et al., 2013; Huntley, Johnson, King, Morris, & Purdy, 2016; Morrish et al., 2009; Scherz et al., 2017). For example, with case management utilization by specialty MDTs, repeat asthma admissions fell by 33% in 2 years. Length of hospital stays also fell by 52% in difficult asthma patients who had prior frequent admissions (Burke et al., 2016). Disconnected services come with mental health stress from patients or clients seeking to negotiate the care service niches separately.

Systems-of-care provided by MDTs comprised of allied health professionals and clinical mental health clinicians providing coordinated or integrated services can utilize their discipline-specific skills sets, knowledge, and training to address mental health needs of persons with complex and chronic conditions (Krupa & Clark, 1995).

This chapter provides an overview of systems-of-care and strength-based qualities that allow effective allied and clinical mental healthcare management to deliver optimal care with sustainability. We provide a brief overview of the evolution of allied and clinical mental healthcare management services in the United States. Next, we discuss the scope and functioning of allied and clinical mental health case management services and related ethical issues. Then we provide a comprehensive digest on types of allied and clinical mental health case management settings and related practices with illustrative case studies. Finally, we consider research and practice issues in allied and clinical mental health case management.

▨ HISTORY OF ALLIED AND CLINICAL HEALTH IN CASE MANAGEMENT

The historical evolution of case management in the United States can be traced as far back as the 19th century when almshouses were established during the Colonial period in order to provide a place for the dependent aging and poor populations to receive care for their illnesses (Linz, McAnally, & Wieck, 1989). Churches or municipalities were the primary providers during this period. Subsequently, state governments provided homes for the aged and infirm. Families carried the burden of care for their vulnerable members from any cause. Social workers were among the first healthcare professionals to recognize the need for a case management approach to the delivery of healthcare services in order to improve the quality of care and health outcomes of impoverished and vulnerable populations (Australian Association of Social Workers, 2015; Society of Social Work Leadership in Health, 2015). A timeline for the development of case management is shown in Figure 3.1.

In 1935, Franklin D. Roosevelt signed the Social Security Act, which was designed to provide old-age pensions and old-age assistance payments to the elderly, the unemployed, and the disadvantaged. This Act gave individuals the ability to receive pensions and cash assistance to procure quality care in emerging private institutions. These nongovernmental care institutions were some of the first to receive federal funds for providing care as long as they adhered to the guidelines set forth by the Act (Doty, 1996).

In 1965, the U.S. Congress passed the Medicare (Title 18) and Medicaid (Title 19) sections of the Social Security Act, which provided funding appropriations for medical and social services. Following this, there was a proliferation of case management providers in both the public and private sectors; however, patients and families were still faced with ongoing challenges in regard to how to navigate their continuum and management of care. Additional legislation continued to be passed in the 1970s, and there arose a need to coordinate the various services and programs offered through diverse agencies and delivery systems. There was a spike in the demand for case managers across a variety of settings including long-term care, inpatient and outpatient hospitalizations, community service settings, home care, and others. Currently, healthcare provisioning is a multibillion dollar business in the United States, and organizations are turning to case managers

19th Century	Private singular charity organizations started to provide case management services to people in need.
1935	Social Security Act attempted to bring together categorical programs (i.e., public assistance and social insurance programs) into logical relationships.
1960s	Great wave of federal legislation for social services occurs. The need for case-management emerges in response to the deinstitutionalization of large numbers of people with severe mental health conditions who required referrals to outpatient and community health services.
1970s	The rapid increase in the number of human service programs results in negative consequences (i.e., fragmented and uncoordinated care systems).
1971	The Secretary of Health, Education, and Welfare declared service integration as a policy objective. Forty-five federally funded projects called Service Integration Targets of Opportunity started to build local interagency linkages.
1980s	The increasing cost of healthcare and decentralization of health services influence the role of case management. Growing bodies of evidence demonstrate that case management can potentially reduce the cost of services for individuals with chronic disabilities.
Late 1980s until now	Case management processes are adapted for implementation in all healthcare areas and practice settings (i.e., acute, subacute, rehabilitation, and community settings). Case management roles are undertaken by individuals from various disciplines to cater to people with different health conditions in diverse contexts and settings.

FIGURE 3.1 The historical evolution of allied health and mental health case management.

SOURCE: Linz, M., McAnally, P., & Wieck, C. (1989). *Case management: Historical, current and future perspectives.* Cambridge, MA: Brookline Books.

to help patients receive the highest quality of care possible while also promoting the most efficient use of resources and services.

In recent years, the realization that case management is a model of care that transcends professional affiliations has created the unique opportunity for members of various allied health and mental health professions to assume certain aspects of the case management role. As early as 1991, the American Occupational Therapy Association published the document *Statement: The Occupational Therapist as Case Manager* and asserted that occupational therapists can serve successfully as case managers (American Occupational Therapy Association, 2017). Baldwin and Fisher (2005) found that the educational premises and standards of occupational therapy programs paralleled the fundamental concepts of case management as defined by the CMSA, including the holistic (i.e., medical, spiritual, and psychosocial) management of chronic and complex conditions. The Australian Physiotherapy Association's position statement supports a physical therapist's role in case management in addition to clinical-based interventions, particularly in the areas of occupational rehabilitation and chronic diseases. Occupational therapists and physiotherapists are well trained to work collaboratively within MDTs, performing comprehensive functional and environmental assessments, designing therapeutic interventions, and developing management plans using a holistic approach to practice (Krupa & Clark, 1995; Robinson, Fisher, & Broussard, 2016; Willard, Spackmen, Schelle, Gillen, & Scaffa, 2014). In these roles, they typically collaborate with medical doctors, social workers, mental health clinicians, families, and community health support agencies.

The determination of which specific allied health professional or mental health clinician is best suited to provide short-term and long-term case management services is dependent upon the specific care needs of the client, the care setting, and the professional background of the clinician providing the service (Gursansky, Kennedy, & Camilleri, 2012; Powell & Tahan, 2010). For example, a client whose chronic obstructive pulmonary disease (COPD) interferes with the performance of activities of daily living and increases the risk of falls would benefit from having an occupational therapist as a case manager. By successfully matching the needs of the client to a case manager with the most relevant professional background, training, skills, and knowledge, clients experience better access to appropriate care, receive improved care coordination, and experience enhanced clinical outcomes while de-escalating healthcare costs. Furthermore, effective case management also may serve to empower clients by providing them with relevant clinical information, support, resources, and resource management strategies that enable them to increase their participation in the decision-making processes and planning for their current and future needs.

Allied health and clinical mental health case managers applying systems-of-care and strength-based practices typically work alongside with, or in lieu of, the family physician and are able to offer additional explanation and coordination of healthcare for the individual client (Dugdale, Epstein, & Pantilat, 1999). When one assesses the total amount of healthcare paperwork, instructions, prescriptions, and appointments that the average client must navigate, it becomes very clear that professional help is needed to navigate these challenges.

ALLIED HEALTH AND CLINICAL MENTAL HEALTH CASE MANAGEMENT: CONTEXT AND SCOPE OF PRACTICE

Case management is aimed to improve the coordination of care for clients with chronic and complex conditions across various healthcare settings (CMSA, 2010). The main goals of systems-of-care and strength-based case management are to focus on providing seamlessly networked services for improving quality of care by providing therapeutic and beneficial care that is responsive to emerging health needs from disease progression, including those that are related to a primary mental health disorder diagnosis.

Context of Allied Health and Clinical Mental Health Case Management

For decades, nurses and social workers have taken the central role in allied healthcare coordination, and they are recognized as experts in care management. However, as the U.S. federal government seeks new ways of controlling escalating healthcare costs while maintaining quality of care (Robinson et al., 2016), case management strategies delivered by MDTs, in collaboration with clinical mental health professionals, have become more prevalent. For this reason, allied health and clinical mental health case managers provide coordinated, client-centered services for improving the quality of care and health outcomes, across the spectrum of health conditions and service systems (Baldwin & Fisher, 2005; Chapleau, Seroczynski, Meyers, Lamb, & Haynes, 2011; Smith, Yeowell, & Fatoye, 2017). The following is a representative list of allied and clinical mental health case management practice settings:

- Hospitals and integrated care delivery systems, including acute care, sub-acute care, long-term acute care facilities, nursing facilities, and rehabilitation facilities;

- Ambulatory care clinics and community-based organizations;

- Public health insurance programs (i.e., Medicare, Medicaid, and state-funded programs);

- Private health insurance programs (i.e., workers' compensation, occupational health, disability, accident and health, long-term care insurance, and group health insurance);

- Independent and private case management companies;

- Government-sponsored programs (i.e., correctional facilities and military healthcare/Veterans Affairs);

- Provider agencies and community facilities (i.e., mental health facilities, home health services, ambulatory, and day-care facilities);

- Geriatric services, including residential and assisted living facilities;

- Long-term care services, including home and community-based services;

- Hospice, palliative, and respite care programs;

- Physician and medical group practices;

- Life care planning programs; and,

- Disease management companies (CMSA, 2010).

Allied health and clinical mental health case management currently is provided at all levels of care from the acute hospital setting to rehabilitation centers and community programs. Moreover, systems-of-care and strength-based case management practices are expanding to emphasize client education and self-advocacy, enabling clients to seek services for emerging health needs, including those that arise from mental health function compromise. Allied health and clinical health professionals bring distinct value and unique expertise to the role of case management not only from their medical, psychosocial, and practical clinical experience, but also from their knowledge of related health services to supplement or complement those that are discipline specific but likely to enhance the overall health and function of the patient or client. Moreover, poor organizational relationships, which include lack of clarity in directions and expectations from supervisors/management, compromise the quality of care for patients or clients by allied and clinical mental health case managers (Salloum, Kondrat, Johnco, & Olson, 2015).

The Role and Scope of Practice of Allied and Clinical Mental Health Case Management

The roles and responsibilities of allied health and clinical mental health case managers vary depending on the care setting (i.e., hospital, community, hospice, and insurer), model of practice used (i.e., brokerage, rehabilitation, clinical, and strength based), target population being served, area of specialty (i.e., mental health, elder care, long-term care, and child welfare), and the profession of the person providing the service (i.e., medical, nursing, allied health professionals, and mental health clinicians). For this reason, some care settings may prioritize mental healthcare needs more than others. A system-of-care is when a specific service deliberately addresses patient and client needs with an appropriate and timely referral. Furthermore, the roles and scope of practice of case managers can be influenced significantly by funding priorities and programs or organizational mandates. This being the case, some service care settings may overlook the mental health function needs of clients that are important for overall quality of treatment care.

A yawning healthcare practice gap occurs when allied health management systems-of-care fail to address the mental health needs of patients or clients that are important for health-related quality-of-life and treatment adherence for comorbid health conditions. For instance, in the context of rehabilitation care, case management often begins in the emergency department, immediately after a patient diagnosis has been confirmed and the patient has been stabilized (Wissel, Olver, & Sunnerhagen, 2013). Emergency rehabilitation will include a coordinated multidisciplinary approach, which often will involve pharmacotherapy, surgical intervention, and physical or occupational therapy. Emergency rehabilitation service case managers fulfill the responsibilities of their discipline while working toward a common goal for a treatment plan for the health function recovery of the patient. Emergency rehabilitation case managers determine the discharge destination of the patient as the level of functional recovery (Jesus & Hoenig, 2015), often without a mental healthcare qualified person on the case management roster. Needless to say, the mental healthcare needs of patients in emergency medical care settings likely are short-changed or ignored from a lack of systems-of-care approach to patient or client management.

Allied and clinical mental health case manager roles are defined operationally by the behaviors and expected outcomes associated with a person's position in a social structure (CMSA, 2010). For instance, the roles of allied health and clinical mental health case managers can be divided into two areas: patient/client and family-system roles, or service-system roles, otherwise known as clinical or administrative roles, respectively (You, Dunt, & Doyle, 2015). Each of these two broad roles carries both potentialities and constraints for addressing existing or emerging mental health function needs of patients or clients.

Clinical Roles

An allied and clinical mental health case manager's clinical roles, such as caregiver, educator, problem solver, and supporter, focus on providing quality care through applying systems-of-care and strength-based interventions. Case managers implementing systems-of-care and strength-based interventions within this capacity are expected to fulfill some of the following responsibilities:

- Conduct comprehensive assessments of the health and psychosocial needs of the client while taking into consideration the needs and expectations of the family or caregivers;

- Identify the current and potential needs of the client in order to develop a case management or clinical pathway plan in collaboration with the client, family, caregivers, and all appropriate healthcare, social, and community service providers;

- Inform and educate the client, family, or caregivers regarding the management of acute or chronic conditions, available treatment options, available health, social, and community resources, insurance benefits, and so forth;

- Assist the client in safe transitioning of care among healthcare settings, service providers, and levels of care to ensure the seamless continuity of care; and,

- Empower the client to engage in self-advocacy and self-determination by exploring options of care when available and alternative plans when necessary to achieve desired outcomes (CMSA, 2010).

Allied and clinical mental health practices subscribe to the dictum "do no harm," which is widely acknowledged alongside several ethical principles of medical and healthcare practice, and which also includes beneficence, respect for autonomy, and justice (Hain & Saad, 2016). However, the extent to which allied and clinical mental health practitioners are trained in interdisciplinary practice ethics in healthcare to guide acceptable professional conduct is questionable. This is primarily because few preservice healthcare professional programs provide direct instruction concerning interdisciplinary systems-of-care oriented practices, with the seeming expectation that practitioners somehow will learn the ethical practices from work experience. Consequently, apparent mental healthcare needs of patients or clients are likely to be overlooked by practitioners overly invested in their discipline-specific roles and functions.

Administrative Roles

Administrative roles, such as gatekeeper, care coordinator, negotiator, and advocate, focus on the coordination of services and the management of resources. Allied health and clinical mental health case managers implementing systems-of-care and strength-based interventions in this capacity are expected to:

- Generate referrals to appropriate health, social, and community services;

- Facilitate efficient and timely communication and coordination of services among providers to minimize fragmentation;

- Manage financial resources, analyze fiscal benefits, maintain cost-effectiveness, and ensure effective resource utilization;

- Advocate for the attainment of resources and the achievement of desired outcomes for the client and the healthcare providers; and,

- Remain up-to-date with policy, funding, and research developments (CMSA, 2010).

In this regard, allied health and clinical mental health case managers apply systems-of-care and strength-based approaches to assist patients or clients to navigate complex health, social, and community service systems. Matters related to the scope of practice in allied health case management continue to evolve with the increasing impetus toward interdisciplinary practices. Regrettably, role ambiguities and conflicts are often the rule rather than the exception (Beard & Barter, 2016; Dasgupta, 2013), hazarding the overall quality of care, with risk for escalating mental healthcare needs from suboptimal care. For instance, when working in a healthcare role, ethical conflicts can arise from systematic constraints on the extent to which a care provider can go beyond the call of duty to care without infringing on client autonomy (Beard & Barter, 2016).

Other administrative practice-related ethical issues arise from the need to maintain continuity of care while facing barriers, such as under-resourcing, high staff turnover, and understaffing (Brady, 2003). This is particularly the case when allied and clinical mental health professionals seek to serve dispersed client populations, such as those in rural or remote locations, and residents of historically disadvantaged neighborhoods (Davis & Bartlett, 2008; Morgan, Innes, & Kosteniuk, 2011), though there is increasing use of tele-health technology to mitigate some of these barriers to systems-of-care oriented services (Inglis, Clark, Dierchx, Prieto-Merino, & Cleland, 2015; Morgan et al., 2011; Reinius et al., 2013). For instance, the community virtual ward (CVW) model has been developed in order to assist healthcare professionals to support and provide treatment to older healthcare clients within their own home environment in order to reduce emergency department presentations and unplanned hospital admissions. The CVW model provides a framework of care that assists healthcare professionals with prioritizing client care coordination and ensuring the timely mobilization of services. This innovative approach to the provision of healthcare services allows allied health professionals and clinical mental health counselors to circumvent some of the continuity-of-care ethical concerns that were noted previously. However, research evidence is needed on the incremental value of the use of CVW in allied health professions and clinical mental health case management.

Ethical practice issues also arrive from allied and clinical mental health practitioners in both service system (administration) roles and client system (clinical) case manager roles, which may require knowledge and skills that can be vastly different from those required by some allied health professionals when fulfilling their traditional professional roles (Krupa & Clark, 1995; Lloyd et al., 2007). Some service-system roles involve managing client budgets, monitoring the use of resources, and being gatekeepers to accessing services, while client-system roles may involve being a crisis manager, counselor, monitor, and educator (CMSA, 2010; You et al., 2015). In this regard, allied and clinical mental health professionals may experience significant challenges to assume systems-of-care and strength-based role and functions new to their scope of practice and training.

From the legal realm come regulatory standards and policies, such as the Health Information Privacy and Accountability Act (HIPAA) of 1996, issued by the U.S. Department of Health and Human Services and aimed at protecting the use and disclosure of the private health information of individuals. While this rule has been deemed successful in protecting the individual's health information from commodification or abuse, it also may limit allied and clinical mental health professionals in collaborations that are intended to address the mental healthcare needs of the patient or client at the planning stage of the case management process. In other words, at least in some ways, this Act may make it more cumbersome for allied and clinical mental health counseling (CMHC) professionals to collaborate on services that are needed by the client or patient. However, what may seem to be a somewhat restrictive function of the act actually affords protection to clients and patients. While professional collaboration generally is encouraged, HIPAA regulations require a signed release of information from the client as a necessary step in protecting clients' and patients' rights.

The Case Management Process

In applying systems-of-care and strength-based approaches, allied and clinical mental health case managers help clients to progress through each phase of the case management process, taking into consideration the health status, needs, values, and wishes of the clients, their families, and caregivers within the service-provider policy framework. Healthcare case management also is "carried out within the ethical and legal realm of a case manager's scope of practice, using critical thinking and evidence-based knowledge" (CMSA, 2010, p. 14). The typical steps in the case management process are included in the following list:

Screening/Intake or On-Boarding
This involves the gathering and reviewing of relevant information related to a client's past and present health conditions, functional abilities, social supports, home environment, current and prior services, and financial and insurance assets. The allied health case manager's objective is to identify client needs for targeted case management services.

Assessment
This entails the gathering of in-depth information about a client's circumstances similar to that gathered during the screening phase. The case manager's objective is to identify the client's needs and assets in order to facilitate the development of a comprehensive case management or clinical pathway plan. The assessment of a client's needs occurs repeatedly throughout the case management process as the client's needs and the situation change.

Planning
This entails establishing, modifying, and prioritizing the client's long-term and short-term goals for intervention in addition to determining the resources and the health, social, and community services required to meet the established goals and achieve the client's desired quality of life.

Implementation
This is about the execution of the case management plan. The allied health or clinical mental health case manager's objectives are to engage in active care coordination.

Monitoring and Review
This spans the activities aimed at monitoring the effectiveness of the case management plan. It also provides the opportunity to revise any irrelevant plans and/or address any unforeseen problems.

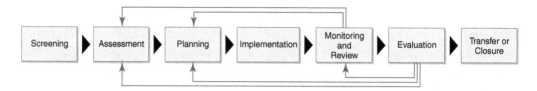

FIGURE 3.2 Systems-of-care and strength-based case management process.

Evaluation

This involves the formal and informal assessment of the effectiveness of the case management plan, applying a systems-of-care and strength-based approach. The allied health or clinical mental health case manager's objective is to determine the effect of the case management plan on improving the client's health condition(s) and quality of life.

Transfer or Closure

This is about the transfer or termination of case management services when all of the client's goals have been met, or the needs of the client have changed, and his or her recovery-oriented assets have been enhanced.

A systems-of-care and strength-based case management process is not a linear one. It is recursive and involves the constant reassessment, planning, monitoring, reviewing, and evaluation of the case management plan to ensure that the clients' desired outcomes are met as illustrated in Figure 3.2.

Regardless of the specific health condition for which a patient or client is receiving care, systems-of-care, and strength-based case management functions must address mental health function needs, as these are critically important for overall health-related quality of life. Depending on the coping resource supports to the patient or client, their mental healthcare needs would fluctuate across the case management process phases, requiring interdisciplinary collaboration to address the needs adequately. Coping refers to the actions and thoughts individuals engage to enable them to deal with stressors. Strength-based case management interventions seek to support patients or clients to adopt and utilize active coping strategies or psychological or behavioral responses that foster a positive mental health attitude toward living with a debilitating health condition.

TYPES AND LEVELS OF ALLIED HEALTH AND CLINICAL MENTAL HEALTH CASE MANAGEMENT APPROACHES

Case management services can be initiated in any treatment setting and can be provided during a single episode of care and/or throughout the care continuum. This ensures that clients receive the right care at the right time and from the right provider for the best price. Systems-of-care and strength-based case management services generally are implemented based on two models of care: internal case management and external case management (Rutter et al., 2004).

Internal Case Management

Internal or "within the walls" case management services are provided mainly within the hospital acute, subacute, and inpatient rehabilitation setting. These services typically are implemented to coordinate internal and transitional hospital services during a single episode of care (Rutter et al., 2004). Efficient and effective internal case management service provision often is provided by nursing staff and, to a lesser extent, by allied health professionals.

The Clinical Setting

Within a clinical setting, the case management process and coordination of clinical care begin at the moment of triage. As previously noted, this process involves facilitating efficient patient flow through the healthcare system, thus ensuring needed assessments along with treatment planning and implementation with the clients, their families, and other health providers for timely referral. This, in turn, can enhance client clinical outcomes, reducing the length of hospitalization, readmission rates, and costs of care delivery (Gursansky et al., 2012; Rutter et al., 2004). To achieve these goals in a systems-of-care manner, case managers working within this capacity are required to:

- Understand and facilitate efficient patient flow;
- Be knowledgeable about various insurance plans;
- Understand the roles of all members of the MDT;
- Be knowledgeable of available community and in-facility resources;
- Be able to interpret the meaning of laboratory test results;
- Be able to develop and implement complex clinical pathway plans; and,
- Have extensive knowledge of all major medical diagnoses, procedures, and medications (Powell & Tahan, 2010; Scherz et al., 2017; Smith, 2011).

While the lead internal allied and clinical health case manager may be nursing staff, clinical mental health counselors play a key role in ensuring the safe and timely discharge of clients from the clinical setting, as typically is the case with clinical mental health counselors working in psychiatric hospitals (Lloyd et al., 2007; Smith, 2011).

Allied health professionals making a transition from providing discipline-specific interventions to engaging in nondiscipline-specific tasks can expect to experience substantial role confusion and role conflict. Role confusion is characterized by feelings of uncertainty on the part of the case managers as to what their role is within a practice setting, in addition to the existence of uncertainty regarding what is expected of them by colleagues (Smith, 2011). Case manager role confusion and role conflict are occupational hazards that persist due to insufficient training for the case management role and variations in role definition, depending on the practice setting. Within the context of a multidisciplinary case management team, some professionals may become conflicted and disempowered due to role overlap. Case Illustration 3.1 is a hypothetical case study in relation to allied health case management in a clinical setting.

CASE ILLUSTRATION 3.1

HOSPITAL-BASED ALLIED HEALTH AND CLINICAL MENTAL HEALTH COUNSELING CASE MANAGEMENT: THE CASE OF SCOTT

Scott is an 80-year-old man who was brought into the hospital by ambulance with increased urinary frequency and urgency and potential delirium on a background of chronic renal failure. Scott was found by police at the scene of a motor vehicle accident after he crashed his car into a tree while attempting to pull over to the side of the road to urinate. Upon admission, Scott was put under the care of an MDT consisting of a geriatric consultant, registrar, junior medical officer, clinical care coordinator, occupational therapist, physiotherapist, and clinical mental health counselor.

During his admission, the occupational therapist and clinical mental health counselor made several attempts to collect information regarding Scott's social situation, home environment, and preadmission functional status. However, they were unsuccessful, as Scott was in a state of hyperactive delirium. The occupational therapists observed that Scott was disorientated to person, place, and time; looked unkempt; and was unable to manage his personal activities of daily living in the ward (i.e., Scott was refusing to shower and was observed to urinate on the floor, despite being given a urinary bottle and being orientated to the location of the toilets in the ward). The physiotherapist was unable to assess Scott's active mobility, due to his restlessness and agitation. The urology team also came to review Scott and, upon their investigation, determined that he needed to have surgery prior to discharge from the hospital, once his delirium had resolved.

The occupational therapist, physiotherapist, clinical mental health counselor, and nursing staff reported their findings, or lack thereof, and expressed their concerns to the treating medical team and clinical coordinator, and advised against the discharge of Scott. The treating medical team, however, did not agree with the allied health professional's recommendations and believed Scott was at this baseline level of functioning and would be at greater risk of infection if his hospital stay were prolonged any further. The medical team also argued that there was nothing that could be done in terms of linking Scott with external services, as he lived out of the area (2 hours away from the hospital). Scott was discharged from the hospital after a 3-day admission, against the recommendation of allied health. Scott was later found seriously unwell in his place of residence by a friend and was admitted into a local hospital, in his area, for critical care.

The scenario above exemplifies the serious consequences of inadequate internal case management in a clinical setting from the nonuse of systems-of-care and strength-based approaches. In this case, while an MDT was assembled to treat Scott, there was no nominated case manager to oversee the appropriate implementation of care and services, as outlined in the clinical pathway, and to facilitate a safe and appropriate discharge. Regrettably, case management plans did not address his apparent, life-threatening mental health function needs.

Despite the shift toward the implementation of a multidisciplinary approach to case management, it is outside the scope of practice of many allied health professionals to (a) fully understand a consumer's clinical course, (b) develop and ensure the successful implementation of comprehensive clinical pathways, and (c) manage the consumer's financial outcomes of care due to lack of specialized knowledge, skills, and training that are required to embody the clinical case manager role within the clinical setting.

External Case Management

External case management services include the coordination of services across several institutions and providers throughout the care continuum (Rutter et al., 2004). External case management services are provided mainly in the community setting. Within this setting, case management services are provided most effectively and efficiently by certified case managers and community-based health professionals.

The Community Setting

Systems-of-care and strength-based community outpatient therapy services have flourished over the last few decades. They have reduced the costs associated with prolonged hospital stays and have provided comprehensive, high quality care to clients with complex needs. While this increase in the number of community allied health services does create more opportunities for clients to receive multidisciplinary care at home, clients commonly are confused by the fragmented health system, inconsistent referral process, and duplicated assessments.

In order to understand the case management component of an allied health professional's day-to-day work, it is essential to have an overview of the chain of care in the community setting. Figure 3.3 offers a flowchart that illustrates the client journey through the community healthcare system and shows the points of engagement with allied health professionals in various community services. It also serves as a simplified summary of the typical categories of community services.

The four categories of community services illustrated in Figure 3.3 are only simplified examples. In reality, each community health service category comprises numerous intervention programs and services that are designed to cater uniquely to the needs of specific target populations. One might look at hospital-directed systems-of-care and strength-based community services, for example; each service niche has unique inclusion criteria and serves a population with specific conditions or impairments. Community programs and services also may vary, based on the duration of service or based on the health supports focus of the program. Systems-of-care and strength-based allied health and clinical mental health case managers working in the community have the responsibility to deliver quality clinical care, in addition to providing clients with any assistance they may require to navigate the healthcare system by providing effective case management, both internally (with the MDT within the service) and externally (with other community services, hospitals, or home care providers).

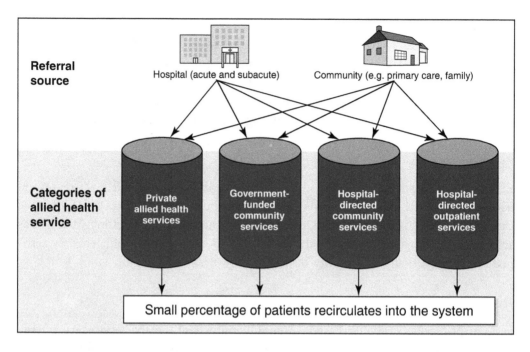

FIGURE 3.3 Referral pathway for community services.

Within Community Program Case Management

For effective systems-of-care and strength-based provision of services, health tasks of a community-living-oriented program relies heavily on effective communication among MDT members. Systems-of-care and strength-based case management in the community adopts a more client-centered care approach when compared to inpatient case management. In the inpatient setting, clients need to follow treatment plans developed by clinicians from differing disciplines in order to meet discharge requirements. For example, physical therapists need clients to achieve optimal mobility, occupational therapists require clients to return to optimum levels of independence in their activities of daily living, and medical teams make sure the patient is medically safe to be discharged. Allied health clinicians conduct their clinical caseload in isolation, and most of the case management collaboration for the allied health staff takes place only during team meetings. In contrast, community rehabilitation programs are heavily client centered and goal oriented. Once a client's goals have been established, the MDT members work collaboratively with each other to help the client achieve his or her goals. This client-centered care approach lays the foundation for case management in the community setting. Allied health professionals and clinical mental health counselors proactively coordinate treatment plans and utilize multidisciplinary professional skills to solve problems and empower clients. Due to its holistic and comprehensive approach, a big emphasis of systems-of-care and strength-based allied health and clinical mental health case management in the community is to coordinate healthcare services with external service providers. For this reason, successful case management of clients in the community setting also requires the establishment of effective referral processes in which allied health professionals and clinical mental health counselors take a comprehensive approach to assessing the needs of their clients and generate appropriate referrals to service providers within the community program and work collaboratively to address the client's goals.

The Axis of Care Coordination

External case management can be divided into two axes of care coordination: the vertical integration coordination of care and the horizontal coordination of care (Lewis et al., 2017) as illustrated in Figure 3.4. Longitudinally, through the vertical continuum of care, the therapist or counselor in a community setting needs to liaise with the treating inpatient team to discuss a client's clinical transfer of care. For example, if a patient is to be discharged from hospital with community follow-up, the members of the treating inpatient team and case manager are required to contact the community allied health or clinical mental health case manager to provide a thorough handover, stating the reason for which the client has been referred to that community service and also stating the patient's goals of treatment. Besides the therapist-to-therapist or counselor-to-counselor vertical integration across primary, community, hospital, and tertiary healthcare services, the allied health or clinical mental health case manager also needs to collaborate proactively with other health and social services along the horizontal axis.

The horizontal axis of coordination of care portrays the breadth of health and social services available in the community. Some examples of horizontal integration of care across health services, social services, and other sectors are illustrated in Figure 3.4. On the horizontal axis, an allied health or clinical mental health case manager might need

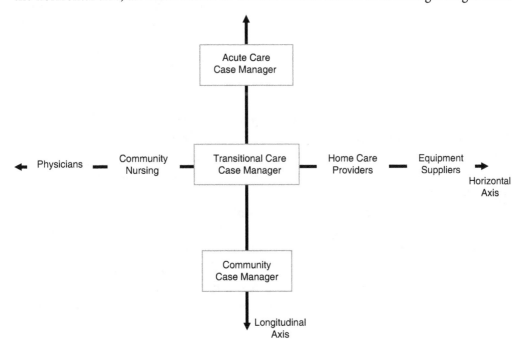

FIGURE 3.4 Axis of care in community-oriented Allied Health Care Model (AHCM).

to communicate with primary care physicians, medical specialists, community nurses, community podiatrists, speech pathologists, dieticians, local pharmacists, equipment suppliers, home care providers, government housing services, home modification services, day-care centers, hoarding and squalor programs, blindness and low vision services, and so on.

Within this model, clinical nurse coordinators and clinical mental health counselors may carry similar case management roles. However, an occupational therapist or physiotherapist may be required to be on call or engage in crisis-management or symptom-monitoring functions typically assigned to nursing, social work, or mental health clinicians. As previously noted, compromise in the overall quality of care may result when allied and mental health professionals who are implementing a system-of-care approach are less well prepared to address mental health function needs of the patient or client. Case Illustration 3.2 is a hypothetical case study in relation to allied health case management in the community setting.

CASE ILLUSTRATION 3.2

EXAMPLE OF AXIS OF CARE ALLIED HEALTH CASE MANAGEMENT: THE CASE OF HOPE

Hope is an 83-year-old female who was admitted to the hospital after experiencing two falls at home. Although Hope complained of bilateral thigh pain during her admission, the x-rays of her hips and pelvis showed no fractures. The physical therapist and occupational therapist who assessed Hope reported that she was independent with her functional mobility and transfers. Hope was discharged home with strong pain relief medication and a follow-up home visit by a physical therapist case manager in order to ensure that she returned to her optimal level of function.

The community physical therapist visited Hope at home, one day after discharge from the hospital, and reported her to have severe pain interfering with her mobility around the home. The physical therapist contacted the inpatient medical team to request a review of Hope's x-rays. A computed tomography (CT) scan was ordered by the medical team and subsequently indicated that Hope had a right hip fracture. Hope was operated on the next day, putting her on course for functional recovery.

This scenario exemplifies the need for systems-of-care and strength-based patient-oriented community-living-focused case management. Although a physical therapist case manager was assigned by the hospital to lead the home care follow-up support for Hope, the physical therapist was able to make the appropriate referrals that Hope required for further investigation and care. However, the care provider team did not address any mental health needs by Hope, which would have been important for better management of the physical recovery functions.

Commodification of Healthcare Services

Healthcare commodification occurs when patient care needs become primarily a monetary gain issue for the care provider. In such cases, patients may be at risk from community healthcare providers offering unneeded case management services primarily for financial gain.

CASE ILLUSTRATION 3.3

EXAMPLE OF COMMODIFICATION OF CARE BY COMMUNITY-BASED HEALTH-CARE PROVIDER: THE CASE OF MR. JONES

Mr. Jones lives in an assisted living center (ALC), is on Medicaid, and other than showing signs of some form of dementia, he seems to be in pretty fair shape. But Mr. Jones had been having increasingly intolerant pain in his left knee joint, so he was taken by the ALC to his family physician. His family physician ruled out arthritis and recommended he visit a brand new orthopedic surgeon named Dr. Smith. The ALC made an appointment with Dr. Smith and transported Mr. Jones to the appointment.

At the appointment, Dr. Smith informed the ALC employee that their patient, Mr. Jones, needed a full-knee replacement, as soon as possible, followed by 3 to 6 months of therapy in his own orthopedic practice therapy center attached to his office. The ALC made all of the arrangements, and Mr. Jones proceeded to have the surgery and therapy without getting a second opinion or having a follow-up MRI. Moreover, the case management protocol did not include the mental health function needs of Mr. Jones, both before and after the full-knee replacement surgery.

The case of Mr. Jones in Case Illustration 3.3 was a breach of ethics as well as overutilization by the ALC. For example, the U.S. Stark Law prohibits physicians to self-refer any Medicare or Medicaid patient to a health service with which the physician has a financial relationship. A qualified second opinion may have ruled out the need for surgery completely for Mr. Jones. Additionally, if therapy were warranted, it could have been completed at any qualified center available (Physician Self-Referral, n.d.). While the ALC provided the minimal care and the case management needed for Mr. Jones, further navigation and assessment into his situation may have shown that only minimal therapy actually was warranted. Overutilization of resources may have occurred, thus putting Mr. Jones at a higher risk than was needed. Furthermore, healthcare product marketing exerts considerable pressure on case managers, wellness coordinators, directors of nursing, and others, which may not be in the best interests of the patient. The case of Mrs. Tonya in Case Illustration 3.4 is illustrative of this.

CASE ILLUSTRATION 3.4

HARMS TO PROFESSIONAL CASE MANAGEMENT BY AGGRESSIVE HEALTHCARE PRODUCT MARKETING: THE CASE OF MRS. TONYA

As the Wellness Coordinator for an independent senior living facility, Mrs. Tonya had marketing representatives coming by almost daily to promote their senior services in hopes that she would then pass them on to the 130 senior adults living under her care. ABC Home Health Agency was the most recognized vendor because they recently had offered to give a substantial building fund donation to Mrs. Tonya's facility if they could become the only home health agency recommended to the residents. Because of this generous offer, Mrs. Tonya's boss told her to recommend only ABC Agency so that they could receive the financial donation. It was only after a family filed suit against the senior living facility and called Adult Protective Services for abuse against their loved one by the ABC Home Health Agency that Mrs. Tonya found out that the ABC agency did not screen their employees properly.

Situations such as this one happen quite often, because the pull of the additional funding in the aging services and housing field is quite appealing. With most of the payment structures and budgets being currently built around the minimal Medicare and Medicaid reimbursement alone, additional financial donations from individuals and companies can alter or sway the best decision-making of those caseworkers and others, who are the front line of protection against poor healthcare practices for patients and residents. Needless to say, Mrs. Tonya's independent living facility underprioritized the mental healthcare needs of residents and their families.

Most allied health professionals and clinical mental health counselors have learned first-hand or have an understanding of the vital importance of effective verbal communication with the patient and the patient's representatives. Language barriers were once a tremendous challenge to all in the healthcare field, but with the creation of language translation apps, software programs, and translator phone services, this challenge has been mitigated to some degree. Communication, however, is not always limited to verbal interactions.

Minimizing the communication barrier with the patient may not be the only challenge that allied health and clinical mental health case management faces in seeking to adopt systems-of-care and strength-based practices. Challenges of financial losses within insurance companies, misunderstandings from housing representatives, disagreement of patient protocols by medical providers, and family members presenting cultural sensitivities all can be potential communication barriers that would affect the allied health and clinical mental health case manager from reaching the best outcome possible for quality care for the client. Case Illustration 3.5 is a hypothetical case study in relation to communication lapses in allied health and clinical mental health case management posing serious potential health risks to a client in a hospital outpatient setting.

CASE ILLUSTRATION 3.5

EXAMPLE OF COMMUNICATION FLOW CHALLENGES: THE CASE OF MR. HARVEY

Mr. Harvey was an 80-year-old male, living in an independent housing facility. With no living relatives nearby, Mr. Harvey relied on the clinical mental health counselor to help him organize his medical care, because the housing facility did not offer him any assistance. The clinical mental health counselor made arrangements for an outpatient surgical procedure that Mr. Harvey needed to have, thus becoming his case manager by default. Unfortunately, it was scheduled during her day off.

The housing facility transported Mr. Harvey to the outpatient surgical facility and dropped him off, as per protocol. After the procedure, the outpatient surgical team placed Mr. Harvey back into the housing facility transport van with a few papers of vital instructions for him to follow. He was dropped off and proceeded up to his room. Later that day, he was found wandering down a hallway looking for help, because he was bleeding profusely from his wound that had reopened. Because he did not understand the instructions given to him by the outpatient surgical center, and because there was no help available at his housing facility, he had to be taken by ambulance to the emergency department for immediate care.

This scenario exemplifies the serious consequences to patient health that can occur from communication lapses in case management care provisioning. In this case, while the housing clinical mental health counselor was the service provider who initially set up the outpatient procedure, the surgical center staff should have confirmed with the housing staff as to who would be following up with Mr. Harvey upon his arrival back home. Most importantly, Mr. Harvey's mental health function needs were a risk for his safety and general well-being, yet they were not addressed by the housing service facility.

ISSUES FOR ALLIED AND CLINICAL MENTAL HEALTH RESEARCH AND PRACTICE

The critical importance of allied health and clinical mental healthcare management is underscored by the fact that individuals with complex and long-term chronic conditions frequently require healthcare and social and community services from multiple healthcare providers across various healthcare sectors (Hirshon et al., 2013). For this reason, allied health and clinical mental health case management systems must provide effective and efficient management for individuals living with long-term health conditions, be they primarily mental or physical (Hudon et al., 2016; Robinson, 2010). We consider three challenges to system-of-care and strength-based approaches to allied and clinical mental health case management, and we discuss these in the following subsections.

Ambiguity of Practice Boundaries With System-of-Care Approaches

More often than not, allied health professionals in community settings assume the role of "case manager" with neither the adequate training nor organizational support required to fulfill the role successfully. The lack of a case manager credentialing regulation potentially places clients at risk of receiving substandard care from case managers who are deficient in educational and professional training for their roles. Moreover, case management programs that focus on decreasing hospital readmission rates among "high risk" patients or clients with multiple morbidities may not address the mental healthcare needs of the patients or clients. Unknown mental health needs may result in patients or clients not seeking readmission, which would harm their overall health and well-being.

Diversity in Case Management Contexts

The multiplicity of roles and the variability of case management responsibilities are limiting to the research evaluation of the effectiveness of systems-of-care and strength-based case management interventions (Agency for Healthcare Research and Quality, 2013). This diversity in case management regimens makes it difficult to (a) isolate which of the components of case management role and process has the greatest influence on its effectiveness and (b) ensure that studies are comparing the effectiveness of equivalent case management models of practice. Moreover, the current research literature is limited by its lack of clarity on findings that are specific to the efficacy of case management models in addressing mental health function needs of different patient or client subgroups. Future research should aim to address explicit mental health outcomes of systems-of-care and strength-based case management approaches among patients presenting with primary mental health conditions or mental health conditions that are secondary to other chronic illness or disease.

Communication Loopholes

Allied health and clinical mental health case management dynamics can be a very fluid situation that ebbs and flows with each patient encounter. As discussed, systems-of-care and strength-based case management roles may have to expand or contract due to multiple variables surrounding each situation. However, ineffective or challenged communication between allied health case managers and clients can exacerbate these relationships and diminish effective decision-making. Furthermore, the allied health and clinical mental health case manager may be the primary communicator of all parties involved in the case including, but not limited to, the client, the family, insurance providers, housing facilities, social services, and healthcare providers. Without effective communication, these interconnected stakeholders may make decisions without updated or factual information, which then can result in lower quality, ineffective care, or poor outcomes for the client.

▨ CONCLUSION

Allied health and clinical mental health counseling (CMHC) professionals increasingly are becoming engaged as case managers by health systems worldwide, applying systems-of-care and strength-based approaches. Good healthcare management also may serve as a mitigating factor for those at risk of health deterioration from preventable causes, the escalation of which has mental health functioning consequences. Allied and clinical mental health case management achieve best outcomes for clients and their allies by facilitating timely quality service coordination, continuity of service, and effective transmission of information between services providers. At each stage of allied health and CMHC case management, mental healthcare needs should be addressed to ensure that intended treatment goals are met by the most efficient means.

Since its emergence in the 18th century, case management has continued to evolve concurrently with changes in healthcare laws, social circumstances, the development of new healthcare delivery models, and advances in technology. While the roots of allied health and CMHC case management germinated over a hundred years ago, allied health professionals are still relatively new at engaging in the provision of case management within community settings.

Within the clinical setting, allied health professionals and mental health clinicians play a key role alongside MDT members in providing coordinated in-hospital care. For allied health professionals and mental health clinicians in the community setting, the utilization of an external case management model of care ensures comprehensive delivery of patient-centered care.

The call for allied health professionals to assume the systems-of-care and strength-based case manager role faces multiple challenges. These challenges include the fact that the education curriculum for occupational therapists and physical therapists remains heavily structured around discipline-specific related knowledge. Case management training and certification programs may facilitate the acquisition of specific skills and knowledge that are significantly different from the clinical training received by allied health therapists.

Current evidence for allied health and CMHC professionals' efficacy in the delivery of case management services is limited but promising. However, further evidence is needed on the effectiveness of systems-of-care and strength-based allied health and clinical mental health case management in improving health outcomes and reducing the cost of healthcare services with subgroups of patients defined by their health and living conditions.

▨ RESOURCES

American Counseling Association: www.counseling.org
   The world's largest association representing counselors and mental health service providers.
American Psychological Association: www.apa.org
   Association for psychologists, provides information on the impact of psychology as it relates to improving social problems and individuals' everyday lives.
Substance Use and Mental Health Services Administration: www.samhsa.gov
   Includes access to comprehensive research related to mental health and substance use, in addition to a National Helpline (treatment locator for clients), 24-hour suicide hotline, and a Disaster Distress Helpline.

▓ REFERENCES

Agency for Healthcare Research and Quality. (2013). *Outpatient case management for adults with medical illnesses and complex care needs: Future research needs*. Portland, OR: Oregon Evidence-based Practice Centre.

American Occupational Therapy Association. (1991). Statement: The Occupational Therapist as Case Manager. *American Journal of Occupational Therapy, 45*(12), 1065–1066. doi:10.5014/ajot.45.12.1065

Association of Schools of Allied Health Professions. (2018). *What is allied health?* Retrieved from http://www.asahp.org/what-is

Australian Association of Social Workers. (2015). *Scope of social work practice: Case management and care coordination*. North Melbourne: Australian Association of Social Workers.

Baldwin, T., & Fisher, T. (2005). Case management: Entry-level practice for occupational therapists? *The Case Manager, 16*(4), 47–51. doi:10.1016/j.casemgr.2005.06.001

Beard, K., & Barter, B. (2016). "What can we do?" Compassionate care and the potential role of clinical psychologists working within intellectual disability services post-Francis and Winterbourne. *Advances in Mental Health and Intellectual Disabilities, 10*(6), 324–332. doi:10.1108/AMHID-09-2016-0027

Brady, F. N. (2003). "Publics" administration and the ethics of particularity. *Public Administration Review, 63*(5), 525–534.

Burke, H., Davis, J., Evans, S., Flower, L., Tan, A., & Kurukulaaratchy, R. (2016). A multidisciplinary team case management approach reduces the burden of frequent asthma admissions. *European Respiratory Journal Open Research, 2*(3), 1–7. doi:10.1183/23120541.00039-2016

Case Management Society of America. (2010). *Standards of practice for case management*. Little Rock, AR: Case Management Society of America.

Centers for Medicare and Medicaid Services. (n.d.) Physician self-referral. Retrieved from https://www.cms.gov/Medicare/Fraud-and-Abuse/PhysicianSelfReferral/index.html?redirect=/physicianselfreferral

Chapleau, A., Seroczynski, A., Meyers, S., Lamb, K., & Haynes, S. (2011). Occupational therapy consultation for case managers in community mental health. *Professional Case Management, 16*(2), 71–79. doi:10.1097/ncm.0b013e3181f0555b

Dasgupta, P. (2013). Effect of role ambiguity, conflict and overload in private hospitals:"Nurses" burnout and mediation through self-efficacy. *Journal of Health Management, 14*(4), 513–534. doi:10.1177/0972063412468980

Davis, S., & Bartlett, H. (2008). Healthy ageing in rural Australia: Issues and challenges. *Australasian Journal on Ageing, 27*(2), 56–60. doi:10.1111/j.1741-6612.2008.00296.x

Doty, P. (1996). *Caring for frail elderly people: Policies in evolution, Chapter 14: United States*. U.S. Department of Health and Human Services. Retrieved from https://aspe.hhs.gov/basic-report/caring-frail-elderly-people-policies-evolution

Dufresne, G. M. (1991). Statement: The occupational therapist as case manager. *The American Journal of Occupational Therapy: Official Publication of the American Occupational Therapy Association, 45*(12), 1065–1066. doi:10.5014/ajot.45.12.1065

Dugdale, D. C., Epstein, R., & Pantilat, S. Z. (1999). Time and the patient physician relationship. *Journal of General Internal Medicine, 14*(Suppl 1), S34–S40. Retrieved from https://www.ncbi.nlm.nih.gov/pmc/articles/PMC1496869

Gabbay, R., Añel-Tiangco, R., Dellasega, C., Mauger, D., Adelman, A., & Van Horn, D. (2013). Diabetes nurse case management and motivational interviewing for change (DYNAMIC): Results of a 2-year randomized controlled pragmatic trial. *Journal of Diabetes, 5*(3), 349–357. doi:10.1111/1753-0407.12030

Gursansky, D., Kennedy, R., & Camilleri, P. (2012). *Practice of case management: Effective strategies for positive outcomes.* Crows Nest, NSW: Allen & Unwin.

Hain, R., & Saad, T. (2016). Foundations of practical ethics. *Medicine, 44*(10), 578–582. doi:10.1016/j.mpmed.2016.07.008

Hirshon, J., Risko, N., Calvello, E., Stewart de Ramirez, S., Narayan, M., Theodosis, T., & O'Neill, J. (2013). Health systems and services: The role of acute care. *Bulletin of the World Health Organization, 91*(5), 386–388. doi:10.2471/BLT.12.112664

Hudon, C., Chouinard, M., Lambert, M., Dufour, I., & Krieg, C. (2016). Effectiveness of case management interventions for frequent users of healthcare services: A scoping review. *British Medical Journal Open, 6*(9), e012353. doi:10.1136/bmjopen-2016-012353

Huntley, A., Johnson, R., King, A., Morris, R., & Purdy, S. (2016). Does case management for patients with heart failure based in the community reduce unplanned hospital admissions? A systematic review and meta-analysis. *British Medical Journal Open, 6*(5), 1–19. doi:10.1136/bmjopen-2015-010933

Inglis, S., Clark, R., Dierckx, R., Prieto-Merino, D., & Cleland, J. (2015). Structured telephone support or non-invasive telemonitoring for patients with heart failure (Review). *Cochrane Database of Systematic Reviews, 10*, CD007228. doi:10.1002/14651858. CD007228.pub3

Jesus, T. S., & Hoenig, H. (2015). Postacute rehabilitation quality of care: Toward a shared conceptual framework. *Archives of Physical Medicine and Rehabilitation, 96*(5), 960–969. doi:10.1016/j.apmr.2014.12.007

Krupa, T., & Clark, C. (1995). Occupational therapists as case managers: Responding to current approaches to community mental health service delivery. *Canadian Journal of Occupational Therapy, 62*(1), 16–22. doi:10.1177/000841749506200104

Lewis, C., Moore, Z., Doyle, F., Martin, A., Patton, D., & Nugent, L. (2017). A community virtual ward model to support older persons with complex health care and social care needs. *Clinical Interventions in Aging, 12*, 985–993. doi:10.2147/cia.s130876

Linz, M., McAnally, P., & Wieck, C. (1989). *Case management: Historical, current and future perspectives.* Cambridge, MA: Brookline Books.

Lloyd, C., King, R., & Ryan, L. (2007). The challenge of working in mental health settings: Perceptions of newly graduated occupational therapists. *British Journal of Occupational Therapy, 70*(11), 460–470. doi:10.1177/030802260707001102

Morgan, D., Innes, A., & Kosteniuk, J. (2011). Dementia care in rural and remote settings: A systematic review of formal or paid care. *Maturitas, 68*(1), 17–33. doi:10.1016/j.maturitas.2010.09.008

Morrish, D., Beaupre, L., Bell, N., Cinats, J., Hanley, D., Harley, C., … Majumdar, S. R. (2009). Facilitated bone mineral density testing versus hospital-based case management to improve osteoporosis treatment for hip fracture patients: Additional results from a randomized trial. *Arthritis & Rheumatism, 61*(2), 209–215. doi:10.1002/art.24097

Powell, S., & Tahan, H. (2010). *Case management: A practical guide for education and practice.* Philadelphia, PA: Wolters Kluwer Health/Lippincott Williams & Wilkins.

Reinius, P., Johansson, M., Fjellner, A., Werr, J., Öhlén, G., & Edgren, G. (2013). A telephone based case-management intervention reduces health care utilization for frequent emergency department visitors. *European Journal of Emergency Medicine, 20*(5), 327–334. doi:10.1097/mej.0b013e328358bf5a

Robinson, K. (2010). Care coordination: A priority for health reform. *Policy, Politics, & Nursing Practice, 11*(4), 266–274. doi:10.1177/1527154410396572

Robinson, M., Fisher, T., & Broussard, K. (2016). Role of occupational therapy in case management and care coordination for clients with complex conditions. *American Journal of Occupational Therapy, 70*(2), 7002090010p1-6. doi:10.5014/ajot.2016.702001

Rutter, D., Tyrer, P., Emmanuel, J., Weaver, T., Byford, S., Hallam, A., … Ferguson, B. (2004). Internal vs. external care management in severe mental illness: Randomized controlled trial and qualitative study. *Journal of Mental Health, 13*(5), 453–466. doi:10.1080/09638230400006759

Salloum, A., Kondrat, D. C., Johnco, C., & Olson, K. R. (2015). The role of self-care on compassion satisfaction, burnout and secondary trauma among child welfare workers. *Children and Youth Services Review, 49*, 54–61. doi:10.1016/j.childyouth.2014.12.023

Scherz, N., Bachmann-Mettler, I., Chmiel, C., Senn, O., Boss, N., Bardheci, K., & Rosemann, T. (2017). Case management to increase quality of life after cancer treatment: A randomized controlled trial. *BioMed Central Cancer, 17*(1), 223. doi:10.1186/s12885-017-3213-9

Smith, A. (2011). Role ambiguity and role conflict in nurse case managers. *Professional Case Management, 16*(4), 182–196. doi:10.1097/ncm.0b013e318218845b

Smith, J., Yeowell, G., & Fatoye, F. (2017). Clinical and economic evaluation of a case management service for patients with back pain. *Journal of Evaluation in Clinical Practice, 23*(6), 1355–1360. doi:10.1111/jep.12797

Society for Social Work Leadership in Health. (2015). *Social Work Best Practice Healthcare Case Management Standards*. Philadelphia, PA: Society for Social Work Leadership in Health Care.

You, E., Dunt, D., & Doyle, C. (2015). What is the role of a Case Manager in community aged care? A qualitative study in Australia. *Health & Social Care in The Community, 24*(4), 495–506. doi:10.1111/hsc.12238

Willard, H., Spackman, C., Schell, B., Gillen, G., & Scaffa, M. (2014). *Willard & Spackman's occupational therapy* (12th ed., pp. 1–58, 265–382). Philadelphia, PA: Wolters Kluwer Health/Lippincott Williams & Wilkins.

Wissel, J., Oliver, J., & Sunnerhagen, K. (2013). Navigating the post stroke continuum of care. *Journal of Stroke and Cerebrovascular Diseases, 22*(1), 1–8. doi:10.1016/j.jstrokecerebrovasdis.2011.05.021

CHAPTER 4

CASE CONCEPTUALIZATION, ASSESSMENT, AND DIAGNOSIS

NANCY FAIR

Counseling values traditionally have stressed the evaluation of clients from a holistic, strength-based perspective; however, the recent problem-focused, medical/illness model trend in clinical mental healthcare environments has dictated the need for counselors to become skilled in case conceptualization, assessment, and diagnosis. This trend has shown some signs of moderation of the mind/body split approach to human distress through an increase in systems-focused treatment that encompasses physical, emotional, and spiritual aspects of healing. Integrated behavioral and primary healthcare systems currently are being utilized within institutions to address treatment failures caused by a lack of continuity-of-care among providers of mental and physical health services. As mental health practitioners, counselors often may be required to work as team members alongside physicians and other providers of services to clients with multiple needs. This chapter addresses the challenges that counseling students may encounter in clinical practice situations that require complex case conceptualization skills. Topics to be explored include elements of comprehensive clinical assessment, such as objective testing, structured and unstructured interviews, and symptom-specific tests, as well as techniques for assessing clients' potential for self-harm or harm to others. The benefits and risks inherent in the process of diagnosing individuals presenting for treatment are examined, along with the clinical tensions that often exist between the needs of clients and the requirements of the mental healthcare system. The chapter begins with learning objectives based upon Council for Accreditation of Counseling and Related Educational Programs (CACREP) standards) and continues with the subject matter described earlier. This is followed by a section exploring future needs for counselor programming, as relevant to the topics discussed in this chapter. Finally, students can find a list of resources and references applicable to case conceptualization, assessment, and diagnosis.

The following CACREP standards are addressed in this chapter:
CACREP 2016:
2F5.b, 2F5.g, 2F5.h, 2F7.a, 2F7.b, 2F7.b, 2F7.c, 2F7.e, 2F7.j, 2F7.k, 5C1.c, 5C3.a
CACREP 2009:
2G5.c, 2G5.d

INTRODUCTION

Case conceptualization is a process that serves as the foundation for understanding the needs of clients and eventually for providing appropriate treatment. The counseling profession traditionally has approached work with clients from a strength-based, wellness perspective that emphasizes a life-span view of human distress rather than medically labeling issues. Changing trends in the provision of healthcare mean that institutional providers are addressing the historically separate fields of medical health and mental health (including addiction treatment) by creating more integrated systems for approaching the human condition. Such integrated systems are seeking to coordinate patient care among providers within a team approach, and counselors are likely to be integral members of such teams. In the future, counselors may find employment in hospitals or other large institutions, and this implies that they will be required to become proficient in the entire patient intake process, which includes assessment and diagnosis.

Providing mental healthcare under the auspices of an integrated behavioral and primary healthcare (IBPH) treatment paradigm may present challenges for the counseling profession in maintaining a collaborative, strength-based approach with clients while jointly cooperating in continuity of care within a larger, medically based system. This chapter examines both the practical and philosophical aspects of the changes counselors face as the mental health field evolves, including systems-based and team approaches to providing mental health services.

A SYSTEMS APPROACH TO CONCEPTUALIZING CLIENTS

The evolving trend toward corporatization and consolidation of many previously free-standing healthcare agencies has been presented as a progressive move that can benefit patients by centralizing care and providing continuity among various providers whose activities would not necessarily have been coordinated in the past. For example, an individual who is receiving services from a psychiatrist in private practice could be prescribed medications with potential side effects that were unknown to the patient's cardiologist unless the patient himself or herself informed one or both physicians. Integrated systems seek to reduce these potential health conflicts by offering patient care in which all providers are connected to and associated with each other and have access to shared medical records.

Other potential benefits of this approach include enhanced provider ability to encourage and monitor patients' medical and mental health needs in a more holistic manner, thereby ensuring that patients receive treatment for co-occurring issues. Schmit, Watson, and Fernandez (2018) compared the effectiveness of an IBPH approach with the traditional methods of treatment and found that patients involved in IBPH had greater improvement in overall functioning over a 12-month period compared with patients in traditional treatment. Patients with mental health issues who were involved in traditional treatment were apparently less likely to seek appropriate medical treatments for physical health problems, leading to a higher mortality rate from treatable health conditions. Despite this result, outcome studies across the various models of integrated care are sparse, and have yet to catch up with this new and rapidly evolving treatment approach.

Case conceptualization within this changing treatment paradigm does not mean that counselors must abandon the traditional values of the profession, but rather that they must learn to balance counseling values with system requirements. This balance means learning to use standardized instruments of assessment, and possibly offering a diagnosis, depending upon the needs and requirements of the counselor's workplace. For instance, in agencies or units where substance abuse is the primary focus of treatment, structured assessments and questionnaires are used, and the diagnosis will reflect the emphasis on addiction. Strength-based values may be embedded in the assessment questions of a particular agency, or they may be expressed through the counselor's personal interaction with clients.

While traditional drug and alcohol treatment programs may seem straightforward in their purpose and scope, counseling within that context may not effectively address co-occurring problems and disorders. It is well documented that the majority of individuals seeking treatment for addictions have histories that include childhood abuse and neglect that form the basis for efforts at self-medication that lead to addiction (Felitti et al., 1998). Flores (2004) has written extensively on the concept of addiction as an attachment disorder, with the premise being that damaging or disruptive attachment in childhood can lead to an individual's attachment to a behavior or substance that offers a predictable self-soothing response in place of inadequate or abusive caregivers. Some eating disorders and gambling addictions may fit this definition as well, and counselors must be aware of the co-occurring mental health and addictions problems that are referred to as a dual diagnosis.

A client who has been assigned a diagnosis of addiction along with another diagnosis, such as depression or bipolar disorder, for example, is often assumed to have two separate illnesses requiring different approaches. However, research has shown that the percentage of clients who qualify for a dual diagnosis is high (Center for Behavioral Health Statistics and Quality, 2015). This has become especially obvious now that posttraumatic stress disorder (PTSD) and complex posttraumatic stress disorder (CPTSD, which has not yet been included in the *Diagnostic and Statistical Manual of Mental Disorders* [*DSM*]) are being identified as major precursors to substance abuse and other behavioral problems. However, many providers, including some integrated health systems, have been slow to incorporate these findings into their system of assessment and diagnosis, which can result in clients accruing multiple, often overlapping or unhelpful, diagnoses as shown in Case Illustration 4.1.

CASE ILLUSTRATION 4.1

OVERLAPPING DIAGNOSES RESULT IN UNHELPFUL MEDICATION

A client sought out individual counseling after having been hospitalized for several weeks following a suicide attempt that was diverted when she changed her mind and called a friend for help. During the hospitalization, the client was assessed by an intake nurse and eventually by a psychiatrist who gave her the following diagnoses based upon her reported history:

1. *Bipolar disorder*
2. *Substance abuse disorder*
3. *PTSD*

According to the client, she was diagnosed with bipolar disorder because she reported that she had mood swings that sometimes included suicidal thoughts and urges. Her frequent misuse of drugs and alcohol to modulate her moods was the basis for her substance abuse diagnosis, and PTSD was added after she disclosed a history of child abuse. For this client, the multiple, overlapping diagnoses were not helpful in that she received side-effect-laden medication for the bipolar diagnosis. She also was directed to drug and alcohol treatment for an assumed substance abuse disorder and was referred to counseling for the PTSD diagnosis. As the client worked in counseling, her use of substances to control her moods dropped off, as did her mood swings, and she soon was able to discontinue the medication. In this client's case, multiple diagnoses could have been avoided or subsumed under the PTSD diagnosis, because all of her symptoms commonly are seen in traumatized people and are not necessarily evidence of separate disorders.

Disasters, war trauma, and other catastrophic occurrences associated with the development of PTSD, as well as childhood abuse resulting in CPTSD, have been identified by the Adverse Childhood Experience (ACE) study (Felitti et al., 1998) as appearing frequently in clinical settings. It is estimated that 60% of adults are exposed to traumatic experiences or other difficulties during childhood. Given these statistics, it is inevitable that counselors will encounter large numbers of clients who report a variety of difficulties that have originated in, or been exacerbated by, traumatic experience. Therefore, counselors will be able to create more effective collaborative, holistic case conceptualizations by incorporating this knowledge of the potential effects of traumatic exposure into the interview and assessment process with clients. While addictions (or other specialty) counselors may not be able to address comprehensively clients' trauma histories or other mental health problems within the scope of their jobs, counseling values are able to be transmitted to the client. This can be done through what Welfare and Borders (2010) call "counselor cognitive complexity," which refers to the counselor's ability to identify and integrate complex, multifaceted, and sometimes contradictory client information in order to understand a client's needs.

Levers (2012) indicates that client needs are situated in and are only understood within the larger bioecological system that includes the following components:

1. The client–clinician dyad and other more or less formal therapy, such as 12-step groups or group therapy;

2. The nexus of personal and treatment issues, which includes matters and individuals associated with the client's life that may affect treatment outcomes, such as the therapeutic milieu, agency administration, and multiple other factors; and,

3. The broader systemic and cultural influences that affect mental health treatment policies, funding, and regulations.

Given these factors, and with the potential to influence the delivery of mental healthcare in multiple and sometimes conflicting ways, counselors must utilize tools of assessment while exercising counselor cognitive complexity (Welfare & Borders, 2010) on behalf of their clients.

ASSESSMENT

Counselors initially may encounter clients in a variety of different ways, depending upon the counselors' employment venues. In an agency setting, clients most likely are screened initially, in person or via phone contact by an intake specialist or receptionist. In some agencies, the terms "intake" and "assessment" are used interchangeably, or they may represent separate parts of the larger assessment process. For the purposes of this chapter, intake is assumed to be the initial agency contact, while assessment refers to subsequent encounters with a counselor for the purpose of evaluating the client's strengths and needs with an eye toward the development of a comprehensive plan for treatment.

Clinical assessment can be seen as having two separate components. The first is the client–counselor clinical interview (Sommers-Flanagan, 2004), which may be structured through the use of an agency questionnaire or form, or the meeting may be an unstructured one in which the counselor simply invites the client to describe what brings him or her to the agency. Whether the first encounter is structured or unstructured may depend upon the context of the interview; for example, crisis counseling is more likely to be unstructured at a walk-in clinic initially, with a structured follow-up later.

The second component of clinical assessment is through the use of formalized assessment tools, such as the *Beck Depression Inventory* (Beck, Steer, & Brown, 1996) or the *Generalized Anxiety Disorder Test* (Spitzer, Kroenke, Williams, & Löwe, 2006). There are many such tests that are not intended to provide a diagnosis, but rather to serve as reliable and valid screening tools for certain key symptoms (Grath-Marnat, 2009). The use of such tools will vary, depending upon the counselor's place of employment. Guo, Wang, and Johnson (2012) propose that the following are components of the counseling process and begin with assessment:

1. Ethical and Legal Issues—would include issues such as regarding a minor brought for assessment, or a client's ability to make judgments on his/her own behalf.

2. Crisis Intervention—includes considerations for immediate care or transfer to another facility, if appropriate.

3. Referral or Discharge—may become necessary at this point if #2 or #4 dictates.

4. Medical Conditions—may necessitate referral or discharge to appropriate medical facility before counseling can begin.

5. Consultation and Supervision—should be ongoing for the counselor.

6. Diagnosis—may be the next step, based upon assessment.

7. Intervention and Treatment Planning—case conceptualization and assessment results will be the driving force in this component.

TIPS FROM THE FIELD 4.1
THE CLIENT–COUNSELOR CLINICAL INTERVIEW

1. Doing an unstructured interview at initial contact can provide counselors with valuable information conveyed by clients' body language, eye contact, and facial expressions that often are missed when we are busy writing or typing.

2. If possible, counselors should fill out the agency's paperwork *with* the client rather than giving it to them to fill out on their own. Counselors' interactions while asking the questions, along with the ability to observe the clients while they answer, can help to build trust and enable counselors to follow up on answers that elicited a reaction.

■ ASSESSING FOR POTENTIAL CLIENT SELF-HARM OR HARM TO OTHERS

It is likely that no topic arouses greater counselor concern than that of possible client dangerousness, to themselves or to others. It is important to note that self-harm can take the form of nonlethal self-injurious behavior, or it can manifest in suicidal ideation or attempts. For purposes of clarification, self-harm is addressed as involving three separate behaviors.

Nonlethal Self-Injury

Research has shown that self-injurious behaviors such as cutting, burning, scratching, or punching serve a purpose for clients that is unrelated to suicidal ideation (Connors, 2000; Miller, 1994). These types of behaviors are best regarded as self-regulatory coping strategies that are not progressive in the sense that they do not "escalate" into suicidal behavior. Clients may hesitate to admit their use of self-injury to counselors, because there has been considerable stigma attached to the behavior, along with misguided interventions, such as involuntary hospitalizations, driven by clinician anxiety and misunderstanding. Clients often are forthcoming in saying that the use of self-injury *precludes* their need for more dangerous behavior. Therefore, clinician attempts at preventing self-injury through threats of hospital commitment or termination of therapy may hinder the therapeutic relationship by forcing the client to lie or to miss scheduled appointments. Verbal or written no-harm contracts can be useful with some clients, provided there are clear steps the client can take to obtain help, and that no punitive actions are associated with failure to honor the contract. Clients who self-injure are likely to have a history of physical, sexual, emotional, or relational trauma, and the use of the behavior usually markedly diminishes on its own as the counseling process unfolds (Brown & Bryan, 2007; Mazelis, 2003); however, such client behaviors need to be assessed carefully, and the new counselor may wish to seek supervision.

In cases in which clients have injured themselves regularly and severely enough to require medical care, further questioning about the need that is filled for the client by the behavior is warranted. For example, a client was cutting herself so deeply that stitches were required on a regular basis. The counselor explored with the client what needs the client thought were being met by this behavior, and the client replied, "I don't want to kill myself. I just need the undivided attention of someone for a little while. Even if the doctor is angry with me for showing up again, it makes me feel seen and heard." Based upon this new understanding of what the client was seeking, the counselor and client were able to explore different ways of feeling seen and heard, such as membership in a group. The client and counselor also developed a detailed safety plan for handling the client's feelings in ways that did not involve self-injury.

Self-injurious behavior also has been labeled *self-mutilation*; however, this term often is perceived to be pejorative by clients, and its use does not allow for the ambiguity of body art, piercings, and other alterations that may serve dual purposes for individuals. Case Illustration 4.2 is an example of this point.

CASE ILLUSTRATION 4.2

WOMEN'S THERAPY GROUP BEHAVIOR WITH DUAL PURPOSES

During the course of a 16-week women's therapy group, the co-facilitators of the group noted high group cohesion, as evidenced by the members' willingness to discuss deep feelings and their unwavering support of each other during the sessions. Shortly after the group terminated, the counselors were made aware of the fact that, after each session, the entire cohort left the building and proceeded to a local tattoo parlor, where one of them got a tattoo while the rest of the group watched. The counselors were shocked by this behavior, and wondered if it had been a case of collective self-injury as a way to process group stress, a unique post-group bonding experience, or some combination of the two.

Suicidal Ideation, Threats, or Attempts

The Centers for Disease Control and Prevention (CDC, 2015) lists suicide as one of the leading causes of death, especially for adolescents and young adults. It is important, however, for counselors to be aware that suicidal thoughts (ideation), threats, and attempts are not synonymous, nor should counselors' reactions to them be identical.

Suicidal ideation refers to clients' self-reported thoughts about considering suicide as a potential solution to life problems. Such ideation is commonly encountered in the mental health field, and may be expressed by clients in statements such as the following:

"I'd be better off dead."
"My family would be better off without me."
"I just don't see any other way out."

Such statements are indirect and require further follow-up by counselors to determine whether the sentiments are just expressions of despair, or if the client has a suicide plan and the means to execute it. Making such a determination is part of the ongoing therapeutic relationship that transcends questionnaires and assessment tools, focusing the counselor's attention on the essential human interaction inherent in the relationship.

Almost all counselors will encounter a suicidal client during their careers (Granello, 2010), and as many as 71%, according to one study (Rogers, Gueulette, Abbey-Hines, Carney, & Werth, 2001), will work with a client who has made at least one suicide attempt. Dozens of assessment tools are available for clinicians' use with children, adolescents, and adults, along with tools for special populations (Granello, 2010). While such assessment strategies tend to focus the clinician's attention on minutiae and details, Granello proposes the following, *12 Core Principles of Suicide Risk Assessment,* as a way to focus the counselor's attention on the context of assessment so as not to lose sight of the process while focusing on content.

Suicide risk assessment:

- *of each person is unique.*

- *is complex and challenging.*

- *is an ongoing process.*

- *errs on the side of caution.*

- *is collaborative.*

- *relies on clinical judgment.*

- *takes all threats, warning signs, and risk factors seriously.*

- *asks the tough questions.*

- *is treatment.*

- *tries to uncover the underlying message.*

- *is done in a cultural context.*

- *is documented.*

A broad contextual view within which to consider a client's potential for suicide, such as that illustrated by the earlier listed principles, will help counselors to distinguish client suicidal ideation and threats from the likelihood of an actual suicide attempt.

Hom, Joiner, and Bernert (2015) note that the single highest predictive factor for suicide attempts is a past incident that has ended in what is termed an "aborted" or "interrupted" attempt. Their research also indicated that the manner in which questions about suicide are asked initially, and in subsequent assessments, will often elicit conflicting answers from individuals, thus making it difficult to categorize, reliably, ideation and attempts.

A confounding factor in assessing an individual's true potential for suicide is the difficulty in determining the client's intent in issuing a threat or making a suicide attempt. Differentiating between attempts that were aborted by the client because of a change of heart, or those that were considered by the client to be "cries for help" can be extremely challenging. Threats can be presented vaguely, and attempts can be indirect, as in the "suicide by cop" terminology currently used to describe some well-publicized ends to criminal sprees. Case Illustration 4.3 shows an example of a client's vague and indirect allusions to impending suicide in which the clinician felt the need to act preventively.

CASE ILLUSTRATION 4.3

COUNSELOR'S PREVENTIVE ACTION MISINTERPRETED

The counselor received a voicemail from a current client expressing concern that her husband would not be able to handle life if she (the client) were not around. The client mentioned vague ideas of stepping in front of a bus or truck and asked that the counselor "take care of" the client's husband, should anything happen to the client. Attempts by the counselor to reach the client were unsuccessful, following which the counselor made the decision to try to contact the client's husband, and, if that failed, to alert police. Contact was established with the client's husband, and the crisis was averted. However, the client later phoned the counselor to express her outrage over the counselor's action, which the client deemed a betrayal of confidence. Further discussion with the client in office sessions centered on the client's intent (to get the counselor's attention) and the unintended outcome that indicated a need for more effective communication between client and counselor.

In cases such as Case Illustration 4.3, counselors must always put client safety first. The risk of the counselor doing nothing was likely greater than the risk of potentially breaching confidentiality due to a misperception regarding the client's intent.

Another example of suicidal behavior that challenges the clinical discretion of clinicians is "accidental" overdose, following which the client immediately contacts paramedics or calls the therapist. Is this a serious suicide attempt that was aborted because of a client change of heart, or is it a cry for help? Such a determination is usually difficult to reach, and the counselor must rely on clinical judgment and the perceived strength of the therapeutic relationship to make a decision on what action to take. Case Illustration 4.4 exemplifies such a decision-making process.

CASE ILLUSTRATION 4.4

KNOWLEDGE OF A CLIENT GUIDES THE COUNSELOR'S DECISION-MAKING PROCESS

The counselor received a phone call after hours from a client who reported that she had just taken an overdose of antianxiety medication and had called the paramedics herself. The client stated that she had been desperate to go to sleep, but was unable to do so, and continued taking more medication until she became tired. At that point, the client stated that she become afraid and called the paramedics. During the phone call, the police and paramedics arrived and asked the therapist if they should involuntarily admit the client to the hospital for attempted suicide. Based upon the counselor's knowledge of the client and the strength of their relationship, the counselor declined to have the client admitted for observation, and the incident was discussed and resolved between client and clinician at future sessions.

Other factors that influenced the counselor's decision to decline hospitalization for the client included the report from the first responders indicating that the client was stable and that she most likely had not taken a lethal dose of her medication. Additionally, this client had no history of suicidal ideation or attempts, but despite these factors, new clinicians should err on the side of client safety if there are any doubts about intent.

Assessment for Homicidal Risk

Although the risk of client suicide is nearly twice that of a client committing homicide or injuring others (Merrill, 2013), it is important for counselors to be aware of a client's potential for becoming dangerous to others. The original Tarasoff (*Tarasoff v. Board of Regents*, 1976) legal ruling outlines a clinician's duty to warn potential victims of homicide or violence and is presented in Box 4.1.

BOX 4.1   *TARASOFF V. BOARD OF REGENTS* RULING (1976)

"When a therapist determines, or pursuant to the standards of his or her profession should determine, that his patient presents a serious danger of violence to another, he incurs an obligation to use reasonable care to protect the intended victim against such danger. The discharge of this duty may require the therapist to take one or more of various steps, depending on the nature of the case. Thus it may call for him to warn the intended victim of the danger, to notify the police, or to take whatever other steps are reasonably necessary under the circumstances."

This deceptively simple paragraph indicates that counselors should follow the guidelines of their profession, which are outlined in Section B.2.a, Serious and Foreseeable Harm and Legal Requirements (American Counseling Association [ACA] Code of Ethics, 2014). If a counselor considers a client's threat of harm to others to be credible, the counselor will, of necessity, have to breach normal privacy and confidentiality rules. In this circumstance, and in the case of suicidal potential discussed previously, counselors should abide by the ACA Code of Ethics (2014, p. 7), which states that, "counselors consult with other professionals when in doubt as to the validity of an exception (to confidentiality)." In addition to helping counselors verify and validate their perspectives on potentially dangerous clients, consultation and supervision offer ways of conceptualizing these difficult cases using existing research literature. For example, Hoff (2009) offers the following points for use in thinking about and assessing potential client lethality:

1. *Clients with no predictable risk of assault or homicide:*
   Client has no assaultive or homicidal ideation, urges, assault or homicide, or history of the same; has a basically satisfactory support system; and is likely to be a social drinker only.

2. *Clients with low risk of assault or homicide:*
    The client has occasional assault or homicidal ideation (including paranoid ideas) with some urges to kill; has no history of impulsive acts or homicidal attempts; has occasional drinking bouts and angry verbal outbursts; and has a basically satisfactory support system.

3. *Clients with moderate risk of assault or homicide:*
    The client has frequent homicidal ideation and urges to kill but no specific plan; has a history of impulsive acting out and verbal outbursts while drinking, on other drugs, or otherwise; has stormy relationship with significant others with periodic high-tension arguments.

4. *Client with high risk of homicide:*
    Client has homicidal plan; has obtainable means; has a history of substance abuse; frequently acts out against others, but has had no homicide attempts; and has stormy relationships and much verbal fighting with significant others, with occasional assaults.

5. *Very high risk of homicide:*
    Client has current high-lethal plan and available means; has a history of homicide attempts or impulsive acting out, plus feels a strong urge to control and "get even" with a significant other; and has a history of serious substance abuse, with possible high-lethal suicide risk.

To summarize, the previous sections of this chapter have served as an introduction and overview of client assessment as a complex and collaborative process. Most counselors begin their careers in agencies or integrated healthcare systems where they need to work as part of a team delivering client care. This makes it likely that assessment and diagnosis, including making decisions about client potential for suicide or homicide, will be a collaborative function of a team that includes supervisors and consultants. In concluding these sections, the chapter moves beyond assessment practices to present an introduction to the process of diagnosis.

TIP FROM THE FIELD 4.2

THE IMPORTANCE OF DEVELOPING EFFECTIVE LANGUAGE

Clients who speak of suicide and/or homicide often do so because they lack effective language for expressing their feelings in other ways. For example, a client's statement, "I just want to die!" may be the only way the client can say that he or she is experiencing deep or overwhelming emotional pain. Helping the person to develop effective language to use within the therapeutic relationship can reduce the need for repetitive crisis assessments and interventions.

■ DIAGNOSIS

Counseling as a profession traditionally has focused on the skills, strengths, and development of individuals, and it has been relatively recently that counselors have begun performing tasks within the mental health system that require knowledge and skill in diagnosis (Mannarino, Loughran, & Hamilton, 2007). Despite this focal expansion, counselors have tried to support the imperative of "respect for human dignity and diversity" in their professional activities (ACA, 2014, p. 2). The expansion of counselor roles within the mental health system has allowed counselors to benefit through increased employment opportunities, reimbursement from insurance companies, and enhanced professional credibility (Hinkle, 1999).

An integral part of this role expansion is familiarity with the principles of diagnosis set forth in the *DSM-5* (American Psychiatric Association [APA], 2013). In using the *DSM-5* as a basis for case conceptualization, diagnosis, and treatment planning, counselors must find ways to maintain their professional standards despite the manual's failure to recognize client strengths and diversity (Erikson & Kress, 2006; Zalaquett et al., 2008). The ACA Code of Ethics (2014, Section E.5.d.) states that counselors may refrain from making or reporting a diagnosis if they believe that it would cause harm to the client or others. Despite the potential tensions inherent in using the *DSM*, it is important that counselors have a basic understanding of the *DSM* system.

The *DSM* System

The following is a list of the disorders that are covered in the chapters contained in the *DSM-5* (APA, 2013):

The complete listing of *DSM-5* chapters is:

- Neurodevelopmental Disorders
- Schizophrenia Spectrum and Other Psychotic Disorders
- Bipolar and Related Disorders
- Depressive Disorders
- Anxiety Disorders
- Obsessive-Compulsive and Related Disorders
- Trauma- and Stressor-Related Disorders
- Dissociative Disorders
- Somatic Symptom Disorders
- Feeding and Eating Disorders
- Elimination Disorders
- Sleep-Wake Disorders
- Sexual Dysfunctions
- Gender Dysphoria

- Disruptive, Impulse Control and Conduct Disorders
- Substance Use and Addictive Disorders
- Neurocognitive Disorders
- Personality Disorders
- Paraphilic Disorders
- Other Disorders

Each of these disorders and its subsets are assigned a number that represents the diagnosis and its features, such as age of onset and complications. This code number also is required by insurance companies for coverage and payment determination, along with the relevant *International Classification of Diseases, 10th Revision* (*ICD-10*; World Health Organization, 1992) code provided in the *DSM-5*. While *DSM* codes only apply to mental disorders, *ICD-10* contains codes for all medical and mental disorders, and insurers are now requiring clinicians to report both codes when submitting mental health diagnoses.

The most recent (fifth) edition of the *DSM* was expanded to include developmental and life-span considerations for determining age of onset, and some culture-linked syndromes (such as belief in demonic possession) are mentioned as subsets of the dissociative disorders category. While the addition of these considerations is helpful in broadening the scope of the *DSM*, the absence of client resilience factors and culturally laden diagnoses from the manual's focus continues to be problematic. The following section examines the strengths and limitations of the *DSM*.

Strengths and Limitations of the DSM System

The primary strength of the *DSM* system is that it provides a common terminology that is widely understood between professionals in discussing their clients. In the United States, it is the most commonly used method for diagnosis (Zalaquett et al., 2008). In this era of integrated mental healthcare, understanding and using this professional language has become more important to counselors working within the system (Hinkle, 1999).

Additionally, the *DSM* has a reciprocal relationship with research intended to enhance diagnostic specificity, but also to develop more effective treatment plans based upon feedback from the mental health professional community. Changes in the *DSM* editions over the years reflect such enhancements as subtypes and differences in age of onset for certain disorders, which in turn influence the direction of research (Moffit, Caspi, Dickson, Silva, & Stanton, 1996).

Limitations of the *DSM* system include its focus on psychopathology of the individual, lack of recognition of client strengths, and the applicability of cultural and developmental issues to the diagnostic process (Ivey & Ivey, 1998). The *DSM's* emphasis on pathology may prevent clinicians from developing a whole-person picture of clients, which is a limitation of the diagnostic language that may be interpreted differently by individual clinicians. Case Illustration 4.5 shows an example of different professional understandings of a client's behavior that resulted in diagnostic damage to the client.

CASE ILLUSTRATION 4.5

DIAGNOSIS HAS LONG-TERM CONSEQUENCES

A client was referred by a psychiatric hospital to an agency that specialized in sexual abuse trauma. In the hospital, the client had been diagnosed as schizophrenic due to her flat affect, repetitive speech patterns, and "odd" behaviors. The client's report of a trauma history motivated the referral, because standard medical treatments were not helping the client. As the client and the agency counselor built a trusting relationship, the client eventually was able to describe her history, which made sense of her flat affect and repetitive speech patterns, both of which represented her fear of hospital personnel and inability to find correct words to talk about her distress. The behaviors that were considered pathological were evidence of her fear, which caused her to hide under furniture when she was frightened. Through several years of counseling, the client was able to regain function and live on her own; however, she found that she was unable to obtain life insurance because of the schizophrenia diagnosis, which remained on her health record despite conversations between hospital and agency personnel. It is critical to mention here that the client was a member of a marginalized group, a fact that may have had a serious impact on the hospital personnel's original diagnosis.

While the *DSM* lists criteria for disorders, there is no link between the disorders and effective subsequent treatment. Lopez et al. (2006) challenged the assumption that clinicians are provided with sufficient information by diagnostic categories alone. A more thorough and collaborative case conceptualization plan that includes resilience factors, developmental concerns, and client strengths and feelings is needed for clinical decision-making.

Hays, Prosek, and McLeod (2010) state that clinical decision-making refers to the complex process that counselors employ in judging the severity of a client's problems, identifying their level of functioning, and making decisions about treatment. Counselor awareness of bias in the mental health system toward racial/ethnic minorities, women, and sexual minorities is critical in the clinical decision-making process. For example, Hispanics have been diagnosed with schizophrenia at 1.5 times the rate of Caucasians, and African Americans are more likely than Caucasians to be diagnosed with schizophrenia, substance abuse, and/or dementia. Women are disproportionately diagnosed with personality disorders; lesbian, gay, and bisexual clients are diagnosed 3 to 4.7 times the rate of heterosexual clients for major depressive disorder and panic disorder. Clients of lower educational levels are diagnosed more often with schizophrenia than with mood disorders. Research that has been done to date suggests that there is a significant relationship between clinician cultural bias and perceived level of client functioning (Hays et al., 2010).

This chapter thus far has delineated some of the strengths and weaknesses of the mental health system as it currently exists. The following section illuminates some of the ongoing clinical tensions of which counselors are likely to become aware as they enter practice and gain clinical experience in assessing and diagnosing clients.

Clinical Tensions

Client Safety Versus Client Confidentiality

Most clinicians will face a difficult decision involving client safety at some point in their careers. The price of safety may come at the cost of the client's confidentiality, as it was described in one of the case examples in this chapter. Despite the anxiety counselors will undoubtedly experience when making such a decision, erring on the side of caution will always be preferable to a possible negative outcome when considering a client's safety.

Pathology Versus Normal Human Experience

Changes in the *DSM* definition of grief have reduced the timeline within which normal grieving is diagnosed as a major depressive disorder to 2 weeks—a change that has created concern among many clinicians. Although the APA defends its time reduction, claiming that clinicians are not "required" to render a diagnosis of depressive disorder, the change appears to be symptomatic of a more general trend in the medicalization of normal human experiences (Greenberg, 2013).

What's Wrong With You? Versus What Happened to You?

The differences in these two questions fundamentally describe two different ways of understanding human distress. A major limitation of the medical model of mental health assessment using the *DSM* system is the necessity of bypassing the "what happened" in favor of labeling the "what's wrong" in individuals (Bloom, 1997). As counselors are aware, doing a balanced assessment requires inquiry into all aspects of a client's life—the "what happened" questions—before assigning a diagnosis. In fact, the client's explication of "what happened" may be healing in and of itself by offering insight and helping the client to make meaning.

Symptoms Versus Coping Strategies

The use of the term "symptoms" in describing human suffering often obscures the adaptive ways in which some behaviors may have helped clients to survive otherwise intolerable conditions. The use of self-injury described previously is one example. Another is the use of alcohol or other addictions as a way to cope temporarily with overwhelming feelings. Research on the concept of addiction as an attachment disorder (Flores, 2004) makes a compelling case for reassessing the classic view of this common problem.

Mental Illness as Primarily Biological Versus Mental Illness as a Biopsychosocial Issue

Despite widespread claims by mainstream mental health organizations that they espouse Engel's (1977) biopsychosocial model for understanding mental illness, research conducted by Ahn, Proctor, and Flanagan (2009) revealed that individual clinicians tend to view mental disorders along a continuum ranging from biological to psychosocial. These beliefs have implications for their views on the effectiveness of therapy versus that of medication, and may affect their choices in treatment planning.

These clinical tensions, among others, continue to present challenges for the future of the clinical mental health field. As counselors become team members in the field of integrative healthcare, they bring to their workplaces the values and principles inherent in the counseling profession, thereby necessitating continued review and revision of counselor education training programs.

▨ FUTURE PROGRAM NEEDS

Myers and Sweeney (2005) propose that counseling for holistic wellness must be conducted within four main levels of context: local, institutional, global, and chronometrical. The local context includes family of origin as well as other affinity groups. The institutional context includes work places, schools, and other community groups such as agencies and hospitals. The global context refers to impactful world events that affect all people, while the chronometrical context includes the effects of life-span development upon individuals' health and wellness. Myers, Sweeney, and Witmer (2000) have suggested that counselors integrate a four-phase approach to wellness into their case conceptualization and assessment. The four phases include the following:

1. Introduction of the wellness model;
2. Assessment of wellness;
3. Design and implementation of interventions; and,
4. Evaluation and follow-up.

This model illustrates the counseling profession's continued dedication to the principles of a strength-based, holistic view of human beings, which may be difficult for mental health counselors to integrate into their work in settings that adhere primarily to a medical model of assessing human distress, as mentioned previously in this chapter. It may be necessary for counselor education programs to assist students by meeting with prospective practicum and internship sites to promote inclusion of holistic views and assessment strategies. Support of counselors-in-training will be crucial for helping students navigate the current paradoxes in integrative systems of healthcare where wellness is valued, but adherence to diagnoses of pathology is required.

In order to be prepare counselors for the complexities of the field, counselor education programs need to provide in-depth training in understanding mental health disorders as they are defined in the *DSM* system, while meeting the competing demand of maintaining the integrity of counseling values (Mannarino et al., 2007). These values are well worth protecting, though they continue to face opposition from the lucrative alliance between psychiatry and the pharmaceutical industry, whose influence maintains the chasm between holistic and biological views of the causes of human distress (Greenberg, 2013; Wyatt & Midkiff, 2006).

Another challenge for counselor education programs is the need for the inclusion of basic trauma training for students prior to their entry into practicum and internship (Ventura, 2010). Despite the well-documented prevalence of trauma (Brown, 2008) and the high likelihood that counselors will encounter traumatized clients, trauma continues to be regarded, for the most part, as a specialty subject and not a part of basic curricula. The lack of training has been found to be potentially damaging, to both clients and clinicians alike, when untrained counselors are faced with wounded clients (Fair, 2017; Ventura, 2010).

CONCLUSION

This chapter has introduced the reader to the ideas of case conceptualization, assessment, and diagnosis in preparation for more advanced courses on these topics. The strengths that professional counselors are prepared to bring to integrative mental healthcare systems have been emphasized, along with the challenges that are likely to be encountered while working within the system. Case examples from clinical practice have been used to illustrate some of the ideas presented, and tips from the field are offered for students' consideration as they prepare to enter practice. Identifying clinical tensions has addressed some of the conflicts that exist within the mental health community.

The challenges facing clinical mental health counselors and counselor education programs mirror those faced by individuals and society in general, as our culture struggles to define itself. Counseling, as a profession, views individuals as change agents in their own lives, with strengths that permit growth within the greater context of family, institution, and society. Professional counselors enter the clinical mental health counseling field uniquely prepared to offer humanistic alternatives to reductionistic views of human distress; clinical mental health counselors have the opportunity to initiate social change through advocacy on their clients' behalf.

RESOURCES

TED Talks

Eleanor Longden: The voices in my head | TED Talk—TED.com
https://www.ted.com/talks/eleanor_longden_the_voices_in_my_head?language=en
Let's end the silence around suicide | TED Talks—TED.com
https://www.ted.com/playlists/let_s_end_the_silence_around_s
Mental Health for all by involving all
https://www.ted.com/talks/vikram_patel_mental_health_for_all_by_involving_all
   ?language=en&utm_campaign=tedspread&utm_medium=referral&utm_source
   =tedcomshare

ACA Resources

Counseling Today (ct.counseling.org)

- "Advocating for 'one-stop' shopping" health care: Q&A with ACA's Interest Network for Integrated Care: compiled by Bethany Bray
- "Using your integrated behavioral health tool box" by David Engstrom
- "Total health care" by Lynne Shalcross
- "Where brain meets body" by Laurie Meyers

Podcasts (counseling.org/knowledge-center/podcasts)

"Integrated Care Applying Theory to Practice" with Russ Curtis and Eric Christian (HT030)

ACA Interest Networks (counseling.org/aca-community/aca-groups/interest-networks)

ACA Interest Network for Integrated Care

REFERENCES

Ahn, W., Proctor, C., & Flanagan, E. (2009). Mental health clinicians' beliefs about the biological, psychological, and environmental bases of mental disorders. *Cognitive Science, 33*, 147–182. doi:10.1111/j.1551-6709.2009.01008.x

American Counseling Association. (2014). *ACA code of ethics*. Alexandria, VA: Author.

American Psychiatric Association. (2013). *Diagnostic and statistical manual of mental disorders* (5th ed.). Arlington, VA: Author.

Beck, A., Steer, R., & Brown, G. (1996). *Manual for the Beck Depression Inventory-II*. San Antonio, TX: Psychological Corporation.

Bloom, S. (1997). *Creating sanctuary: Toward the evolution of sane societies*. New York, NY: Routledge.

Brown, L. (2008). *Cultural competence in trauma therapy: Beyond the flashback*. Washington, DC: American Psychological Association.

Brown, L., & Bryan, T. (2007). Feminist therapy approaches to working with self-inflicted violence. *In Session: Journal of Clinical Psychology, 63*, 1121–1133. doi:10.1002/jclp.20419

Center for Behavioral Health Statistics and Quality. (2015). *Report on SAMHSA 2014 National Survey of Drug Use and Health*. Retrieved from https://www.samhsa.gov/data/sites/default/files/NSDUH-MHDetTabs2014/NSDUH-MHDetTabs2014.htm

Centers for Disease Control and Prevention. (2015). *Understanding suicide: Fact sheet*. Retrieved from https://www.cdc.gov/violenceprevention/pdf/suicide_factsheet-a.pdf

Connors, R. (2000). *Self-injury: Psychotherapy with people who engage in self-inflicted violence*. Lanham, MD: Jason Aronson.

Engel, G. (1977). The need for a new medical model: A challenge for biomedicine. *Science, 196*(4286), 129–136. doi:10.1126/science.847460

Erikson, K., & Kress, V. (2006). *Beyond the DSM story: Ethical quandaries, challenges, and best practices*. Thousand Oaks, CA: Sage.

Fair, N. (2017). *The lived experience of trauma counselor supervisors* (Unpublished doctoral dissertation). Duquesne University.

Felitti, V., Anda, R., Nordenberg, D., Williamson, D., Spitz, A., Edwards, V., … Marks, J. (1998). Relationship of childhood abuse and household dysfunction to many of the leading causes of death in adults: The adverse childhood experiences (ACE) study. *American Journal of Preventive Medicine, 14*(4), 245–258.

Flores, P. (2004). *Addiction as an attachment disorder.* Lanham, MD: Jason Aronson.

Granello, D. (2010). The process of suicide risk assessment: Twelve core principles. *Journal of Counseling & Development, 88,* 363–370. doi:10.1002/j.1556-6678.2010.tb00034.x

Grath-Marnat, G. (2009). *Handbook of psychological assessment.* Hoboken, NJ: John Wiley & Sons, Inc.

Greenberg, G. (2013). *The book of woe: The DSM and the unmaking of psychiatry.* New York, NY: The Penguin Group.

Guo, Y., Wang, S., & Johnson, V. (2012). Clinical assessment in the counseling process: A teaching model. *VISTAS 2012, 1,* 1–6.

Hays, D., Prosek, E., & McLeod, A. (2010, Winter). A mixed methodological analysis of the role of culture in the clinical decision-making process. *Journal of Counseling & Development, 88,* 114–121. doi:10.1002/j.1556-6678.2010.tb00158.x

Hinkle, J. (1999). A voice from the trenches: A reaction to Ivey and Ivey (1998). *Journal of Counseling & Development, 77,* 474–483. doi:10.1002/j.1556-6676.1999.tb02475.x

Hoff, L. (2009). *People in crisis: Clinical and diversity perspectives.* New York, NY: Routledge.

Hom, M., Joiner, T., & Bernert, R. (2016). Limitations of a single-item assessment of risk of suicide attempt history: Implications for standardized suicide risk assessment. *Psychological Assessment, 28*(8), 1026–1030. doi:10.1037/pas0000241

Ivey, A., & Ivey, M. (1998). Reframing *DSM-IV*: Positive strategies from developmental counseling and therapy. *Journal of Counseling & Development, 76,* 334–350. doi:10.1002/j.1556-6676.1998.tb02550.x

Levers, L. (2012). Conclusion: An integrative systemic approach to trauma. In L. L. Levers (Ed.), *Trauma counseling: Theories and interventions* (pp. 579–585). New York, NY: Springer Publishing Company.

Lopez, S., Edwards, L., Teramoto Pedrotti, J., Prosser, E., LaRue, S., Vehige Spalitto, S., & Ulven, J. (2006). Beyond the *DSM-IV*: Assumptions, alternatives, and alterations. *Journal of Counseling & Development, 84,* 259–267. doi:10.1002/j.1556-6678.2006.tb00404.x

Mannarino, M., Loughran, M., & Hamilton, D. (2007, October). *The professional counselor and the diagnostic process: Challenges and opportunities for education and training.* Paper based on a program presented at the Association for Counselor Education and Supervision Conference, Columbus, OH.

Mazelis, R. (2003). *Understanding and responding to women living with self-inflicted violence. Women, Co-Occurring Disorders and Violence Study.* Washington, DC: Substance Abuse and Mental Health Services Administration.

Merrill, G. (2013). *Assessing client dangerousness to self and others: Stratified risk management approaches.* Retrieved from http://socialwelfare.berkeley.edu/sites/default/files/users/gregmerrill/Assessing%20client%20dangerousness%20to%20self%20and%20others%2C%20stratified%20risk%20management%20approaches%2C%20Fall%202013.pdf

Miller, D. (1994). *Women who hurt themselves: A book of hope and understanding.* New York, NY: Basic Books.

Moffit, T., Caspi, A., Dickson, N., Silva, P., & Stanton, W. (1996). Childhood onset versus adolescent onset antisocial conduct problems in males: Natural history from ages 3 to 18 years. *Development and Psychopathology, 8*(2), 399–424. doi:10.1017/S0954579400007161

Myers, J., & Sweeney, T. (2005). The indivisible self: An evidence-based model of wellness (reprint). *Journal of Individual Psychology, 61,* 269–279.

Myers, J., Sweeney, T., & Witmer, J. (2000). The wheel of wellness: A holistic model for treatment planning. *Journal of Counseling & Development, 78*, 251–266. doi:10.1002/j.1556-6676.2000. tb01906.x

Rogers, J., Gueulette, C., Abbey-Hines, J., Carney, J., & Werth, J. (2001). Rational suicide: An empirical investigation of counselor attitudes. *Journal of Counseling & Development, 79*, 365–372. doi:10.1002/j.1556-6676.2001.tb01982.x

Schmit, M., Watson, J., & Fernandez, M. (2018). Examining the effectiveness of integrated behavioral and primary health care treatment. *Journal of Counseling & Development, 96*, 3–14. doi:10.1002/jcad.12173

Sommers-Flanagan, J. (2004). *Advanced ethical considerations in the use of evidenced-based practices and in crisis/humanitarian work.* Retrieved from https://www.researchgate.net/ profile/John_Sommers-Flanagan/publication/238072859_Advanced_Ethical_Considerations _in_the_Use_of_Evidenced-Based_Practices_and_in_CrisisHumanitarian_Work/links/ 0c96052940f171df23000000/Advanced-Ethical-Considerations-in-the-Use-of-Evidenced -Based-Practices-and-in-Crisis-Humanitarian-Work.pdf

Spitzer, R., Kroenke, K., Williams, J., & Löwe, B. (2006). A brief measure for assessing generalized anxiety disorder: The GAD-7. *Archives of Internal Medicine, 166*(10), 1092–1097. doi:10.1001/archinte. 166.10.1092

Tarasoff v. The Board of Regents of the University of California. (1976). 17 Cal. 3d 425, 551 p. 2d 334, 131 Cal. Rptr. 14. (Original work published 1974)

Ventura, E. (2010). *The experiences of counseling victims of trauma as perceived by master's level post-practicum students* (Unpublished doctoral dissertation). Duquesne University.

Welfare, L., & Borders, L. (2010). Counselor cognitions: General and domain-specific complexity. *Counselor Education and Supervision, 49*(3), 162–178. doi:10.1002/j.1556-6978.2010. tb00096.x

World Health Organization. (1992). *ICD-10: Classification of mental and behavioral disorders.* Geneva: Author.

Wyatt, W., & Midkiff, D. (2006). Biological psychiatry: A practice in search of a science. *Behavior and Social Issues, 15*, 132–151. doi:10.5210/bsi.v15i2.372

Zalaquett, C., Fuerth, K., Stein, C., Ivey, A., & Ivey, M. (2008). Reframing the *DSM-IV-TR* from a multicultural/social justice perspective. *Journal of Counseling & Development, 86*, 364–371. doi:10.1002/j.1556-6678.2008.tb00521.x

CHAPTER 5

CRISIS, DISASTER, AND TRAUMA ISSUES IN CLINICAL MENTAL HEALTH COUNSELING

LISA LOPEZ LEVERS

This chapter provides an overview of how clinical mental health counselors work with crisis, disaster, and trauma issues. A focus is placed on the pragmatic, neurobiological, and existential natures of crisis, disaster, and trauma along with the ways that these dynamics are implicated in numerous counseling scenarios. Basic crisis intervention skills are presented, disaster response is discussed, and the importance of understanding trauma is emphasized. The chapter anticipates that students will have an advanced course that covers these important topics more fully. The following Council for Accreditation of Counseling and Related Educational Programs (CACREP) standards are addressed in this chapter:

    CACREP 2016:
        2F1.c, 2F3.e, 2F3.g, 2F5.l, 2F5.m, 2F7.c, 2F7.d, 5C2.f, 5C2.g
    CACREP 2009:
        2G1.c, 2G3.c, 2G3.d, 2G5.g

LEARNING OBJECTIVES

After reviewing this chapter, the reader should be able to:

1. Demonstrate an introductory awareness of some of the major constructs related to crisis, disaster, and trauma counseling;

2. Identify basic crisis intervention skills;

3. Understand disaster response planning and strategies; and,

4. Articulate fundamental principles concerning trauma counseling.

▨ INTRODUCTION

Many clients experience one or more crises that may bring them into counseling; clients also may experience crises while they already are in counseling for other reasons. As both human-made and natural disasters continue to increase around the globe, it is likely that the practice of most professional counselors will be touched, in some way, by disaster-response activity of some type. And because the human experience of trauma is ubiquitous, professional counselors definitely will be involved with assisting clients who are recovering from traumatic events of all types. For these reasons, the information in this chapter is very important for students of clinical mental health counseling (CMHC) to absorb. However, the knowledge imparted in this chapter anticipates that students will have an advanced course in their counselor education programs that covers these important topics in greater detail, and so this is intended as an introduction to crisis, disaster, and trauma counseling.

The CACREP standards (2016) require professional counselors to possess certain competencies related to crisis, disaster, and trauma across specialty areas and at the doctoral level. Professional counselors working in CMHC are responsible for understanding the effects of crisis, disaster, and trauma on diverse individuals across the life span; this includes the impact of crisis and trauma on individuals with mental health diagnoses, on individuals with disabilities, and on marriages, couples, and families. For professional counselors who take on counseling roles and responsibilities in schools, it is imperative to understand the operational aspects of a particular school's emergency management plan in relationship to crisis, disaster, and trauma. For professional counselors who take on counseling roles and responsibilities at colleges and universities, it is crucial to understand the specific institution's emergency management plan in relationship to crisis, disaster, and trauma. All professional counselors must understand the procedures for identifying trauma and abuse and for reporting abuse as legally and ethically mandated. Further, professional counselors are expected to be acquainted with crisis intervention, trauma-informed service delivery, and community-based strategies, such as *Psychological First Aid* (National Child Traumatic Stress Network & National Center for Posttraumatic Stress Disorder [PTSD], 2006). At the doctoral level, professional counselors must have at least baseline knowledge about leadership roles in and strategies for responding to crises and disasters. In addition, trauma-informed pedagogy is an essential consideration for professional counselors teaching in university counselor education programs or offering training in community settings (Levers, 2012b).

Responding to crisis, disaster, and trauma necessitates an understanding from a bio-ecological perspective; the individual or group and any associated clinical issues exist in reciprocal relationship to larger social systems and dynamics. Not all crisis situations are necessarily traumatizing, but if left unresolved, a crisis easily can cause an individual to feel traumatized. All trauma events involve some element of crisis. By definition, all disaster events include some dimension of crisis; however, while not all disasters necessarily are traumatizing, under certain conditions such as active warfare or a hurricane, or in the *absence* of certain conditions, such as a sense of safety, a disaster very well may be traumatizing. Because clients are vulnerable when experiencing crisis, disaster, or trauma, adherence to ethical practice is an important part of the counseling process. The remaining sections of this chapter examine the following issues: Crisis Intervention, Disaster Response, and Trauma. These major sections are followed by a conclusion summarizing the most important aspects of these issues.

CRISIS INTERVENTION

Crisis is an interesting construct, from the perspective of its paradoxical nature, that is, from the standpoint that it can have positive or negative outcomes. The Merriam-Webster Dictionary (2019) defines "crisis" in the following ways:

1. *(a)* the turning point for better or worse in an acute disease or fever;

   (b) a paroxysmal attack of pain, distress, or disordered function;

   (c) an emotionally significant event or radical change of status in a person's life;

2. the decisive moment;

3. *(a)* an unstable or crucial time or state of affairs in which a decisive change is impending, *especially* one with the distinct possibility of a highly undesirable outcome;

   (b) a situation that has reached a critical phase. (Merriam-Webster, 2019, crisis, para. 1–3)

This popularized understanding of crisis helps to emphasize the potentially paradoxical nature of experiencing crisis and offers a basis by which a clinical mental health counselor potentially can assist a client in addressing, managing, and transforming a crisis into a moment for growth.

Gilliland and James (1997) define a crisis as the "perception of an event or situation as an intolerable difficulty that exceeds the person's resources and coping mechanisms" (p. 3). They further assert that "Unless the person obtains relief, the crisis has the potential to cause severe affective, cognitive, and behavioral malfunctioning" (p. 3).

Gilliland and James (1997) suggest that all individuals may face any of the following types of crises:

- Developmental crises, as they relate to the "normal flow of human growth"

- Situational crises, that arise from "uncommon and extraordinary events"

- Existential crises that comprise the "inner conflicts and anxieties" associated with "important human issues of purpose, responsibility, independence, freedom, and commitment" (p. 19)

While the clinical literature naturally emphasizes the conflictual nature of a crisis, it is important to maintain the strength-based perspective that a crisis also can initiate circumstances for creating meaningful change. A helpful operational definition of a crisis is one emphasizing that a crisis also can be a turning point in a person's life (Case Illustration 5.1).

CASE ILLUSTRATION 5.1

SUZY: A MOTHER'S TRAUMA BECOMES A SURVIVOR MISSION

At 19 years of age, Suzy died from a heroin overdose, and Suzy's mother wrote a frank and honest obituary about Suzy's death. In response to this courageous act, Suzy's mother heard from many people across the globe and wrote publicly about how this epidemic of opiate overdose is affecting the lives of so many families. By telling Suzy's story and giving a voice to Suzy's pain, Suzy's mother was able to help many other people, who, like so many grieving family members in this situation, feel as if they are alone. Suzy's mother sensed that if she could help just one person, it would make her own loss more bearable; at the same time, she knew that she also was speaking to the families of the nearly 75,000 other people who had died from opiate overdose that year.

The unusual action of Suzy's mother was courageous and compassionate. By sharing her personal crisis, she was able to touch the lives of many others in similar circumstances. Many people would be traumatized by such an experience as the loss of a child. Instead, Suzy's mother was able to turn her profound loss into what Judith Lewis Herman (1992/1997) has called a "survivor mission."

Clearly, assisting clients to manage their crises is a pertinent clinical skill. Purvis (1994) offers the following useful definition:

> Crisis management is the careful and tactful management of a situation in which there is trouble or danger that has the possibility of serious and negative consequences. The possible serious and negative consequences might include litigation, injury to individuals and/or property, death of an individual, disruption of the normal routine, and loss of confidence and trust in an individual or an institution. It is important to note that serious and/or negative consequences associated with a crisis situation can be valid or imagined, depending on the mind-set of the individual directly involved in the crisis or a person totally removed from the event. In either situation, it is extremely important for those assisting in a crisis to be fully aware of this very important aspect and respond in a professional, legal, humane, and ethical manner. (p. 23)

Imagined danger can have an equally profound effect on one person, as much as being in the throes of a real crisis can have on another. It is essential that clinical mental health counselors be well equipped with crisis intervention skills. Crisis intervention should be presented as an entire course or in a robust module within another clinical counseling course in every counselor education program. There are a number of crisis intervention models that can be useful in assisting clients to manage and work through their crises. One general model for conceptualizing a client's concerns is the *Integrative ACT Intervention Model* (Roberts, 2002), which includes the following three stages: (a) assessment, (b) crisis intervention, and (b) trauma treatment services. Gilliland and James (1997) have articulated their Six-Step Model of Crisis Intervention, which offers the following six steps:

- Defining the problem,

- Ensuring client safety,

- Providing support,

- Examining alternatives,

- Making plans, and

- Obtaining commitment.

Roberts (2002) also has designed a *Seven-Step Crisis Intervention Model*, which is more detailed than his *Integrative ACT Intervention Model* and suggests the following seven steps:

- assess lethality,

- establish rapport,

- identify problems,

- deal with feelings,

- explore alternatives,

- develop an action plan, and

- follow up.

Psychological First Aid (National Child Traumatic Stress Network & National Center for PTSD, 2006) is an evidenced-based modular program that has been used widely in responding to crisis, disaster, terrorism, and other emergencies (the manual is listed in the Resources section at the end of this chapter). It was developed jointly by the National Child Traumatic Stress Network and the National Center for PTSD, a section of the United States Department of Veterans Affairs, in 2006. It also has been used extensively by the International Federation of Red Cross and the Red Crescent Societies.

Regardless of which model of crisis intervention is chosen by the counselor, it is important to maintain a focus on client needs. It is also imperative for professional counselors to be familiar with the specific mechanisms and dynamics of the model and to ensure that the model is compatible with their broader clinical framework. In many ways, effective crisis intervention skills form the foundation for effective responses to disaster situations.

DISASTER RESPONSE

For a variety of reasons, it is much more likely now, than ever before, that clinical mental health counselors will be faced with responding to disasters and with counseling clients whose lives have been affected by disasters. The United Nations Office for Disaster Risk Reduction (UNOSDR, 2009, p. 9) defines a disaster as: "A serious disruption of the functioning of a community or a society causing widespread human, material, economic or environmental losses which exceed the ability of the affected community or society to cope using its own resources." Both natural and human-made disasters are apt to bring sudden and calamitous damage, loss, misfortune, or destruction, often placing victims in life-threatening situations.

In the last few decades, the lines of distinction between natural and human-made disasters have become more blurred, as increasingly more robust scientific evidence points to anthropogenic causes for many of the climate change-related "natural" disasters that continue to occur at a more rapid pace. Generally speaking, disasters affect entire communities, along with the individuals who live in those communities. Organized disaster response has been a relatively new role for professional counselors. While disaster response certainly is within the scope of practice for professional counselors, little concerning disaster (or crisis and trauma) is reflected in the professional accreditation standards. Likewise, the profession's code of ethics offers little guidance for ethical conduct or practice issues (Tarvydas, Levers, & Teahen, 2018). Tarvydas et al. (2017) have begun to address these ethical/professional lacunae by suggesting ethical guidelines for mass trauma and complex humanitarian emergencies.

It is beyond the scope of this chapter to address all types of disaster. Because climate change is having such a devastating effect on the planet, and because climate change has been linked, in complex ways, with many acts of human aggression, including war and the necessity for so many people around the world to seek refuge by migrating to other locations, this topic has been selected for discussion here as representative of the knowledge base that clinical mental health counselors should possess. In the remaining part of this section, climate change and the need to embrace a move from disaster preparedness to adaptation are discussed.

Climate Change

Climate change has been linked with increased incidences of natural disasters and human conflict and aggression. Interconnections among climate change, disaster risk, and environmental and human factors are highly complex (Boikanyo & Levers, 2017); however, the scientific evidence concerning the existence of anthropogenic climate change is clear. (For a social science friendly discussion of major scientific findings related to climate change, see Levers & Drozda, 2018.)

Climate change is a global humanitarian threat, and the increasing frequency with which anthropogenic climate change-related disasters are occurring suggests a much greater need for disaster preparedness and response. In fact, disaster preparedness has become a key public health issue that is interdisciplinary in its scope, that requires contextual assessment, and that demonstrates the need for a shift from postimpact reaction to adaptation and building community resilience (Rodin, 2014; Teahan, Levers, & Tarvydas, 2017). Climate change is a global problem involving the following grave implications: environmental concerns, social dynamics, economic issues, political matters, and the distribution of goods. Depending upon the severity of a given disaster, these implications have the potential to degrade any semblance of a quality of life.

From Disaster Preparedness to Adaptation

Professional counselors and clinical mental health counselors need to begin to conceptualize a more adaptation-oriented paradigm for disaster preparedness, and Bronfenbrenner's bioecological model offers such a framework. Within the structure of this model, the individual's needs are nested within broader community and societal needs; these sets of needs, along with the effects of the individual on the environment as well as environmental effects on the individual, exist within a reciprocal relationship. Disaster response is a highly systemic enterprise. In line with the current trends in clinical mental health treatment and community-based interventions, disaster preparedness and disaster response rely upon an integrated system-of-care approach in the same way as many of the topics discussed in this textbook.

It is important to analyze a community's vulnerability to natural and human-made disasters in terms of (a) susceptibility, that is, the degree of exposure to danger and the environmental risk factors, and (b) resilience, that is, the capability to cope, the capacity to recover, and protective factors that exist in the environment (Teahan et al., 2017). It is particularly important for professionals to consider the ways in which the most vulnerable persons (e.g., infants, elders, people with disabilities, and those living in poverty) need to be accounted for and protected during a disaster situation. According to the United Nations (UN), "Protecting and assisting the most vulnerable people on Earth is becoming increasingly complicated with the emergence of a number of complex and interconnected global mega-trends...[including] population growth, urbanization, food and energy insecurity, water scarcity, and climate change" (UN, n.d., *New trends require new strategies*, para. 1). This amplifies the importance of systemic disaster preparation planning.

Disaster services must be tailored to the unique communities for which they are provided (Teahan et al., 2017). Many challenges that face disaster survivors stem from disruptions in their daily life routines, disruptions that actually are caused by the disaster. It is important to consider the level of readiness, locally and globally, for the kinds of climate change-related disasters that already are occurring. New trends require new strategies, and some of the strategic needs upon which the society must focus include devising and maintaining the following:

- Designing strategic and systemic networks, across local platforms and within regional and national arenas;

- Shifting from a sole focus on postdisaster impact activity to one that includes prevention, systematic preparedness, adaptation, and an ecological perspective; and,

- Building resilient communities (Rodin, 2014).

Professional counselors and clinical mental health counselors can assist with disaster planning and response phases, including disaster planning mitigation, predisaster preparedness, disaster response, and postdisaster recovery, both short term and long term. Further actions can be taken to enhance social–ecological resilience by developing better response practices, by creating greater awareness of climate change and adaptation, and by promoting frameworks for resilience (Teahan et al., 2017).

An important advocacy issue in the disaster response arena is that the American Counseling Association (ACA) code of ethics does not provide adequate ethical guidelines for mass trauma and complex humanitarian emergencies (Tarvydas et al., 2017,

2018; Teahan et al., 2017). The absence of ethical guidelines places counselors who respond to disasters in potentially precarious positions. The need also exists for better understanding of the intersectionality of professional counselors' skill bases and the crisis- and trauma-related needs of those being affected by a disaster. The counseling profession needs to advocate for greater awareness of critical needs in this area, development of situation- and context-specific interventions, and continued research regarding the effects of disaster on individuals and systems.

▤ TRAUMA

Trauma is ubiquitous. As the Dalai Lama (2003) insightfully points out, "Pain is inevitable, suffering is optional" (quotation widely attributed to His Holiness, the Dalai Lama). The human condition lends itself to painful experiences, but it is not necessary for people to continue to suffer when help is available. This is the case with trauma, and professional counselors can be of profound assistance in helping people who suffer emotional pain, due to traumatic events, to recover from their traumatic experiences. In fact, many people possess innate resilience, even in the face of trauma, and professional counselors and clinical mental health counselors can facilitate clients' growth in the transformation from being a victim to being a survivor, in transforming the trauma event into personal meaning making. This section of the chapter provides the following: an introduction to the construct of trauma; a description of loss, grief, and suffering; and discussions of developmental issues, stressors, lived experience of trauma, PTSD, immigrants and refugees, marginalized populations, and neuroscience and Polyvagal Theory.

Introduction to Trauma

Briefly put, trauma is a physiological and emotional reaction to a horrific event (APA, 2019). Traumatic experiences may involve gendered violence, racial and ethnic violence, and age-related violence (child or elder abuse); cultural implications may be instrumental in the trauma dynamics, and media influences may shape perceptions about traumatic incidences. Trauma events include some of the following examples (this, by no means, is intended as an exhaustive list):

- Sexual abuse;
- Physical abuse;
- Domestic or intimate partner violence;
- Community, workplace, or school violence;
- Medical or health-related trauma;
- Motor vehicle accidents;
- Acts of terrorism;
- War experiences;
- Natural and human-made disasters;

■ Homicides and suicides; and,

■ Other traumatic losses.

The suffering that accompanies any of these types of traumatic experiences can be reduced and even extinguished—not necessarily forgotten but managed well enough that trauma survivors can resume productive lives. For this reason, it is important that traumatized individuals receive some type of clinical intervention sooner rather than later. The longer the delay, the more likely the possibility becomes that a traumatized person may develop PTSD. Clinical mental health counselors deal with trauma in its early stages as well as with PTSD (students will learn more about related diagnostics in a course that focuses on clinical diagnosis).

It is important that clinical mental health counselors bear in mind that not everyone who experiences trauma develops PTSD. As previously mentioned, for a variety of both nature and nurture reasons, many individuals possess greater resilience and are better able to cope with the effects of traumatic experiences. Research has suggested that between 30% and 70% of individuals who experience trauma also report positive change and growth as they emerge from the traumatic experience (Joseph & Butler, 2010). Although it remains somewhat controversial, Calhoun and Tedeschi (1998) initiated the concept of posttraumatic growth (PTG), which represents the positive psychological change that may result from an individual's engagement with a traumatic event. Tedeschi and Calhoun (2004) define PTG as:

> …the experience of individuals whose development, at least in some areas has surpassed what was present before the struggle with crises occurred. The individual has not only survived, but has experienced changes that are viewed as important, and that go beyond the status quo. Posttraumatic growth is not simply a return to baseline—it is an experience of improvement that for some persons is deeply profound. (p. 4)

PTG has been associated with a number of interrelated constructs, including resilience, hardiness, and a sense of coherence (Almedom, 2005). Although PTG has been reported in an array of samples, it remains controversial due to measurement challenges (Park & Lechner, 2006). PTG usually is assessed by self-report, through interviews or questionnaires, and skeptics question the validity of the construct (e.g., Frazier & Kaler, 2006). A web-based study of 1,739 adults concluded that growth following trauma may entail the strengthening of character (Peterson, Park, Pole, D'Andrea, & Seligman, 2008). PTG is not necessarily a consequence of trauma; rather, it is one possible outcome of the process of working through the aftermath of trauma. The various risk factors and protective factors existing in a person's life at the time of a trauma event and immediately after, contribute to the degree to which the trauma has a lesser or greater impact. Professional counselors and clinical mental health counselors need to consider the resilience and hardiness of their clients and to maintain a growth-oriented and meaning-making perspective when working with clients who have been traumatized.

Responding to and treating trauma is a multidisciplinary endeavor, and various professionals offer assistance within a variety of professional roles. While this includes professional counselors and clinical mental health counselors, some of the other helping roles may encompass those held by psychologists, social workers, psychiatrists, physicians, nurses, police personnel and other first responders, journalists, community leaders, and members of the clergy and other spiritual healers. Professional counselors need to understand that trauma is a complex clinical issue that involves obtaining a detailed client history, employing sound diagnostic skills, and using evidence-based and best-practice treatments. It is important to understand that trauma affects people on multiple levels: personal (cognitively, affectively, existentially, and spiritually), physical, relational, social, and cultural. It is of equal importance to understand that the multidimensionality of the effects of trauma requires a bioecological perspective and systemic as well as individualistic responses. Precisely because trauma is both an individual and a systemic issue, counselors and counselor educators must consider the cultural dimensions of trauma, the social justice dimensions of trauma, the spiritual and existential dimensions of trauma, and the pedagogical dimensions of trauma (Levers, 2012b). By understanding trauma from this broad bioecological perspective, counselors can assist clients and the systems in which clients and counselors function with meaningful transformations (Levers, 2012a).

Loss, Grief, and Suffering

According to Walter and McCoyd (2009, p. 1), "Loss is at the heart of life and growth." A similar sentiment might be expressed concerning the experience of trauma: Loss, grief, and suffering are at the center of experiencing trauma. Not all experiences of loss, grief, and suffering necessarily involve trauma. However, loss, grief, and suffering are implicit aspects of trauma, across the varying circumstances that may manifest as traumatic experience. The purpose of this point is to underscore the importance of these constructs and to illuminate their centrality to the experience of trauma (Levers, 2012b).

Elisabeth Kübler-Ross (1969) wrote *On Death and Dying: What the Dying Have to Teach Doctors, Nurses, Clergy and Their Own Families* in 1969. This was the source of the now widely accepted and reified stages of (a) denial and isolation, (b) anger, (c) bargaining, (d) depression, and (e) acceptance. Professional helpers were eager to view these concepts as linear stages through which clients would progress. However, this was never the intention of Kübler-Ross. She conducted interviews of patients facing death in order to understand their experiences and illuminate the phenomena. Therapists eventually learned that clients facing loss and grief issues do not necessarily experience any or all of these, and further, individuals may not experience these stages sequentially.

John Bowlby later (1980/1998) postulated these stages of loss:

- Numbness (defined as being shocked and stunned, not as denial),
- Separation anxiety (viewed as yearning/searching),
- Despair and disorganization (as the loss sinks in, the person attempts to recognize the loss and to develop a "new normal" without the object of the loss), and
- Acquisition of new roles/reorganization (the bereaved begins to relinquish efforts aimed at preparing for the deceased's return, such as getting rid of the loved one's clothing; this movement toward new aspects of life and relationships with others is seen as moving through reorganization).

More recently, William Worden (2008) has popularized his task-based grief theory and intervention framework. Worden developed his theory in response to some of the stage- and phase-based models of the late 1960s through the early 1990s, thus offering clinicians a more behavior-based perspective upon which to make clinical intervention decisions. Worden's model includes the following steps:

1. Accept the reality of the loss,

2. Experience the pain of the grief, and

3. Adjust to a world without the deceased.

Developmental Issues

Greater attention to the validity of traumatic experiences in recent decades has permitted an increased realization of the frequency with which early childhood trauma occurs. From a purely psychological perspective, a child's development is interrupted or even arrested by the negative consequences of any type of child maltreatment. For example, through the lens of Erikson's (1950) stages of human development, significant developmental tasks may not be completed, in which case the individual experiences the opposing dynamic of the developmental task (e.g., instead of learning to trust in caretakers and the environment, the infant instead learns mistrust) and is not able to move to subsequent developmental stages. From a more bioecological or systemic perspective, everything that applies to the individual's psychological development is still taken into account but so are systemic and environmental influences, as well as both risk factors and protective factors. The multiple environmental impacts of any trauma experienced in childhood may be worsened or mediated, depending on developmental stage, risk factors in the environment, and the presence or potential presence of protective factors. The following subsections address the relevance of attachment theory and the Adverse Childhood Experiences (ACE) study.

Attachment Theory

Attachment was a concept originally proposed by the late John Bowlby in 1958; it is highly relevant to the discussion of early childhood trauma. The term has been used when referring to the emotionally close and important social relationships that people have with each other. Bowlby's (1958) work offered the basis for identifying four basic characteristics of attachment that have assisted professionals in understanding the importance of bonding in the relationship between a child and his or her caregiver: having a safe haven, having a secure base, engaging in proximity maintenance, and showing separation distress.

The aim of attachment theory was to explain how relationships form and the role that they play in the individual's development. Bowlby originally proposed attachment theory as a basis for understanding social relationships across the life span; however, much of the early work regarding attachment was focused upon parent–child relationships, especially mother–infant dyads. It long has been thought that if attachment is seriously interrupted, as is often the case with early childhood trauma, significant developmental problems may emerge. Given recent neurological research regarding the effects of trauma on the brain, more is understood about the integrative effects of a particular individual's attachment and neurobiology (e.g., Newman, Sivaratnam, & Komiti, 2015).

ACE Study

A landmark study (Felitti et al., 1998) illuminated what many clinicians had been realizing about client trauma histories, long before the evidence was aggregated systematically. Fortunately, Felitti and his colleagues took the time and initiative to investigate what they also had been observing in clinical settings: Many individuals have endured adverse childhood experiences, and there are health consequences.

The Adverse Childhood Experiences (ACE) study (Felitti et al., 1998) was undertaken from 1995 to 1997 by the Centers for Disease Control and Prevention (CDC) and Kaiser Permanente, a managed healthcare consortium. The investigation involved over 17,000 subjects, which is an unusually high number, thus suggesting that the results of the study are quite robust. ACEs can have profound influences on future violence, both victimization and perpetration, as well as on health and potential opportunity over the life span; this makes adverse childhood experiences an important public health issue. According to a CDC website (2016, "About adverse childhood experiences", para 2), ACEs have been linked to the following outcomes:

- Risky health behaviors,
- Chronic health conditions,
- Low life potential, and
- Early death.

The greater the number of ACEs that a person has experienced, the higher the risk becomes for experiencing these outcomes. Figure 5.1 represents the pyramid of whole-life health risks and social impairments that may result from the core ACE that forms the base of the pyramid.

A high ACE score is an indicator for high risk across the life span. According to the American Society for the Positive Care of Children (ASPCC) website (2018, "A note from American SPCC," para. 3), the Substance Abuse and Mental Health Services Administration (SAMHSA) offers the following: "Adverse childhood experiences (ACEs) are stressful or traumatic events, including abuse and neglect. They may also include household dysfunction such as witnessing domestic violence or growing up with family members who have substance use disorders." Individuals who have experienced ACEs are likely to develop a wide range of health problems. The prevalence of health problems is higher for those scoring a higher number of ACEs, and this includes problems associated with substance misuse. The original ACE study (Felitti et al., 1998) has identified the following most common ACEs:

- Physical abuse,
- Sexual abuse,

- Emotional abuse,

- Physical neglect,

- Emotional neglect,

- Intimate partner violence,

- Mother treated violently,

- Substance misuse within household,

- Household mental illness,

- Parental separation or divorce, and

- Incarcerated household member.

Clearly, there is a strong association between the health-related effects of ACEs and stress, and this illuminates how stress is implicated in the experience of trauma.

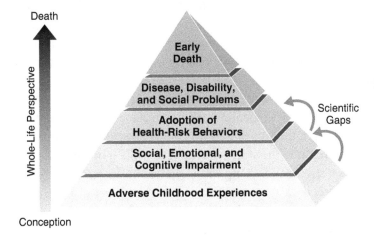

FIGURE 5.1 Adverse childhood experiences (ACEs) pyramid.

SOURCE: American Society for the Positive Care of Children (ASPCC). (2018, March 15). *Adverse childhood experiences (ACEs) are a significant risk factor for substance use disorders and can impact prevention efforts.* Retrieved from https://americanspcc.org/2018/03/15/adverse-childhood-experiences-aces -are-a-significant-risk-factor-for-substance-use-disorders-and-can-impact-prevention-efforts/

Stressors

Stress is a normal part of life; everyone experiences stress. In fact, some stress, termed "eustress" (Selye, 1956), actually is productive, for example, the "stress" that one experiences when the alarm clock goes off in the morning. This small amount of positive stress is enough to get the person out of bed and to prepare for the workday; without a bit of eustress, the temptation to remain in bed might win out. But the complexities of modern life produce a lot of stressors that, cumulatively, can be harmful. Not all stress leads to trauma, though a particular stressor or set of stressors can become traumatizing. The notion of adverse life experiences helps us to understand that there is a continuum from normal stress to trauma, with the concept of adverse life experiences offering a midpoint between stress and trauma. Many clients seek help after a stressor has affected them to the point of being able to identify an adverse life experience; a clinical mental health counselor can assist in managing the stress in ways that may prevent the adverse life experience from becoming traumatizing.

One "clinical tension" that is intrinsic to the topic of trauma relates to what Francine Shapiro (1997) has referenced as *Large-T* traumas versus *Small-t* traumas. Small-t traumas represent those adverse life experiences that do not qualify, necessarily, for a diagnosis of PTSD, but they certainly can be distressing and may require clinical attention (e.g., racial or gender discrimination, cyberbullying, work-related verbal abuse, loss of a pet). Large-T traumas are the types of traumatic events that typically are associated with PTSD (e.g., sexual assault, witnessing violence, experiencing war or a natural disaster). An associated clinical tension relates to how trauma is defined more narrowly, in terms of how it qualifies as a clinical diagnosis, versus how it is defined more broadly, that is, how a client actually may experience an adverse incident as traumatizing. Psychosocial trauma is a subjective and relative phenomenon. Definitions vary, depending on whether the focus is on *Diagnostic and Statistical Manual, Fifth Edition (DSM-5; American Psychiatric Association [APA])* diagnostic criteria of PTSD, on a life-span stage (e.g., adult versus children), or on the context of the potentially traumatic event.

It is essential that clinicians understand that stress is both a psychosocial and a physiological construct. The clinical mental health counselor may be tempted to view a client's stress only through the lens of focusing on feelings and emotional impact or to try to get the client to reframe the stress, cognitively, while ignoring the biological distress that accompanies a stressor. Ongoing stress can lead to anxiety, which, in turn, can lead to serious health problems (e.g., high blood pressure, heart disease, diabetes, obesity). While an in-depth discussion of the biochemistry of stress and anxiety is beyond the scope of this chapter, it is important to understand that, when experiencing a stressor, the person's hormonal system releases cortisol and adrenaline that then can trigger the fight-or-flight response (Children's Bureau, 2015; Tomko, 2012).

Lived Experience of Trauma

The *DSM-5* (APA, 2013) provides specific criteria for particular trauma-related diagnoses. Yet humans' lived experiences of trauma are not so neatly packaged; diagnostics are linear and explicit, while the phenomenology of lived trauma is much more fluid. Psychologically traumatic experiences demand extraordinary efforts to cope, and traumatic events call basic human relationships into question in profound ways (Courtois, 1988/1996). Decades ago, Courtois posited that traumatic events can destroy the victim's fundamental assumptions about the following profound existential conditions:

- The safety of the world (basic trust),
- The positive value of the self (self-esteem), and
- The meaningful order of creation (how one's life is "supposed" to be, and how it is "supposed" to make meaning).

In earlier versions of the *DSM*, that is, the *DSM-IV-TR*, the *DSM-IV*, and the *DSM-III* (PTSD was not yet identified in the *DSM-II* and the *DSM-I*), the core experiences of trauma were viable considerations within the diagnostic process. These core experiences included (a) terror, which encompasses a sense of disempowerment, helplessness, and abandonment, and (b) disconnection. In its latest iteration, *DSM-5*, subjective components of the definition of trauma have been eliminated (Pai, Suris, & North, 2017).

Posttraumatic Stress Disorder

Tehrani and Levers (2016) have asserted how essential it is for professionals who engage with trauma to understand the phenomenology of trauma. They have stated that "Perceptions of trauma experience have remained relatively constant throughout recorded history; however, the landscape of diagnostic classification regarding trauma has undergone recent change" (Tehrani & Levers, 2016, p. 105). Although clients' trauma-related concerns have been addressed by helping professionals for many years, PTSD was not even officially recognized until 1980, when it first was listed in the *DSM-III* (APA, 1980).

The diagnostic construct has continued to evolve, with later inclusions in the *International Classification of Diseases, 10th Revision* (*ICD-10*; World Health Organization, 1992) and in subsequent editions of the *DSM*. The most significant change in the diagnostic perspective of trauma occurred with the publication of the *DSM-5* (APA, 2013); in this most recent version of the *DSM*, PTSD was removed from its previous category as an anxiety disorder in *DSM-IV-TR* (APA, 2000) and placed in the chapter on "Trauma- and Stressor-Related Disorders." However, this chapter immediately follows chapters on "Anxiety Disorders" and "Obsessive-Compulsive and Related Disorders" and precedes the chapter on "Dissociative Disorders"; the introduction to the trauma chapter has noted that the placement of the chapter indicates a close relationship among these sets of diagnoses (APA, 2013). Understanding this relationship is important for those working with trauma in order to rule out unsuitable diagnoses and to make accurate diagnoses (Tehrani & Levers, 2016). The trauma- and stressor-related disorders included in the current *DSM-5* (APA, 2013) include the following:

- Reactive attachment disorder,
- Disinhibited social engagement disorder,
- Posttraumatic stress disorder,
- Acute stress disorder,
- Adjustment disorders,
- Other specified trauma- and stressor-related disorder, and
- Unspecified trauma- and stressor-related disorder.

Changes to the diagnosis of PTSD in the *DSM-5* (APA, 2013) have stirred controversy (Pai et al., 2017), on the one hand, and some appreciation for the greater emphasis on dissociative symptomatology (Dorahy & van der Hart, 2015; Friedman, 2013) on the other. Momentum favoring the inclusion of a posttraumatic complex trauma diagnosis continues (Giourou et al., 2018).

In Herman's (1992/1997) seminal book on trauma and recovery, she asserted that the many symptoms of PTSD fall into the following three main categories:

- Hyperarousal,

- Intrusion (intrusive symptoms include *flashbacks* and *nightmares*), and

- Constriction (constrictive symptoms can include *numbing, a detached state, and depression*).

This set of categorizations has remained helpful to clinicians in diagnosing trauma-related cases, especially complex trauma. Herman further identified the cyclical nature of long-term untreated PTSD, as the person fluctuates between intrusive and constrictive sets of symptoms. This has pointed to the importance of obtaining a thorough trauma history upon intake; without knowledge of the client's trauma history, a person presenting with intrusive symptoms may appear agitated or anxious and be misdiagnosed, while a person presenting with constrictive symptoms may appear depressed and likewise may be misdiagnosed.

In Herman's (1992/1997) original work, decades ago, she identified three stages of recovery that remain robust today. These stages included the following:

- Establishing Safety,

- Reconstructing the Trauma Story, and

- Reconnecting With Ordinary Life.

Stage I: Establishing Safety has involved naming the problem, restoring control, establishing a safe environment, and ensuring that all elements of the first stage have been completed before moving on. *Stage II: Reconstructing the Trauma Story* has involved remembering, transforming traumatic memory, and mourning/grieving the traumatic loss. *Stage III: Reconnecting With Ordinary Life* has involved learning to fight or not fight (comprehending the function of the autonomic nervous system [ANS] in the trauma response, which is explained later in this section), reconciling with oneself, reconnecting with others, finding a survivor mission, and resolving the trauma (Herman, 1992/1997).

The three stages that were identified by Herman (1992/1997) are compatible with strength-based, systemic, and resilience-producing approaches to resolving trauma. They also are compatible with the best practices associated with trauma counseling. *Integrative* approaches to therapy currently are considered to be the best practices in trauma counseling interventions (Levers, 2012a), and these include the following:

- Relational and cognitive behavioral interventions;

- Trauma-informed and trauma-specific care;

- Observed and experiential integration (OEI) model; and,

- Cognitive behavioral therapy (CBT) and adjunct therapies, for example eye movement desensitization and reprocessing (EMDR), dialectical behavior therapy (DBT), and exposure therapy.

In addition to the listed best-practice interventions, clinicians have been finding that a number of complementary and alternative medicine (CAM) treatments may be efficacious in managing and treating trauma (Strauss, Coeytaux, McDuffie, Nagi, & Wing, 2011; Wahbeh, Senders, Neuendorf, & Cayton, 2014). Some of the more helpful anxiety- and trauma-related CAM interventions have included mindfulness practices, acupuncture, tai chi, yoga, and meditation. Cannabidiol (CBD oil, which is the phytocannabinoid constituent of cannabis, but without the psychoactive effects of tetrahydrocannabinol) also has shown promise in the treatment of PTSD (Bitencourt & Takahashi, 2018), as has medicinal marijuana (Shishko, Oliveira, Moore, & Almeida, 2018).

Immigrants and Refugees

Immigrants and refugees have emerged more recently as groups that, respectively, may or are likely to experience trauma. Incidents at the southern border of the United States and throughout Europe illustrate how prejudice, bias, and xenophobia can serve as a justification to persecute people who, largely, are trying to flee horrible conditions in home countries where conditions such as poverty and political oppression make life unbearable (e.g., Case Illustration 5.2). Anthropogenic climate change has contributed to increasingly larger migration trends around the globe (Boikanyo & Levers, 2017; Levers & Drozda, 2018; Tarvydas et al., 2017, 2018). Levers and Hyatt-Burkhart (2011) have identified the potential for psychosocial trauma as a part of some immigration experiences and have pointed to the need for immigration reform.

CASE ILLUSTRATION 5.2

MARQUITA AND ISABELLA: SEPARATION OF A MOTHER AND THREE-YEAR-OLD AT THE U.S. BORDER

Three-year-old Marquita and her mother, Isabella, fled their drug-cartel-controlled small town in a Central American country after Isabella had been gang-raped at knifepoint. Isabella was terrified and just wanted to get to her brother's home in the southwestern part of the United States. She had heard that if she could manage to get to the Texas border, she could apply for refugee status with the U.S. government and remain in a detention camp, while the paperwork was being processed and while she located her brother. When she reached the border, Marquita was taken from her immediately. Marquita was screaming "Mamma, no!" as she was torn from Isabella's arms. Isabella tried to run after the border agent who took Marquita from her, but Isabella was held back by other agents as the agent with Marquita carried her away. Isabella was placed in a detention camp and continuously inquired about her daughter's whereabouts, begging to see her. Isabella was so distraught about this unexpected situation that she would have returned to her home immediately, but not without Marquita. Isabella remained in the detention camp for months, begging to be reunited with her daughter. Isabella finally was informed that the border agents had not tracked the children taken from their parents and that they did not know the location of Marquita.

Issues concerning traumatized immigrants and refugees are not likely to subside soon. Clinical mental health counselors interested in working with traumatized individuals may wish to consider immigrants and refugees as important contemporary populations in need of services. The treatment of immigrants and refugees in the United States and in other parts of the world clearly is a social justice issue warranting serious attention. Such treatment constitutes a humanitarian crisis.

Marginalized Populations

The historical period of colonialism, driven by dominating colonizers, created the circumstances under which marginalized populations emerged without the same rights as the colonizers. Such populations include Native American Indians, First Nations peoples, and other indigenous peoples; African Americans, whose ancestors were slaves; Jewish people, along with Roma and others who were persecuted during the Holocaust; Hispanics and Latinx; South Africans who lived under apartheid; Aboriginal peoples; those living in poverty without equitable access to healthcare and education; and others. Many of the people referenced here are the descendants of groups who were persecuted for racial, ethnic, religious, and other reasons; these ancestors experienced trauma and brutality, and their descendants have experienced the transgenerational effects of epigenetics and historical trauma (DeGruy, 2005; Mohatt, Thompson, Thai, & Tebes, 2014; SAMHSA, 2018; Shrira, 2019). Social and cultural trauma are relatively recent conceptualizations within the trauma discourse and merit further investigation (Igreja & Baines, 2019), as does the issue of resilience—peoples who survived social, cultural, and historical trauma also have adapted in amazing ways. The issues associated with marginalized populations constitute another set of contemporary social justice issues with which clinical mental health counselors need to become familiar.

Neuroscience and Polyvagal Theory

Better understandings of physiological and hormonal responses to stress, anxiety, and trauma have led to increased knowledge about how the brain is implicated in the effects of trauma (Children's Bureau, 2015; Newman et al., 2015; Tomko, 2012). In scans of a healthy brain juxtaposed with the brain of someone who has been abused (Perry, 2002), even a non-neurologist easily can spot the differences. Neuroscience research has helped in cultivating a better apprehension of ways that the brain affects social relationships (e.g., Cozolino, 2006; Fishbane, 2007; Goleman, 2006; Siegel, 2007). Recent advances in neuroscience are helping us to understand why some people are so much more susceptible to developing symptoms of PTSD, while others remain so much more resilient (Rattel et al., 2019).

Perhaps one of the most intriguing and promising contributions to the field of traumatology, in recent years, is Polyvagal Theory, developed by Professor Stephen Porges (2011). Polyvagal Theory relies on an understanding of the vagus nerve, which may be the most important body nerve that most people probably do not know that they have.

The functions and mechanisms of the vagus nerve have important implications for how humans respond to, experience, and process stress, anxiety, and trauma.

The vagus nerve has important links to the brain, heart, lungs, and other major organs; it even links to the middle and inner ear—vibrations in the ear can have a calming effect on the vagus nerve, which accounts for the soothing effect of certain types of music or the body-calming effect of an ancient syllable such as "om" (i.e., the resonant vibration of the 'm'). The practice of mindfulness has been successful in its use with anxiety- and trauma-related conditions, and its efficacy also can be explained with reference to the vagus nerve (Forner, 2019).

The vagus nerve is the longest nerve in the autonomic nervous system (ANS) and interacts with two major parts of the ANS: the parasympathetic nervous system (PNS) and the sympathetic nervous system (SNS). These two nervous systems have three circuits or functions that are instrumental in understanding not just the brain's response to trauma, but the whole body's response to stress, anxiety, and trauma:

- Social–communicative engagement (ability to interpret facial and social cues),
- Mobilization (fight or flight), and
- Immobilization ("shutdown"—inability to fight or flee).

The ANS regulates body functions that are generally beyond conscious control, such as normal breathing and heartbeat. The PNS is responsible for the *rest and digest* system; it *conserves energy* by slowing the heart rate, increasing intestinal and gland activity, and relaxing sphincter muscles in the gastrointestinal tract. Conversely, the SNS is responsible for what commonly is referenced as the *fight or flight response*—when the body panics due to lack of safety or to danger cues in the environment. The SNS *energizes* or *activates* body mechanisms by increasing muscle blood flow and tension, dilating the pupils, accelerating heart rate and respiration, and increasing perspiration and arterial blood pressure.

The nervous system continually picks up and assesses information in the environment, and the responses are not voluntary (Porges, 2011). In other words, this processing is not cognitive or intentional, but rather, it is happening at the neural level. "Perception" is not quite the right word to use, because the process is not a cognitive one; therefore, Porges coined the term "neuroception." Neuroception allows the body to define risk, at the autonomic neural level, in the following three essential ways: (a) threat perception, (b) threat sensitivity, and (c) self-image.

At the neuroception level, the ANS detects safety, or lack thereof, and engages the PNS or the SNS, depending upon environmental cues. An individual's response to a stressor, to danger, or to a potentially threatening or traumatizing event is beyond conscious control and is not processed at a cognitive level—it is happening at the neuroceptive ANS level. This explains why two people experiencing the same incident may have very different responses. It also offers evidence for refuting some of the intense victim blaming, which has persisted and become rampant, fueled by privilege and power, even in light of scientific findings (Bob, 2019).

TIP FROM THE FIELD 5.1

DESCRIBING THE NORMAL AUTONOMIC NERVOUS SYSTEM RESPONSE IN THE CONTEXT OF A TRAUMATIC EVENT

I was providing a full-day community violence workshop, with the director of an agency with which I volunteer. The agency operates a rapid-response-to-gun-violence service to the county. We were offering the workshop when the director received a call, notifying him of an active shooting. He had to leave the workshop, and I did not know the exact location (only the neighborhood, close to my neighborhood) of the shooting until I was driving home that evening, and traffic was being diverted at the corner where the *Tree of Life Synagogue* is located. I realized, in a panic, that this is where the director and our response team were. I pulled around the corner, parked my car, pulled out my cell phone, and was about to call to say that I was around the corner and would rush over to help them. My neuroceptors were engaged; I was in a panic (I have good friends who attend this synagogue—I would only learn later about the utter devastation of the massacre). Fortunately, my higher brain took control, I put my cell phone away, and I drove home. For a variety of reasons, an unplanned/just-jump-in response to a disaster is not a good idea; had I rushed to the site, I would not have been prepared, like the team, and I could have gotten in the way. At the same time, I wanted to do something, so I found some ways to volunteer my services.

In the context of availing myself to assist, in the aftermath of the massacre, I met with a person who was having a strong anxiety response to what had happened. After gleaning a sense of the person's state, I offered a description of how the person's ANS, particularly the SNS, was responding to the horror of what had occurred. As the person understood the autonomic response, I could see the anxiety dissipate from the person's face. The person barely could utter the words "Do you mean that my response is normal?" As I assured the person that yes, indeed, the person was having a normal (ANS/SNS/vagus nerve) response to this despicable tragedy, I witnessed the calming effect. I saw greater results in this 25-minute conversation than I have seen with much longer traditional talk therapies, under similar circumstances.

The construct of dissociation has become an increasingly dominant point in the discussion of trauma, in general, and is paid greater attention, specifically, in the *DSM-5* (APA, 2013) discussion of PTSD. It also is an instrumental concept within the framework of Polyvagal Theory. Dissociation is an altered state of consciousness that can serve as a biological protection mechanism. In this state, conscious awareness splits apart from feelings or memories that may be scary or terrifying to the person. A continuum of symptoms may become manifest, from relatively mild sensations of fogginess, sleepiness, or difficulty concentrating to a feeling of numbness or being separated from others, from the world, or even from parts of oneself. In extreme altered states, a person may even "lose time" or experience amnesia.

Other theoretical systems only talk about the fight or flight concept, whereas Polyvagal Theory accounts for a broader range of responses that actually match the wider scope of trauma experiences (Porges, 2011). Rather than focusing on only fight or flight, Polyvagal Theory acknowledges a more inclusive continuum of responses, particularly dissociative responses. So it may be helpful to think of the neurobiology of trauma as manifesting itself in stages, with greater degrees of dissociation occurring in later stages. Schauer and Elbert (2010) refer to the stages of trauma responses as the 6 *"Fs" of trauma response*, and these include the following:

- Freeze,
- Flight and fight,
- Fright,
- Flag, and
- Faint.

Freeze is an orienting response, involving the initial neuroception of danger—the *deer-in-the-headlights* phenomenon. With hormones shooting throughout the body and the SNS activating, the threatened person prepares either to fight or to flee. Mild stages of dissociation mediate these first three defensive responses. It is within the final three responses that dissociation becomes increasingly stronger. According to Schauer and Elbert (2010), fright involves unresponsive immobility; the person is beginning to become overwhelmed by the threat. In the flag stage, the threat has become so extreme that the SNS's arousal is beginning to shut down, and the PNS begins to be engaged. Schauer and Elbert (2010, p. 117) state that this stage "of the defense armament encompasses forms of dissociation and is characterized by reduced sympathetic arousal and passivity or a 'shut-down' peripherally dominated by vagal activity." If the threat or danger continues unabated, a full shutdown may occur in the final, faint stage, and the person literally may faint, experiencing vasovagal syncope (Schauer & Elbert, 2010).

CONCLUSION

This chapter has offered discussions of crisis, disaster, and trauma and has identified some of the key concepts for professional counselors and clinical mental health counselors working in these areas of professional counseling. Some of the major approaches to crisis intervention were presented. An adaptation-resilience building framework for conceptualizing disaster response was provided. The issue of psychosocial trauma was discussed from a multidimensional perspective, and some of the key aspects of trauma were elaborated. The most salient issues involving crisis, disaster, and trauma were explored, with a focus on their implications for the CMHC profession.

Perhaps the most important frontier in crisis, disaster, and trauma counseling is the necessity for more and expanded original and translational research related to the latest neuroscience. The field of professional counseling needs to incorporate the latest neuroscience into our current knowledge and practice sets in order to address crisis, disaster, and trauma in the most efficacious and efficient ways. Such professional advancement is compatible with an integrated system-of-care approach and is in line with the current trends in CMHC treatment and community-based interventions.

RESOURCES

Adverse Childhood Experiences Study. Retrieved from https://developingchild.harvard.edu/resources/aces-and-toxic-stress-frequently-asked-questions

American Psychological Association. (2019). *Trauma.* Retrieved from https://www.apa.org/topics/trauma

American Society for the Positive Care of Children. (2018, March 15). *Adverse childhood experiences (ACEs) are a significant risk factor for substance use disorders and can impact prevention efforts.* Retrieved from https://americanspcc.org/2018/03/15/adverse-childhood-experiences-aces-are-a-significant-risk-factor-for-substance-use-disorders-and-can-impact-prevention-efforts/

Brigham and Women's Hospital. "Long-term trauma outcomes heavily impacted by gender and education level." *ScienceDaily.* Retrieved on January, 3, 2019 from www.sciencedaily.com/releases/2019/01/190103185543.htm

Centers for Disease Control and Prevention. (2016). *Violence prevention: About the CDC-Kaiser ACE Study.* Retrieved from https://www.cdc.gov/violenceprevention/childabuseandneglect/acestudy/about.html

Centers for Disease Control and Prevention. (2019). *Essentials for childhood: Creating safe, stable, nurturing relationships and environments.* Retrieved from https://www.cdc.gov/violenceprevention/childabuseandneglect/essentials.html

Dr. Stephen Porges: What is the Polyvagal Theory? [Video]. Retrieved from https://www.youtube.com/watch?v=ec3AUMDjtKQ

Elsevier. (2019, February 14). Neural processing with trauma and adversity interact to increase core symptom of PTSD. *ScienceDaily.* Retrieved from www.sciencedaily.com/releases/2019/02/190214115541.htm

Forner, C. (2019). What mindfulness can learn about dissociation and what dissociation can learn from mindfulness. *Journal of Trauma & Dissociation, 20*(1), 1–15. Retrievedfromhttps://www.tandfonline.com/doi/pdf/10.1080/15299732.2018.1502568?needAccess=true

Frankl, V. (2006). *Man's search for meaning.* Boston, MA: Beacon Press. (Original work published 1946)

Harvard. Retrieved from www.developingchild.harvard.edu

Levers, L. L. (Ed.). (2012). *Trauma counseling: Theories and interventions.* New York, NY: Springer Publishing Company.

Long-term trauma outcomes heavily impacted by gender and education level. Retrieved from https://www.sciencedaily.com/releases/2019/01/190103185543.htm

National Child Traumatic Stress Network & National Center for PTSD. (2006). *Psychological first aid: Field operations manual* (2nd ed.). Retrieved from https://www.ptsd.va.gov/professional/treat/type/PFA/PFA_2ndEditionwithappendices.pdf

National Institute for the Clinical Application of Behavioral Medicine (NICABM). Retrieved from http://www.nicabm.com

National Institutes of Health. (2018, June). Dealing with trauma: Recovering from frightening events. *NIH News in Health.* Retrieved from https://newsinhealth.nih.gov/sites/nihNIH/files/2018/June/NIHNiHJun2018.pdf

National Scientific Council on the Developing Child. (2018). *Understanding motivation: Building the brain architecture that supports learning, health, and community participation: Working Paper No. 14*, Center on the Developing Child, Harvard University. Retrieved from https://46y5eh11fhgw3ve3ytpwxt9r-wpengine.netdna-ssl.com/wp-content/uploads/2018/12/wp14_reward_motivation_121118_FINAL.pdf

Trauma Informed Community Development. Paul Abernathy. TEDxPittsburgh. [Video]. Retrieved from https://www.youtube.com/watch?v=kcbu58p0fbA

▨ REFERENCES

Almedom, A. M. (2005). Resilience, hardiness, sense of coherence, and posttraumatic growth: All paths leading to "light at the end of the tunnel"? *Journal of Loss and Trauma, 10*, 253–265. doi:10.1080/15325020590928216

American Psychiatric Association. (1980). *Diagnostic and statistical manual of mental disorders* (3rd ed.). Washington, DC: Author.

American Psychiatric Association. (2000). *Diagnostic and statistical manual of mental disorders* (4th ed., Text Revision). Washington, DC: Author.

American Psychiatric Association. (2013). *Diagnostic and statistical manual of mental disorders* (5th ed.). Washington, DC: Author.

American Psychological Association. (2019). *Trauma*. Retrieved from https://www.apa.org/topics/trauma

American Society for the Positive Care of Children (ASPCC). (2018, March 15). *Adverse childhood experiences (ACEs) are a significant risk factor for substance use disorders and can impact prevention efforts*. Retrieved from https://americanspcc.org/2018/03/15/adverse-childhood-experiences-aces-are-a-significant-risk-factor-for-substance-use-disorders-and-can-impact-prevention-efforts/

Bitencourt, R. M., & Takahashi, R. N. (2018). Cannabidiol as a therapeutic alternative for post-traumatic stress disorder: From bench research to confirmation in human trials. *Frontiers in Neuroscience, 12*, 502. Retrieved from https://www.ncbi.nlm.nih.gov/pmc/articles/PMC6066583/pdf/fnins-12-00502.pdf

Bob, C. (2019). *Rights as weapons: Instruments of conflict, tools of power*. Princeton, NJ: Princeton University Press.

Boikanyo, M. N., & Levers, L. L. (2017). The effects of climate change on water insecurity in Botswana: Links to the criminal justice system. In G. Magill & K. Aramesh (Eds.), *The urgency of climate change: Pivotal perspectives* (pp. 434–449). Newcastle upon Tyne: Cambridge Scholars Publishing.

Bowlby, J. (1958). The nature of the child's tie to his mother. *The International Journal of Psychoanalysis, 39*, 350–373.

Bowlby, J. (1998). *Attachment and loss: Vol. 3 Sadness and depression. Attachment and loss*. London: Pimlico. (Original work published 1980)

Calhoun, G. C., & Tedeschi, R. G. (1998). Posttraumatic growth: Future directions. In R. G. Tedeschi, C. L. Park, & L. G. Calhoun (Eds.), *Posttraumatic growth: Positive change in the aftermath of crisis* (pp. 215–238). Mahwah, NJ: Lawrence Erlbaum Associates, Inc.

Centers for Disease Control and Prevention. (2016). *Violence prevention: About Adverse Childhood Experiences*. Retrieved from https://www.cdc.gov/violenceprevention/childabuseandneglect/acestudy/aboutace.html

Children's Bureau. (2015, April). Understanding the effects of maltreatment on brain development. *Child Information Gateway, Issue Brief*. Retrieved from https://www.childwelfare.gov/pubPDFs/brain_development.pdf

Courtois, C. A. (1996). *Healing the incest wound: Adult survivors in therapy*. New York, NY: W. W. Norton & Company. (Original work published 1988)

Council for the Accreditation of Counseling and Related Educational Programs. (2016). *2016 CACREP standards*. Retrieved from http://www.cacrep.org/wp-content/uploads/2017/08/2016-Standards-with-citations.pdf

Cozolino, L. (2006). *The neuroscience of human relationships: Attachment and the developing social brain*. New York, NY: W. W. Norton & Company.

Dalai Lama. (2003). *How to practice: The way to a meaningful life*. New York, NY: Atria Books.

DeGruy, J. (2005). Post traumatic slave syndrome: America's legacy of enduring injury and healing. Milwaukie, OR: Uptone Press.

Dorahy, M. J., & van der Hart, O. (2015). DSM-5's 'PTSD with dissociative symptoms': Challenges and future directions. *Journal of Trauma & Dissociation, 16*(1), 7–18. doi:10.1080/15299732.2014.908806

Erikson, E. H. (1950). *Childhood and society*. New York, NY: W. W. Norton & Company.

Felitti, V. J., Anda, R. F., Nordenberg, D., Williamson, D. F., Spitz, A. M., Edwards, A. M., ... Marks, J. S. (1998). Relationship of childhood abuse and household dysfunction to many of the leading causes of death in adults: The adverse childhood experiences (ACE) study. *American Journal of Preventive Medicine, 14*(4), 245–258. doi:10.1016/S0749-3797(98)00017-8

Fishbane, M. (2007). Wired to connect: Neuroscience, relationships, and therapy. *Family Process, 46*(3), 395–412. doi:10.1111/j.1545-5300.2007.00219.x

Forner, C. (2019). What mindfulness can learn about dissociation and what dissociation can learn from mindfulness. *Journal of Trauma & Dissociation, 20*(1), 1–15. Retrieved from https://www.tandfonline.com/doi/pdf/10.1080/15299732.2018.1502568?needAccess=true

Frazier, M. F., & Kaler, P. (2006). The meaning in life questionnaire: Assessing the presence of and search for meaning in life. *Journal of Counseling Psychology, 53*(1), 80–93. doi:10.1037/0022-0167.53.1.80

Friedman, M. J. (2013). Finalizing PTSD in *DSM-5*: Getting here from there and where to go next. *Journal of Traumatic Stress, 26*, 548–556. doi:10.1002/jts.21840

Gilliland, B. E., & James, R. K. (1997). *Crisis intervention strategies* (3rd ed.). Pacific Grove, CA: Brooks/Cole Publishing Company.

Giourou, E., Skokou, M., Andrew, S. P., Alexopoulou, K., Gourzis, P., & Jelastopulu, E. (2018). Complex posttraumatic stress disorder: The need to consolidate a distinct clinical syndrome or to reevaluate features of psychiatric disorders following interpersonal trauma? World Journal of Psychiatry, 8(1), 12–19. doi:10.5498/wjp.v8.i1.12

Goleman, D. (2006). *Social intelligence: The new science of human relationships*. New York, NY: Bantam Books/Random House.

Herman, J. L. (1992/1997). *Trauma and recovery: The aftermath of violence--from domestic abuse to political terror*. New York, NY: Basic Books. (Original work published 1992)

Igreja, V., & Baines, E. (2019). Social trauma and recovery: Emergent themes. In R. R. Grinker, S. C. Lubkemann, C. B. Steiner, & E. Gonçalves (Eds.), *A companion to the anthropology of Africa* (pp. 251–270). Hoboken, NJ: John Wiley & Sons, Inc.

Joseph, S., & Butler, L. D. (2010, Summer). Positive changes following adversity. *PTSD Research Quarterly, 21*(3), 1–8. Retrieved from https://pdfs.semanticscholar.org/5e22/33dbdc6afc820c45bf098bb89fe3bad71c05.pdf

Kübler-Ross, E. (1969). *On death and dying: What the dying have to teach their doctors, nurses, clergy and their own families*. New York, NY: Macmillan Publishing.

Levers, L. L. (2012a). Conclusion: An integrative systemic approach to trauma. In L. L. Levers (Ed.), *Counseling survivors of trauma: Theories and interventions*. New York, NY: Springer Publishing Company.

Levers, L. L. (2012b). Introduction to understanding trauma. In L. L. Levers (Ed.), *Counseling survivors of trauma: Theories and interventions* (pp. 1–22). New York, NY: Springer Publishing Company.

Levers, L. L., & Drozda, N. A. (2018). Embracing a human ecological approach to anthropogenic climate change: The mandate for moving beyond empathy and raising levels of compassion. In G. Magill & J. Potter (Eds.), *Integral ecology: Protecting our common home* (pp. 83–131). Newcastle upon Tyne: Cambridge Scholars Publishing.

Levers, L. L., & Hyatt-Burkhart, D. (2011). Immigration reform and the potential for psychosocial trauma: The missing link of lived human experience. *Analyses of Social Issues and Public Policy, 12*(1), 68–77. doi:10.1111/j.1530-2415.2011.01254.x

Merriam-Webster. (2019). Crisis. *The Merriam-Webster Dictionary*. Retrieved from https://www.merriam-webster.com/dictionary/crisis

Mohatt, N. V., Thompson, A. B., Thai, N. D., & Tebes, J. K. (2014). Historical trauma as public narrative: A conceptual review of how history impacts present-day health. *Social Science Medicine, 106*, 128–136. Retrieved from https://www.ncbi.nlm.nih.gov/pmc/articles/PMC4001826/pdf/nihms569976.pdf

National Child Traumatic Stress Network & National Center for PTSD. (2006). *Psychological first aid: Field operations manual* (2nd ed.). Retrieved from https://www.ptsd.va.gov/professional/treat/type/PFA/PFA_2ndEditionwithappendices.pdf

Newman, L., Sivaratnam, C., & Komiti, A. (2015). Attachment and early brain development – neuroprotective interventions in infant–caregiver therapy. *Translational Developmental Psychiatry, 3*(1), 1–13. Retrieved from https://www.tandfonline.com/doi/pdf/10.3402/tdp.v3.28647?needAccess=true

Pai, A., Suris, A. M., & North, C. S. (2017). Posttraumatic stress disorder in the *DSM-5*: Controversy, change, and conceptual considerations. *Behavioral Sciences*. Retrieved from https://www.ncbi.nlm.nih.gov/pmc/articles/PMC5371751/pdf/behavsci-07-00007.pdf

Park, C. L., & Lechner, S. C. (2006). Measurement issues in assessing growth following stressful life experiences. In L. G. Calhoun & R. G. Tedeschi (Eds.), *Handbook of posttraumatic growth: Research & practice* (pp. 47–67). Mahwah, NJ: Lawrence Erlbaum Associates Publishers.

Perry, B. D. (2002). Childhood experience and the expression of genetic potential: What childhood neglect tells us about nature and nurture. *Brain and Mind, 3*, 79–100. doi:10.1023/A:1016557824657

Peterson, C., Park, N., Pole, N., D'Andrea, W., & Seligman, M. E. (2008). Strengths of character and posttraumatic growth. *Journal of Traumatic Stress, 21*(2), 214–217. doi:10.1002/jts.20332

Porges, S. W. (2011). *The Polyvagal Theory: Neurophysiological foundations of emotions, attachment, communication, self-regulation.* New York, NY: W. W. Norton & Company.

Purvis, J. R. (1994). Crisis management. *Encyclopedia of human behavior: Volume 2.* New York, NY: Academic Press.

Rattel, J. A., Miedl, S. F., Franke, L. K., Grünberger, L. M., Blechert, J., Kronbichler, M., … Wilhelm, F. H. (2019). Peritraumatic neural processing and intrusive memories: The role of lifetime adversity. *Biological Psychiatry: Cognitive Neuroscience and Neuroimaging, 4*(4), 381–389. doi:10.1016/j.bpsc.2018.12.010

Roberts, A. R. (2002, Spring). Assessment, crisis intervention, and trauma treatment: The integrative ACT model. *Brief Treatment & Crisis Intervention, 2*(1), 1–21. doi:10.1093/brief-treatment/2.1.1

Rodin, J. (2014). *The resilience dividend: Being strong in a world where things go wrong.* New York, NY: Public Affairs.

Schauer, M., & Elbert, T. (2010). Dissociation following traumatic stress: Etiology and treatment. *Zeitschrift für Psychologie/Journal of Psychology, 218*(2), 109–127. doi:10.1027/0044-3409/a000018

Selye, H. (1956). *The stress of life*. New York, NY: McGraw-Hill Books.

Shapiro, F. (1997). *EMDR: The breakthrough "eye movement" therapy for overcoming anxiety, stress, and trauma*. New York, NY: Basic Books.

Shishko, I., Oliveira, R., Moore, T. A., & Almeida, K. (2018). A review of medical marijuana for the treatment of posttraumatic stress disorder: Real symptom relief or just high hopes? *Mental Health Clinician, 8*(2), 86–94. Retrieved from https://www.ncbi.nlm.nih.gov/pmc/articles/PMC6007739/pdf/i2168-9709-8-2-86.pdf

Shrira, A. (2019). Parental PTSD, health behaviors and successful aging among offspring of Holocaust survivors. *Psychiatry Research, 271*, 265–271. doi:10.1016/j.psychres.2018.11.060

Siegel, D. J. (2007). *The mindful brain: Reflection and attunement in the cultivation of wellbeing*. New York, NY: W. W. Norton & Company.

Strauss, J. L., Coeytaux, R., McDuffie, J., Nagi, A., & Wing, L. (2011, August). *Efficacy of complementary and alternative medicine therapies for posttraumatic stress disorder*. Washington, DC: Department of Veterans Affairs. Retrieved from https://www.ncbi.nlm.nih.gov/books/NBK82774/pdf/Bookshelf_NBK82774.pdf

Substance Abuse and Mental Health Services Administration. (2018). *Behavioral Health Services for American Indians and Alaska Natives: For Behavioral Health Service Providers, Administrators, and Supervisors: TIP 61*. Retrieved from https://store.samhsa.gov/system/files/tip_61_aian_full_document_020419_0.pdf

Tarvydas, V., Levers, L. L., & Teahen, P. R. (2017). Ethical guidelines for mass trauma and complex humanitarian emergencies. *Journal of Counseling and Development, 95*, 260–268. doi:10.1002/jcad.12140

Tarvydas, V., Levers, L. L., & Teahen, P. R. (2018). Ethics narratives from lived experiences of disaster and trauma counselors. In J. Webber & J. B. Mascari (Eds.), *Disaster mental health counseling: A guide to preparing and responding* (4th ed., pp. 97–109). Alexandria, VA: American Counseling Association Foundation.

Teahan, P. R., Levers, L. L., & Tarvydas, V. (2017). Disaster, climate change, and public health: Building social-ecological resilience. In G. Magill & K. Aramesh (Eds.), *The urgency of climate change: Pivotal perspectives* (pp. 133–160). Newcastle upon Tyne: Cambridge Scholars Publishing.

Tedeschi, R. G., & Calhoun, G. C. (2004). Posttraumatic growth: Conceptual foundations and empirical evidence. *Psychological Inquiry, 15*(1), 1–18. doi:10.1207/s15327965pli1501_01

Tehrani, N., & Levers, L. L. (2016). Working through the pain. In D. A. Lane, M. Watts, & S. Corrie (Eds.), *Supervision in the psychological professions: Building your own personalized model* (pp. 104–124). Berkshire: Open University Press/McGraw-Hill Education.

Tomko, J. R. (2012). Neurobiological effects of trauma and psychopharmacology. In L. L. Levers (Ed.), *Counseling survivors of trauma: Theories and interventions* (pp. 59–75). New York, NY: Springer Publishing Company.

United Nations Office for Disaster Risk Reduction. (2009). *Terminology of disaster risk reduction*. Retrieved from https://www.unisdr.org/files/7817_UNISDRTerminologyEnglish.pdf

Wahbeh, H., Senders, A., Neuendorf, R., & Cayton, J. (2014). Complementary and alternative medicine for post-traumatic stress disorder symptoms: A systematic review. *Journal of Evidence-Based Complementary & Alternative Medicine, 19*(3), 161–175.

Walter, C. A., & McCoyd, J. L. M. (2009). *Grief and loss across the lifespan: A biopsychological perspective*. New York, NY: Springer Publishing Company.

Worden, J. W. (2008). *Grief counseling and grief therapy: A handbook for the mental health practitioner* (4th ed.). New York, NY: Springer Publishing Company.

World Health Organization. (1992). *The ICD-10 classification of mental and behavioural disorders: Clinical descriptions and diagnostic guidelines*. Geneva: World Health Organization.

SECTION III

PRACTICE ISSUES

COMMUNITY-BASED MENTAL HEALTH COUNSELING, RECOVERY MODELS, AND MULTIDISCIPLINARY COLLABORATION

ELIAS MPOFU | JUSTIN WATTS | QIWEI LI |
NGOZI JANE-FRANCES CHIMA ADARALEGBA | PATRICK IGBEKA

This chapter considers community-based mental healthcare practices for optimal functioning of people in their communities. First, we address community mental health in the context of the activities and participation to which people aspire, regardless of their specific mental health impairment; within this context, their personal factors are considered as well as the lived environment. Second, we discuss mental health recovery models for satisfying personal and community functioning. Finally, we identify types of collaborative community mental healthcare practices and offer associated evidence.

The following Council for Accreditation of Counseling and Related Educational Programs (CACREP) standards are addressed in this chapter:
CACREP 2016:
2F1.b, 2F1.c, 2F3.d, 2F3.h, 2F5.k, 5C2.a, 5C2.c, 5C2.e, 5C3.d
CACREP 2009:
2G2.a, 2G3.g

LEARNING OBJECTIVES

After reviewing this chapter, the reader should be able to:

1. Define mental health in the context of community;

2. Differentiate between mental health functioning and diagnosable mental health disorders;

3. Discuss mental health needs in the context of community;

4. Evaluate the roles of activity and participation in the restoration and maintenance of mental health issues;

5. Characterize the nature of recovery in the context of community mental health needs; and,

6. Discuss collaborative mental healthcare models.

INTRODUCTION

Community-based mental health services offer structure and support to individuals with mental health issues in order to help them achieve an optimal level of functioning. Levels of functioning can be enhanced when communities provide a foundation for achieving a sense of being for and with others (Mantovani, Pizzolati, & Gillard, 2017). Community is more than just a place where people live; it is a space in which people construct their lives for and with others who share broadly common values/interests and goals/actions for realizing life goals (Mitchell & Haddrill, 2006). Communities provide social capital resources for health and well-being, along with other important resources aimed at meeting the mental health needs of community members. For instance, communities that are socially disadvantaged have fewer physical and social resources, which greatly inhibits participation in both physical and social activities (Sheffield & Peek, 2009). Meaningful personal and community functioning is premised on healthy mental functioning and on the capacity of community members to carry out basic self-care and successfully engage in major life domains (Table 6.1).

For many decades, mental healthcare practices have privileged clinical psychiatric care with little regard for community-oriented mental healthcare (Rosen, O'Halloran, Mezzina, & Thompson, 2015). There is presently a major shift toward community-oriented mental healthcare, which aims to support people with specific mental health conditions in order to foster the greatest quality of life possible within communities (Fairweather, Cressler, Meissner, & Maynard, 2013; Mpofu, 2015). Despite the significance of community mental healthcare services, there is currently an enormous gap between mental health needs and available resources in the community setting (Thyloth, Singh, & Subramanian, 2016).

LEGAL AND PROFESSIONAL ISSUES

The community mental health movement started in 1963 in the United States after President John F. Kennedy signed the Community Mental Health Act (CMHA; Dixon & Goldman, 2003). Prior to this act, many individuals with disabilities and mental illness were isolated in asylums that failed to provide treatment or any type of productive activities for those who were institutionalized (Substance Abuse and Mental Health Services Administration [SAMHSA], 2013). The CMHA provided a comprehensive foundation for community-focused mental healthcare in every U.S. state. This Act served as a springboard for advanced training for mental health practitioners, increased research on mental health and mental illness, influenced an emphasis on prevention, and ultimately led to deinstitutionalization, which has resulted in the decongestion of large state mental hospitals, thus placing the responsibility of mental healthcare on the community (Dixon & Goldman, 2003).

In 2008, Senator Edward Kennedy and Representative Patrick Kennedy oversaw updates to the CMHA of 1963 by implementing the Mental Health Parity and Addiction Equity Act, which requires that insurance agencies treat mental health and substance use disorders in the same fashion that other illnesses and diseases are addressed. These updates were intended to address concerns due to fragmented service delivery and issues related to certain disorders "falling through the cracks" of the healthcare system. These pivotal pieces of legislation have set the foundation for many advances in community systems of care in providing equitable treatment for individuals with mental health issues, in addition to new legislation in addressing current concerns related to mental health coverage for individuals with and without insurance coverage, Medicare, or Medicaid. Changes in policies and the involvement of nongovernmental institutions and organizations have contributed to the current, improved state of community-based mental health services. Currently, community mental health programs attempt to assist people in meeting their mental health needs for everyday functioning (Drake & Latimer, 2012). These programs also strive to attain full social and economic inclusion (Nieminen et al., 2012; Seebohm, Gilchrist, & Morris 2012).

The World Health Organization's International Classification of Functioning, Disability and Health (WHO ICF, 2001) defines mental health functions as being comprised of two major domains: *global* and *specified*. Global mental functions refer to predispositions of consciousness, awareness, social engagement, and temperament that are important for everyday functioning. A person's general sense of mental health well-being defines his or her sense of connectedness or belongingness (Mitchell & Haddrill, 2006). Specified mental functions refer to individual attention, memory, emotion, and perception, which include mental and personality disorders. Disorders of specified mental health functions account for approximately 13% of the global burden of disease (Ng et al., 2014). Those with disorders of specified mental health functions typically require treatment, care, and support by mental health providers, family, and significant others (Corrigan, Druss, & Perlick, 2014). Community life also influences the prevalence and severity of specific mental health functions, as with the management of psychiatric illness.

The quality of lived social and physical environments influences both the physical and mental health of individuals and their significant others. For instance, perceptions of social and physical safety, housing, transportation, and distribution of human services influence the mental health well-being of residents (Kelly, Perkins, Fuller, & Parker, 2011). Communities with high levels of physical illness also demonstrate high rates of mood disorders, such as depression and anxiety (Methley, Campbell, Cheraghi-Sohi, & Chew-Graham, 2017).

▩ ACTIVITY AND PARTICIPATION IN COMMUNITY MENTAL HEALTH

People's mental health influences the activities in which they choose to engage, along with the degree to which they participate in their communities. According to the WHO ICF (2001), the term "activity" involves execution of a task or action by an individual (e.g., riding a bicycle or walking). The term "participation" refers to involvement in a life situation that broadly encompasses key areas of everyday life. Individuals might have limitations regarding participation in certain activities that may be a result of general or specified mental health conditions. The WHO ICF (2001) defines participation restrictions as challenges an individual may experience that limit involvement in certain life situations. The WHO ICF also defines nine domains of activities and outlines examples of actions essential to participate in these activities (Table 6.1).

The first set of four domains and functions cover *activity functions*, whereas the latter set of five domains cover *participation functions*. There is an interplay between activity limitations and participation restrictions in the community context (Figure 6.1). For instance, engagement in leisure-time physical activity, such as playing sports, is associated with higher levels of mental health (Marlier et al., 2015). Similarly, when individuals are community engaged, they tend to have higher levels of general mental health. Case Illustration 6.1 is illustrative.

TABLE 6.1 The World Health Organization's International Classification of Functioning (WHO ICF) Activities and Participation

DOMAINS	EXAMPLES OF ACTIONS/TASKS
Activities	
Learning and applying knowledge	Basic learning, applying knowledge
General tasks and demands	Recreation and leisure, undertaking multiple tasks, carrying out daily routine
Communication	Conversation and use of communication devices and techniques
Mobility	Carrying, moving, and handling objects
Self-care	Washing oneself, eating, dressing
Participation	
Domestic life	Caring for household objects, household tasks
Interpersonal interactions and relationships	General and specific interpersonal relationships
Major life areas	Education, economic life, and employment
Community, social, and civic life	Community life, recreation and leisure, and religion

SOURCE: Adapted from World Health Organization. (2001). *International Classification of Functioning, Disability and Health*. Retrieved from https://apps.who.int/iris/bitstream/handle/10665/42407/9241545429.pdf;jsessionid=25740D4E9A37B6B253A5D6ECEFD82007?sequence=1

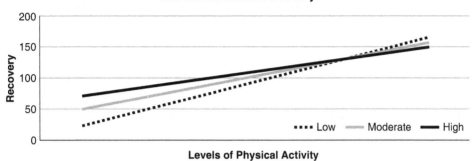

FIGURE 6.1 Interaction between physical activities and levels of mental health.

CASE ILLUSTRATION 6.1

ANNA: COMMUNITY INVOLVEMENT AS A TREATMENT FOR SPECIFIC MENTAL HEALTH FUNCTIONS

Anna is a 34-year-old female who recently joined a volunteer organization that engages in community improvement projects to keep neighborhoods and parks clean and beautiful. She has made a few friends through the organization and maintains several hours a week in volunteering while also attending social events through the organization. Prior to her engagement with the organization, Anna was experiencing depressed mood for most of the day. She reported losing interest in most activities, and experiencing increased fatigue, difficulty sleeping, and difficulty concentrating on anything. When she initially was diagnosed with Major Depressive Disorder, Anna reported that she "no longer had the interest or energy to do anything." She began to withdraw from friends and started to have issues at work. A close friend encouraged her to join the volunteer organization. Over time, this began to give her a sense of purpose and connection, which has helped her to begin addressing her symptoms, in addition to seeking counseling and other supports. She noted that "it's nice to get up and get moving, meet new people, and feel a sense of pride for accomplishing something and making my community beautiful."

The case of Anna exemplifies the presentation of specified health functions involving emotion regulation. It also demonstrates the fact that community engagement may be a partial solution for thought and mood disorders through the restoration of a sense of belongingness and agency involving others. Traditional mental healthcare has prioritized treatment and care for emotional functions with psychopharmacological medications and intensive cognitive behavioral therapies at the relative neglect of informal engagement in community activities, which would treat the specific mental health functions while also enhancing the person's overall functioning.

Activities and Community Mental Health Functions

An individual's degree of mental health functioning has a major impact on the degree of engagement in basic life activities. However, the relationship between mental health functioning and community engagement is bidirectional. The ability to perform general tasks in and withstand the demands of community settings is associated with the general mental health functions of energy and drive. For instance, mobility limitations, such as difficulties in using public transportation due to mental health impairment, may result from reduced mental health functions (Stegenga et al., 2012; Thorpe et al., 2011). Similarly, mental health condition limitations from a specified emotional disorder, such as depression and anxiety, would affect the ability to complete tasks on time and to manage and develop interpersonal relationships (Carrière et al., 2011; Norton et al., 2012). Conversely, consistent physical exercise is linked to reduced depression (Hamer, Stamatakis, & Steptoe, 2009).

Participation and Community Mental Health Functions

As previously noted, community participation influences both global and specific mental health functions. For instance, participation in domestic life activities improves an individual's confidence and encourages a sense of fulfillment and belonging in the community (Firth et al., 2016). One's global (general mental health) and specific mental health functions (mental disorders) influence the quality of one's interpersonal/interactional relationships. Successful community living depends on global (general) mental health functions and/or well-managed specific health functions or disorders. Conversely, people with lower engagement in major life domains of work, education, and employment may be restricted in their general psychosocial functioning. Participation in community, social, and civic life is related to healthy functioning with mental health disorders. For instance, a study by Tjonstrandi, Bejerholm, and Eklun (2011) found that people with psychiatric disabilities who had more opportunities to socialize at community day centers had superior mental health functioning. Similarly, improvements in cognitive and intellectual functioning are associated with availability of physical activity resources, such as recreational centers and parks (Clarke, Weuve, Barnes, Evans, & Mendes de Leon, 2015).

Community Environment and Mental Healthcare

Community mental health outcomes are shaped by interactions between people and the environments in which they live, work, and play (Clarke & Nieuwenhuijsen, 2009). As noted previously, both physical functioning and the social–environmental context influence health and well-being. The WHO ICF (2001) considers the environment to be comprised of an individual's natural surroundings (including those that are human made), technology, support and interpersonal relationships, as well as political systems and policies. The environment either can act as a barrier to or can assist in facilitating positive mental health functioning of individuals (WHO ICF, 2001). A healthy community environment fosters social interactions, nurtures social capital, and provides a sense of belonging for the community (Wong, Yu, & Woo, 2017). By contrast, some communities may lack a supportive, nurturing environment and may be full of chronic psychosocial stressors that are likely to have a negative impact on the global mental health functions of individuals (Ilies, Aw, & Lim, 2016).

As noted previously, social capital and social support consistently help to improve people's mental health (Rothon, Goodwin, & Stansfeld, 2011). Higher rates of positive social interactions and consistent social inclusion have a positive impact on the mental health of an individual (Wong et al., 2017). Individuals who work in environments with greater social support from supervisors and colleagues and who experience greater job security often report improvement in mental health functioning.

In addition to the social environment, the physical environment (e.g., buildings, transportation, and accessibility of recreational facilities) also can affect global health functions, specifically psychosocial and intellectual functions. For instance, while accelerated urbanization may contribute to livable communities and overall improved health of some residents (Chen, Chen, Landry, & Davis, 2014), it may also result in homelessness for others, which can have an adverse effect on the mental health of community members.

Policies and programs that involve a strict focus on the individual have yielded insignificant results when compared with community-oriented policies that utilize community resources and social capital, as the quality of mental health reported by community members is affected by these social factors (Marmot, Friel, Bell, Houweling, & Taylor, 2008). For example, home allocation services in Australia, Canada, and the United States have reduced homelessness and associated mental health problems among citizens (Metraux, Cusack, Byrne, Hunt-Johnson, & True, 2017). Public housing programs in the United States have an opportunity to create people-friendly communities where members enjoy superior health and a lower prevalence of chronic physical health diseases.

In 1996 the U.S. Congress passed legislation that created parity in mental health coverage with the intent to meet the increasing demand for mental health services to individuals within the community. This amendment is known as the Mental Health Parity Act (MHPA) of 1996. Prior to this act, individuals with mental health needs were not covered by insurers or experienced dollar limitations on coverage that limited access to mental healthcare. Congress passed the Mental Health Parity and Addictions Equity Act (MHPAEA) in 2008, which was a revision to the MHPA. This act required that health insurers, who covered mental health treatment, provide the same level of benefits for mental and/or substance use treatment and services as they did for medical/surgical care. The MHPAEA did not mandate coverage for mental health diagnoses and substance use disorders. This Act only required that the financial requirements and treatment limitations were no more restrictive than the predominant financial requirements and treatment limitations for medical and surgical benefits covered by the plan. The Affordable Care Act (ACA) of 2014 mandated that most individual and small group health insurance plans cover mental health and substance abuse treatment. The ACA was needed for the purposes of streamlining mental health support services provided by managed healthcare organizations, unlike CMHA, which was utilized primarily for promoting community living with mental health diagnoses.

▨ RECOVERY AND MENTAL HEALTH FUNCTIONS

The conceptualization and treatment of mental illness has undergone a dramatic change over the last several decades. As opposed to describing mental illness as a chronic (long-term), degenerating (worsening) disease, research and treatment efforts have started to understand these issues through the lens of recovery and rehabilitation (Jenkins & Carpenter-Song, 2005). The focus is shifting from primarily symptom alleviation to recovery; this shift in research and service provision involves a sustained effort to restore factors that individuals perceive to be essential to their own mental health and well-being (Sklar, Groessl, O'Connell, Davidson, & Aarons, 2013). The process of recovery from mental illness is multifaceted and unique to each individual, as the resources that an individual has or may need will vary drastically from person to person. Recovery from mental health-related issues involves a process by which an individual utilizes a combination of personal assets and available resources to restore and maintain mental health (Crowley, 2000; Deegan, 1996; Jacobson & Curtis, 2000).

Sources of recovery or social/recovery capital include personal assets (e.g., psychological resilience, empowerment, or learned resourcefulness) and environmental factors (social support and community mental health; Brown & Baker, 2018; Cloud & Granfield, 2008; Ellison, Belanger, Niles, Evans, & Bauer, 2018; SAMHSA, 2013). For instance, SAMHSA (2012) has outlined 10 guiding principles that support recovery from mental health and substance-related issues. These guiding principles involve the following components: (a) person centered (i.e., the concept of recovery is highly individualized and distinct for each individual), (b) empowerment (i.e., the individual has agency over decision-making and control over his or her life), (c) hope (a belief in one's capacity to recover), (d) self-direction (i.e., an individual has the autonomy to determine his or her goals for recovery), (e) strengths based (i.e., recovery builds on many different capacities and coping abilities), (f) respect (i.e., dignity, lacking stigma, and free from discrimination), (g) responsibility (individual accountability for one's life), (h) peer support (mutual support from peers), and (i) holistic (recovery involves mind, body, spirit, and community). In addition to these components of recovery, SAMHSA (2012) also outlined the following four dimensions of recovery: (a) health (overcoming and managing one's disease), (b) home (having a safe, stable place to live), (c) purpose (having fulfilling life roles that contribute to a meaningful life), and (d) community (interaction with the environment, a sense of connectedness).

"Recovery capital" is a concept that initially was introduced in the addictions field (Cloud & Granfield, 2008) and that now has major implications for the field of mental health. In essence, recovery capital involves personal or environmental resources that can support an individual's recovery from substance use or mental health-related issues. Recovery capital, in essence, works much like a bank account; the more resources individuals have at their disposal, the more likely they are going to be able to navigate distressing situations and, ultimately, increase the likelihood of recovery. Examples of recovery capital include any of the following: (a) social capital (i.e., social resources such as friends, family, and peer support groups), (b) physical capital (i.e., acceptable housing, financial assets, and transportation), (c) human capital (i.e., skills, knowledge, health, mental health, and employment skills), and (d) cultural capital (i.e., cultural and environmental conditions that contribute to well-being; Brown & Baker, 2018; Cloud & Granfield, 2008). These factors also provide a springboard from which practitioners, who are working with individuals with mental health-related issues, may identify areas that may be lacking in order to facilitate growth and support for individuals.

Integrated Recovery-Oriented Model (IRM)

IRMs are collaborative models that are designed to increase access to comprehensive mental health services. These models focus on an individual's changing needs for recovery, in addition to facilitating contact with comprehensive services that are designed to enhance the holistic needs of clients with mental health-related issues. IRMs are intended to restore, maintain, and augment functioning with collaborative restoration of skills, competencies, and active community reconnection (Liberman & Kopelowicz, 2005). The three key components of the IRM—healing, empowerment, and responsibility—have shown evidence for effectiveness (Slade et al., 2014). Healing is a process of recovery that results from individuals increasing their capacity to cope with mental health issues in the context of community living. Healing is associated with enhanced self-care practices, such as accepting a wellness lifestyle. Empowerment involves self-determination related to recovery goals, and it entails developing and achieving a sense of courage to take risks and deal with issues as they arise. Finally, a sense of responsibility for personal recovery is a profoundly social process, based on capitalizing personal strengths and social connectedness (Wehmeyer, Kelchner, & Richards, 1996). With IRMs, these personal and social functions are achieved promoting dignity, respect, trust, and love of self and community.

Activity and Participation for Recovery

Individuals in recovery are able to experience enhanced mental health functioning, engage in preferred activities, and participate in community living events. For instance, engagement in learning and applying knowledge allows individuals to benefit from education and employment. Activities are vital in battling the high levels of social isolation and low levels of community engagement that often are experienced by people in mental health recovery (Townley, Kloos, & Wright, 2009). An increase in community activities can elevate existential, functional, and social levels of engagement while potentially decreasing psychiatric symptoms and distress. For instance, a person in recovery is capable of engaging in domestic activities, which also could assist him or her with maintaining and promoting mutually beneficial interpersonal relationships.

Personal factors such as race, gender, age, educational level, and coping style must be taken into consideration concerning activity and participation in recovery. While race, gender, and age describe an individual's identity, educational level and coping style can have an influence on the recovery process with regard to a person's ability to master, minimize, or tolerate stress and conflict. In addition, recovery models may work differently for people from diverse ethnic and cultural backgrounds, who are at differing stages of recovery and may be experiencing different types of mental illness. Case Illustration 6.2 is illustrative.

CASE ILLUSTRATION 6.2

ANGELA: ACKNOWLEDGING SYMPTOMS OF ANXIETY AND SHIFTING FOCUS ONTO HEALTHY ACTIONS

Angela is a 23-year-old female who recently lost her mother to cancer. Angela and her mother were very close, and her mother served as her main source of social support over the years. When Angela was 15 years old, she was diagnosed with generalized anxiety disorder (GAD). She constantly worried about situations, had difficulty relaxing and sleeping, and tended to be nervous and on edge, especially in social situations. At times, her anxiety was severely debilitating. After her mother died, she noticed that her symptoms increased dramatically; she attempted to control situations that were impossible to control, in order to bring some sense of relief and predictability to her life. Upon meeting with a clinical mental health counselor, she was able to identify several aspects of her life that needed to change in order for her to begin to address her symptoms. First and foremost, she identified that she had little social support. She then decided to reach out to family, to join a support group for young adults who are grieving the loss of a parent, and to start to go to counseling. She also began to read a bit more about anxiety and to meet with a doctor to discuss her symptoms. She learned that anxiety is a disorder with physiological, psychological, and biological underpinnings that can be treated. This knowledge inspired hope. She also started to work on finding purpose and meaning through her mother's loss and started to volunteer for a local cancer support organization providing transportation for patients to medical appointments.

It is important to identify several aspects of the recovery process in relation to Angela's case. She had dealt with anxiety for several years, but after her mother's passing, her symptoms worsened. She noticed that she was trying to control different aspects of her life; from her perspective, if things were predictable, her anxiety tended to decrease (her mother's untimely death likely contributed to this, as fear of another significant event greatly increased her anxiety). She quickly learned that many aspects of her life were not within her control. A key aspect of Angela's recovery was utilizing this form of control in a positive manner, by shifting her focus onto aspects of her life that she could control. In this case study, social support, connectedness, and seeking counseling and consultation related to her disorder were all significant aspects of her recovery process, in addition to gaining hope that recovery was possible. She also found meaning and purpose in helping others who had gone through similar circumstances to her mother; focusing on others' needs shifted the focus from her own situation in a positive way.

■ MULTIDISCIPLINARY COLLABORATION

Collaborative mental healthcare services are aimed at mental health function recovery, therein addressing the person's activity limitations and participation restriction, in the context of his or her lived environment and considering personal factors. To achieve these positive outcomes related to mental health, the use of multidisciplinary and inter-disciplinary models provides the best promise for comprehensive healthcare services to people with mental health issues. Multidisciplinary collaborations, in the context of community mental healthcare, involve mental healthcare services that are provided by multiple professional or paraprofessional workforces who collaboratively work to serve individuals at the community level (Schultz et al., 2014).

The significance of multidisciplinary collaborations in mental healthcare arises from the fact that people with mental health issues may have co-existing physical conditions that require services from different healthcare professionals. Receiving services from multiple health providers at different locations can be quite costly. This fragmented type of service delivery often leads to duplicated services and gaps in service provision, as there is frequently little or unclear communication among treatment team members (team members may include clinical mental health counselors, medical doctors, psychologists, occupational therapists, nurses, social workers, community health workers, family members, and patients). Those with serious mental health needs typically experience barriers to mental healthcare that stem from the division between community-based mental healthcare services and the primary care provider (Newcomer & Hennekens, 2007).

Collaboration among healthcare providers and other members of the treatment team is a best practice; such professional collaboration can offer an additional layer of community support for people with mental healthcare needs. Collaborative mental healthcare services involve primary care providers, mental health specialists, and case managers who coordinate services and also provide assistive services such as patient education, follow-ups of outcomes, adjustments, and evaluations (Katon, Unützer, Wells, & Jones, 2010; Njeru et al., 2016; Thota et al., 2012). Due to issues related to confidentiality, it is important for mental health service providers to speak with clients about the importance of opening lines of communication among different providers to ensure optimal service delivery. In many cases, a mental health service provider can work with the client to sign a consent form allowing the provider to speak with other members of the treatment team.

Multidisciplinary Collaborative Teams

Multidisciplinary, collaborative health service approaches aim to improve access to healthcare, provide continuity of care, and thereby produce better outcomes. Multidisciplinary, collaborative health services extract knowledge from various disciplines (Choi & Pak, 2006). Treatment team members contribute expertise according to their disciplines, often using discipline-oriented terms and practices. Members may focus on specific aspects of client needs that apply to their discipline, and expect other team members to address other aspects of treatment that relate to their specific discipline. A multidisciplinary, collaborative approach is premised on the belief that each treatment team member addresses his or her area of expertise to the presenting health problem or issue in order to achieve holistic or comprehensive treatment.

However, multidisciplinary treatment team members may or may not be invested in crossing expertise boundaries to advantage the client. For example, a treatment team comprising medical doctors, psychologists, clinical mental health counselors, nurses, social workers, and case managers, working with a person with mental health needs who lives in the community, may each seek to address discipline-specific issues as follows. The medical doctor may prescribe medication and address concerns related to the individual's physical health primarily and mental health needs only secondarily, unless treating a mental health disorder. Mental health specialists (e.g., psychologists and clinical mental health counselors) typically provide mental health counseling (Thota et al., 2012), and may not ask questions concerning physical health conditions that bear upon the presenting psychiatric symptoms. Nurse practitioners may assist with promotional programs for people with mental health disorders (Grundberg, Hansson, Hilleras, & Religa, 2016), independent of social workers and case managers who are involved in the treatment decision-making to ensure that the client has access to different aspects of the prescribed course of action (Ambrose-Miller & Ashcroft, 2016). These oversights by multidisciplinary team members, if unchecked, raise ethical issues about them doing harm to the client through omission rather than commission.

Interdisciplinary Collaborative Teams

An interdisciplinary team in a single location provides care for people with mental health needs, allowing for comprehensive assessment and treatment of both physical and mental health needs (Pomerantz, Kearney, Wray, Post, & McCarthy, 2014). The interdisciplinary team members have regular meetings during which they share information important for comprehensive treatment planning according to their collective expertise (Collins, Hewson, Munger, & Wade, 2010; Reynolds, Chesney, & Capobianco, 2006). In contrast to multidisciplinary teams, interdisciplinary treatment teams focus on leveraging treatment team expertise within a specific discipline to allow for cross-learning, so that the person receiving services experiences maximum benefit from several individuals within the treatment setting. For instance, a medical doctor who is considering treatment options for a person with mental health needs who has been able to remain within the community might consider mood disorder management to increase social engagement (Castien, Hanssen, & Fett, 2017) and improve the patient's ability to carry out activities of daily living (Kim & Choi, 2015). An occupational therapist at the same practice might assist the same individual to manage his or her personal activities and livelihood issues (Seberg & Eriksson, 2018). A psychologist at the same practice might work with allied healthcare providers (e.g., nurses, occupational therapists, and social workers) to address personal and environmental factors influencing the person's activities of daily living, family support with home living issues, and engagement in significant life roles (e.g., vocational and employment counseling). Interdisciplinary care teams are less likely to commit treatment omissions by not knowing what other team members are contributing to the care support effort as might happen with multidisciplinary teams.

Collaborative mental healthcare services in a community context also must address the interface among care programs working with the person with mental health conditions (Pollard et al., 2014). Doherty, McDaniel, and Baird (1996) proposed three core parts of collaboration, including the following: (a) locations (different locations vs. a single location), (b) services (unintegrated services vs. integrated services), and (c) communications among healthcare professionals (little communication vs. close communication). For example, minimal collaboration (i.e., healthcare providers work at individual locations with scattered services and little communication) could be harmful to people who are receiving community-based treatment. A close collaboration, in which healthcare providers are working in an integrated system and providing unified services by sharing organizational culture and decision-making across healthcare teams, provides people who are receiving community-based treatment with superior care.

Communication among health service providers about diagnoses, treatment plans, and medical instructions for patients and families reduces the risk of medical errors, duplication of services, and conflicting management recommendations (Pollard et al., 2014). In such cases, the diagnoses of patients' health conditions will be shared by other care providers, including sharing of treatment plans, prescriptions, and follow-up recommendations. Therefore, communication among all care providers is essential, because the collaboration will be successful only when information related to diagnoses, medical recommendations, and treatment plans transfer efficiently and effectively from part to part. However, communication among core parts of the treatment team is not always easy; without a qualified communication coordinator or case manager, obstructed, fragmented, or incomplete communication may lead to ambiguous and likely negative outcomes (Mitchell & Patience, 2008).

CASE ILLUSTRATION 6.3

EDDIE: COMBINING MEDICATION AND MENTAL HEALTH COUNSELING TO TREAT BIPOLAR DISORDER

Eddie is a 45-year-old man who was diagnosed with bipolar disorder. Eddie experienced a great deal of distress from his mental health issues. On one hand, he reported experiencing very "extreme lows" that he attributed to depression, but on the other hand he reported experiencing "extreme highs" during which he felt grandiose. At times, during these highs, he engaged in risky sexual encounters and heavy substance use. Eddie sought treatment from his primary care physician, who referred him to a psychiatrist for medication. Eddie reported that he did not like taking his medications. At times he would take them inconsistently, or stop taking them altogether, only to find himself with worsening symptoms. He reported that the medications made him feel "flat," neither high nor low. He reported that before medication, "the lows were bad, I hated feeling depressed, but at least I knew that it would not last forever, I could look forward to the highs!"

For many individuals with bipolar disorder, treatment adherence to mediation management can be a major issue. In this case, it would benefit Eddie to seek mental health counseling (to address dysfunctional thoughts that might be contributing to negative feelings, to develop problem-solving skills, to increase social skills and structure while providing psy-choeducation on the disorder), in addition to taking medications. Signing a consent form for open communication among practitioners might help him to increase communication among service providers. This would allow his mental health practitioner to assist Eddie in developing skills to communicate with medical providers, and potentially to adjust the type or dose of medication that he is receiving. It also would allow the mental health practitioner to build a strong therapeutic relationship with Eddie to discuss, nonjudgmentally, the rea-sons why he might stop taking his medications while introducing psychoeducation related to bipolar disorder and the importance of mediation relative to holistic recovery.

■ COMMUNITY-BASED INTERDISCIPLINARY MODELS FOR PEOPLE WITH MENTAL HEALTH CONDITIONS

In this section, we provide a brief overview of the following interdisciplinary models in community mental healthcare: shelter-based collaborative mental healthcare, the cardiometabolic risk assessment and treatment through a novel integration model for underserved populations with mental illness (the CRANIUM model; Mangurian, Niu, Schillinger, Newcomer, & Gilmer, 2017), the ElderLynk community outreach model (McGovern, Lee, Johnson, & Morton, 2008), The National Council for Community Behavioral Healthcare model (2009), and community mental health teams (CMHTs; Bháird et al., 2016; Rao, 2014; Woody, Baxter, Harris, Siskind, & Whiteford, 2018).

Shelter-based collaborative mental healthcare is an integrated multidisciplinary col-laborative care (IMCC) that benefits people who are experiencing homelessness and who subsequently have a higher risk of mental illness and substance use disorders (Fazel, Khosla, Doll, & Geddes, 2008). In this Canadian community-based and shelter-based model of collaboration for mental healthcare, shelter employees work closely with pri-mary care providers from local communities in a collaborative team whose medical rec-ords are stored and shared electronically. Shelter staff also take on the responsibilities of consultant, educational support, and indirect patient discussion. This model facilitates referrals and interdisciplinary care, enhances the communication among care providers, harmonizes care plans, and therefore provides more integrated and comprehensive care for people who are experiencing homelessness.

The CRANIUM model (Mangurian et al., 2017) is an example of an integrative inter-disciplinary care model that consists of four components including (a) a patient-cen-tered team (patients, healthcare providers, and coordinators), (b) population-based care (patient enrollment), (c) screening protocols (stepped care approach), and (d) treatment protocols (evidence-based approaches for cardiometabolic screening and treatment among people with mental healthcare needs). This model uses "E-Consultant," which connects the primary care providers through an exchange center. E-Consultant is a set of services that allows telecommunication through various devices such as laptops, phones, and so forth (Meenan et al., 2009). By adopting such technologies, patients are able to connect to all providers on the treatment team at the same time and to receive comprehensive health services that include initiating medical diagnoses, reporting laboratory results, and getting referrals (Mangurian et al., 2017).

Other examples of interdisciplinary collaborative models include the ElderLynk community outreach model (McGovern et al., 2008), which focuses on mental health treatment for people over the age of 65 who are living in rural counties in Missouri. Geriatric nurses manage treatment plans and coordinate a community-based interdisciplinary team that consists of a psychiatrist, a geriatrician, a psychologist, and a social worker who provide counseling for the client. A parish nurse connects the clients to faith communities where their spiritual needs may be addressed (McGovern et al., 2008). The National Council for Community Behavioral Healthcare's community-based mental health center approach is another interdisciplinary model that allows mental health clinicians to work with hospital-based primary care providers, offering community living supports by nurse caseworkers.

▓ ISSUES FOR RESEARCH AND OTHER FORMS OF SCHOLARSHIP

Evidence suggests that research has focused on mental health disorders that are prevalent among individuals in communities; studies largely have been based on diagnostic systems rather than on the mental health and wellness of the community (Ng et al., 2014). Even less has been documented, concerning the general mental health function of ordinary community citizens not having psychiatric diagnoses (Rosen et al., 2015). The privileging of mental disorder indexing compared to the indexing of the general mental health function of communities is explained, in part, by prevalent pathology rather than health promotion healthcare systems and related case treatment reimbursement plans. Health systems are more likely to index what they are paid to do. However, the sum total of individuals in the community with mental health disorders is not the same as the general mental health of their community. According to the WHO ICF (2001), people's general mental health is derived from the interaction between their personal predispositions and the environment in which they live. The effect on persons, by environmental interactions, might accentuate or modulate the general mental health functioning of individual members and/or the collective community. Studies are needed to construct robust community mental health indicators that are premised more on general mental health functioning rather than on the prevalence of specific mental health disorders in the community. The construction and implementation of a community mental health index would be important for the design of mental health-friendly communities, which would add to the quality of life and productivity of communities (Fairweather et al., 2013). Yet, professional training in community mental health remains focused on mental health treatment rather than health promotion. Mental health promotion at the community level makes for sustainable community health at a lower cost to the community members through equipping people to live well rather than focusing on treatment-oriented approaches aimed at managing preventable mental health disorders.

The concept of recovery holds much promise for constructing and implementing community mental health support interventions that recognize mental health functioning as a process rather than an end (Ellison et al., 2018). As previously discussed, the mental health of communities and member individuals is continuously evolving, calling for timely supports for well-being. However, recovery is multifaceted and premised on personal factors of self-efficacy, hope, resilience, grit, and type of diagnoses. Mental health recovery also is explained by co-existing health conditions such as substance abuse and chronic diseases. This means determining what constitutes recovery for different individuals will vary by their personal circumstances (Brown & Baker, 2018). Yet, recovery-oriented practices might prioritize specific diagnosis over the community health circumstances important for personally satisfying community life. There is a need for research to increase our understanding of how subtle microprocesses of recovery are operating, such as how hope is reawakened and sustained with lifestyle chnages or how contextual changes are associated with community mental health well-being.

Finally, community mental health is a burgeoning field of practice in which professional mental healthcare providers work in collaboration with citizen coalitions for health. Mental healthcare collaborations between professionals and citizen coalitions for health have the advantage of benefiting from the expertise of professional counselors as well as from community citizens who possess the lived knowledge of mental well-being in their community (Rapkin, 2015). However, ethical questions might arise regarding where to draw the line between professional accountability and the unique mental health needs of specific communities, some of which might require external oversight for the safety of individual community members (Bickenbach, 2015). There is need for guidelines to navigate the thin line between community partnerships for health and local health practices that carry potential risks to vulnerable citizens in the absence of external, regulatory oversight.

CONCLUSION

Community is both the cradle and theater for mental well-being. People's general health functions are important for their personal and community living. For this reason, the management of mental health-related issues at the community level has significant implications for both personal and community well-being. Mental health recovery is enhanced when individuals become increasingly engaged with their communities. Individuals can aspire to a level of mental health at least equal to that of their community, with opportunities for superior mental health and well-being drawn from their personal and community resources. The WHO ICF provides a framework in which mental health at the community level is defined not only by specified mental health needs, requiring intensive treatment care, but also by the general mental health and well-being of the community.

Engagement in community and civic activities promotes well-being through social capital and increased social support systems, which in turn increases an individual's capacity to cope with problems of living. Mental health recovery is a unique and individual experience that should be the result of collaborative engagement with community resources for health and well-being. Interdisciplinary mental health treatment teams provide community-based health and social supports for people with mental health needs. Collaborative multidisciplinary mental health services, in the community context, can be productive for cross-learning to optimize the mental health well-being of community residents.

RESOURCES

American Counseling Association: https://www.counseling.org

American Psychological Association: https://www.apa.org
  Association for psychologists, which provides information on the impact of psychology as it relates to improving social problems and individuals'everyday lives.

Centers for Disease Control and Prevention—Mental Health: https://www.cdc.gov/mentalhealth
  Includes access to comprehensive research related to mental health and substance use, in addition to a national helpline (treatment locator for clients), 24-hour suicide hotline, and a disaster distress helpline.

Integrated Behavioral Health Project (IBHP): www.ibhp.org

Integrated Primary Care, Inc.: www.integratedprimarycare.com

MentalHealth.gov: https://www.mentalhealth.gov

Mental Health and Mental Illness: Collaborative Care for the Management of Depressive Disorders: https://www.thecommunityguide.org/findings/mental-health-and-mental-illness-collaborative-care-management-depressive-disorders

National Institute of Mental Health: https://www.nimh.nih.gov/index.shtml

New AAMC, APA Collaboration Expands Mental Health Educational Resources: www.apa.org/news/press/releases/2013/06/mental-health.aspx

Substance Use and Mental Health Services Administration: https://www.samhsa.gov

TeamSTEPPS: Team Strategies and Tools to Enhance Performance and Patient Safety: https://www.ncbi.nlm.nih.gov/books/NBK43686

TeamSTEPPS: https://www.ahrq.gov/teamstepps/index.html
  The world's largest association representing counselors and mental health service providers

REFERENCES

Ambrose-Miller, W., & Ashcroft, R. (2016). Challenges faced by social workers as members of interprofessional collaborative health care teams. *Health and Social Work, 41*(2), 101–109. doi:10.1093/hsw/hlw006

Bháird, C., Xanthopoulou, P., Black, G., Michie, S., Pashayan, N., & Raine, R. (2016). Multidisciplinary team meetings in community mental health: A systematic review of their functions. *Mental Health Review Journal, 21*(2), 119–140. doi:10.1108/MHRJ-03-2015-0010

Bickenbach, J. E. (2015). Ethics and equity in community health. In E. Mpofu (Ed.), *Community oriented health services: Practices across disciplines* (pp. 63–86). New York, NY: Springer Publishing Company.

Brown, B., & Baker, S. (2018). The social capitals of recovery in mental health. *Health, 1*, 1–19.

Carrière, I., Gutierrez, L. A., Pérès, K., Berr, C., Barberger-Gateau, P., Ritchie, K., & Ancelin, M. L. (2011). Late life depression and incident activity limitations: Influence of gender and symptom severity. *Journal of Affective Disorders, 133*(1–2), 42–50. doi:10.1016/j.jad.2011.03.020

Castien, N., Hanssen, E., & Fett, A. (2017, March). *Real-word social engagement trust, and attachment in Schizophrenia: Reduced trust in close relationships.* Poster session presented at the International Congress on Schizophrenia Research, San Diego, CA.

Chen, J., Chen, S., Landry, P. F., & Davis, D. S. (2014). How dynamics of urbanization affect physical and mental health in urban China. *China Quarterly, 220*(November 2014), 988–1011. doi:10.1017/S0305741014001465

Choi, B., & Park, A. (2006). Multidisciplinarity, interdisciplinarity and transdisciplinarity in health research services education and policy: Definitions objectives and evidence of effectiveness. *Clinical& Investigative Medicine, 29*(6), 351–564.

Clarke, P., & Nieuwenhuijsen, E. R. (2009). Environments for healthy ageing: A critical review. *Maturitas, 64*(1), 14–19.doi:10.1016/j.maturitas.2009.07.011

Clarke, P. J., Weuve, J., Barnes, L., Evans, D. A., & de Leon, C. F. M. (2015). Cognitive decline and the neighborhood environment. *Annals of Epidemiology, 25*(11), 849–854. doi:10.1016/j.annepidem.2015.07.001

Cloud, W., & Granfield, R. (2008). Conceptualizing recovery capital: Expansion of a theoretical construct. *Substance Use & Misuse, 43*(12/13), 1971–1986. doi:10.1080/108260808022 89762

Collins, C., Hewson, D. L., Munger, R., & Wade, T. (2010). *Evolving models of behavioral health integration in primary care.* New York, NY: Milbank Memorial Fund. Retrieved from http://dx.doi.org/10.1599/EvolvingCare2010

Corrigan, P. W., Druss, B. G., & Perlick, D. A. (2014). The impact of mental illness stigma on seeking and participating in mental health care. *Psychological Science in the Public Interest, 15*(2), 37–70. doi:10.1177/1529100614531398

Crowley, K. (2000). *The power of pro-recovery in healing mental illness.* San Francisco, CA: Kennedy Carlisle.

Deegan, P. (1996). Recovery as a journey of the heart. *Psychiatric Rehabilitation Journal, 19*(3), 91–97. doi:10.1037/h0101301

Dixon, L. B., & Goldman, H. H. (2003). Forty years of progress in community mental health: The role of evidence-based practices. *Australian and New Zealand Journal of Psychiatry, 37*(6), 668–673. doi:10.1111/j.1440-1614.2003.01274.x

Doherty, W. J., McDaniel, S. H., & Baird, M. A. (1996). Five levels of primary care: Behavioral healthcare collaboration. *Behavioral Healthcare Tomorrow, 5*(5), 25–27.

Drake, R. E., & Latimer, E. (2012). Lessons learned in developing community mental health care in North America. *World Psychiatry, 11*(1), 47–51.

Ellison, M. L., Belanger, L. K., Niles, B. L., Evans, L. C., & Bauer, M. S. (2018). Explication and definition of mental health recovery: A systematic review. *Administrative Policy of Mental Health, 45*, 91–102. doi:10.1007/s10488-016-0767-9

Fairweather, G. W., Sanders, D. H., Cressler, D. L., & Maynard, H. (2013). *Community life for the mentally ill: An alternative to institutional care.* New York, NY: Routledge.

Fazel, S., Khosla, V., Doll, H., & Geddes, J. (2008). The prevalence of mental disorders among the homeless in Western countries: Systematic review and meta-regression analysis. *PLoS Medicine, 5*(12), e225. doi:10.1371/journal.pmed.0050225

Firth, J., Carney, R., Jerome, L., Elliott, R., French, P., & Yung, A. R. (2016). The effects and determinants of exercise participation in first-episode psychosis: A qualitative study. *BMC Psychiatry, 16*(1), 36. doi:10.1186/s12888-016-0751-7

Grundberg, Å., Hansson, A., Hillerås, P., & Religa, D. (2016). District nurses' perspectives on detecting mental health problems and promoting mental health among community-dwelling seniors with multimorbidity. *Journal of Clinical Nursing, 25*(17–18), 2590–2599. doi:10.1111/jocn.13302

Hamer, M., Stamatakis, E., & Steptoe, A. (2009). Dose-response relationship between physical activity and mental health: The Scottish Health Survey. *British Journal of Sports Medicine, 43*(14), 1111–1114. doi:10.1136/bjsm.2008.046243

Ilies, R., Aw, S. S. Y., & Lim, V. K. G. (2016). A naturalistic multilevel framework for studying transient and chronic effects of psychosocial work stressors on employee health and well-being. *Applied Psychology, 65*(2), 223–258. doi:10.1111/apps.12069

Jacobson, N., & Curtis, L. (2000). Recovery as policy in mental health services: Strategies emerging from the states. *Psychiatric Rehabilitation Journal, 23*(4), 333–341. doi:10.1037/h0095146

Jenkins, J., & Carpenter-Song, E. (2005). The new paradigm of recovery from schizophrenia: Cultural conundrums of improvement without cure. *Culture, Medicine and Psychiatry, 29*, 379–413. doi:10.1007/s11013-006-9000-8

Katon, W., Unützer, J., Wells, K., & Jones, L. (2010). Collaborative depression care: History, evolution and ways to enhance dissemination and sustainability. *General Hospital Psychiatry, 32*(5), 456–464. doi:10.1016/j.genhosppsych.2010.04.001

Kelly, B. J., Perkins, D. A., Fuller, J. D., & Parker, S. M. (2011). Shared care in mental illness: A rapid review to inform implementation. *International Journal of Mental Health Systems, 5*(Journal Article PG-31), 31. doi:10.1186/1752-4458-5-31

Kim, B. J., & Choi, Y. (2015). The relationship between activities of daily living (ADL), chronic diseases, and depression among older Korean immigrants. *Educational Gerontology, 41*(6), 417–427. doi:10.1080/03601277.2014.982006

Liberman, R. P., & Kopelowicz, A. (2005). Recovery from schizophrenia: A concept in search of research. *Psychiatric Services, 56*(6), 735–742. doi:10.1176/appi.ps.56.6.735

Mangurian, C., Niu, G., Schillinger, D., Newcomer, J. W., & Gilmer, T. (2017). Understanding the cost of a new integrated care model to serve CMHC patients who have serious mental illness. *Psychiatric Services, 68*(10), 990–993. doi:10.1176/appi.ps.201700199

Mantovani, N., Pizzolati, M., & Gillard, S. (2017). Engaging communities to improve mental health in African and African Caribbean groups: A qualitative study evaluating the role of community well-being champions. *Health & Social Care in the Community, 25*(1), 167–176. doi:10.1111/hsc.12288

Marlier, M., Van Dyck, D., Cardon, G., De Bourdeaudhuij, I., Babiak, K., & Willem, A. (2015). Interrelation of sport participation, physical activity, social capital and mental health in disadvantaged communities: A SEM-analysis. *PLoS One, 10*(10), 1–18. doi:10.1371/journal.pone.0140196

Marmot, M., Friel, S., Bell, R., Houweling, T. A., & Taylor, S. (2008). Closing the gap in a generation: Health equity through action on the social determinants of health. *The Lancet, 372*(9650), 1661–1669. doi:10.1016/S0140-6736(08)61690-6

McGovern, R. J., Lee, M. M., Johnson, J. C., & Morton, B. (2008). ElderLynk: A community outreach model for the integrated treatment of mental health problems in the rural elderly. *Ageing International, 32*(1), 43–53. doi:10.1007/s12126-008-9004-5

Meenan, R. T., Stevens, V. H., Funk, K., Bauck, A., Jerome, G. J., Lien, L. F., … Svetkey, L. P. (2009). Development and implementation cost analysis of telephone-and internet-based interventions for the maintenance of weight less. *International Journal of Technology Assessment in Health Care, 25*(3), 400–410. doi:10.1017/S0266462309990018

Methley, A. M., Campbell, S., Cheraghi-Sohi, S., & Chew-Graham, C. (2017). Meeting the mental health needs of people with multiple sclerosis: A qualitative study of patients and professionals. *Journal of Disability and Rehabilitation, 39*(11), 1097–1105. doi:10.1080/09638288.2016.1180547

Metraux, S., Cusack, M., Byrne, T. H., Hunt-Johnson, N., & True, G. (2017). Pathways into homelessness among post-9/11-era veterans. *Psychological Services, 14*(2), 229–237. doi:10.1037/ser0000136

Mitchell, F., & Patience, D. A. (2008). Conjoint multi-disciplinary assessment in a community mental health team. *Social Work in Health Care, 35*(1–2), 605–613. doi:10.1300/J010v35n01_14

Mitchell, R., & Haddrill, K. (2006). WHO Safe Communities–Should we expand the definition of a "community"? *International Journal of Injury Control and Safety Promotion, 14*(1), 60–63. doi:10.1080/17457300600775585

Mpofu, E. (2015). (Ed.). *Community oriented health services: Practices across disciplines.* New York, NY: Springer Publishing Company.

National Council for Community Behavioral Healthcare. (2009). National Council Magazine. Winter. Retrieved from https://www.thenationalcouncil.org/wp-content/uploads/2018/10/BehavioralHealthandPrimaryCareIntegrationandthePCMH-2009.pdf

Newcomer, J. W., & Hennekens, C. H. (2007). Severe mental illness and risk of cardiovascular disease. *JAMA, 298*(15), 1794. doi:10.1001/jama.298.15.1794

Ng, M., Fleming, T., Robinson, M., Thomson, B., Graetz, N., Margono, C., … Abraham, J. P. (2014). Global, regional, and national prevalence of overweight and obesity in children and adults during 1980–2013: A systematic analysis for the Global Burden of Disease Study 2013. *The Lancet, 384*(9945), 766–781. doi:10.1016/S0140-6736(14)60460-8

Nieminen, I., Ramon, S., Dawson, I., Flores, P., Leahy, E., Pedersen, M. L., & Kaunonen, M. (2012). Experiences of social inclusion and employment of mental health service users in a European Union project. *International Journal of Mental Health, 41*(4), 3–23. doi:10.2753/IMH0020-7411410401

Njeru, J. W., DeJesus, R. S., St. Sauver, J., Rutten, L. J., Jacobson, D. J., Wilson, P., & Wieland, M. L. (2016). Utilization of a mental health collaborative care model among patients who require interpreter services. *International Journal of Mental Health Systems, 10*(1), 4–9. doi:10.1186/s13033-016-0044-z

Norton, J. L., Ancelin, M. L., Stewart, R., Berr, C., Ritchie, K., & Carrière, I. (2012). P-620-Anxiety: A risk factor for the incidence of activity limitations in the elderly. *European Psychiatry, 27*, 1. doi:10.1016/S0924-9338(12)74787-9

Pollard, R. Q., Betts, W. R., Carroll, J. K., Waxmonsky, J. A., Barnett, S., deGruy, F. V., … Kellar-Guenther, Y. (2014). Integrating primary care and behavioral health with four special populations: Children with special needs, people with serious mental illness, refugees, and deaf people. *American Psychologist, 69*(4), 377–387. doi:10.1037/a0036220

Pomerantz, A. S., Kearney, L. K., Wray, L. O., Post, E. P., & McCarthy, J. F. (2014). Mental health services in the medical home in the Department of Veterans Affairs: Factors for successful integration. *Psychological Services, 11*(3), 243–253. doi:10.1037/a0036638

Rao, T. (2014). The role of community nursing in providing integrated care for older people with alcohol misuse. *British Journal of Community Nursing, 19*(2), 80–84. doi:10.12968/bjcn.2014.19.2.80

Rapkin, B. (2015). The role of community health workers in implementing community-oriented primary and preventive services across the life-span. In E. Mpofu (Ed.), *Community oriented health services: Practices across disciplines* (pp. 87–116). New York, NY: Springer Publishing Company.

Reynolds, K. M., Chesney, B. K., & Capobianco, J. (2006). A collaborative model for integrated mental and physical health care for the individual who is seriously and persistently mentally ill: The Washtenaw Community Health Organization. *Families, Systems, & Health, 24*(1), 19–27. doi:10.1037/1091-7527.24.1.19

Rosen, A., O'Halloran, P., Mezzina, R., & Thompson, K. S. (2015). International trends in community-oriented mental health services. In E. Mpofu (Ed.), *Community oriented health services: Practices across disciplines* (pp. 315–344). New York, NY: Springer Publishing Company.

Rothon, C., Goodwin, L., & Stansfeld, S. (2012). Family social support, community "social capital" and adolescents' mental health and educational outcomes: A longitudinal study in England. *Social Psychiatry and Psychiatric Epidemiology, 47*(5), 697–709. doi:10.1007/s00127-011-0391-7

Schultz, C., Walker, R., Bessarab, D., McMillan, F., MacLeod, J., & Marriott, R. (2014). *Interdisciplinary care to enhance mental health and social and emotional well-being.* Canberra: Department of the Prime Minister and Cabinet.

Seberg, M., & Eriksson, B. G. (2018). Reablement in mental health care and the role of the occupational therapist: A qualitative study. *SAGE Open, 8*(2), 215824401878464. doi:10.1177/2158244018784644

Seebohm, P., Gilchrist, A., & Morris, D. (2012). Bold but balanced: How community development contributes to mental health and inclusion. *Community Development Journal, 47*(4), 473–490. doi:10.1093/cdj/bss023

Sheffield, K. M., & Peek, M. K. (2009). Neighborhood context and cognitive decline in older Mexican Americans: Results from the Hispanic Established Populations for Epidemiologic Studies of the Elderly. *American Journal of Epidemiology, 169*(9), 1092–1101. doi:10.1093/aje/kwp005

Sklar, M., Groessl, E., O'Connell, M., Davidson, L., & Aarons, G. A. (2013). Instruments for measuring mental health recovery: A systematic review. *Clinical Psychology Review, 33*, 1082–1095. doi:10.1016/j.cpr.2013.08.002

Slade, M., Amering, M., Farkas, M., Hamilton, B., O'Hagan, M., Panther, G., … Whitley, R. (2014). Uses and abuses of recovery: Implementing recovery-oriented practices in mental health systems. *World Psychiatry, 13*(1), 12–20. doi:10.1002/wps.20084

Stegenga, B. T., Nazareth, I., Torres-González, F., Xavier, M., Švab, I., Geerlings, M. I., … King, M. (2012). Depression, anxiety and physical function: exploring the strength of causality. *Journal of Epidemiology and Community Health, 66*(7), e25. doi:10.1136/jech.2010.128371

Substance Abuse and Mental Health Services Administration. (2013). Reflecting on JFK's legacy of community based care. Retrieved from https://www.samhsa.gov/homelessness-programs-resources/hpr-resources/jfk%E2%80%99s-legacy-community-based-care

Substance Abuse and Mental Health Services Administration. (2017). *SAMHSA's working definition of recovery: 10 guiding principles.* Retrieved from https://store.samhsa.gov/system/files/pep12-recdef.pdf

Thorpe, R. J., Jr., Koster, A., Kritchevsky, S. B., Newman, A. B., Harris, T., Ayonayon, H. N., … Health, Aging, and Body Composition Study. (2011). Race, socioeconomic resources, and late-life mobility and decline: Findings from the Health, Aging, and Body Composition study. *Journals of Gerontology Series A: Biomedical Sciences and Medical Sciences, 66*(10), 1114–1123. doi:10.1093/gerona/glr102

Thota, A. B., Sipe, T. A., Byard, G. J., Zometa, C. S., Hahn, R. A., McKnight-Eily, L. R., … Williams, S. P. (2012). Collaborative care to improve the management of depressive disorders: A community guide systematic review and meta-analysis. *American Journal of Preventive Medicine, 42*(5), 525–538. doi:10.1016/j.amepre.2012.01.019

Thyloth, M., Singh, H., & Subramanian, V. (2016). Increasing burden of mental illnesses across the globe: Current status. *Indian Journal of Social Psychiatry, 32*(3), 254. doi:10.4103/0971-9962.193208

Tjonstrandi, C., Bejerholm, U., & Eklun, M. (2011). Participation in day centres for people with psychiatric disabilities: Characteristics of occupations. *Scandinavian Journal of Occupational Therapy, 18*(4), 243–253. doi:10.3109/11038128.2011.583938

Townley, G., Kloos, B., & Wright, P. (2009). Understanding the experience of place: Expanding methods to conceptualize and measure community integration of persons with serious mental. *Health & Place, 15*(2), 520–531. doi:10.1016/j.healthplace.2008.08.011

Wehmeyer, M. L., Kelchner, K., & Richards, S. (1996). Essential characteristics of self-determined behavior of individuals with mental retardation. *American Journal on Mental Retardation, 100*, 632–642.

Wong, M., Yu, R., & Woo, J. (2017). Effects of perceived neighbourhood environments on self-rated health among community-dwelling older Chinese. *International Journal of Environmental Research and Public Health, 14*(6), 1–17. doi:10.3390/ijerph14060614

Woody, C. A., Baxter, A. J., Harris, M. G., Siskind, D. J., & Whiteford, H. A. (2018). Identifying characteristics and practices of multidisciplinary team reviews for patients with severe mental illness: A systematic review. *Australasian Psychiatry, 26*(3), 267–275. doi:10.1177/1039856217751783

World Health Organization. (2001). International Classification of Functioning, Disability and Health: ICF. Retrieved from https://apps.who.int/iris/bitstream/handle/10665/42407/9241545429.pdf;jsessionid=25740D4E9A37B6B253A5D6ECEFD82007?sequence=1

CHAPTER 7

RECORD KEEPING AND DOCUMENTATION

ERIC W. OWENS

This chapter discusses the importance of the record keeping and documentation processes for clinical mental health counselors. Specifically, record keeping practices and policies are reviewed. Also included are legal and ethical issues related to appropriate documentation and record keeping, including the Health Insurance Portability and Accountability Act (HIPAA), subpoenas, and court orders. The following Council for Accreditation of Counseling and Related Educational Programs (CACREP) standards are addressed in this chapter:

> *CACREP 2016:*
> *2F1.i, 5C1.c, 5C2.l, 5C2.m, 5C3.c*
> *CACREP 2009:*
> *2G2.m*

LEARNING OBJECTIVES

After reviewing this chapter, the reader should be able to:

1. Understand the purpose, process, and importance of accurate and thorough record keeping;

2. Distinguish the content of clinical records and identify what is included in a client's clinical file;

3. Recognize the ethical obligation of professional counselors related to record keeping; and,

4. Appreciate the legal elements of record keeping and how professional counselors can adhere to the laws regarding clinical documentation.

INTRODUCTION

Most people enter the counseling profession with the desire to help others. Students and counselors-in-training focus their energies on learning theory and practicing techniques. Counselor preparation programs emphasize the seemingly unending catalogue of knowledge and skills that are essential to being an effective and ethical practitioner. Good counselors balance client concerns with strengths, track all of the data clients present, develop diagnoses and treatment plans, craft and implement interventions, and then assess the effectiveness of treatment, with the intention of revisiting all of it until that satisfying moment when clients meet their goals! This process takes a great deal of time, energy, and continuous feedback in order to be successful.

Equally exciting is the world of record keeping and documentation, right?

For many students, the answer is probably, "Uh, no." Many counselors-in-training do not consider the administrative elements of the profession, which can be time consuming and burdensome. But the value of keeping good documentation of one's work as a clinical mental health counselor cannot be understated. Every element of the counseling process (e.g., evaluating client concerns and strengths, tracking client data, diagnosis, treatment planning) is all more effective with good documentation. Documentation allows clinicians to provide high quality care without relying solely on their memories to recall treatment details. Good record keeping is also an ethical and legal requirement.

THE PURPOSE OF RECORD KEEPING

There are a variety of reasons to keep good clinical records. While there are a host of legal and ethical reasons to maintain documentation of clinical work, one of the most important reasons is that documentation allows one to be a better practitioner for clients. From the beginning of the counseling relationship, the client puts trust in the counselor. Part of this trust includes believing that the clinician will work in an ethical and professional way and will behave in the client's best interest. A critical part of that process is the development and maintenance of a therapeutic alliance.

When we consider the elements of a strong therapeutic alliance, they will differ for each client, but an important element is almost always that the client wants to feel heard, understood, and respected. This may beg the question, "What in the world does this have to do with keeping records of sessions?" Case Illustration 7.1 provides an example of how clinical records can be instrumental in maintaining that therapeutic alliance, or in this case, how the lack of proper documentation can negatively impact that relationship.

CASE ILLUSTRATION 7.1

THE CASE OF THE OVERWORKED COUNSELOR

Dr. Snyder is a Licensed Professional Counselor working in a university counseling center. His background is in clinical mental health counseling and he has years of experience working in agencies, private practice, and school-based programs. He has been working in this counseling center for almost a decade and has seen his caseload grow each year. It seems that more and more students are coming in for counseling, and the concerns with which they present are more complex than ever. This year, Dr. Snyder is seeing six to seven clients each day, 5 days each week, and is also providing on-call emergency coverage one weekend each month.

To say Dr. Snyder is overwhelmed is an understatement. He is still doing good clinical work and helping his clients as well as he can, given the circumstances. However, with all the clients he has, there is little time to keep up with documentation. Dr. Snyder hasn't been able to write a thorough progress note in several weeks and has been working from memory with most of his clients. Because there are no insurance companies requiring documentation for reimbursement, he's found that he's able to manage his caseload without keeping notes.

After three back-to-back clients, he walks in to the waiting room to get Dave, his next client, and walks Dave back to his office. They sit and Dr. Snyder realizes he doesn't remember Dave at all! The name looked familiar on his calendar, but it is only Dave's second session and Dr. Snyder can't remember what happened in the intake. Dr. Snyder tries to cover by asking Dave "How are you? Do you want to pick up where we left off last time?" but Dave simply replies, "I can't believe you would ask me that? I'm terrible. After what we talked about last time, you really would just start by asking me how I am and if I want to pick up where we ended?" Dave gets up abruptly and leaves. Dr. Snyder is left at a loss for words and feeling as if he's failed this client. Dr. Snyder knows that had he kept notes of their last session, he would have been able to remember Dave and this outcome could have been avoided.

Keeping good records is about more than simply remembering details of client sessions. Luepker (2012) outlines six reasons that keeping clinical records is essential:

1. *Clinical records help facilitate the communication process between the client and counselor. Good record keeping demonstrates a commitment to the welfare of the client, and discussing records with clients can open dialogue and create an atmosphere of "safety and mutual respect." (p. 2)*

2. *Records are an important part of the diagnosis and treatment planning process. Systematic review of records allows the counselor to evaluate and revise treatment plans as necessary.*

3. *Good documentation facilitates continuity of care. The better the record keeping, the more likely it is that another practitioner can understand what has happened during the therapeutic process and can provide appropriate treatment based on previous sessions. In cases where the clinician no longer can provide treatment, client records may be the only tool a new counselor has to pick up where treatment left off.*

4. *Case files can be used in the clinical supervision process. Counselors and supervisors can review client records in order to provide feedback to the counselor and develop future strategies for treatment.*

5. *Documentation is often required for third-party billing. Insurance companies will likely require a diagnosis and/or treatment plan in order to reimburse the clinician for services.*

6. *Documentation is the best defense counselors have against accusations of illegal and unethical behavior. Should a client file a lawsuit or ethics complaint against the counselor, the documentation kept during the therapeutic process may be the difference between losing or winning in court or in an ethics hearing.*

CONTENT OF CLINICAL RECORDS

Having established the importance of good record keeping, an obvious question might be, "What are characteristics of good counseling records?" Luepker (2012) explains that counseling records should "convey, in humane, legible, and plain language, accurate and contemporaneous answers to 'who, why, what, when, and how?'" (p. 22). The best counseling records tell a story, providing the reader with a thorough understanding of the client, the client's needs, and the process that has taken place to help the client meet treatment goals. Luepker (2012) identifies six key characteristics of good clinical records:

1. They are legible. When clinicians use handwritten notes, they are often difficult to read. The use of electronic health records (EHR; described in the section of this chapter related to legal issues) can eliminate this concern.

2. Clinical notes are germane. Good records are limited in scope to the most important issues that occur in the therapeutic process. They include risk factors such as suicidal ideation, psychopharmacology, risk-taking behaviors, and noncompliance with treatment or medication.

3. They are reliable. Clinical notes should be as empirical as possible. They should be clear in describing data as a subjective inference, an objective observation, or a clinical assessment on the part of the counselor. Clinicians should avoid drawing conclusions or developing assessments that cannot be supported by the data.

4. Records are logical. Clinical counseling should follow a rational progression. Such a progression might include the following elements: clinical assessment, development of a diagnosis, creation of a treatment plan, intervention strategies used, assessment of outcomes, re-evaluation of diagnoses and treatment plans, and eventually termination. Counselors' notes should follow a similar, logical, progression.

5. Documentation should be prompt. Clinicians should not wait for days or even weeks to "catch up" on their note-taking. The clinical hour is 45 to 50 minutes for the purpose of allowing counselors to record their progress notes in the

time between the end of one session and the start of another. While some clinicians may take notes during the session, others argue that doing so can interrupt attention to the client and be distracting to the process.

6. Records should be chronological. By keeping records in chronological order, others can see that they have been maintained appropriately and have not been altered.

Another question students and trainees often ask is "What kind of information is documented in good counseling records?" There are different ways of conceptualizing client records. For example, one means of understanding client case files is through the lens of problem-oriented medical records (POMRs; Cameron & Turtle-Song, 2002). POMR approaches to record keeping are typically used by physicians and other health-care professionals and contain four distinct elements: database, problem list, initial plans, and SOAP (subjective, objective, assessment, and plan) notes (Cameron & Turtle-Song, 2002). While this is one way of approaching counseling documentation, the focus on problems rather than a holistic, client-centered perspective can make the POMR method problematic for professional counselors. SOAP notes, however, are commonly accepted record keeping processes and will be described in the section of this chapter describing progress notes.

While the format of clinical notes may vary based on clinician or agency, a good client case file will contain the following: (a) informed consent documentation, (b) intake information, (c) assessment/evaluation information, (d) treatment plans, (e) progress notes, (f) a termination summary, and (g) other client data. What follows is a discussion of each of these elements of client documentation. The descriptions are not meant to be exhaustive, but they are designed to give the reader some sense of the elements that are contained in each of these sections of a clinical record.

Informed Consent

One of the most important elements of the client file is the inclusion of informed consent documentation. Including all consent forms in the client file is not only an important legal consideration, it also can give the clinician the opportunity to refer to those documents should questions arise. Informed consent is the foundation of the therapeutic relationship; no clinical work can occur until this process is completed. Informed consent documentation gives clients important information about their rights and protects the practitioner by documenting the agreement into which both parties have voluntarily entered. Finally, the contractual nature of consent documents may provide motivation to the client to engage in the counseling process (Luepker, 2012). The informed consent documents contained within the client file may include some or all of the following (Luepker, 2012):

■ Consent to provide treatment: This document is the core of the informed consent process and outlines the rights of the client, responsibilities of the clinician, and the process and purpose of treatment.

■ Consent for billing: This document outlines costs, who is responsible for payment, information needed to process insurance claims, and so forth.

■ Consent for treatment of a minor child: When the client is a minor, the counselor must receive consent from a child's legal guardian. The age of consent for mental health treatment varies from state to state; it is critical that clinical mental health counselors understand the laws for consent to treatment in their states.

■ Consent for disclosure to third parties: Before a counselor may release any information to a third party (e.g., spouse, school administrator, psychiatrist, or family physician), the client must sign a release to disclose that information. Authorizations generally include the following information: the client's full name and address, some identifier such as a birthdate, name and address of the recipient of the information, the specific information requested, the purpose for release, a date of expiration, signatures, and a statement explaining that the client can revoke the authorization at any time.

■ Records of disclosure: When disclosures are made to third parties, those disclosures should be documented. This reporting should include the following: time and date of the disclosure, how the information was disclosed (e.g., fax, email, telephone), the purpose for the disclosure, the organization and/or individual to whom the data were disclosed, the information that was disclosed (e.g., diagnosis, clinical assessment, progress notes, termination summary), and a copy of the signed and dated authorization for said release.

Intake Information

The data required during clinical intake will vary from agency to agency and practice to practice. However, there are certain data that should always be included in a clinical intake. These data include demographic information, such as name, date of birth, gender, address, contact information (such as email address and telephone number), medical information including primary care provider, emergency contacts, data on family members (e.g., spouse, children, and other family members in the home), marital status, guardian information for minors, and other demographics.

Intake data should also include information about the client's presenting concerns. While data about client concerns may be complex and be truly understood only after the therapeutic relationship develops, at intake the client is asked to provide some information about what brought them to counseling. Presenting problems may include descriptions such as depression, anxiety, marital concerns, problems at work or school, or experience of trauma. Another element of the client concern is the history of those concerns. Counselors should document when the concern began, what was happening when the concern began, what the client has done to try to cope with the issue, and a description of the severity of the concern.

Intake information also includes a brief description of the client's life history, including significant issues that occurred in childhood. These data give context for understanding the client as well as some appreciation of hurdles the client has overcome in the past and how these experiences might be influencing the present concern. These data may include concerns at birth, during childhood, or through adolescence. Life history also includes data on the family of origin, work history, and functioning at work or school.

During intake, the counselor will also want to document any medical concerns and medications that the client is taking or has taken recently. Counselors should also document substance use such as nicotine, alcohol, and other drugs. Frequency of use, duration of use, or amount of time since the client quit using the substance should be noted. Counselors should also document their observations during the initial interview. The intake may include physical characteristics such as body build, hair and eye color, clothing, grooming, and hygiene. The intake may also include a mental status examination (MSE). An MSE is a formal assessment of the client's mental functioning during the intake interview and may include data about affect, mood, insight, judgment, focus, concentration, memory, impulse control, or other factors.

Finally, the intake documentation should note client strengths. These data are critical to understanding how the client has overcome challenges in the past and may be influential in addressing the current presenting concern. Client strengths are also important for understanding the client's capacity for resilience. Strengths often are overlooked during the intake process but are necessary to understanding the client as more than a litany of problems. Strengths may include the following: insight, intelligence, academic success and degrees earned, social supports, community supports, spirituality, and readiness for change through the therapeutic process.

Assessment/Evaluation Information

The data described in this section may be included in the intake section of the documentation, or may be included in a separate section. Assessments may include data such as the clinical diagnosis assigned to the client, symptoms (including severity and duration), as well as any diagnostic assessment or inventory data that have been collected. Examples of assessments and inventories include the Minnesota Multiphasic Personality Inventory (MMPI-2), Beck Depression Inventory (BDI), or intelligence assessments such as the Wechsler Intelligence Scale for Children (WISC-V) and the Wechsler Individual Achievement Test (WIAT-III). Personality inventories such as the Myers–Briggs Type Indicator (MBTI) or the Big Five Personality Test might also be included.

Treatment Plans

The creation and documentation of a treatment plan is essential to successful outcomes in the counseling process; the treatment plan is the "roadmap" of the process. The plan is developed based on the client's diagnosis and symptoms and provides both the client and the counselor with direction in the forms of goals and intervention strategies. Both diagnoses and treatment plans are fluid documents; they should be revisited regularly and revised as necessary (Luepker, 2012). As treatment progresses, client responses to treatment (both positive and negative) should be noted and the plan should be updated accordingly.

Treatment plans may vary but usually will include data that are relevant to the client's symptoms as well as strategies for resolving them. Treatment plans typically include a list of the client's presenting symptoms or issues, including duration and severity. For each of these presenting issues, goals and associated objectives are developed and included in the plan, as well as a timeline for achieving each goal. The treatment plan also will include the strategies or interventions the clinician intends to use to help the client achieve the goals, which may be described in terms of a theoretical modality or framework (e.g., cognitive behavioral therapy, reality therapy). The treatment plan also should include progress toward goals and objectives and be updated regularly as the client advances through the therapeutic process.

Progress Notes

Progress notes document what occurred in each counseling session and identify progress toward client goals (Cameron & Turtle-Song, 2002; Luepker, 2012). Progress notes can take many different formats. Some clinicians will write a brief paragraph describing what occurred in each session. Other progress notes take on specific formatting that include particular elements of the counseling session. One such example is the use of DAP notes; DAP is an acronym that stands for Data, Assessment, and Plan. Using this method, the clinician documents session *data* in one section of the note, the clinician's clinical *assessment* in a second section, and *plans* for future intervention in the third section. Similarly, the BIRP format includes documentation on the client's *behavior*, the *intervention* used, the client's *response* to the intervention, and the *plan* for upcoming sessions.

A commonly accepted practice for writing progress notes is the use of the SOAP format. SOAP is also an acronym that stands for: *subjective* data, *objective* data, *assessment*, and *plan* (Weed, 1964). Using the SOAP format, the counselor would first document the subjective data in the session. Subjective data can be difficult to differentiate from objective data; a good rule is to think of subjective information as those data shared with the counselor by the client or others (Cameron & Turtle-Song, 2002). The objective data recorded in the next section of the note are factual data that can be described in concrete and quantifiable terms. Consider here the information that can be seen or heard in session, as well as data that can be counted or measured (Cameron & Turtle-Song, 2002). The assessment section of the progress note contains the counselor's clinical assessment, including the synthesis and analysis of the data that were collected during the session. This section also may contain conclusions the counselor is drawing from the data and may also include information about diagnoses that the clinician is attempting to rule in or out of the assessment. Finally, the plan section of the note includes information about what the counselor intends to do in future sessions, as well as a prognosis on client outcomes.

For more information on writing SOAP notes, the reader is encouraged to review the work of Cameron and Turtle-Song (2002) that is included in the Resources section at the end of this chapter. An important consideration for counselors involves how to document specific statements made by the client or that the client attributes to someone else.

Caution should be exercised when using direct quotes. Specific quotations make a record more difficult to follow, and research suggests that it is very difficult to retain client quotations verbatim (Hart, Berndt, & Caramazza, 1985). Quotations may not be correct; therefore, extensive use of them may call the accuracy of the record into question.

A final consideration regarding progress notes involves the continuing process of risk assessment. Counselors' notes should include assessment of risk such as suicidal ideation or intent, homicidal ideation or intent, or other high risk behaviors. How these data are documented may vary depending on the agency or practice in which one works, but the continued assessment of client risk to self or others is an important legal and ethical consideration that should not be overlooked when completing progress notes.

Termination Summary

When documenting the termination process, it is important to remember that clients terminate counseling for a host of reasons. Gabbard (2009) identifies several reasons that may result in closure of the counseling relationship. Clients and counselors may agree that the client has met identified goals and that counseling is no longer needed for the presenting concern. A client may be limited in the number of sessions by a third-party payer. Clients may simply stop attending counseling, perhaps believing that the process is not helpful and choosing to terminate before goals are met. Therapists may also choose to terminate after referring a client to a more appropriate therapeutic resource.

Regardless of the reason for termination, the clinician should document the termination of the therapeutic relationship. This termination summary should include the issues and concerns for which the client presented for counseling along with a description of the treatment that was provided. The termination note also should identify progress toward the identified goals and the reasons for termination. Finally, the counselor should identify any direction provided to the client upon termination, such as follow-up care, medication management, plans should relapse occur, safety planning, and how to return to counseling should the client choose to do so.

Other Client Data

Finally, there may be elements of the counseling relationship that should be documented and maintained in the client's file but that may not fit into one of the aforementioned categories. Examples of these types of data include:

- Records of any referrals made;
- Any action taken when clients pose a threat to self or others;
- Specific data regarding suicidal ideation, gesturing, or attempts;
- Any action taken under the clinician's duty to warn (e.g., threats to self or others);
- Any mandated reports that are made regarding child abuse or abuse of the elderly;

- Information related to ethical concerns that may arise;

- Communications from clients that occur outside of session (e.g., email, telephone calls, etc.); and,

- Materials that may be developed or used as therapeutic interventions such as journals, writings, drawings, photographs, and so forth.

Having established that good documentation is an important element of being an effective and professional counselor, there are other important reasons to maintain good client records. One reason is that record keeping and documentation is an ethical responsibility of all counselors, as described in the following section.

ETHICAL ISSUES IN RECORD KEEPING

The American Counseling Association's (ACA) *2014 ACA Code of Ethics* (ACA, 2014) is quite clear in delineating the ethical responsibilities of professional counselors in relation to record keeping. In fact, the introductory section of the *Code of Ethics* identifies the responsibilities of counselors to maintain records of client sessions.

A.1.b. Records and Documentation
Counselors create, safeguard, and maintain documentation necessary for rendering professional services. Regardless of the medium, counselors include sufficient and timely documentation to facilitate the delivery and continuity of services. Counselors take reasonable steps to ensure that documentation accurately reflects client progress and services provided. If amendments are made to records and documentation, counselors take steps to properly note the amendments according to agency or institutional policies. (ACA, 2014, p. 4)

Here, the *Code of Ethics* identifies the importance of record keeping in the effective and professional delivery of services to clients. The accuracy of those records is critical for ensuring that clients receive the best possible services. The *Code of Ethics* provides a great deal of specific guidance in Section B.6. Sections B.6.a to B.6.i identify a variety of explicit requirements for professional counselors in relation to documentation of client contact.

B.6.a. Creating and Maintaining Records and Documentation
Counselors create, safeguard, and maintain records and documentation necessary for rendering professional services. (ACA, 2014, p. 7)
B.6.b. Confidentiality of Records and Documentation
Counselors ensure that records and documentation kept in any medium are secure and that only authorized persons have access to them .(ACA, 2014, p. 8)

In these sections, the *Code of Ethics* identifies both the necessity for documenting the services counselors provide and the essential nature of the confidentiality of those records. Regardless of how professionals maintain their documentation (e.g., electronically, in a computer-assisted system, on paper, via computer), those documents must be secure. Legal requirements for securing documents are discussed in the section of this chapter on legal issues as well as the limits to confidentiality under the law.

Sections B.6.c (Permission to Record) and B.6.d (Permission to Observe) outline counselors' responsibilities in securing permission to use live observation or audio/video recordings in the consultation or supervision processes (ACA, 2014). Section B.6.e identifies how clients can and should have access to their records, if they wish to do so, and Section B.6.f directs counselors to assist clients in understanding their records.

B.6.e. Client Access

Counselors provide reasonable access to records and copies of records when requested by competent clients. Counselors limit the access of clients to their records, or portions of their records, only when there is compelling evidence that such access would cause harm to the client. Counselors document the request of clients and the rationale for withholding some or all of the records in the files of clients. In situations involving multiple clients, counselors provide individual clients with only those parts of records that relate directly to them and do not include confidential information related to any other client. (ACA, 2014, p. 8)

B.6.f. Assistance With Records

When clients request access to their records, counselors provide assistance and consultation in interpreting counseling records. (ACA, 2014, p. 8)

These sections of the *ACA Code of Ethics* make it clear that professional counselors have a responsibility to share records with their clients when requested and to assist clients in understanding those records, assuming that the client is competent and such a disclosure would not cause harm to the client or to others. These can be challenging considerations, especially in cases where something in the record might be challenging emotionally to the client. As with all ethical dilemmas, it is important in these cases to follow an accepted ethical decision-making process (e.g., Welfel, 2015) and seek consultation and/or supervision. Case Illustration 7.2 provides an example of how counselors may work with clients in reviewing and understanding records for the benefit of both client and clinician.

CASE ILLUSTRATION 7.2

WHAT DOES MY FILE SAY ABOUT ME?

Dr. Parsons is a Licensed Professional Counselor who has been working in private practice for many years. She is well trained, experienced, and keeps copious and accurate notes of all her client sessions. She re-examines treatment plans throughout her work and attempts to keep open and honest communication with her clients about their diagnoses, goals, objectives, and her assessment of their progress.

During a session with a client named Chris, Dr. Parsons casually commented on her process of keeping client records. Chris replied, "I think it would be great to see what's in that file. I feel like I've made a lot of progress since we started working together, and it would be really interesting to go back and look at where I started. Besides, I'd like to know what my file says about me."

Dr. Parsons could feel herself get tense and her anxiety rise. While she keeps accurate notes, she also knows that when she keeps notes, she includes her own assessment of client progress, and she hasn't seen the growth in Chris that she would have hoped. Her clinical assessments are documented throughout the case notes, and she's concerned about sharing her unfiltered assessments with Chris. Dr. Parsons tells Chris that she'll have to pull everything together and that perhaps they can review the file during their next session.

In the interim, Dr. Parsons seeks out supervision, both to address the practical issue of whether to share the case file as well as to process her own anxiety and insecurity about doing so. Through the supervision process, Dr. Parsons realizes that her anxiety is not so much about what is in the notes, but it is instead a response to her concern that sharing her own assessment might upset Chris or even set back his progress in therapy.

After exploring these issues in supervision, Dr. Parsons makes the decision to share the entire case file with Chris, and to discuss their difference in opinion about his progress. Dr. Parsons takes the time to explain how the file is structured, explains clinical terminology found in the file, and opens a dialogue about their difference in opinion about the progress Chris has made. The resulting conversation becomes a catalyst for their continued work. Chris recognizes that there's still much he needs to do, and by reviewing the file together, Chris and Dr. Parsons are able to re-evaluate goals, create new objectives, and identify means of better assessing Chris' progress. Over the next weeks, Chris begins to meet objectives and clinical goals, progressing faster than he had previously.

Sections B.6.g and B.6.h address the storage, transfer, and disposal of client records.

B.6.g. Disclosure or Transfer
Unless exceptions to confidentiality exist, counselors obtain written permission from clients to disclose or transfer records from clients to legitimate third parties. Steps are taken to ensure receivers of counseling records are sensitive to their confidential nature. (ACA, 2014, p. 8)

Examples of issues related to transfer of records might occur when a client changes counselors or moves from one level of care to another (e.g., a client leaves a partial hospitalization program and enters outpatient counseling). In these cases, the *Code of Ethics* requires counselors not only to make sure they receive permission to transfer those records, but that the receiver of the records also is acting ethically and is likely to treat those documents with care and respect and to maintain the confidence of the materials contained within the file.

B.6.h. Storage and Disposal After Termination
Counselors store records following termination of services to ensure reasonable future access, maintain records in accordance with federal and state laws and statutes such as licensure laws and policies governing records, and dispose of client records and other sensitive materials in

a manner that protects client confidentiality. Counselors apply careful discretion and delib-
eration before destroying records that may be needed by a court of law, such as notes on child
abuse, suicide, sexual harassment, or violence. (ACA, 2014, p. 8)

Here, the *Code of Ethics* directs professionals to ensure that records are disposed of properly when it is appropriate to do so. The amount of time that counselors must keep documents is dependent on state and federal law, as well as the nature of the material contained in the record. For example, if the law does not require disposal, counselors are encouraged to consider extenuating circumstances such as the nature of the content of those records. For example, should a record be needed for a legal proceeding (e.g., a custody hearing, a criminal trial) and destruction is not required, it may be important, and even necessary, for the counselor to maintain that record until such time as it is no longer needed. An important consideration in this section of the *Code of Ethics* is the law in the counselor's jurisdiction that govern client records. States have different statutes regarding how long client records must be maintained, and individual agencies may have their own policies as well.

Finally, Section B.6.i states that counselors must have contingencies to protect the confidential nature of client records "in the event of the counselor's termination of practice, incapacity, or death" (ACA, 2014, p. 8). Counselors must have plans in place for how their records will be stored, secured, and accessed should they no longer practice. The *Code of Ethics* suggests the appointment of a custodian to oversee the records in such cases (ACA, 2014). Counselors should consider who might serve as such a custodian. In agencies there are typically policies in place to address such contingencies, but for those counselors practicing independently, they must ensure that protocols are in place for their records, as well.

Finally, as this discussion moves from ethical concerns to legal issues, it is important to make a distinction between ethics and the law. Professional ethics are codes written by professional organizations (e.g., the ACA) that guide professional practice. Ethics tend to be subjective, and it is sometimes difficult to apply ethical codes to real-life situations, because they are, by their nature, open to a degree of interpretation. Violations of ethical codes do not, in and of themselves, result in legal issues; violating an ethical code may result in the loss of one's credentials (e.g., license, certificate) or other sanctions from state-level credentialing bodies.

In contrast, laws are written by local, state, and federal governments to regulate the behavior of citizens. While violating an ethical code may result in serious penalties, violations of the law may result in criminal or civil action. Criminal violations can include fines, probation, or incarceration, while violations of civil laws may result in lawsuits. Laws are interpreted by courts through legal proceedings, where precedents are set that can establish expected behavior in the future.

Sometimes, ethics and laws are contradictory. An example of this incongruence might be found in issues related to confidentiality. Of course, professional counselors maintain the confidence of their clients; confidentiality is essential to the success of the therapeutic process. However, at times counselors may be expected to breach that confidence, such as in the case of a court proceeding. Confidentiality is not a legal absolute; it does not afford a counselor the same legal privilege held by attorneys and members of the clergy. Section I.1.c of the *Code of Ethics* speaks to such situations.

I.1.c. Conflicts Between Ethics and Laws

If ethical responsibilities conflict with the law, regulations, and/or other governing legal authority, counselors make known their commitment to the ACA Code of Ethics *and take steps to resolve the conflict. If the conflict cannot be resolved using this approach, counselors, acting in the best interest of the client, may adhere to the requirements of the law, regulations, and/or other governing legal authority. (ACA, 2014, p. 19)*

Here, the *Code of Ethics* makes it clear that if the law and the *Code of Ethics* are contradictory, counselors can follow the law without breaching their ethical responsibilities. However, it also should be noted that the counselor must take efforts to resolve the conflict first, that they should be acting in the best interest of their clients, and that they do not necessarily have to breach the ethical code.

LEGAL ISSUES

Snider (1987) identified record keeping as one of the top five areas of legal liability for professional counselors. As such, the legal concerns surrounding client records and documentation are worthy of discussion. This section of the text focuses on federal statutes related to healthcare and counseling notes (i.e., HIPAA) and issues related to subpoenas of client records.

It should be noted that these are not the only legal topics about which clinical mental health counselors must be aware. Each state has its own laws and regulations related to documentation and maintenance of client records. It is imperative that counselors understand the legal requirements in the state or states in which they practice. Additionally, state-level administrative offices may license agencies and other organizations that provide therapeutic services. These organizations also may have legal record keeping requirements that must be met by the agency, and therefore, by the clinicians who work for that agency. Clinical mental health counselors must be aware of the laws that govern practice in their state as well as the legal obligations of agencies for which they work.

Health Insurance Portability and Accountability Act of 1996

As healthcare professionals, clinical mental health counselors are subject to the legal requirements of HIPAA, enacted to protect the privacy of healthcare information and ensure the security of healthcare records (Corley, 2013; U.S. Department of Health and Human Services [DHHS], 2013). Anyone who has visited a doctor's office in the 21st century is aware of HIPAA, even if they did not realize it at the time. When most people visit a medical office, they sign a form allowing their provider to release certain information to their insurance company; this is required under HIPAA. Computer screens with client or patient information are typically not viewable to anyone other than the person at the computer. Full names often are not called in waiting rooms. These are also signs that a healthcare provider is abiding by HIPAA regulations.

HIPAA is a complex law, but the section appropriate to our discussion of record keeping and documentation includes Title II: *Preventing Health Care Fraud and Abuse: Administrative Simplification; Medical Liability Reform.* This section outlines five rules for healthcare professionals, two of which are of importance in this discussion. The two rules of importance to clinical mental health counselors are the *Privacy Rule* and the *Security Rule.*

The Privacy Rule was established by the DHHS in 2002 to protect clients' personal health information and to guarantee client rights regarding the release of that information (Corley, 2013; DHHS, 2013). Specifically, the Privacy Rule established regulations around the protection of counseling notes, which was based in part on the U.S. Supreme Court ruling *Jaffee v. Redmond* (Corley, 2013). In the ruling the Court found that the confidential and protected nature of the psychotherapy relationship is critical to the success of the process. The Privacy Rule requires counselors to obtain written consent prior to releasing any portion of a client's record to a third party, in most cases. The information contained within a client's record, including demographic information such as a client's name, is called protected health information (PHI; Freeburg & McCaughan, 2008).

The Privacy Rule allows a provider 30 days to disclose information, when requested by the client, and establishes exceptions to allow the disclosure of PHI in cases where other laws supersede HIPAA, such as when a counselor is required to report child abuse (HIPAA, 2007). Also, the Privacy Rule requires counselors to keep records of any disclosure of PHI to third parties. Elements of the Privacy Rule often are included in the informed consent process when clients first enter the counseling relationship, explaining how records are maintained and when confidentiality might be breached under the law and the *Code of Ethics.*

It is noteworthy to identify a distinction made in the HIPAA legislation between client case files and what are termed "psychotherapy notes" (HIPAA, 2007, p. 864). HIPAA identifies *psychotherapy notes* as different records from those in the client's clinical file. Instead, psychotherapy notes are those notes taken by a counselor that are used only for the clinician's own purposes, such as for consultation or supervision. These notes are kept separate from the client's file and may include items such as countertransference issues, names of individuals who are important in the client's life, or topics the counselor might want to explore in future sessions (Luepker, 2012).

The Security Rule protects the security of client records and PHI. As more providers switch to EHRs, the security of those records is of greater concern. The Security Rule identifies three specific types of security safeguards: *administrative safeguards, physical safeguards,* and *technical safeguards* (HIPAA, 2007). The law defines administrative safeguards as "administrative actions, and policies and procedures, to manage the selection, development, implementation, and maintenance of security measures to protect electronic protected health information and to manage the conduct of the covered entity's workforce in relation to the protection of that information" (DHHS, 2007, p. 2).

Administrative safeguards include elements such as identifying a Privacy Official who is responsible for maintaining PHI and security of records (Freeburg & McCaughan, 2008). These safeguards also include the following: conducting risk analyses, regular training on HIPAA and record keeping, password security, security provisions with any outside contractors, and the development of written policies regarding data security (DHHS, 2007). Administrative safeguards also include the development of contingency plans in the event of data breaches and the use of internal audits to ensure security. In short, administrative safeguards are the policies and procedures that the healthcare provider uses to ensure security, as well as planning in case that security is breached.

Physical safeguards are the elements of the Security Rule that protect PHI from physical threats and monitor access to protected data (Freeburg & McCaughan, 2008). Physical safeguards include the use of technology to secure EHRs and the systems on which those records are maintained. Examples of physical safeguards might include the proper destruction of unused computers and storage devices, the protection of data from computer technicians, and the implementation of the *double lock rule* (Freeburg & McCaughan, 2008). The double lock rule suggests that all PHI should be behind two "locks" or safeguards. For example, written records might be kept in a locked file cabinet that is maintained in a locked room.

Finally, technical safeguards refer to the technology used to secure records and the policies and procedures for its use (HIPAA, 2007). HIPAA has been amended in several ways by the Health Information Technology for Economic and Clinical Health (HITECH) Act of 2010 (Lawley, 2012). Technical safeguards are the measures counselors take to ensure that their computer systems and other technologies are reasonably and appropriately protected. When considering technical safeguards, counselors should consider issues such as server security, antivirus software, malware protection, and security against hacking and technology breaches. Additionally, counselors must be sure that when they use technology to transmit information (e.g., computers, fax, phone) that they are guaranteeing that the data are being transmitted securely and are being received by the party for whom it was intended (Freeburg & McCaughan, 2008).

As technology develops, counselors need to consider how these advances will have an impact on the expansion of technical safeguards (Lawley, 2012). For example, many people back up data through online (i.e., cloud) storage systems. However, in order to do this legally, the system being used must be HIPAA compliant. Similarly, smartphones are now ubiquitous in our society, but is the technology secure enough to pass the requirements of HIPAA? Also, the use of encryption can be a technological safeguard, but the encryption system must meet HIPAA requirements (Lawley, 2012). These issues are not addressed in the *2014 ACA Code of Ethics* but are addressed under HIPAA and HITECH and are of the utmost importance to legal and ethical counseling practice.

Subpoenas

The mere mention of a legal term such as subpoena in this text may cause a bit of anxiety, but the fact is that many professional counselors have received subpoenas and have managed the process without difficulty. A subpoena is a legal request for information; it can include appearing before the court to testify, or it can be a request for documents or other written materials (Erford, 2014). When someone receives a subpoena, instinct might suggest immediate compliance with the request, but counselors should consider all available options before breaching confidentiality. A court order (described in the following paragraphs) is also a legal request for information but should be addressed differently.

Regarding subpoenas, first the counselor should read through the subpoena thoroughly; the attorney who filed the subpoena might be requesting a case file, progress notes, specific testimony, a deposition, or some other information (Sori & Dermer, 2006). Next, the counselor should speak with the client or the client's attorney, *only if* the client has signed a release to speak with the lawyer. Clients may have requests for how they want the counselor to respond to the subpoena. If the client agrees to the release of their confidential information, they can sign a release form that allows the counselor to comply.

If the client does not want to release the information, the client's attorney can file documents with the court to quash the subpoena, which if granted, releases the counselor from having to disclose the requested information (Erford, 2014). In some cases, a judge may issue a court order, requiring the counselor to produce the requested information. Failure to do so could result in the counselor being held in contempt of court, a criminal offense. In any case where counselors receive subpoenas or court orders, they should seek supervision, request legal guidance from their own attorney or their agency's attorney, and should carefully record all actions taken and documents received or disclosed.

CONCLUSION

While it is true that many students and counselors-in-training do not consider the administrative requirements of our work, these requirements are still vital elements of the therapeutic process. Documentation and record keeping are not only legal and ethical mandates, they are also instrumental in providing competent, quality care to clients. But good record keeping processes are complex, time consuming, but most importantly, protect the client and the counselor. Client records are comprised of many different features that must be maintained regularly, punctually, and accurately.

As the information in this chapter has described, this process cannot be overlooked and should not be dismissed. The *2014 ACA Code of Ethics* is clear that professional counselors must take documentation seriously. State and federal law mandates that clinical mental health counselors maintain client records. But most importantly, our clients need us to keep good records of their treatment. Those records are the roadmap for our work; they show the beginning, the middle, and the end of the process. Should we need to refer to those documents, they guide us, reminding us of the goals of the process and the path that we are following with our clients. If we cannot continue the journey with them, client records show other clinicians the road that we mapped out together and can guide another counselor on the journey with the client. The goal of counseling is to facilitate change for the client; quality record keeping is an instrumental element of that process.

■ RESOURCES

On the Web

American Counseling Association. (2014). *2014 ACA code of ethics.* Alexandria, VA: Author. Retrieved from https://www.counseling.org/resources/aca-code-of-ethics.pdf

Cameron, S., & Turtle-Song, I. (2002). *SOAP note template.* Retrieved from https://durhamcollege.ca/wp-content/uploads/SOAP_Note_Template.pdf

Freeburg, M. N., & McCaughan, A. M. (2008). HIPAA for dummies: A practitioner's guide. In G. R. Walz, J. C. Bleuer, & R. K. Yep (Eds.), *Compelling counseling interventions: Celebrating VISTAS' fifth anniversary* (pp. 305–312). Ann Arbor, MI: Counseling Outfitters. Retrieved from http://www.counseling.org

U.S. Department of Health and Human Services. (2007). *HIPAA security series: Administrative safeguards.* Retrieved from https://www.hhs.gov/sites/default/files/ocr/privacy/hipaa/administrative/securityrule/adminsafeguards.pdf?language=es

U.S. Department of Health and Human Services. (2018). *Health information privacy.* Retrieved from http://www.hhs.gov/ocr/hipaa

In Print

Cameron, S., & Turtle-Song, I. (2002). Learning to write case notes using the SOAP format. *Journal of Counseling & Development, 80,* 286–292. doi:10.1002/j.1556-6678.2002.tb00193.x

Lawley, J. S. (2012). HIPAA, HITECH, and the practicing counselor: Electronic records and practice guidelines. *The Professional Counselor, 2,* 192–200. doi:10.15241/jsl.2.3.192

Luepker, E. T. (2012). *Record keeping in psychotherapy and counseling: Protecting confidentiality and the professional relationship* (2nd ed.). New York, NY: Routledge.

Welfel, E. R. (2015). *Ethics in counseling and psychotherapy: Standards, research, and emerging issues* (6th ed.). Belmont, CA: Cengage.

■ REFERENCES

American Counseling Association. (2014). *2014 ACA code of ethics.* Alexandria, VA: Author.

Cameron, S., & Turtle-Song, I. (2002). Learning to write case notes using the SOAP format. *Journal of Counseling & Development, 80,* 286–292. doi:10.1002/j.1556-6678.2002.tb00193.x

Corley, S. O. (2013). Protection for psychotherapy notes under the HIPAA Privacy Rule. *Health Matrix, 22,* 489–589.

Erford, B. T. (2014). *Orientation to the counseling profession: Advocacy, ethics, and essential professional foundations* (2nd ed.). Upper Saddle River, NJ: Pearson.

Freeburg, M. N., & McCaughan, A. M. (2008). HIPAA for dummies: A practitioners guide. In G. R. Walz, J. C. Bleuer, & R. K. Yep (Eds.), *Compelling counseling interventions: Celebrating VISTAS' fifth anniversary* (pp. 305–312). Ann Arbor, MI: Counseling Outfitters.

Gabbard, G. O. (2009). What is "good enough" termination? *Journal of the American Psychoanalytic Association, 57,* 575–594. doi:10.1177/0003065109340678

Hart, J., Berndt, R., & Caramazza, A. (1985). Category specific naming deficit following cerebral infractions. *Nature, 316,* 339–340. doi:10.1038/316439a0

Health Insurance Portability and Accountability Act, 45 C.F.R. § 164. (2007). Retrieved from https://www.gpo.gov/fdsys/pkg/CFR-2011.../CFR-2011-title45-vol1-part164.pdf

Lawley, J. S. (2012). HIPAA, HITECH, and the practicing counselor: Electronic records and practice guidelines. *The Professional Counselor, 2*, 192–200. doi:10.15241/jsl.2.3.192

Luepker, E. T. (2012). *Record keeping in psychotherapy and counseling: Protecting confidentiality and the professional relationship* (2nd ed.). New York, NY: Routledge.

Snider, P. D. (1987). Client records: Inexpensive liability protection for mental health counselors. *Journal of Mental Health Counseling, 9*, 134–141.

Sori, C. F., & Hecker, L. L. (2006). Ethical and legal considerations when counseling children and families. In C. F. Sori (Ed.), *Engaging children in family therapy* (pp. 159–176). New York, NY: Routledge.

U.S. Department of Health and Human Services. (2007). *HIPAA security series: Administrative safeguards.* Retrieved from https://www.hhs.gov/sites/default/files/ocr/privacy/hipaa/administrative/securityrule/adminsafeguards.pdf?language=es

U.S. Department of Health and Human Services. (2013). *Understanding health information privacy.* Retrieved from http://www.hhs.gov/ocr/privacy/hipaa/understanding

Weed, L. L. (1964). Medical records, patient care and medical education. *Irish Journal of Medicine, 462*, 271–282. doi:10.1007/BF02945791

Welfel, E. R. (2015). *Ethics in counseling & psychotherapy: Standards, research, & emerging issues* (6th ed.). Belmont, CA: Cengage.

CHAPTER 8

LEGAL ISSUES, ETHICS OF PRACTICE, AND COUNSELOR BEHAVIORS

SARA P. JOHNSTON | VILIA M. TARVYDAS

This chapter focuses on the legal and ethical issues that are salient to clinical mental health counselors. Specifically, this chapter discusses the American Counseling Association (ACA) Code of Ethics (2014), the American Mental Health Counselors Association (AMHCA) Code of Ethics (2015), state licensure and national certification, confidentiality, mandated reporting, duty to warn, and scope of practice. The chapter also focuses on the responsibility of counselors to engage in ethically based practice. Covered topics include values clarification, bias assessment, boundary awareness and maintenance, and the importance of self-reflection. The following Council for Accreditation of Counseling and Related Educational Programs (CACREP) standards are addressed in this chapter:
CACREP 2016:
2F1.i, 5C2.l
CACREP 2009:
2G1.j

LEARNING OBJECTIVES

After reviewing this chapter, the reader should be able to:

1. Summarize the major characteristics of the three components of professional standards;

2. Discuss the elements and processes of ethics governance;

3. Explain ethical decision-making as a value-laden, but rational, procedure;

4. Describe moral, ethical, and legal stances and their relationship to ethical dilemmas and ethical decision-making;

5. Apply knowledge of moral, ethical, and legal stances to a case scenario; and,

6. Apply an ethical decision-making model to a case scenario.

▧ INTRODUCTION

This chapter provides the clinical mental health counselor with an overview of the legal and ethical issues that undergird clinical practice. Counselors who have knowledge about the legal and ethical requirements for practice in their state and local jurisdictions are more likely to exhibit ethical behaviors in practice, within their profession, and as members of their communities.

The practice of professional counseling is governed at the national and state levels by a variety of governing boards and regulatory agencies. To ensure that they are practicing ethically and competently, counselors must be knowledgeable regarding the regulatory process and its relationship to legal issues, ethics of practice, and counselor behaviors. The purpose of this chapter is to provide counselors with an understanding of current legal and ethical issues that clinical mental health counselors are likely to see in practice, whether they practice in a healthcare setting, in the community, or in private practice. This first section of the chapter describes the legal and ethical governance systems that oversee the practice of counseling to provide a framework for understanding counselor licensure and certification. Next, the chapter discusses specific legal and ethical considerations related to counseling, including professional codes of ethics, mandated reporting, confidentiality, and scope of practice. In addition, the chapter connects the ACA and AMCHA ethical codes and the CACREP standards to several topics in ethical practice, including values clarification, bias assessment, boundary awareness and maintenance, and self-reflection. The chapter concludes with a case scenario to illustrate chapter concepts and a Resources section to provide further information.

▧ PROFESSIONAL STANDARDS AND THE COUNSELING PROFESSION

The primary purpose of professional standards is the protection of the public. This protection serves both counselors and clients. The practice of counseling is both an art and a science—requiring the practitioner to make both value-laden and rational decisions. Rather than being incompatible stances, both facts and values must be considered in juxtaposition to one another in order for counselors to engage in rational decision-making (Gatens-Robinson & Rubin, 1995). Within ethical deliberation, the practitioner blends such elements as personal moral sensitivities and philosophies of practice with clinical behavioral objectivity and the quest for efficient care of clients (Tarvydas & Johnston, 2018).

The nature and complexity of standards of practice for all healthcare professions have changed and grown over the last several decades. The phrase *professional standards* no longer simply means specifically the ethical standards of the profession. This term is a general term, meaning professional criteria that indicate acceptable professional performance (Powell, 1996), and may encompass ethical and/or clinical care standards. There are three types of standards that are relevant to describing professional practice: (a) the internal standards of the profession; (b) clinical standards for the individual practitioners within a profession; and (c) external, regulatory standards. Taken together, these professional standards increase the status of the profession and its ability for self-governance, as well as enhancing the external representation and accountability for the profession's competence with clients, the general public, employers, other professionals, external regulators, and payers (Rinas & Clyne-Jackson, 1988).

Internal Standards of the Profession

The internal standards of the profession form the underpinnings of the appropriate role and functions of the profession. Internal standards focus on advancing the professionalism of the members of the discipline. The intent of internal standards is to set a profession-wide standard of practice and to assist individual professionals in defining their professional identity and obligations. Prominent examples of internal standards include the profession's code of ethics and any guidelines for specialty practice relevant to the discipline (Tarvydas & Johnston, 2018). Internal standards are developed by the profession as part of the self-governing process. For example, the ACA *Code of Ethics* (2014), the overarching code to which all counselors adhere, is developed and revised on a regular basis by a committee or task force comprised of counselors who work as educators, practitioners, or researchers in the discipline. In addition, specialty areas of counseling practice develop and revise codes of ethics related to practice of a specific specialty. For example, clinical mental health counselors are held to both the internal standards contained within the ACA *Code of Ethics* (2014) and the AMCHA *Code of Ethics* (2015).

Clinical Standards for Professionals

The clinical standards for individual professionals are similar to the internal standards described in the previous section, in that both are directly relevant to services delivered to the client or patient. As counseling practice increasingly involves collaborative practice with other healthcare professions, clinical standards have expanded to include both individual and interprofessional standards of clinical care. Clinical standards may be specific to a particular setting or client population—they evaluate the competency of individual professionals based on the specific care rendered, and they have a client- or patient-care outcome measurement focus. Peer review processes and standards, as well as clinical care pathways, are examples of this type of standard (Tarvydas & Johnston, 2018). All healthcare professionals, including counselors, rely on their respective codes of ethics to provide guidance on understanding and applying ethical principles to clinical practice. Beginning clinical mental health counselors often struggle with learning how to apply ethical principles to clinical practice in general, and, more specifically, how to apply ethical principles to specific client populations or client issues. Later sections of this chapter will provide an in-depth review of ethical principles and ethical decision-making as they relate to clinical practice issues in clinical mental health counseling.

External Regulatory Standards

Ethical and legal institutions that govern the practice of professional counseling include state licensure boards, national accreditation and certification agencies, as well as professional organizations, such as the ACA or the AMHCA. It is important to note that ethical and legal institutions recognize that professions have the responsibility to self-govern. This means that a profession provides guidance to ethical and legal institutions on the external regulatory standards that govern professional practice. External regulatory standards define ethical and competent professional practice. External regulatory standards also specify requirements for professional practice, often referred to as *credentials*, and enforce the *credentialing* requirements. Often, one of the most confusing concepts for new counselors is *credentials and credentialing*. A credential simply indicates that a counselor's education and experience has been reviewed by a professional or legal body, and that the counselor legitimately possesses specific knowledge and skills that meet the minimum standards of the profession (Remley & Herlihy, 2007). There are many types of credentials. Some are *mandatory*, meaning a counselor must possess the credential in order to practice legally as a counselor; to practice in a specific setting, such as a school; or to work with a specific diagnosis, such as substance abuse. Other types of credentials are optional or *voluntary*, which means that a counselor is not required to possess the credential in order to practice legally as a counselor (Remley & Herlihy, 2007). Voluntary credentials include professional certification by certification bodies, such as the National Board for Certified Counselors (NBCC) and the Commission on Rehabilitation Counselor Certification (CRCC).

State Licensure

State licensure boards are an important part of external regulatory standards. States have a duty to protect the health and welfare of their citizens. Licensure boards ensure that persons presenting them selves as counselors have the appropriate experience and training to engage in counseling activities, and that properly trained counselors provide services to clients in a safe and ethical manner (ACA, 2014; Cottone & Tarvydas, 2007; Remley & Herlihy, 2007; Welfel, 2010). Each state sets its own educational, experience, and testing requirements for licensure as a counselor. Employers and insurance companies also may specify minimum qualifications for counselors employed in certain settings or for counselors who work with a specific client or client issue. For example, in order to bill insurance companies for their services, clinical mental health counselors who practice in a community mental health center may be required to hold state licensure as a professional counselor.

Accreditation

Educational programs that adhere to specific educational and training standards, set by an accreditation board, are accredited programs. The CACREP accredits counselor education programs. The 2016 CACREP standards promote a unified counseling profession, ensuring that students graduate with a strong professional counselor identity and have opportunities for specialization in one or more CACREP specialty areas (e.g., addiction counseling, clinical mental health counseling, clinical rehabilitation counseling; CACREP, 2015).

Educational standards evolve to reflect changes in professional practice, ethical code revisions, and state licensure requirements. For example, it has become increasingly common over the past decade for states to require applicants for professional counselor licensure to be graduates of CACREP-accredited programs (Johnston, Tarvydas, & Butler, 2015). Currently, many counselor education programs are making the transition from the 2009 CACREP standards to the 2016 CACREP standards, which requires those programs to understand and meet the changes made to the standards. Most graduates of CACREP programs practice in states where state licensure as a mental health counselor is a prerequisite to practice. The 2016 CACREP standards reflect the current emphasis on licensure and on specialty practice. States set the minimum educational and clinical requirements for licensure and define scope of practice. For example, counselors may be allowed to diagnose in certain states, but not others.

CACREP specialty standards provide guidance to counselors on what is required to advance their scope of practice in specialty areas. CACREP sets standards that cover professional identity, specialization, and contextual considerations. For example, CACREP (2016) has set standards related to the specialization of clinical mental health counseling, including the "roles and settings of mental health counselors, legal and ethical considerations specific to mental health counseling, and techniques and interventions for prevention and treatment of a broad range of mental health issues" (pp. 24–25). It is counselors' responsibility to ensure that they are meeting the national, state, and specialty standards for practice. Enrolling in a CACREP-accredited program is one of the best ways that counselors-in-training can ensure that they are fully prepared for practice as professional counselors.

Certification

Unlike state licensure, which is valid only in the state in which the license was granted, voluntary national certification is valid across the entire nation. Certification is granted to applicants by a national certification body, such as the NBCC, after a review of the applicant's education, experience, and score on a required national credentialing exam (Remley & Herlihy, 2007). National certification agencies use the same education, experience, and testing requirements for all counselors regardless of the state in which they practice (Remley & Herlihy, 2007).

Professional Organizations

One purpose of professional organizations is to maintain and enforce a mandatory code of ethics. The ACA *Code of Ethics* is one example of a mandatory code of ethics (ACA, 2014). Professional organizations are membership organizations, meaning counselors must pay a membership fee to join. In addition to providing a mandatory code of ethics, professional organizations also develop and implement an enforcement process for their members, and, in the case of the ACA, the enforcement for referred complaints of its specialty memberships (e.g., addiction counseling and clinical mental health counseling). Professional organizations consult with certification and licensing bodies as well as the specialty professional organizations; this aims to ensure active participation of all parties in the ethics enforcement process, and to incorporate specialty viewpoints into professional codes of ethics. Professional organizations may provide referral to other jurisdictions for complaints against accused parties, as appropriate, and also may provide educational programs to ensure that members continue to develop and improve their professional knowledge and skills (Cottone & Tarvydas, 2016; Tarvydas & Johnston, 2018).

Codes of Ethics

National certification agencies, such as the NBCC, and professional organizations, such as the ACA and the AMHCA, develop and enforce mandatory codes of ethics that outline the components of ethical practice. *Mandatory* codes of ethics require that all certificants or members follow the organization's code of ethics or be subject to sanctions that range from suspension or revocation of certification or membership to referral to state licensure officials for disciplinary action (for current versions of professional codes of ethics, see the ACA [www.counseling.org], the NBCC [www.nbcc.org/ethics], and the AMHCA [www.amhca.org/learn/ethics]). For example, professional organizations that receive an ethical complaint involving sexual or other abuse of a client are mandated to report the complaint to the counselor's state licensing board. The licensing board then will refer the matter to the state department of justice for civil or criminal prosecution (NBCC, 2014; Remley & Herlihy, 2007). *Aspirational* codes of ethics, in contrast, are ideal standards based on common morals that guide professional practice and are voluntary. An example of a professional organization with an aspirational code of ethics involves the *Best Practice Guidelines* (2007) of the Association for Specialists in Group Work (ASGW), which is a division of the ACA. The ASGW does not engage in enforcement tasks related to their membership because enforcement is handled by ACA. Instead, the ASGW has developed and disseminated *Best Practice Guidelines* that addresses issues encountered within the group counseling specialty, such as group dynamics (Tarvydas & Johnston, 2018; Thomas & Pender, 2008).

Relevant Standards

Clinical mental health counselors often work with clients who are experiencing serious difficulties in their lives, such as childhood trauma, domestic violence, and substance abuse. If, during the course of a counseling session, a client discloses information that involves a threat to self (self-injury or suicidal ideation), or threats to underage or vulnerable individuals (children, elderly, or disabled individuals), the counselor must make a decision about whether to report the information to others outside the counseling relationship to protect the client's or other individuals' well-being or safety. In order to make an ethical decision about whether to report a client issue to law enforcement or another agency, counselors must understand the ethical concept of confidentiality and the two related concepts of duty to warn and mandatory reporting.

Confidentiality

The ethical concept of confidentiality requires professionals, including counselors, to keep the client information that they have obtained within the context of a professional relationship private. When confidentiality is referenced in a legal context, such as state statutes governing counseling practice, it is known as *legal confidentiality* (Cottone & Tarvydas, 2007, 2016). Most counselors become familiar with the ethical and professional requirement of confidentiality from a traditional, rule-based ethics perspective, which views the protection of client confidentiality through the lens of risk management. In other words, confidentiality is a practice in which counselors engage in order to reduce the risk of client complaints, including malpractice or other civil lawsuits (Duffy, 2007; Johnston et al., 2015). While it is developmentally appropriate for beginning counselors to be focused on reducing their risk of being sued, seasoned counselors develop a much broader and deeper understanding of confidentiality as an "ethic of care rooted in concern for the dignity and safety of the client" (Duffy, 2007, p. 91). Counselors who view confidentiality through the ethic-of-care lens understand that counseling is a value-laden profession. An ethic-of-care approach to confidentiality is referred to as an "integrative-contextual perspective" (Duffy, 2007, p. 91), which requires practitioners to engage in ongoing self-reflection about how their personal ethical values inform their practice. Counselors who understand that counseling is a value-laden profession, and who practice under an integrative-contextual perspective, view confidentiality as fundamental to the development of trust and rapport within the counselor–client relationship. Under an integrative-contextual perspective, counselors understand the importance of allowing the client to decide when and with whom to share confidential information (Duffy, 2007). There are two key limitations to confidentiality: duty to warn and mandatory reporting.

Duty to Warn: Counselors must inform their clients about the limits of confidentiality. An important limit to confidentiality is the *duty to warn*. "Duty to warn" requires counselors to take specific steps to "warn any identifiable victim of a client from harm" (Pietrofesa, Pietrofesa, & Pietrofesa, 1990, p. 135). Costa and Altekruse (1994) recommend that counselors follow a nine-step process in the implementation of duty to warn requirements: First, before beginning a counseling relationship with a client, counselors obtain informed consent from the client. Second, after informed consent is obtained, and before counseling begins, counselors discuss their treatment plan with the client, including providing information to the client about the potential for consultation with other providers. Third, throughout the course of the counseling sessions with the client, the counselor thinks ahead by developing contingency plans to meet the needs of the client and to address any issues as they arise. Fourth, before beginning their professional careers, counselors should obtain professional liability insurance. Fifth, counselors should ensure that their scope of practice and specialty training is appropriate for the client population with whom they work in their specific practice. Sixth, counselors should involve the client in decisions about the client's treatment plan. Seventh, counselors should obtain a detailed history on all new clients, updating the history as needed to reflect any significant changes in the client's life. Eighth, counselors document their case notes and any other relevant documents, such as consent forms, in writing. Finally, counselors work with their supervisors and their agencies to implement a procedure to warn. Counselors who follow the nine-step process and who have established good rapport and trust with a client may be able to involve the client in finding solutions to the situation that do not put the client or another individual in danger. However, counselors should take additional care when working with clients who are experiencing symptoms that may affect their ability to make rational decisions. In cases of imminent danger or harm to the client or another individual, a breach of confidentiality may be the most prudent and ethical choice (Cottone & Tarvydas, 2016).

Mandatory Reporting: Another limit to confidentiality involves state statutes governing *mandatory reporting*, which is the requirement of all healthcare providers to report known or suspected abuse of a minor or of an adult who is a member of a vulnerable population (e.g., individuals with disabilities and elderly individuals; Duffy, 2007). All 50 states have some type of mandatory reporting requirement in their statutes governing healthcare practice. Typically, states provide a hotline or other means for reporting suspected abuse, and, in most states, professionals who break confidentiality in order to report known or suspected abuse are protected from legal action for the breach. Mandatory reporting statutes were established with the understanding that many victims of abuse are unable to advocate for themselves. Professionals who are trained to recognize the signs and symptoms of abuse can advocate on behalf of potential victims. It is important to note that mandatory reporting statutes do not contain the requirement that the healthcare provider present proof of known or suspected abuse, only that the healthcare provider report the known or suspected abuse to the proper authorities, who then will conduct an appropriate investigation (Duffy, 2007).

Scope of Practice

Working with clients within a specific knowledge and experience base is known as practicing within one's *scope of practice*. Counselors' scope of practice includes the education and training they have completed as well as any credentials they have earned that qualify them to work with a specific client issue or a particular client population. For example, counselors who are interested in working with clients who have been diagnosed with a substance abuse disorder have received training in the neurobiology of addiction and specific treatment modalities, and may be required to be licensed as chemical dependency counselors in the state in which they practice. Clinical mental health counselors receive education and training in the diagnosis and treatment of mental illness and typically are required to hold state licensure as a licensed mental health counselor. Counselors who practice within their scope of practice limit their exposure to legal complaints (Cottone & Tarvydas, 2007). Professional organizations (e.g., ACA), licensing boards (individual states), and national certification bodies (e.g., CRCC and NBCC) and accreditation agencies (e.g., CACREP and Council on Rehabilitation Education [CORE]) define the scope of practice for counseling in general. The scope of practice is a written statement that outlines the knowledge and skills that define the counseling profession and the practice of counseling. The scope of a *specialty practice*, such as mental health counseling and school counseling, is defined by state licensing and credentialing bodies, as well as professional organizations governing the particular specialty (Cottone & Tarvydas, 2007, 2016; Remley & Herlihy, 2007; Tarvydas & Johnston, 2018).

Counselors should be familiar with how their particular states define the scope of counseling practice within their own *jurisdictions*, or, in other words, their particular geographic locations (Garner, 2005). Counselors can find their state's laws governing counseling practice within their individual state's bureau of licensure. Licensure laws often are adopted from national professional counseling organizations (ACA, 2014). Each state may add rules or statutes for its own purposes, for example, a rule to prohibit falsifying information on an application. The ACA has published a manual titled *Licensure Requirements for Professional Counselors* (2016), which provides contact information for each state's licensure board, as well as information on professional associations, scope of practice, and insurance reimbursement.

■ CLINICAL PRACTICE ISSUES

The first section of the chapter described counseling as a value-laden profession that requires professionals to reflect on and understand their own values as they work with clients with diverse backgrounds, life experiences, and values. The development of a strong professional identity rests on clear professional standards of practice. Clients need solution-focused, respectful, nonexploitative, empowering, and, therefore, ethical relationships with their counselors (Tarvydas & Johnston, 2018).

This section of the chapter extends the concept of counseling as a value-laden profession to clinical practice issues in clinical mental health counseling practice. This section provides an overview of the ethical, legal, and moral stances in ethics and ethical decision-making. Next, this section works through a case example to illustrate some of the clinical tensions that counselors may encounter in their work with clients, in particular when working with clients who are members of marginalized groups. Finally, this section of the chapter describes how counselors can recognize the ethical, moral, and legal aspects of a clinical practice issue; how counselors can engage in a values clarification process; and how counselors can use an ethical decision-making model to avoid potential ethical pitfalls, work through ethical dilemmas, and promote client welfare throughout the counseling process.

Ethical, Moral, and Legal Aspects of Clinical Practice

Clients require the services of professional counselors who are grounded firmly in the awareness of their value-laden mission and who are willing and able to assist people by applying appropriate knowledge and competencies (Gatens-Robinson & Rubin, 1995). Counselors are required to make decisions that affect the quality of life and well-being of their clients. The process of decision-making can be difficult; often, agency policies and procedures do not provide sufficient guidance. In addition, many decisions regarding client well-being require counselors to balance the moral, ethical, and legal aspects of the various stakeholders to make the best decision in a given case.

Ethics is commonly confused with religion. While it is true that traditional religious values such as "Thou shall not kill," and "Love your neighbor" inform ethics, ethics is broader in that it covers both religious and nonreligious individuals. Ethics also may be confused with the law. Again, while it is true that ethics informs laws and legal systems, ethics is broader than any one set of laws. Ethics may also deviate from the law. For example, before the Civil War in the United States, slavery was legal but not ethical. The Civil War in the United States was the result of a conflict between those who believed that slavery should continue to be legal and those who believed that slavery was wrong and should be abolished. Finally, societal norms may be assumed to be ethical, but this may not always be the case. There are many examples of societal norms that serve to reinforce stereotypes about and discrimination against certain groups of people. For example, in the mid-20th century, there were socially accepted White Supremacist movements in the American South and in Germany that encouraged the rise of the Ku Klux Klan and the Nazi regime, respectively. The Nazis and the Ku Klux Klan used negative societal beliefs about groups of individuals, including Jews, people with disabilities, and racial/ethnic minorities, to promote a political and economic agenda that encouraged discrimination, hatred, and violence against targeted groups of people. More recently, the United States has witnessed a conflict between individual and societal norms on issues ranging from the increased number of shootings of African American men by police officers, which resulted in the Black Lives Matter movement; to the rights of LGBT citizens to marry legally, or, if allowed to marry legally, their right to order a wedding cake without being turned away due to their sexual identity; and to the rights of documented and undocumented immigrants to remain in the United States (Johnston & Hartley, 2018). Each of these issues includes ethical, moral, and legal considerations, and each issue is value laden, or based on an assumed acceptance of certain values.

For purposes of this chapter, ethics is defined as long-held standards of right and wrong that govern human behavior. Ethical standards provide guidance to individuals on what to do ("Do good") and what not to do ("Do no harm"). Ethical standards are based on the broader ethical principles of autonomy, justice, fidelity, beneficence, nonmaleficence, which are discussed in detail in the Ethical Stance section of the chapter.

Ethics also refers to the development of individual ethical, societal, and professional standards. Professional organizations develop their own set of ethical standards that guide professional practice, and are contained within the profession's code of ethics. Ethical decision-making is the process professionals engage in as they evaluate and choose the most ethical course of action in a given situation (Johnston & Hartley, 2016; Tarvydas & Johnston, 2018).

Counseling professionals often struggle with ethics and ethical decision-making when faced with an ethical dilemma in practice. Often, ethical dilemmas involve emotional or sociocultural issues that tug at the heartstrings or produce feelings of anger or outrage. Individuals who pursue careers in the counseling field are often natural advocates who strive to be fair and just in their interactions with others. However, without an understanding of how to advocate effectively for their clients, counseling professionals may inadvertently violate agency policies, professional codes of ethics, and in some cases, break the law (Johnston & Hartley, 2016). In such cases, it is important that counselors make use of intuitive and criticalevaluative levels of ethical decision-making, thus incorporating both conscious and nonconscious thoughts and emotions (Kitchener, 1984). Knowledge of ethical and legal stances, awareness of values and the values clarification process, and application of an ethical decision-making model may assist counselors in resolving ethical dilemmas and making difficult decision. Later in the chapter, a case study and ethical decision-making model is provided to illustrate the steps in resolving an ethical dilemma.

Moral, Ethical, and Legal Stance

When resolving ethical dilemmas, it is important to understand how and why we make a particular decision; in other words, it is imperative to know from where the decision originates. It also is important to understand what the consequences of the decision may be. Difficult decisions originate from one of three stances: moral, ethical, or legal. These three stances, or groups, are what we use to justify the decisions that we make. Each of the three stances derives from a specific body of knowledge or code (Cottone & Tarvydas, 2016; Johnston & Hartley, 2018).

Moral Stance

The moral stance derives from individual, societal, and religious values (e.g., "Thou shall not kill"). Morals inform ethics, but, again, ethics is broader than one set of morals or one religion. For example, Buddhist, Christian, Islamic, Jewish, and Native American religions all prohibit the intentional taking or harming of a life. However, there may be differences among religions with respect to whether or not there are any exceptions to the prohibition against the intentional harming or taking of a life (Cottone & Tarvydas, 2016; Johnston & Hartley, 2018). It is also important to understand that morals and morality may change over time as society changes. For example, less than 50 years ago, in many communities, women were not allowed to wear pants to school or work, and less than 100 years ago, women were considered to have questionable morals if they wore nail polish or lipstick.

Ethical Stance

The ethical stance derives from ethics and ethical standards. There are five ethical principles that commonly are found across professions: Do no harm (nonmaleficence); do good (beneficence); be fair (justice); allow individual choice (autonomy); and be loyal (fidelity). Professions, such as medicine, nursing, and counseling, incorporate ethics and ethical standards into a formalized code of ethics that govern their behavior in their practice as professionals. For example, the codes of ethics for medicine, nursing, and counseling all contain an ethical standard that requires the professional to practice in a way that will not harm the patient or client—nonmaleficence (do no harm; Tarvydas & Johnston, 2018).

Legal Stance

The legal stance derives from the law and legal standards. For example, intentional homicide violates both state and federal laws. Keep in mind that both morals ("thou shall not kill") and ethics and ethical standards ("do no harm," nonmaleficence) inform laws that prohibit the intentional harm or killing of an individual (Cottone & Tarvydas, 2016; Johnston & Hartley, 2017).

It is important to consider that morals, ethics, and laws may vary by groups of individuals, by geographic location (within the same country and between countries), and by culture. For example, Western cultures may have very different morals, ethics, and legal standards concerning individual rights and independence than do cultures that place more importance on collective or interdependent relationships. For example, in Japan, which is a collective or interdependent culture, the needs of the community or the family are placed above the needs of the individual. Families consider it an honor and a duty to care for an elder family member. Assistive living centers and other facilities that provide housing for elderly people are not common. In contrast, in the United States, which values independence and individual freedom, individual needs are placed above the needs of society and sometimes above the family as well. Individual success in school or work is valued. Elderly family members may not want to live with their children or grandchildren because they "do not want to be a burden." It is important to note that neither approach is wrong; rather, these are cultural differences, of which counselors need to be mindful when working with clients.

Values Clarification

To resolve moral, ethical, and legal conflicts within counseling practice, counselors must first recognize their own values and understand the implications of their values in practice. Values clarification involves assessing one's own values within the client–counselor relationship as how those values relate to professional practice (Cottone & Tarvydas, 2016). Values clarification helps individuals clarify their beliefs through a process of assigning value rather than on the content of what is valued (Cottone & Tarvydas, 2016; Raths, Harmin, & Simon, 1966). The process of values clarification involves reconciling disparate and often competing values orientations. When reconciling their own values with the values of clients, counselors must recognize that: (a) There are no absolute values which are objectively true or good; rather, values originate within individual experience or within sociocultural systems; (b) Individuals are responsible for choosing, interpreting, and holding their own values; individuals are not responsible for changing another's values; (c) counselors recognize that they may view their clients through the lens of illness or pathology, which may deemphasize the role of the counselor's values in the counseling process; and (d) counselors work toward accepting clients for who they are, rather than judging them for beliefs or behaviors that do not conform to the counselor's values or preferences (Dell, 1983; Huber, 1994). The above four value assumptions provide counselors with a framework for the values reconciliation process. Values reconciliation includes the following core components: the recognition of mutual obligations and entitlements within the relationships among the parties, or the "give and take" of human interactions; the acknowledgment of those things to which others are entitled and the valid claims of others; and the balance of fairness (Huber, 1994). Although the process of critically evaluating the four assumptions and engaging in the values reconciliation process may appear to add greatly to counseling's complexity, in reality these considerations recognize and respect the shared nature of the important relationship between people of diverse backgrounds. Value issues between counselor and client, which may originate from numerous sources of interpersonal diversity, have the potential to enrich the counseling relationship, if directly addressed within the valuing process (Cottone & Tarvydas, 2007, 2016). For example, a counselor who grew up in a culture that values the Protestant Work Ethic (Weber, Baehr, & Wells, 2002), which asserts that hard work and frugality are an indication of an individual's moral character, may need to reconcile those values with those of clients who value travel or leisure activities and view work as simply a means to an end.

Ethical Dilemmas

When a conflict occurs between actual behavior and behavior that is prescribed within the confines of a profession, such as the law, medicine, nursing, psychology, and counseling, such a conflict is termed an *ethical dilemma*. An ethical dilemma is a case or situation that involves a conflict between two or more ethical principles (ACA, 2014). Ethical principles are derived from morals that society, as a collective body, deems important and necessary for the well-being of its members or citizens. Morals inform ethical principles that individuals and societies use to guide behavior. Ethical principles often are codified into ethical codes, such as the ACA *Code of Professional Ethics* (2014) and the AMHCA *Code of Ethics* (2015). Members of professional organizations must adhere to the code in their professional practice. Ethical principles are also the foundation of many procedures, policies, and laws that form our institutions and government. For example, the ethical principle, "Do no harm" (nonmaleficence) forms the basis for laws that prohibit individuals from intentionally or unintentionally harming other human beings. As previously stated in the chapter, and presented in the following as a review, there are five ethical principles that commonly are found across professions: Do no harm (nonmalefi-cence); do good (beneficence); be fair (justice); allow individual choice (autonomy); and be loyal (fidelity; Johnston & Hartley, 2018; Tarvydas & Johnston, 2018).

Multicultural and Stakeholder Considerations

Ethical dilemmas often involve controversial or traumatic situations, such as abortion, euthanasia (assisted suicide), and the rights of individuals from the LGBT community to marry or have the right to serve in the military. Ethical dilemmas involve morals and values—both individual morals and values and societal or collective morals and values. For example, individuals living in Western societies are more likely to value inde-pendence, which may lead to a societal view, supported by legislation, that individuals should not rely on government to fund their retirements; rather, individuals should be responsible for setting up their own retirement plans and save for them. Individuals liv-ing in a collectivist society, in contrast, may have access to "cradle-to-grave" governmen-tal programs that reflect the societal view that government has the responsibility to care for its citizens throughout the life span. Societal views on the proper role of government in providing for its citizens may be influenced by individual and societal morals (Cot-tone, 2001; Liu & Toporek, 2018; Tarvydas & Johnston, 2018).

Counselors must not assume that their clients share the same individual and socie-tal morals as the counselor. Counselors must assess and respect the client's worldview and refrain from imposing their worldview on the client. Every ethical dilemma has the potential to incorporate a number of worldviews, including the worldviews of the coun-selor, the client, the client's family, the agency, the community, and the government and legal systems. Differing worldviews are often referred to as "stakeholder perspectives." Stakeholders are defined as any person, persons, agency, institution, or government who has an interest in the outcome of an ethical dilemma. An ethical decision-making model can be useful in working through the conflicts among morals and ethics, conflicts between ethical principles, and for understanding stakeholder perspectives (Tarvydas & Johnston, 2018).

Ethical Decision-Making Model

An ethical decision-making model consists of a series of steps that facilitate decision-making. An ethical decision-making model contains the following four steps:

1. Determine whether an ethical dilemma exists.
   a. Is there a conflict between two or more ethical principles?
   b. If yes, what are the principles in conflict, and why are they in conflict?
2. Examine contextual issues.
   a. What are the potential sources of bias, sociocultural considerations, or multicultural considerations?
   b. Who are the stakeholders, and what are their perspectives?

3. Formulate a course of action.

   a. Gather all data, consult with supervisors and colleagues.

   b. Make a decision.

4. Implement and evaluate the course of action (Cottone, 2001; Tarvydas & Johnston, 2018).

It is important to note that ethical decision-making often involves choosing from several courses of action, none of which offers a perfect solution to the dilemma. Ethical decision-making requires decision-makers to be comfortable with ambiguity. In other words, the most ethical course of action may not be black or white, but gray (Tarvydas & Johnston, 2018).

In sum, ethical counseling practice requires counselors to be aware, understand, and apply their knowledge of moral, ethical, and legal stances; the values clarification process; ethical principles and ethical dilemmas; and ethical decision-making models. Case Illustration 8.1 is an example of one counselor's experience with identifying and addressing a values difference in practice.

CASE ILLUSTRATION 8.1

JOE AND CARA: NAVIGATING A DIFFERENCE IN VALUES AND THE ROLE OF CONSULTATION IN ETHICAL DILEMMAS

Cara is a 19-year-old sophomore at a local community college who receives counseling for anxiety and depression at a community agency. Joe is a new master's-level clinical mental health counseling graduate who is working on accruing the required practice hours to obtain state licensure as a Licensed Mental Health Counselor. Cara has been working with Joe for a few weeks. At her most recent session, Cara told Joe that she has been struggling with her sexual identity since high school and is ready to begin dating women. Cara also stated that she believes having a more active social life will help with her feelings of isolation. Joe has some concerns about Cara's plans. He tells his supervisor that he is not supportive of Cara dating women because "dating may lead to sex, and sex between two women or two men is illegal." Joe goes on to state that if he supports Cara's decision to date, it would be unethical, because he would be violating the ethical principle of "do no harm" (nonmaleficence). He claims that he is taking both an ethical and legal stance with regard to his decision about Cara and asks his supervisor to support his decision. Joe's supervisor counters that she believes he is confusing an ethical and legal stance with a moral stance. She explains that there are no laws in the state prohibiting premarital sex among consenting adults, whether the adults are of the same gender or of different genders, and that the client is of legal age. In addition, she reminds Joe that the agency's code of ethics states that client choice is respected and encouraged (autonomy). Finally, she notes that because Joe is a state licensed mental health counselor, a National Certified Counselor under NBCC, and a member of the ACA, he is bound by the state's counselor ethics, the ACA Code of Ethics, and the NBCC Code of Ethics—none of which expressly prohibit same-sex relationships or premarital sex. She directs Joe to section A.4.b of the ACA Code of Ethics.

> *Personal Values. Counselors are aware of—and avoid imposing—their own values, attitudes, beliefs, and behaviors. Counselors respect the diversity of clients, trainees, and research participants and seek training in areas in which they are at risk of imposing their values onto clients, especially when the counselor's values are inconsistent with the client's goals or are discriminatory in nature. (ACA, 2014, p. 5)*

In this case, the supervisor is correct; Joe is confusing a moral stance on the subject of premarital sex with an ethical and legal stance, because there are no ethical standards or laws prohibiting an adult client from engaging in premarital sex. To continue working effectively with Cara, Joe will need to assess the consequences of basing his decision about Cara's dating on a moral stance.

Intrinsic and Extrinsic Consequences

In this case, Joe's decision to take a moral stance in this situation may have several consequences for him, the client, and the agency. For example, the consequence to Joe is that in supporting the client's choice to date, he is violating his morals, which may be emotionally difficult and stressful for him. An individual may feel guilt or shame when violating his or her own morals. Such distress is an example of an intrinsic consequence, which is simply a consequence that originates from within an individual. On the other hand, if Joe chooses not to support the client's choices because of his moral stance on premarital sex, he risks violating the agency's code of ethics and the client's legal rights. Joe's decision to take a moral stance in the case may cause the agency to discipline or fire Joe, and/or the client may file a grievance or a lawsuit against Joe and the agency, charging that the agency did not respect her choice or autonomy. These actions are examples of extrinsic consequences, which are consequences that originate from outside an individual.

Resolving Moral, Ethical, and Legal Conflicts

Ethical decision-making skills are improved when counselors have a clear understanding of the moral, ethical, and legal stances in a case, as well as the potential consequences for taking a particular stance in a case. Many times, counseling professionals may know which decision is the best decision in a case, yet conflicts among morals, ethics, and laws may make it difficult for counselors to "do the right thing." Counselors who are unable to reconcile conflicts among morals, ethics, and values may become frustrated, cynical, and dissatisfied with their work when they find themselves making decisions that go against what they feel is the right decision in a case. Learning how to resolve moral, ethical, and legal conflicts in a counseling setting may improve service delivery and reduce the risk of professional burnout (Cottone & Tarvydas, 2016; Johnston & Hartley, 2018).

Counselor–Client Values Conflicts

Counselors who are experiencing values conflicts within the counselor–client relationship can use a reflective process to resolve those conflicts. As the case of Joe and Cara demonstrates, counseling professionals may confuse a moral stance with a legal or ethical stance, which may lead to decisions that are at best based on faulty assumptions or incorrect information, and at worst not in the best interests of the client. Counseling professionals must take the time to reflect on the stance that underlies each decision that they make to ensure that they are not confusing stances or missing factual information that could affect their stance. Upon reflection, Joe realizes that his objection to Cara's dating derives primarily from a moral stance, specifically, his religious beliefs that premarital sex and sex between members of the same gender are both immoral (Kitchener, 1984). Joe now understands that he and Cara have a values conflict that he must resolve before he can work with Cara in an effective and ethical manner.

Training, Consultation, and Supervision

Joe must next determine whether or not the values conflict can be resolved by additional education and training, counseling and guidance, additional supervision, and consultation with supervisors and other colleagues. If Joe is unable to resolve the values conflict, as a last resort he may need to refer Cara to another counselor. Referral to another counselor means that Joe will need to engage in a process that includes compiling a list of counselors who are qualified to work with Cara and who are accessible to Cara, meaning that they accept her insurance and are located within a reasonable distance of Cara's home. Joe must then discuss with Cara the reasons for his referral to another counselor, provide Cara with the list of available counselors, and allow Cara to make a decision about whether or not she wishes to continue working with Joe or to terminate her counseling relationship with Joe and begin working with a new counselor. As mentioned, referral to another counselor should be a last resort, and should only be considered in cases where counselors believe that their continued relationship with the client would not be beneficial to the client. To continue working effectively with Cara, Joe must be able to resolve any values conflicts between his own morals and the ethical and legal requirements to which he is bound by the agency, his profession, and the laws of the state. Joe must determine whether or not he is able to set aside his own religious beliefs about dating and premarital sex in order to support Cara's choice to date. Joe may be unable to set aside his religious beliefs. In this case, Joe must decide whether he is able to continue working with Cara, and, more broadly, working for the agency, or remaining in the counseling field (Johnston & Hartley, 2018; Tarvydas & Johnston, 2018).

Joe may decide to resolve the values conflict between his morals and the ethical and legal requirements that he is bound to uphold in his work. He may seek support and guidance in working through the conflict by obtaining counseling or by seeking consultation with his supervisor or colleagues. Conversely, Joe may decide that he is unable to resolve the values conflict between his morals and the ethical and legal requirements that he is bound to uphold in his work. Joe may request that Cara be referred to another counseling professional. There may be consequences to this decision, however, because Joe may be bound by professional, agency, and legal codes or requirements that prohibit counseling professionals from using the referral process to discriminate against a client or group of clients who are members of a legally protected class of individuals (e.g., gender, race/ethnicity, age, sexual orientation, or religion). If Joe states that he is unable to work with Cara due to his religious beliefs, Cara may perceive Joe's refusal to work with her as discriminatory. Joe's decision to refer Cara to another counselor may cause Cara emotional distress, in that she may feel shamed or judged by the referral. Cara may have grounds for filing a complaint against Joe and the agency, charging that she was not treated fairly due to her gender or sexual orientation (ACA, 2014). The supervisor may decide that Joe's religious beliefs prevent him from providing appropriate services to clients in accordance with agency policy and state laws, and Joe may be fired. Joe, however, may believe that he is being discriminated against based on his religious beliefs and contest his firing (Johnston & Hartley, 2018).

Ultimately, Joe makes the decision to work through his conflict by obtaining additional supervision and consultation. As he has worked through the conflict between his morals and his ethical and legal responsibilities to the client and the agency, he still has concerns that if he supports Cara's decision to begin dating, there is the potential that she may be exposed to situations for which she is not emotionally ready, and which may exacerbate her symptoms of depression and anxiety. He is struggling with how to balance respecting his client's choices (autonomy) with his duty to protect her from harm (nonmaleficence). Joe must resolve this ethical dilemma between autonomy and nonmaleficence before working with Cara on her decision to begin dating.

Ethical Decision-Making Model

Joe uses the ethical decision-making model to assist him in working through the ethical dilemma in Cara's case. First, Joe determines that there is a conflict between autonomy and nonmaleficence. He wants to support Cara's decision to begin dating (autonomy), but not at the expense of potential harm to Cara's mental health and progress in school, especially if she becomes involved in a relationship that ends badly that she is not emotionally prepared to handle (nonmaleficence).

Second, Joe considers the contextual issues related to the case. Contextual issues include factual information related to policies, codes, and laws that may be important to the case; potential sources of bias, including negative attitudes toward or stereotypes about specific groups of people; and multicultural considerations, such as differing worldviews. Understanding the contextual issues can assist Joe in determining who the stakeholders are in the case. In the case example, the stakeholders would include the counselor, the client, the clients' family (if the client is underage), the supervisor, the agency, the community, and the legal system (Cottone, 2001; Liu & Toporek, 2018; Tarvydas & Johnston, 2018).

If Cara were underage, Joe would need to determine whether there are laws in his state that require Cara's parents or guardians to be informed about matters affecting Cara. Joe also would need to assess Cara's attitudes and beliefs about dating and relationships. Joe should consider whether or not it is important for him to disclose his religious views about same-sex relationships and premarital sex, which may be a source of potential bias. Depending on Cara's situation, Cara's teachers, school counselor (if underage), and medical providers may be stakeholders in the case. Joe may need to gather information from them about any educational or medical considerations. Joe must be aware of any multicultural considerations that may impact Cara's views on dating, relationships, and sex. The more information Joe is able to gather about the contextual issues in the case, the better informed he will be about client and stakeholder worldviews (Cottone, 2001; Liu & Toporek, 2018; Tarvydas & Johnston, 2018).

The third step is that Joe would use the information that he gathered in Steps 1 and 2 to formulate a plan of action. Joe would meet with his supervisor to go over the details of the case, the dilemma, and the information that he gathered. Joe decides not to disclose his religious beliefs to Cara at the current time; however, he will have a broader discussion with Cara about her beliefs and values about dating, relationships, and sex. Joe realizes that because he is a man, there may be some issues related to sex that Cara may be more comfortable discussing with a woman. Joe can offer Cara the opportunity to discuss any sensitive topics with his supervisor, who is female. Joe believes that his plan of action would allow Cara to make her own choice about dating, relationships, and sex, which respects her autonomy. Joe supports Cara in making an informed and educated choice, which addresses Joe's concern about the potential for dating to cause Cara emotional harm that may exacerbate her depression and anxiety (Cottone, 2001; Tarvydas & Johnston, 2018).

Before implementing his plan of action, Joe asks his supervisor for her input and feedback. This collaboration is known as consultation. Joe is wise to ask his supervisor to consult with him on the ethical dilemma before implementing the plan. His supervisor may be able to point out factual errors, suggest additional resources, and address potential biases. Counselors can gain assistance on how best to complete each of the steps in the ethical decision-making model by seeking additional information from professional resources and from colleagues and supervisors. The process of consultation is important to professional practice; indeed, many professions' codes of ethics recommend consultation to resolve ethical dilemmas and improve service delivery.

CONCLUSION

Counselors are required to make decisions that affect the quality of life and well-being of their clients. The process of decision-making can be difficult, because many ethical decisions in counseling practice involve value-laden issues and conflicts. In addition, many decisions require counselors to balance the moral, ethical, and legal aspects of the various stakeholders to make the best decision in a given case. To enhance decision-making and manage the conflicts inherent in ethical dilemmas, counselors may benefit from understanding how moral, ethical, and legal considerations, as well as intrinsic and extrinsic consequences, may affect decision-making in a given case. In cases that involve ethical dilemmas, counselors also may benefit by using a decision-making model. Ethical decision-making models provide a framework for understanding the conflict between ethical principles in a case; contextual, stakeholder, and sociocultural factors related to the case; possible courses of action; and a plan for implementing the course of action. Ethical decision-making models encourage counselors to consult with trusted colleagues, supervisors, and professional resources to obtain facts, as well as different perspectives. Some professional organizations, such as the ACA, offer members free access to resources to help with ethical decision-making, including helplines and advisory opinions. Such resources are an avenue to clarify professional obligations, especially in situations when the decisions involve values conflicts between counselors and clients.

RESOURCES

Accrediting Bodies

Council for Accreditation of Counseling and Related Educational Programs. (2015): https://www.cacrep.org

National Certification

National Board for Certified Counselors: https://www.nbcc.org/Resources/Applicants

Professional Associations

American Counseling Association: www.aca.org

State Licensure

American Counseling Association; State Licensure: https://www.counseling.org/knowledge-center/licensure-requirements

REFERENCES

American Counseling Association. (2014). *Code of ethics.* Alexandria, VA: Author.
American Counseling Association. (2016). *Licensure requirements for professional counselors. A state-by-state report.* Alexandria, VA: Author.
American Mental Health Counselors Association. (2015). *Code of ethics.* Alexandria, VA: Author. Retrieved from http://connections.amhca.org/HigherLogic/System/DownloadDocumentFile.ashx?DocumentFileKey=d4e10fcb-2f3c-c701-aa1d-5d0f53b8bc14
Costa, L., & Altekruse, M. (1994). Duty-to-warn guidelines for mental health counselors. *Journal of Counseling and Development, 72,* 346–350. doi:10.1002/j.1556-6676.1994.tb00947.x
Cottone, R. R. (2001). A social constructivism model of ethical decision-making in counseling. *Journal of Counseling & Development, 79,* 39–45. doi:10.1002/j.1556-6676.2001.tb01941.x

Cottone, R. R., & Tarvydas, V. M. (2007). *Counseling ethics and decision making* (3rd ed.). Upper Saddle River, NJ: Merrill/Prentice-Hall.

Cottone, R. R., & Tarvydas, V. M. (2016). *Counseling ethics and decision-making* (4th ed.). New York, NY: Springer Publishing Company.

Council for Accreditation of Counseling and Related Educational Programs. (2015). *2016 CACREP standards.* Retrieved from https://www.cacrep.org

Dell, P. (1983). From pathology to ethics. *The Family Therapy Networker, 7*(6), 29–31, 64.

Duffy, M. (2007). Confidentiality. In L. Sperry (Ed.), *The ethical and professional practice of counseling and psychotherapy* (pp. 91–108). Upper Saddle River, NJ: Pearson Education.

Garner, B. A. (2005). *Black's law dictionary* (8th ed.). St. Paul, MN: West.

Gatens-Robinson, E., & Rubin, S. E. (1995). Societal values and ethical commitments that influence rehabilitation service delivery behavior. In S. E. Rubin & R. T. Roessler (Eds.), *Foundations of the vocational rehabilitation process* (pp. 157–174). Austin, TX: Pro-Ed.

Huber, C. H. (1994*). Ethical, legal, and professional issues in the practice of marriage and family therapy* (2nd ed.). Upper Saddle River, NJ: Merrill/Prentice Hall.

Johnston, S. P., & Hartley, M. T. (2018). Ethics and facilitating services for clients. In K. B. Wilson, C. L. Acklin, & S. Chao (Eds.), *Case management for the health, human, and vocational rehabilitation services* (pp. 124–137). Linn Creek, MO: Aspen Professional Services.

Johnston, S. P., Tarvydas, V. M., & Butler, M. (2015). Managing risk in ethical and legal situations. In M. Stebnicki & I. Marini (Eds.), *Professional counselors desk reference* (2nd ed., pp. 99–111). New York, NY: Springer Publishing Company.

Kitchener, K. S. (1984). Ethics in counseling psychology: Distinctions and directions. *Counseling Psychologist, 12*(3), 43–55. doi:10.1177/0011000084123002

Liu, W. M., & Toporek, R. L. (2018). Advocacy. In V. M. Tarvydas & M. T. Hartley (Eds.), *The professional practice of rehabilitation counseling* (pp. 257–272). New York, NY: Springer Publishing Company.

National Board for Certified Counselors. (2014). *Ethics.* Retrieved from https://www.nbcc.org/Ethics

Pietrofesa, J. J., Pietrofesa, C. J., & Pietrofesa, J. D. (1990). The mental health counselor and "duty to warn." *Journal of Mental Health Counseling, 12*(2), 129–137.

Powell, S. K. (1996). *Nursing case management: A practical guide to success in managed care.* Philadelphia, PA: Lippincott-Raven.

Raths, L., Harmin, M., & Simon, S. (1966). *Values and teaching: Working with values in the classroom.* Upper Saddle River, NJ: Merrill/Prentice Hall.

Remley, T. P., & Herlihy, B. (2007). *Ethical, legal, and professional issues in counseling* (2nd ed.). Upper Saddle River, NJ: Pearson Education.

Rinas, J., & Clyne-Jackson, S. (1988). *Professional conduct and legal concerns in mental health practice.* East Norwalk, CT: Appleton & Lange.

Tarvydas, V. T., & Johnston, S. P. (2018). Ethics and ethics decision-making. In V. M. Tarvydas & M. T. Hartley (Eds.), *The professional practice of rehabilitation counseling* (pp. 313–342). New York, NY: Springer Publishing Company.

Thomas, R. V., & Pender, D. A. (2008). Association for Specialists in Group Work: Best practice guidelines 2007 revisions. *The Journal of Specialists in Group Work, 33,* 111–117. doi:10.1080/01933920801971184

Weber, M., Baehr, P. R., & Wells, G. C. (2002). *The Protestant ethic and the "spirit" of capitalism and other writings.* New York, NY: Penguin.

Welfel, E. R. (2010). *Ethics in counseling and psychotherapy: Standards, research, and emerging issues* (4th ed.). Belmont, CA: Thomson Brooks/Cole.

SECTION IV

WORKING WITHIN SYSTEMS

CHAPTER 9

CLIENT ADVOCACY, ACCESS, EQUITY, AND RESILIENCE

CARLOS P. ZALAQUETT

This chapter addresses the importance of advocacy and social justice advocacy, and the strategic positionality of the clinical mental health counselor as an advocate for addressing social and institutional barriers that reduce client access, equity, and success. Advocacy competencies and approaches to advocate for clients care are identified, and the ways that they foster resilience and growth are emphasized. Specific cases illustrate clients' and professionals' understandings of and access to a variety of community-based resources. The chapter also addresses strategies to advocate for the profession and for clinical mental health counseling professionals. The following Council for Accreditation of Counseling and Related Educational Programs (CACREP) standards are addressed in this chapter:
   CACREP 2016:
      2F1.e, 2F2.h, 2F3.i, 2F5.k, 5C3.e
   CACREP 2009:
      2G1.h, 2G1.i, 2G2.d, 2G2.e, 2G2.f

LEARNING OBJECTIVES

After reviewing this chapter, the reader should be able to:

1. Explain the critical role of advocacy for the mental health field;

2. Define advocacy and social justice advocacy;

3. Describe the clinical mental health counselor advocate;

4. Identify the American Counseling Association's (ACA) *social justice advocacy competencies*;

5. Analyze potential strengths and limitations of social justice advocates; and,

6. Outline possible issues for clinical mental health counseling advocacy.

▨ INTRODUCTION TO ADVOCACY AND SOCIAL JUSTICE ADVOCACY

Advocacy is key for the clinical mental health counseling profession. Counseling professionals recognize the significant influence that sociopolitical systems have upon the mental health of individuals, couples, groups, communities, and society (ACA, 2014; American Mental Health Counseling Association [AMHCA], 2017; CACREP, 2016). They realize that working with a client one-on-one is not always enough and that challenging the prevailing environment may be necessary in order to make significant differences (Chung & Bemak, 2012; Lee, 2019; Zalaquett, Ivey, & Ivey, 2019).

All counseling organizations have agreed that it is essential for counselors to intervene with clients beyond the individual level, to address the role of factors such as inequalities, oppression, discrimination, barriers, or access to services that affect the lives of clients (Chang, Crethar, & Ratts, 2010, p. 83). Furthermore, as the evolution of advocacy in counseling has progressed, the term *advocacy* has become identified with counselors' actions to champion the profession of counseling and related associations, and the term *social justice advocacy* was introduced to identify advocacy in the service of client and groups (Toporek, Lewis, & Crethar, 2009). Social justice advocacy includes "the action taken by a counseling professional for the purpose of removing external and institutional barriers to clients' well-being" (Toporek et al., 2009, p. 6). The two overarching goals of social justice advocacy are: (a) to increase a client's sense of personal power, and (b) to foster environmental changes that reflect greater responsiveness to a client's personal needs (Lee, 2019). Efforts to advance social justice advocacy among counselors have increased in recent years (Ratts, Singh, Nassar-McMillan, Butler, & McCullough, 2016).

Clinical mental health counselors are in a fundamental position to advocate for their profession, associations, groups, and their clients. Equipped with a bioecological perspective, clinical mental health counselors understand how clinical issues are affected by the social systems in which their clients are immersed (see Chapter 11). Furthermore, by virtue of their professional training, competencies, and roles, clinical mental health counselors can identify societal aspects that affect the well-being of individuals and groups, in both positive and negative ways, and, in turn, serve as clinical mental health counselor advocates.

Clinical mental health counselor advocates have the responsibility to intervene when negative effects are identified. This expectation explicitly is mentioned in the ACA *Code of Ethics*: "Counselors are expected to advocate to promote changes at the individual, group, institutional, and societal levels that improve the quality of life for individuals and groups and remove potential barriers to the provision or access of appropriate services being offered" (ACA, 2015, p. 4). The standards of the CACREP (2016) and the professional standards of the AMHCA (2015) articulate similar expectations.

TIP FROM THE FIELD 9.1

THE ADVOCATE ROLE OF THE CLINICAL MENTAL HEALTH COUNSELOR

The AMHCA *Code of Ethics* defines the advocate role of clinical mental health counselors as follows:

2. Advocate

Mental health counselors may serve as advocates at the individual, institutional, and/or societal level in an effort to foster sociopolitical change that meets the needs of the client or the community.

a)   Mental health counselors are aware of and make every effort to avoid pitfalls of advocacy including conflicts of interest, inappropriate relationships and other negative consequences. Mental health counselors remain sensitive to the potential personal and cultural impact on clients of their advocacy efforts.

b)   Mental health counselors may encourage clients to challenge familial, institutional, and societal obstacles to their growth and development and they may advocate on the clients' behalf. Mental health counselors remain aware of the potential dangers of becoming overly involved as an advocate.

c)   Mental health counselors may only speak on their behalf and are clear, cautious, and authorized to speak on the behalf of any counseling organization.

d)   Mental health counselors endeavor to speak factually and discern facts from opinions. (AMHCA, 2015, p. 4)

The AMHCA *Code of Ethics* description of the role of an advocate highlights the importance of considering the clients' context and avoiding treating clients in isolation, because the clients' issues may stem from the oppression and discrimination these clients experience from the social systems with which they interact (Ratts & Hutchins, 2009). The Code further stipulates the importance of maintaining appropriate professional counselor–client boundaries, which has very important and essential implications for work in the field.

■ THE CLINICAL MENTAL HEALTH COUNSELOR ADVOCATE

Clinical mental health counselor advocates acknowledge the need to confront inequalities, oppression, discrimination, and limited access to health systems at the individual (micro), community (meso), and public policy (macro) levels, as outlined by the ACA *Advocacy Competencies*. They work to change the conditions of the systems that have an impact on their clients, work to empower their clients so that they can advocate for themselves, and work to effect changes within their profession so that they can become more effective agents of change (Lewis, Arnold, House, & Toporek, 2002).

Clinical mental health counselors understand that each of their clients is a part of the environments that may be oppressing them socially, culturally, or economically (Chang et al., 2010). The need for advocacy may include initiatives to increase mental healthcare in schools; to remove health and work inequalities; to promote gender equity; to combat racism; and to implement social action strategies with lesbian, gay, bisexual, transgender, queer, asexual, and other sexual orientation (LGBTQA+) communities, older adults, clients with disabilities, and counseling services for undocumented immigrants. Clinical mental health counselors avoid traditional intrapsychic or individualistic approaches to mental healthcare, because these approaches may deny clients, especially marginalized clients, of the realities in which they live and from which they suffer. These approaches fault the clients for their issues, perpetuate a blame-the-victim attitude, use culturally biased diagnostic criteria, and preserve social injustice and cultural oppression within the counseling profession (Greenleaf & Williams, 2009). Clinical mental health counselor advocates recognize that diagnoses such as depression, anxiety, and oppositional defiant disorder may be the result of the stress experienced by populations that lack power, are oppressed, or are marginalized (Greenleaf & Williams, 2009).

Research on health inequalities shows how marginalized populations are frequently under-, over-, or misdiagnosed with psychopathology within the healthcare professions (Greenleaf & Williams, 2009). Furthermore, findings from various studies show the connection between social oppression—including classism, ethnic/racial discrimination, ageism, and sexism, to mention a few—and negative health outcomes such as depression, anxiety, posttraumatic stress disorder, substance use, and suicide (Greenleaf, Williams, & Duys, 2015). Many of the marginalized populations under discussion here are "beneficiaries" of historical or transgenerational trauma, which is a direct consequence of earlier colonialism and oppression (see Chapter 5 for a fuller discussion).

Social justice advocacy "uses social advocacy and activism as a means to address inequitable, social, political, and economic conditions that impede the academic, career, and personal/social development of individuals, families, and communities" (Ratts & Hutchins, 2009, p. 160). Social justice advocacy typically is initiated at the client level, using appropriate self-empowerment techniques; however, clinical mental health counselor advocates need to be prepared to address systems of oppression, discrimination, and privilege, at multiple levels, in order to advance the well-being of their clients. To achieve this goal, clinical mental health counselor advocates need to have the awareness, knowledge, skills, and actions to do so (Decker, Manis, & Paylo, 2016). Case Illustration 9.1, presented at the end of the chapter, illustrates a counselor's social justice advocacy on behalf of those who use a service dog for a medical or psychological purpose. Tip from the Field 9.2 presents the advocacy competencies model to help clinical mental health counselors sharpen their advocacy skills.

TIP FROM THE FIELD 9.2

EXAMPLE OF SOCIAL JUSTICE ADVOCACY BY A CLINICAL MENTAL HEALTH COUNSELOR

According to Toporek et al. (2009), the ACA's (2003) set of advocacy competencies could serve as a framework for counselor social justice advocacy efforts to promote systemic changes in the child welfare system. Ackerman's (2017) efforts to improve the child welfare system provide a good example of social justice advocacy. Her call to action identified the following major concerns regarding the welfare system and offered a plan for action:

(1) *Racial disproportionality:* Children of color (33% of the total child population in the United States) make up more than 55% of children in foster care. These children have fewer contacts with caseworkers, fewer written case plans, and fewer developmental or psychological assessments, and they receive fewer visits with their birth families and remain in foster care longer than White children, with similar conditions.

(2) *Organizational issues:* High number of cases, poor working conditions, and public criticism of the child welfare system produce a negative effect on social workers, creating job stress and burnout, thus reducing performance effectiveness and increasing personnel turnover rates.

(3) *The inaccessibility of adequate services for families:* Families involved with the child welfare system report higher numbers of barriers to attending child mental health service appointments and have a high risk of premature treatment termination.

(4) *The recruitment and retention of foster parent caregivers:* Negative perceptions about the child welfare system, poor preparation for foster-care roles, low foster parent reimbursement rates, and the high cost of housing negatively affect recruitment and retention of foster parents. Many foster parents quit fostering within the first year of service.

After describing the disproportionate removal of children of color as a crisis in the child welfare system, Ackerman (2017) called for action to address racism, discrimination, and the differential treatment of children and families of color. She has offered an integrated model for counselor advocacy within the child welfare system and has reminded professionals that counselors are uniquely qualified to engage in social justice advocacy efforts on behalf of children.

Clinical mental health counselors are uniquely qualified to work with child welfare workers and foster families in order to improve training and stress management. Furthermore, they have expertise in assessing trauma exposure and severity, and using trauma-focused treatments, which are relevant competencies for offering counseling to children with complex trauma histories. More clinical mental health counselors should advocate for internal counseling positions within child welfare organizations.

THE ACA'S SOCIAL JUSTICE ADVOCACY COMPETENCIES

The ACA's Advocacy Competencies (Lewis et al., 2002) offer 43 specific behaviors to guide counselors, in general, and clinical mental health counselor advocates in particular, to act at three levels of intervention: the client or student, the school or community, and the public. Social justice advocacy competencies is the term that currently is used for interventions at the client, group, or public level. The competencies are organized into six domains: (a) client empowerment, (b) client advocacy, (c) community collaboration, (d) systems advocacy, (e) public information, and (f) social/political advocacy (Toporek et al., 2009). Figure 9.1 shows a 3 × 2 matrix of the domains, where the horizontal axis identifies the level of engagement, from micro to macro, and the vertical axis identifies whether the action is with, or on behalf of, the client. The top identifies the level of

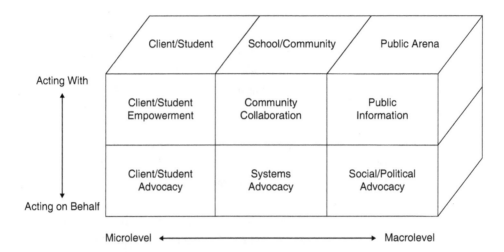

FIGURE 9.1 American Counseling Association's advocacy competency domains.

SOURCE: Lewis, J., Arnold, M. S., House, R., & Toporek, R. (2002). *ACA advocacy competencies*. Retrieved from https://www.counseling.org/Resources/Competencies/Advocacy_Competencies.pdf

intervention and the six domains identify the specific counselor competencies that are relevant to that domain. Table 9.1 provides a sample of those competencies per domain.

Clinical mental health counselors can use the social justice advocacy competencies to empower clients by helping them to identify their own personal strengths and resources, and to learn the skills necessary to take action and promote change. Throughout this process, clients will become aware of their own abilities to advocate for themselves and will grow more resilient.

The current multicultural and social justice competencies (Ratts et al., 2016) assert that multicultural and social justice counselor advocates (a) address the intrapersonal processes that have an impact on clients, (b) address inequities at the institutional level (e.g., schools, churches, and community organizations), (c) address norms, values, and regulations that impede the development of individuals, groups, and communities, (d) address public policy issues that impinge on client development with and on behalf of clients, and (e) address international and global events, affairs, and policies that hinder client development with and on behalf of clients. Counselors believe that every client, regardless of race, ethnicity, gender identity, socioeconomic status, and beliefs, has the right to quality education, healthcare services, and employment opportunities (Lewis, Ratts, Paladino, & Toporek, 2011). Clinical mental health counselor advocates act with the specific goal of ensuring that clients have the opportunity to reach their personal, social, and career potentials, free from unnecessary barriers.

◼ POTENTIAL STRENGTHS AND LIMITATIONS OF SOCIAL JUSTICE ADVOCATES

Effective clinical mental health counselor social justice advocates work directly with clients, families, and groups and contribute to changing social policies through professional

TABLE 9.1 Examples of the 43 advocacy competencies (Lewis et al., 2002) within each advocacy domain, listed by their original numbers

CLIENT/STUDENT	SCHOOL/COMMUNITY	PUBLIC ARENA
Client/Student Empowerment In direct interventions, the counselor is able to: 1. Identify strengths and resources of clients and students. 3. Recognize the signs indicating that an individual's behaviors and concerns reflect responses to systemic or internalized oppression. 6. Help students and clients develop self-advocacy action plans.	**Community Collaboration** When working collaboratively with community partners, the counselor is able to: 16. Develop alliances with groups working for change. 17. Use effective listening skills to gain understanding of the group's goals. 21. Assess the effect of counselor's interaction with the community.	**Public Information** In informing the public about the role of environmental factors in human development, the advocacy-oriented counselor is able to: 30. Recognize the impact of oppression and other barriers to healthy development. 31. Identify environmental factors that are protective of healthy development. 34. Disseminate information through a variety of media.
Client/Student Advocacy In environmental interventions on behalf of clients and students, the counselor is able to: 8. Negotiate relevant services and education systems on behalf of clients and students. 9. Help clients and students gain access to needed resources. 12. Identify potential allies for confronting the barriers. 13. Carry out the plan of action.	**Systems Advocacy** In exerting systems-change leadership at the school or community level, the advocacy-oriented counselor is able to: 22. Identify environmental factors impinging on students' or clients' development. 24. In collaboration with other stakeholders, develop a vision to guide change. 28. Recognize and deal with resistance.	**Social/Political Advocacy** In influencing public policy in a large, public arena, the advocacy-oriented counselor is able to: 41. With allies, prepare convincing data and rationales for change. 42. With allies, lobby legislators and other policy makers. 43. Maintain open dialogue with communities and clients to ensure that the social/political advocacy is consistent with the initial goals.

SOURCE: Lewis, J., Arnold, M. S., House, R., & Toporek, R. (2002). *ACA advocacy competencies*. Retrieved from https://www.counseling.org/Resources/Competencies/Advocacy_Competencies.pdf

writings and collaboration with the social systems affecting clients. Clinical mental health counselor advocates are well trained in counseling skills and multicultural competencies; recognize human suffering; use effective communication skills; use a systems-of-sociocultural-influence perspective; identify mental health disparities; have individual, group, and organizational intervention skills; are competent in social justice advocacy skills; have the ability to deal with conflict; know effective psychoeducational methods to empower clients with self-advocacy skills; collaborate with clients in a diversity-sensitive manner; and act with the best interest of the client in mind (Brubaker, Puig, Reese, & Young, 2010; Chung & Bemak, 2012). At a personal level, counselor advocates are intentional, motivated, persistent, tenacious, flexible, patient, assertive, organized, resourceful, creative, display humility, and have a profound respect for others (Chung & Bemak, 2012). Ineffective clinical mental health counselor advocates are guided by personal or hidden agendas oriented toward personal gains, have some desire to fulfill personal motivations, need to promote themselves, augment their notoriety, or increase their personal power (Smith, Reynolds, & Rovnak, 2009).

TIP FOR THE FIELD 9.3

POSSIBLE ISSUES FOR CLINICAL MENTAL HEALTH COUNSELOR ADVOCACY

Jim Messina (2019), one of the founders of the AMHCA, has offered a list of potential targets for social advocacy by clinical mental health counselors. This list has focused on addressing the long-standing social stigma associated with mental health services as well as on helping clients and their families to cope with the effects of stigma. Messina also advises clinical mental health counselors to proactively assist clients who have been victimized or marginalized in any way, and to think through these issues with preventive measures in mind. This list is helpful in terms of thinking through many of the professional advocacy issues that continue to demand the attention of clinical mental health counselors. The full list can be found at the following website: http://coping.us/cmhcprofessionalization/advocacyissuesforcmhcs.html

The ACA advocacy competencies naturally have steered counselors to populations such as those mentioned in Messina's list. In their ACA *Advocacy Competencies*, Lewis et al. (2002) have articulated an imperative for recognizing and validating the systemic influence of cultural, political, social, and economic factors upon people and their communities. They have suggested that such an imperative pushes counselors to engage in activism that, in turn, can assist the clients with whom counselors work to empower themselves. These advocacy competencies can be found at the following website: www.counseling.org/docs/default-source/competencies/aca-2018-advocacy-competencies.pdf?sfvrsn=1dca552c_6

Two Ongoing Advocacy Efforts

Two ongoing advocacy efforts continue to require the attention of the professional counseling field: including clinical mental health counselors in Medicare and facilitating and implementing a strategy for the national portability of professional counselor licenses. These important issues are outlined, briefly, as follows.

Inclusion of Clinical Mental Healthcare Counselors in Medicare

Medicare, the largest healthcare program in the United States, reimburses psychiatrists, psychologists, clinical social workers, and psychiatric nurses for outpatient behavioral mental health services. The program does not reimburse clinical mental health counselors for similar services. Advocacy for parity of clinical mental health counselors with other professions is an ongoing effort.

Licensure Portability

A national licensure portability program is necessary in a world with a mobile workforce, thus emphasizing the need to ensure a minimum quality of preservice preparation for professional mental health providers. Being a clinical mental health counselor should have the same meaning from state to state. A portable license would affirm minimum standards for safe practice, create consistency in licensure standards across all the U.S. states, protect clients, and increase public access to qualified care.

Discussion

Clinical mental health counselors are well qualified to provide the mental health services covered by Medicare. Medicare beneficiaries need more mental health services than are available currently, and they should have the right to access the type of mental health caregiver, across the various mental health disciplines, who best meets their needs. Licensed clinical mental health counselors are trained to diagnose and treat mental health disorders and are available to serve clients in rural and underserved areas, which are areas of high need for services. Clinical mental health counselors need to support ongoing and upcoming efforts to gain access to Medicare and license portability.

CASE ILLUSTRATION 9.1

CHALLENGES FACED BY SERVICE DOG HANDLERS AND THEIR ADVOCATES
By K. Lynn Pierce

Todd is a young professional who uses a service dog for medical alert assistance. His service dog is able to let him know when his vital signs are outside of his normal threshold. He can also retrieve objects or get help for Todd in an emergency. Because many people are unaware of the laws pertaining to service dogs, Todd routinely encounters access issues where owners of businesses attempt to exclude him, often referencing problems with other animals in the past. He is afraid of standing up for himself in these situations and will often leave and go somewhere else, because a storeowner once called the police. The police didn't know the laws either and made him leave. He sometimes risks leaving his service dog at home to avoid the embarrassment of being asked to leave.

Todd has found that his service dog has a drastic impact on his ability to network and develop his professional identity. At conferences, people around him discuss research and projects. He is almost never asked about anything except his service dog. He has to maintain his service dog's training and his own safety by preventing distractions but knows he is sometimes seen as rude when he asks people not to pet her or talk to her. Because of a lack of awareness of service dog etiquette, he finds himself constantly othered (to be viewed as and treated as different or lesser) because of his need for a service dog as an assistive device. He frequently is excluded from opportunities to engage as others do or to receive the same access, services, and experiences as others.

As a counselor and a counselor educator in training, I have worked with and advocated for individual handlers like Todd, as well as counselors and other service providers who work with this demographic. Service dogs increasingly are used for a variety of disabilities.

In the case of those with mental health concerns that can be helped by a service dog, counselors play an important role in providing access to resources. They can help their client determine whether a service dog is the right treatment choice, direct the client toward quality information and resources, and may provide a recommendation for a training program that may take on the client as a prospective service dog handler. Having this knowledge allows counselors to provide more comprehensive care.

In my advocacy work supporting service dog handlers, I have worked on a number of levels and in different ways to support clients and the needs of the community of individuals who use service dogs. I have educated mental health professionals about service dog laws and etiquette and provided consultation for clinicians whose goal is to assess a client's suitability as a service dog handler. For existing handlers like Todd, providing a safe environment might involve ensuring that colleagues know the basics of etiquette and that Todd has a way to escape a negative interaction with another client in the waiting room. In working with Todd, some goals may be to increase resources for self-advocacy, to process the trauma inflicted by the high levels of discrimination that service dog handlers experience, and to make plans to address likely barriers moving forward.

On a broader level, I have seen success in educating professionals who are most likely, inadvertently, to cause barriers to necessary services/support to service dog handlers due to lack of awareness and education. Counselors are in a position to form alliances with police departments, behavioral health units, medical professionals, and other service providers. We also can ensure that access to information about marginalized populations is available and disseminated in our profession. Our research can provide the basis for new policies for and new understandings about underrepresented groups in the broader society.

For advocacy-oriented counselors, one key is to continue to seek new opportunities for advocacy and new alliances. Public perception, embedded stigma, and far-reaching laws and policies are not going to be changed drastically in a short period of time. I have watched as people I have educated have begun to educate others. Through my community connections, I hear positive stories that are the result of my work or the work of others who are doing similar things. I have found that I need to recalibrate my expected outcomes to be open to the evidence that shows that I am making an impact. This recalibration allows me to be a more empowered advocate, when at times it would be easy to become frustrated and discouraged. It also informs my future advocacy work, as I am more aware of small results and can build purposefully upon those toward bigger successes.

To learn more about how counselors can work effectively and compassionately with service dog handlers, see "Understanding and Working with Service Dog Handlers" in Counseling Today.

RESOURCES

ADA National Network. (2014). *Service animals and emotional support animals*. Retrieved from https://adata.org/publication/service-animals-booklet

Assistance Dogs International. (2019). *Home*. Retrieved from http://www.assistancedogs international.org

Counseling Today. Retrieved from https://ct.counseling.org/2018/10/understanding-and -working-with-service-dog-handlers

Mills, M. (2017). Invisible disabilities, visible service dogs: The discrimination of service dog handlers. *Disability & Society, 32*, 635–656. doi:10.1080/09687599.2017.1307718

Pierce, K. L. (2018, October). Understanding and working with service dog handlers.

U.S. Department of Justice. (2011). *ADA requirements: Service animals*. Retrieved from https://www.ada.gov/service_animals_2010.htm

CONCLUSION

This chapter addressed the importance of advocacy skills and emphasized using social justice advocacy competencies in the work with clients. Clinical mental health counselor advocates rely on the advocacy competencies to guide their assistance to clients in removing barriers and to secure deserving resources, or to advocate on behalf of clients, groups, or communities. Clinical mental health counselors are in a privileged position to address social and institutional barriers depriving clients, especially clients from underprivileged groups, access to quality mental health services. Clinical mental health counselor advocates use their awareness, knowledge, and competencies to address inequalities, to help clients gain knowledge of available resources, and to promote the development of self-advocacy skills and stronger resiliency in clients. Clinical mental health counselor advocates also work with allies on behalf of their clients. They become the voice of marginalized groups to identify and remove barriers to mental healthcare, increase quality of required services, and influence policies and regulations to ensure best treatments and quality services for those in need. Advocacy for the profession is also an important function of clinical mental health professionals. Clinical mental health counselors are trained and licensed to provide services in multiple types of behavioral health organizations, to be covered by Medicare, to serve populations in need of services, with sensitivity to diversity, and to work in underserved areas. Clinical mental health counselor advocates are guided by the belief that every client, regardless of race, ethnicity, gender identity, socioeconomic status, and beliefs, has the right to quality healthcare services, and they advocate to ensure that each client has the opportunity to reach his or her personal, social, and career potential, free from unnecessary barriers.

RESOURCES

American Counseling Association's (ACA) Government Affairs: https://www.counseling .org/government-affairs/actioncenter. ACA supports the counseling profession through government affairs initiatives at the federal and state levels. ACA's voting system represents an effective way to communicate with legislators and policy member to advance policies that increase counselors access to behavioral health services, develop parity with other professionals, and create better systems of care.

American Mental Health Counselors Association Advocacy Handbook: Federal Advocacy Handbook for the American Mental Health Counselors Association. https:// higherlogicdownload.s3.amazonaws.com/AMHCA/6664039b-12a0-4d03-8199 -32c785fe1687/UploadedImages/Documents/AdvocacyHandbook.pdf. The handbook offers best ways to navigate the legislative system and send advocacy messages that get the attention of the relevant legislators.

American Mental Health Counselors Association's Policy Agenda: http://www.amhca.org/ advocacy/policyagenda. Find current information on AMHCA's advocacy initiatives in Congress and state legislatures.

Chung, R. C-Y., & Bemak, F. (2012). *Social justice counseling: The next steps beyond multiculturalism.* Thousand Oaks, CA: Sage. The book addresses issues of social class, race, and ethnicity, and others from a social justice perspective.

Courtland C. Lee (Ed.) (2019). *Counseling for social justice* (3rd ed.). Hoboken, NJ: Wiley. A thorough examination of social justice counseling from local and global perspectives. Ideas for promoting social justice and challenging oppression and marginalization with individual clients and communities are presented.

Donald, E. J., & Moro, R. R. (2011). *Engaging students and supervisees in social justice: The social justice toolbox.* Article 10. Vistas Online. Retrieved from https://www.counseling .org/docs/defaultsource/vistas/article_10.pdf?sfvrsn=1c003afc_12. A collection of tools to become actively involved in social justice advocacy.

Medicare Coverage for Clinical Mental Health Counseling, a Gulf Coast Mental Health Counselors' call for legislative action to include clinical mental health counseling under Medicare coverage. This video, created by the legislative committee of GCMHC, can be accessed here: https://www.youtube.com/watch?v=wjfILTJ-o-w&feature=youtu.be

Multicultural Counseling and Social Justice Competencies: http://toporek.org/index.html. The website, produced by Rebecca Toporek, offers a wide variety of resources to develop multicultural, social justice, advocacy, and counseling competence.

NBCC Government Affairs: https://www.nbcc.org/GovtAffairs. NBCC supports the counseling profession through government affairs initiatives at the federal and state levels. NBCC works with public and private stakeholders to implement policies that increase access of counselors to existing agencies or funders (e.g., Medicare), add more funding to counselors, and create better systems of integrated care.

World Health Organization. (2003). *Advocacy for mental health.* https://www.who.int/mental _health/policy/services/1_advocacy_WEB_07.pdf. Information about the importance of mental health advocacy to promote the human rights of persons with mental disorders and to reduce stigma and discrimination. Provide various actions aimed to change structural and attitudinal barriers to achieving positive mental health outcomes in populations.

REFERENCES

Ackerman, A. M. (2017). An integrated model for counselor social justice advocacy in child welfare. *The Family Journal, 25,* 389–397. doi:10.1177/1066480717736061

American Counseling Association. (2015). *ACA code of ethics.* Alexandria, VA: Author.

American Mental Health Counselors Association. (2015). *Code of ethics.* Retrieved from https://www.amhca.org/HigherLogic/System/DownloadDocumentFile.ashx?Document FileKey=5ff5bc94-e534-091e-c7c1-e3ea45cf943e&forceDialog=0

American Mental Health Counselors Association. (2017). *AMHCA standards for the practice of clinical mental health counseling.* Retrieved from http://www.amhca.org/learn/standards

Brubaker, M. D., Puig, A., Reese, R. F., & Young, J. (2010). Integrating social justice into counseling theories pedagogy: A case example. *Counselor Education and Supervision, 50*(2), 88–102. doi:10.1002/j.1556-6978.2010.tb00111.x

Chang, C. Y., Crethar, H. C., & Ratts, M. J. (2010). Social justice: A national imperative for counselor education and supervision. *Counselor Education & Supervision, 50*, 82–87. doi:10.1002/j.1556-6978.2010.tb00110.x

Chung, R. C., & Bemak, F. P. (2012). *Social justice counseling: The next steps beyond multiculturalism*. Thousand Oaks, CA: SAGE.

Council for Accreditation of Counseling and Related Educational Programs. (2016). *2016 standards*. Alexandria, VA: Author.

Decker, K. M., Manis, A. A., & Paylo, M. J. (2016). Infusing social justice advocacy into counselor education: Strategies and recommendations. *Journal of Counselor Preparation and Supervision, 8*(3). doi:10.7729/83.1092

Greenleaf, A. T., & Williams, J. M. (2009). Supporting social justice advocacy: A paradigm shift towards an ecological perspective. *Journal for Social Action in Counseling and Psychology, 2*, 1–14.

Greenleaf, A. T., Williams, J. M., & Duys, D. K. (2015). Awareness of counselor trainees on clients' social barriers. *Journal of Counselor Practice, 6*, 25–38. doi:10.22229/ctc592017

Lee, C. C. (Ed.). (2019). *Counseling for Social Justice* (3rd ed.). Alexandria, VA: American Counseling Association Foundation.

Lewis, J., Arnold, M. S., House, R., & Toporek, R. (2002). *ACA advocacy competencies*. Retrieved from https://www.counseling.org/docs/default-source/competencies/aca-2018 -advocacy-competencies.pdf?sfvrsn=1dca552c_6

Lewis, J. A., Ratts, M. J., Paladino, D. A., & Toporek, R. L. (2011). Social justice counseling and advocacy: Developing new leadership roles and competencies. *Journal for Social Action in Counseling and Psychology, 3*, 5–16.

Messina, J. (2019). *Social advocacy issues for which CMHCs could advocate*. Retrieved from http://coping.us/cmhcprofessionalization.html

Ratts, M. J., & Hutchins, A. M. (2009). ACA advocacy competencies: Social justice advocacy at the client/student level. *Journal of Counseling and Development, 87*, 269–275. doi:10.1002/j.1556-6678.2009.tb00106.x

Ratts, M. J., Singh, A. A., Nassar-McMillan, S., Butler, S. K., & McCullough, J. R. (2016). Multicultural and social justice counseling competencies: Guidelines for the counseling profession. *Journal of Multicultural Counseling and Development, 44*, 28–48. doi:10.1002/ jmcd.12035

Smith, S. D., Reynolds, C. A., & Rovnak, A. (2009). A critical analysis of the social advocacy movement in counseling. *Journal of Counseling & Development, 87*, 483–491. doi:10.1002/j.1556-6678.2009.tb00133.x

Toporek, R. L., Lewis, J. A., & Crethar, H. C. (2009). Promoting systemic change through the ACA Advocacy Competencies. *Journal of Counseling & Development, 87*, 260–268. doi:10.1002/j.1556-6678.2009.tb00105.x

Zalaquett, C. P., Ivey, A., & Ivey, M. B. (2019). *Essential theories of counseling and psychotherapy: Everyday practice in our diverse world*. San Diego, CA: Cognella Academic Publishing.

CHAPTER 10

PROFESSIONAL ROLES AND FUNCTIONS IN CLINICAL MENTAL HEALTH COUNSELING

REGINA R. MORO

This chapter takes an in-depth look at the variety of functions, counseling and administrative roles, and tasks that may be required of counselors in clinical mental health settings. Pertinent issues include balancing consumer care with administrative duties, balancing employee well-being with productivity standards/financial concerns, ethical marketing and recruitment, and remaining current in the field while in nonclinical roles. The following Council for Accreditation of Counseling and Related Educational Programs (CACREP) standards are addressed in this chapter:
CACREP 2016:
2F1.b, 2F1.i, 5C2.a
CACREP 2009:
2G1.a, 2G1.b

LEARNING OBJECTIVES

After reviewing this chapter, the reader should be able to:

1. Name common roles and functions of clinical mental health counselors.

2. Discuss the clinical tensions experienced among clinical mental health counselors in relation to their job roles.

3. Synthesize an understanding of the complex role a clinical mental health counselor serves in relation to best practices, professional ethics, and legislative regulations.

4. Recommend roles and functions that a clinical mental health counselor could perform in a larger system of care.

▒ INTRODUCTION

This chapter explores the professional roles and functions of clinical mental health counselors working in integrated systems of care. The common English phrase, "the more things change, the more they stay the same," captures the essence of this chapter well. Our professional roles have evolved over time, and there is a great variety among the roles and functions of clinical mental health counselors in each and every different system of work. However, there are also great commonalities that continue to define our identity as professionals.

As a master's student doing my first field placement in a college counseling center, I remember being amazed by the professional counselors with whom I was working. I was in awe of their ability to function in so many different roles and to shift between the roles with such fluidity. Although I learned about the variety in roles during my orientation course, it was completely different to witness personally and then to experience juggling so many different hats on a day-to-day, and sometimes an hour-to-hour, basis. Shifting from individual counseling sessions, to writing notes, to staffing meetings made my head spin! I also felt quite overwhelmed when I would talk with my peers about their own field placements. It sounded as if so many of us were having such different experiences, yet so much was also the same. I have come to realize that much of my perception of the differences was about the different systems of care in which we all were doing our placements. Counselors have the ability to wear so many different hats, yet systems of care often dictate exactly how we function in our day-to-day roles.

Scope of Practice

The American Mental Health Counselors Association (AMHCA) Standards for the Practice of Clinical Mental Health Counseling defines the scope of practice of the profession. According to AMHCA (2017a):

> The practice of clinical mental health counseling includes, but is not limited to, diagnosis and treatment of mental and emotional disorders, psycho-educational techniques aimed at the prevention of mental and emotional disorders, consultations to individuals, couples, families, groups, organizations and communities, and clinical research into more effective psychotherapeutic treatment modalities. (p. 2)

While the AMHCA provides this definition of the scope of practice and highlights roles and functions of clinical mental health counselors, it is important to acknowledge that the AMHCA is a membership association, not a regulating body. The practice of counseling is regulated independently by each state. All licensed counselors need to be familiar with their own state's scope of practice for the credentials that they hold.

The AMHCA (2017a) definition for scope of practice provides an umbrella for all of the roles and functions possible for a clinical mental health counselor. The AMHCA (2017b) has issued a list of services offered by these professionals: "assessment and diagnosis, psychotherapy, treatment planning and utilization review, brief and solution-focused therapy, alcoholism and substance abuse treatment, psychoeducational and prevention programs, crisis management" (para. 2). Over 30 years ago, West, Hosie, and Mackey (1987) conducted a national survey of clinical directors at multiservice mental health agencies. The authors' purpose was to explore the job roles of employees with master's degrees in counseling. Respondents identified that both clinical and administrative services were provided by the counselors. Clinical services included completing intakes; participating in client staffing meetings; crisis intervention; assessment services; providing individual, group, and marriage and family therapy; and providing consultation and education (West et al., 1987). Administrative services identified by the directors included providing supervision for other professionals, coordinating the services offered by the agency, evaluating the efficacy of the services provided to the clients, and assisting with budgetary issues for the functioning of the agency (West et al., 1987).

Many of these common roles and functions have been explored in this book. For example, in Chapter 4, students learned about case conceptualization, assessment, and diagnosis. And in Chapter 7, students read about record keeping and documentation, which is a huge part of the day-to-day role of clinical mental health counselors. I review some details of the more common roles in the following; however, I offer a more expansive look at how clinical mental health counselors perform these roles and functions in complex systems of care.

Clinical Roles in Integrated Systems of Care

Often, there is a distinction drawn between clinical and administrative roles in clinical mental health counseling. This distinction most commonly is noted in discussions regarding the difference between clinical and administrative supervision of counselors. Tromski-Klingshirn (2007) states that clinical supervision, and thus clinical roles, is focused on the counseling relationship, client well-being, assessment and intervention, clinical skills, and treatment outcomes.

Within an integrated system of care, it is likely that the roles and daily functions of clinical mental health counselors are more clearly delineated than in a private practice or a smaller agency. Although clinical mental health counselors have the ability to perform many roles due to their extensive training in all of the complex skills needed, there are likely to be institutional boundaries for delegating responsibilities among multiple providers. This delegation of responsibility occurs through housing specific roles in large departments. In my experience as a counselor and a supervisor, I have encountered departments responsible for the following functions: (a) intake, assessment, and diagnosis; (b) treatment planning; (c) billing and insurance (sometimes called care coordination); and (d) clinical services (referring to psychotherapy). Counselors typically are employed in a specific department, which accordingly delineates their job roles and functions. I explore each of these in detail.

Intake, Assessment, and Diagnosis

Counselors employed in the intake, assessment, and diagnosis units are responsible for these distinct services. This department also may be composed of separate units, with specific counselors designated as intake counselors and as assessment and diagnosis counselors. Some of the responsibility for these services depends on the qualifications of the person hired in the role, state regulations regarding the scope of practice surrounding assessments, and the regulations of the assessment developers regarding who is deemed qualified to be an administrator of that assessment tool.

The providers completing assessment services can include bachelor's-level paraprofessionals, master's- and doctoral-level clinicians (counselors, social workers, and marriage and family therapists), doctoral-level psychologists, and psychiatrists who hold medical degrees. Paraprofessionals are defined as "providers without postgraduate training in a designated mental health specialization program" (Montgomery, Kunik, Wilson, Stanley, & Weiss, 2010, p. 46).

TIP FROM THE FIELD 10.1

WORKING COLLABORATIVELY WITH OTHER PROVIDERS

It is important that clinical mental health counselors are able to work collaboratively with all providers in their systems. In the intake, assessment, and diagnosis arena, clinical mental health counselors collaborate in a variety of ways, such as by completing intakes and assessments, consulting with paraprofessionals and other clinicians on cases, and compiling their findings and making recommendations for client treatment. Providers may be responsible for one or more of these activities, and in larger systems of care, it is likely that a clinical mental health counselor's role will be specific to one activity, compared with clinical mental health counselors employed in smaller agencies who may have responsibility for the entire assessment process.

The CACREP requires specialized training in assessment, testing, and diagnosis (CACREP, 2016, Standards 2. D.7.a-m). Therefore, clinical mental health counselors who have graduated from CACREP-accredited programs have received specialized training in assessment and diagnosis. In addition, professional counseling organization ethical codes regulate the assessment and diagnosis services provided by clinical mental health counselors. The American Counseling Association (ACA, 2014) *Code of Ethics*, Section E, and the AMHCA (2015) *Code of Ethics*, Section D, cover assessment and diagnosis service provision. These thorough training and ethical regulations make clinical mental health counselors vital resources in these departments.

Treatment Planning

Collaborative treatment planning, in which counselors and clients work together to form a plan for service provision, is a vital activity of all counselors working with clients and is an ethical mandate (ACA, 2014; AMHCA, 2015). While treatment planning is often a part of the assessment and diagnostic process, I am focusing on this separately to highlight the process in a larger system of care. Several professionals are likely to be responsible for the variety of components, including the intake. For example, as a member of a treatment team in an integrated setting, a counselor may work collaboratively with psychiatrists, social workers, nursing professionals, or other medical providers. Nursing professionals likely will be responsible for gathering medical information such as vital signs (e.g., blood pressure and heart rate). A psychiatrist may be involved if medication has been, or will be, part of a client's treatment. Social work professionals may have a variety of different roles, including helping to navigate systems of care in which a client may be involved. A clinical mental health counselor who is responsible for the treatment plan for a client needs to work collaboratively with the client to review the information received from other professionals, potentially consult further with these professionals or previous providers, and make an informed and intentional plan for services.

Competent treatment planning, in our growing world of integrated care systems, requires that clinical mental health counselors possess knowledge about common medical terminology, risks, and illnesses experienced by patients (AMHCA, 2017a). Clinical mental health counselors who possess this medical knowledge are able to discuss client concerns with medical providers. This knowledge also positions clinical mental health counselors to look at the holistic view of the client, which includes medical/biological, psychological, sociological/cultural, and spiritual elements. This holistic view allows for a comprehensive treatment planning process.

TIP FROM THE FIELD 10.2

DIFFERENTIATING BETWEEN MEDICAL AND MENTAL DISORDERS

Many common medical disorders can be misidentified as mental disorders. Pollak, Levy, and Breitholtz (1999) provide a list of common misidentified medical disorders attributed to mental disorders (e.g., sleep apnea, hyper-/hypothyroidism). Students are encouraged to review the article and prepare for how to avoid misidentifying medical issues as mental disorders.

Case Illustration 10.1 highlights the treatment planning process within an integrated system of care for the client Hannah. Jamie, Yolanda, and Muhammad work collaboratively to gather and organize intake information in order to outline a comprehensive plan of care for Hannah.

CASE ILLUSTRATION 10.1

THE CASE OF HANNAH: COLLABORATIVE TREATMENT PLANNING

Hannah seeks services at the behavioral health clinic of a larger medical facility. Hannah initially sought services in the primary care medical clinic due to weight gain and reports feeling "tired all the time" in recent months. All patients in the medical facility receive refer- rals to the behavioral health clinic. Following a medical examination, the family medicine doctor provided that referral to Hannah.

As a clinical mental health counselor employed at the behavioral health clinic, Jamie works primarily in the Assessment and Treatment Coordinating Unit. Jamie's job title is Treatment Coordinating Counselor, and her role is to oversee the assessment process and to compile all findings and work with the client to form a comprehensive treatment plan. She the first contact with clients in the clinic. When Jamie meets with Hannah for the first time, she provides an overview for her about what she can expect in the clinic. Jamie informs Hannah that she will first meet with a paraprofessional, Muhammad, who will complete the intake evaluation. Muhammad will take Hannah to meet with Yolanda, a licensed clin- ical mental health counselor, who will complete a series of assessments for common mental health issues. Common assessments conducted by Yolanda include:

- *Beck Depression Inventory-II (Beck, Steer, & Brown, 1996)*
- *Beck Anxiety Inventory (Beck & Steer, 1993)*
- *Alcohol Use Disorders Identification Test (Babor, Higgins-Biddle, Saunders, & Monteiro, 2001)*
- *Drug Abuse Screening Test-10 (Skinner, 1982)*
- *Mood Disorder Questionnaire (Hirschfield et al., 2000)*
- *Columbia-Suicide Severity Rating Scale (Posner et al., 2011)*
- *Primary Care Posttraumatic Stress Disorder (PTSD) Screen (Prins et al., 2003)*

While many of these assessments can be completed by self-report, the clinic has found that there is a benefit to doing these assessments as a part of the clinical interview with a licensed clinician who is able to use her specialized training as a clinical mental health counselors for this process. Yolanda not only completes the assessment interviews but scores, interprets, and writes a summary of the assessments for Jamie.

While Hannah is with Yolanda, Jamie receives the intake paperwork from Muhammad. Jamie learns that Hannah previously had sought counseling services 9 years ago while in her first semester of college. She informed Muhammad that she continued in counseling throughout that year, and that was the last contact she has had with a mental health profes- sional. Jamie decides that having Hannah sign a Release of Information (ROI) to get a treat- ment summary from the counseling center would be helpful. In addition, Jamie gets an ROI for Hannah's medical records from the primary care wing of the organization. Jamie also makes a note to remind the medical clinic to request Hannah's previous medical records, if they are not included in the report. Although the behavioral health clinic and the primary care medical clinic are a part of the larger organization, the clinic keeps separate records from the medical files. This separation is what makes the ROIs necessary.

As Hannah's treatment coordinator, Jamie uses her specialized knowledge as a clinical mental health counselor to review all of the information that she has received (i.e., intake summary, completed assessment report, medical records from in-house clinic, and prior counseling summary), and to consider possible treatments. Jamie did not receive any records regarding her previous medical history, and she makes a note to follow up with the medical clinic.

Jamie learns that Hannah initially sought medical care for weight gain and feelings of lethargy that have persisted for the past 3 months. The intake interview informs her that Hannah is a 27-year old Asian American woman, is an only child, has one living parent (mother deceased 20 years ago in a car accident), completed a master's degree in library science, and is currently employed as a librarian at the local public library, a position that she has held since graduating with her master's degree. Hannah reports during her intake that she met all developmental milestones and has no legal history or remarkable medical history. "I've been super healthy all of my life," Muhammad wrote as a direct quote from Hannah during the intake. The treatment summary from the college counseling center indicated that Hannah completed 19 sessions with a counselor. The presenting problem was listed as a roommate conflict and homesickness. There was no formal diagnosis, and there was no reported referral for follow-up care ("terminated due to returning home for summer"). Yolanda's report provided scores for all administered examinations, and Jamie's training as a clinical mental health counselor allowed her to interpret these. The only score that was clinically relevant was on the Beck Depression Inventory-II, on which Hannah scored a 13 (mild mood disturbance). As a part of Yolanda's report, she also detailed the Mental Status Exam and stated that Hannah's appearance and self-care were all normal and average and that she had normal attention, concentration, and memory. She was oriented times five (time, person, place, situation, and object). Her eye contact was fleeting, she had responsive facial expression, and she was cooperative with the exam. Her affect was appropriate, and her mood appeared mildly depressed. Her thoughts and language were normal and appropriate, judgment and decision-making were normal, and her intelligence was noted as above average. The medical records from her recent visit indicate that the physician intends to prescribe an antidepressant but is waiting on the results of a comprehensive blood test to rule out hypothyroidism.

As Hannah's Treatment Coordinating Counselor, is there further information Jamie would want to review to plan Hannah's treatment? Who would Jamie need to collaborate with in order to gain that information? What recommendations might Jamie make for Hannah's treatment?

Clinical Services

The clinical services offered by clinical mental health counselors in integrated systems of care can include individual, group, couple, and family counseling, as well as consultation and psychoeducation services. In order to practice ethically, clinical mental health counselors must be competent to provide services to clients (ACA, 2014; AMHCA, 2015). Training in CACREP-accredited programs requires intensive clinical training totaling 700 hours, with at least 280 hours in direct service provision (CACREP, 2016). However, CACREP (2016) does not dictate in which clinical capacity these hours need to be accrued, only that it must include "experience leading groups" (p. 16). Therefore, for clinical mental health counselors to practice ethically, it is necessary for them to gain sufficient training and supervision in the clinical modalities that are a part of their job role.

Consultation

For clinical mental health counselors working in integrated systems of care, consultation is a crucial job role. Consultation was mentioned earlier as an element of assessment and treatment planning; however, let us rewind and explore in more detail what consultation is. Dougherty (2009) defines consultation as "a helping relationship in which human service/mental health professionals work with individuals and/or groups in a variety of settings (such as agencies, schools, and businesses) to help them work more effectively" (p. 1). Clinical mental health counselors working as consultants in integrated systems of care use their advanced knowledge and skills in mental health to offer a unique lens that often is missing and may lead to ineffective care delivery.

Case Illustration 10.2 illuminates the importance of cultural sensitivity in care coordination. Brandon, a clinical mental health counselor working as part of an integrated treatment team, is able to offer a culturally informed view of one patient the team is concerned about.

CASE ILLUSTRATION 10.2

THE CASE OF JOSE: CULTURAL CONSULTATIONS

Brandon is a clinical mental health counselor employed at a large urban hospital in the southeastern part of the United States. He works in the cancer center and provides individual counseling services to patients while they are hospitalized. During Brandon's weekly staffing rounds, in which the team reviews all patient cases, he becomes concerned when he hears that Jose, a 57-year-old Latino male who has been hospitalized for 3 weeks, has not been eating. The charge nurse reports that Jose previously had been eating all meals well; however, over the past 3 days, he has not touched his lunch or dinner. The medical staff discusses complications from his medications, as well as the need for potential scans to investigate whether or not the cancer has spread. As he listens to this staffing discussion, he is quite concerned that no one has discussed Jose's religious beliefs as a potential reason for his refusal to eat. During Brandon's work with Jose, he has learned of his conversion to the Islamic faith 20 years ago, and he is also are aware that during the holy month of Ramadan, which is currently occurring, Muslims fast from sunrise to sunset. During this staffing, Brandon is able to inquire about the meal delivery times, and find out that breakfast is delivered before sunrise, allowing him to eat, but that his dinner has been arriving 2 hours before sunset. Brandon states that he will stop by Jose's room to explore this issue further. This consultation activity that Brandon provided was in part due to his specialized training in Social and Cultural Diversity as required by CACREP (2016).

TIP FROM THE FIELD 10.3

UNDERSTANDING SPECIFIC ROLES AND RESPONSIBILITIES

Personally, I have worked in systems in which my role was limited to one specific function and another system in which my role was quite comprehensive. One experience that I had in a larger system of care was at a Level 1 trauma center, where patients who were severely physically injured were treated. In such a large system of care, each employee had a designated role within a specific department. I was a clinical mental health counselor who specialized in addiction, and my role usually was limited to screening and intervening with patients who were injured and subsequently hospitalized due to their risky alcohol and drug use. In this system, it was clearly delineated which unit was responsible for what service provision.

All members of the larger team met for medical rounds each morning to discuss the patients on the trauma-service unit. Attending this meeting were the medical doctors (interns, residents, fellows, and attending physicians), medical students, nursing staff (charge nurse and nurse practitioners), the care coordinators (often social workers responsible for insurance and discharge planning), and our counseling staff. In this role, it was important for me to develop knowledge about medical jobs in general (e.g., difference between a medical intern and resident, or differences between nursing levels), and I needed to understand medical terminology. This knowledge allowed me to follow the flow of the conversation. In addition, it was important that I understood my own role and was prepared with my information about the patients in our service area. I primarily was responsible for information about the alcohol and drug use of patients, and would check the blood and urine results prior to attending this meeting, as well as providing any other information that was available from the family about the patient's use. Understanding patients' use patterns was important for a few different reasons. The initial concern is to explore if the patient may be at risk from withdrawing from substances they do not have access to while hospitalized. Withdrawal from certain substances (i.e., alcohol and benzodiazepines) can be deadly for some patients if no medical intervention occurs. As a clinical mental health counselor with my specialized addiction knowledge, I could alert the medical staff if withdrawal may be a concern in order for an appropriate withdrawal protocol to be started. Understanding patients' use patterns also would help me identify patients with whom I would be able to talk and offer a brief counseling intervention. This intervention would be a chance for the patient and myself to explore how the patient's use might be causing harm and to explore the reduction of risky use patterns. Being clear on my role was important, and this clarity regarding the specifics of my role was an important discussion I often had with supervisees who were training on our team.

Administrative Roles in Integrated Systems of Care

Administrative supervision, and thus the administrative roles of a clinical mental health counselor, is concerned with the general work functioning of the clinical mental health counselor as an employee of the system (Tromski-Klingshirn, 2007). Examples of administrative roles include completing paperwork (in addition to regular progress note documentation), marketing and recruitment, and research activities. Counselors who do not have an awareness of some of these potential roles may feel disillusioned once they enter the world of work. Disillusionment may occur when beginning counselors, who initially chose the counseling profession to have contact with clients, recognize that the totality of the job of a clinical mental health counselor also includes a significant amount of time not in direct contact with the clients they set out to serve. However, all counselors need to recognize how important these other activities are in ultimate service to the clients they are passionate about helping.

Documentation

Chapter 7 of this text explored record keeping and documentation in depth. Here, we discuss some of the nuances of documentation as it relates to clinical mental health counselors working in integrated systems of care. For many counselors, one big change has been the rise in electronic health records (EHRs). Such records also are referred to as electronic medical records (EMRs). There has been rapid adoption of EHRs programs, particularly by hospital systems in the United States that received financial incentives from Medicare and Medicaid for adoption (Adler-Milstein et al., 2017). Ethically, counselors must keep records and documentation of the clinical services that they provide to clients, and they must ensure that these records are confidential and are accessible only by authorized users (ACA, 2014; Section B.6).

Clinical mental health counselors need to be familiar with privacy laws at both the national and state levels. Knowledge of the Health Insurance Portability and Privacy Act (HIPAA) and the Health Information Technology for Economic and Clinical Health Act (HITECH) is crucial. In addition, those clinical mental health counselors who also are providing substance use disorder services need to be familiar with Title 42 of the Code of Federal Regulations Part 2, which regulates the confidentiality of the records of those clients being treated for substance use disorders. These regulations are important for clinical mental health counselors to consider when completing documentation using an integrated EHR system, specifically when considering who has access to view documentation once it has been entered into the system. In large healthcare systems, EHRs are effective in assisting various healthcare providers on a treatment team to communicate with one another about patients in a timely manner. However, in large systems this intentionally designed ease of communication also means that many people potentially can view any information that is entered for a patient, perhaps even one whom they are not treating. Clinical mental health counselors need to ask about what protections are enabled in the software system to limit who views the information they input in order to protect the patient's right to confidentiality. For example, in one hospital system where I worked, there were extra steps enabled for any patient who was on the psychiatry service. Because psychiatric records were specially protected, an EHRs user would have to verify their identity in order to access those specific patient records. Ethical practice of a clinical mental health counselor would include asking the employer about specific questions regarding access to client records, including electronically stored records.

Marketing and Recruitment

A vital component to being able to practice as a clinical mental health counselor in a clinical employment setting is that there are clients to counsel! In order to interest clients in services, marketing and recruitment efforts need to be completed, often by everyone who works in the system. Marketing efforts can be simple, such as wearing shirts or other "swag" items with the business logo on them in order to increase the system's visibility, or it might involve a more complex role, such as managing a social media platform for the system. The most recent ethical code from ACA (2014) included a new section helping to advise counselors on these roles, Section H: Distance Counseling, Technology, and Social Media. While there are many benefits to social media, there are also potential ethical issues, of which clinical mental health counselors need to be aware.

Social media is of particular interest to clinical mental health counselors, who need to think thoroughly through the implications of having an online presence. The ACA (2014) *Code of Ethics* requires that counselors include information about their use of social media as part of the informed consent process with clients. While working in a larger system of care, this informed consent regarding social media may feel as though it is not the clinical mental health counselor's responsibility, as a clinical mental health counselor may be only one of hundreds of employees. However, confidentiality is the responsibility of all people in all parts of the system and can be jeopardized in an instant. Case Illustration 10.3 highlights a risk to confidentiality that can occur through a business social media account. Jessica, a clinical mental health counselor, is highlighted in an employee spotlight and a former client posts a public comment on the post.

CASE ILLUSTRATION 10.3

THE CASE OF JESSICA: SOCIAL MEDIA RISKS

Jessica is a clinical mental health counselor who is employed in a local hospital. Jessica works as a Behavioral Health Consultant, offering brief counseling services throughout the hospital system, as requested by the medical staff. One day she may be providing crisis intervention services in the emergency department. The next day she may be providing grief counseling to a family who lost their grandmother to a long battle with cancer. The marketing unit of the hospital has asked Jessica if it could do a provider spotlight on their Facebook page. Jessica is excited about the idea of highlighting her work to help to advocate for her profession. The marketing department requests a biography, a statement from Jessica about her role, and a professional headshot. The spotlight is posted on the social media accounts for the hospital. There are many comments from the public, such as, "This is a great service! Good to know for the future." However, one comment in particular catches Jessica's attention. The comment is from a user named "Nadia Smith" and states, "Hi Jessica! It is so good to see how great you are doing! I appreciate all you did for me and my family while I was in the Emergency Room a few weeks ago." Not only does a digital connection now exist between Jessica and Nadia (a former client) but it is unknown whether Nadia was aware of this risk to her confidentiality. Nadia has now made a public comment that acknowledges that she and her family were the recipients of counseling services. What is not known is if Nadia had been aware of how public this comment was, and if she had considered the ramifications of telling a great number of people about her use of counseling services. Nadia may not have thought about the unfortunate judgment or stigma that she may be exposed to regarding her disclosure. It is the duty of counselors to educate their clients about these risks (Natwick, 2017).

The ACA (2014) Code of Ethics further outlines ethical practices for advertising and soliciting clients. Joy Natwick (2017) discusses the ethical implications of online reviews and testimonials, which are often a part of a business marketing strategy. According to Natwick (2017), "The ethics code states that counselors do not solicit testimonials; if a client wants to give a testimonial, counselors should do their best to educate the client on the risks and benefits of doing so" (p. 22). While working in an integrated system of care, clinical mental health counselors may find the importance of educating the marketing professionals about the ethical code to highlight where they may be limited in their roles.

Research

The CACREP (2016) standards require that clinical mental health counselors participate in education on research and program evaluation as a part of their core educational experience. Having this training affords clinical mental health counselors the ability to be able to take on an important role in clinical settings. In recent years, there has been a push to train clinical mental health counselors in evidence-based practices (EBPs) and implement these services in large systems of care (Kim et al., 2018). While clinical mental health counselors certainly can be the ones to be trained and deliver EBPs, they also may be called upon to lead, or assist with, initiatives to evaluate the implementation of the practice in their organization. Duties that might be included in program implementation include choosing psychometrically sound measurement instruments for the variables under evaluation, inputting data into a statistical program, data analysis, report writing, and presenting the findings to key stakeholders of the organization. While there is a push for EBPs, not all research or program evaluation is focused on them. Clinical mental health counselors can also use their research knowledge and skills in other ways, including adopting measurements to study outcomes of their clients to understand the efficacy of their clinical practice. As with all practices, it is crucial for counselors to review the ethics of conducting research and program evaluation.

The administrative duties covered here are not all of the options available, as every job is unique. A large role that clinical mental health counselors often are asked to take on, perhaps after a few years, is that of supervision, both clinical and administrative. Chapter 13 explores supervision in more detail, and we encourage all students to research their particular state's requirements for becoming a certified/licensed supervisor. Regarding roles and function in general, it is important that clinical mental health counselors understand that they may be asked to do more than provide counseling and write case notes. Understanding the variations in and the complexities of the field of clinical mental health counseling may be the secret to a successful career as a clinical mental health counselor.

Clinical Tensions

The roles and functions of clinical mental health counselors in integrated systems of care are often sources of clinical tensions for individuals who find themselves navigating these spaces. The reader already has been exposed to some of the specific sources of tension related to specific roles, such as with assessments and diagnosis in Chapter 4. The focus here is on the tensions related to working in a complex system.

One tension experienced by clinical mental health counselors employed in complex systems of care may relate to the protection of client data. This tension may stem from working with collaborative teams or as a result of the rise in EHR systems. The promise of and legal protection regarding confidentiality is foundational to our work, and with it we gain the trust of our clients. When working in integrative treatment teams, other professionals may be familiar with privacy; however, they often are not informed about the limits to confidentiality. Clinical mental health counselors in such settings are encouraged to have transparent conversations with their colleagues about the information that they will be sharing, as well as the information that they will not be sharing. It also is important that information regarding what materials will be shared by clinical mental health counselors and with whom they will be shared is provided to clients within the informed-consent process.

Another way in which counselors may experience tension related to confidential data is due to the rise in EHR systems. The use of integrated EHRs in the sharing of information can be a double-edged sword. On one hand, the sharing of information can allow medical providers to provide more efficient medical care if they are informed about any mental health needs. However, at the same time, we must ask ourselves about the best way to inform other providers of clients' mental health issues. Integrated treatment does not solely need to rely on EHR systems to convey information. There are other ways to collaborate and provide integrated treatment, such as through collaborative meetings. Not many professionals are eagerly awaiting another meeting invitation, but if the end result is more efficient treatment, there is likely to be buy-in from the key stakeholders of client care. Having an in-person meeting would allow clinical mental health counselors to provide insight into mental health issues that may hinder overall treatment while also allowing clinical mental health counselors to protect client data. The EHR systems may be an appropriate place to document patient vital signs (e.g., heart rate, blood pressure, weight) and records from medical visits, including medical illness diagnoses, but it might not be the appropriate place to have clinical mental health counseling progress notes documented. All information we gather in client contacts is not relevant to the work medical providers do, and it is our responsibility to be thoughtful and intentional with the information that we share in collaborative treatment teams.

Clinical mental health counselors in integrated systems of care may experience a conflict between balancing their own self-care and meeting the productivity standards required of the position. Counselors of all specialties need to take active steps to foster their well-being. Research regarding the burnout experiences of counselors has identified multiple predictors of emotional exhaustion. Luther et al. (2017) found that working overtime was associated with greater emotional exhaustion, lower personal accomplishment, greater perceived work conflicts, and lower job satisfaction. Kim et al. (2018) also found that weekly hours of total work and caseload were associated with increased reports of emotional exhaustion. Finally, Green, Albanese, Shapiro, and Aarons (2014) found that clinicians need to have a clear idea of their specific job responsibilities, as role conflict (prioritizing administrative duties over client concerns) and role overload (too many tasks with too little time) were strongly associated with emotional exhaustion for the participants in their study.

As clinical mental health counselors, we need to take proactive steps to prevent burnout, such as having transparent conversations with our clinical and administrative supervisors about our roles and speaking up when we are feeling overwhelmed. For those counselors still in training, it is crucial that a plan for self-care is developed prior to when it is needed. In a recent episode of the Thoughtful Counselor podcast (Shook, 2018), Jessica Smith discussed her experience with burnout. She recounts a conversation that she once had with someone who said, "Having a supervisor say to me 'How do you do self-care?' And in that moment you are doing all you can to survive. So, to add one more thing when you're struggling to get your notes done, when you're struggling to leave on time …" (Shook, 2018, pp. 39:34). Unfortunately, many of us do not plan for burnout, we think we are immune to this, and yet, many of us end up finding ourselves in this very position. Chapter 14 explores self-care and professional development to help the reader consider these plans for caring for oneself. I have learned to have open and honest conversations with my clinical and administrative supervisors during these times. And finally, it is essential to understand that, although we have been trained for multiple roles and functions, it does not have to be our responsibility to perform them all. One great perk of working within a larger system of care is that we have a team with whom to collaborate.

In general, many clinical mental health counselors may experience the clinical tensions associated with conflicts that arise within their job roles and functions. The expectations from the administrators of the system may differ from the expectations of the clinical mental health counselors. It is important to acknowledge professional differences and to provide necessary advocacy related to our profession and what is common among clinical mental health counselors.

CONCLUSION

While this chapter provided an overview of the common roles and functions expected of a clinical mental health counselor, I have found, through my own clinical experience and as a clinical supervisor and educator, that each and every counselor has to learn his or her own process for juggling all of the roles that are expected of clinical mental health counselors. Through our training, we are prepared to work comprehensively in many different roles as clinical mental health counselors. The options are expanding as our work settings continue to integrate within larger systems of care in the coming years.

RESOURCES

Cohen, D. J., Davis, M. M., Hall, J. D., Gilchrist, E. C., & Miller, B. F. (2015). *A guidebook of professional practices for behavioral health and primary care integration: Observations from exemplary sites.* Rockville, MD: Department of Health and Human Services Agency for Healthcare Research and Quality. Retrieved from https://integrationacademy.ahrq.gov/sites/default/files/AHRQ_AcademyGuidebook.pdf

Department of Health and Human Services. (2018). *Information related to mental and behavioral health, including opioid overdose.* Retrieved from https://www.hhs.gov/hipaa/for-individuals/mental-health/index.html

Department of Health and Human Services Office of the National Coordinator for Health Information Technology. (n.d.). *Understanding the value of health IT: Educational module for behavioral health providers.* Retrieved from https://www.healthit.gov/sites/default/files/playbook/pdf/educational-module-Behavioral-Health-Providers.pdf

Kottler, J. A. (2010). *On becoming a therapist* (4th ed.). San Francisco, CA: Jossey-Bass.

Matthew, D. B. (2015). *Overcoming barriers to collaboration among behavioral health and primary care providers.* Retrieved from https://www.pcpcc.org/sites/default/files/HIPAA%20Presentation%20-%20March%2027%202014%20-%20Updated.pdf

Pollak, J., Levy, S., & Breitholtz, T. (1999). Screening for medical and neurodevelopmental disorders for the professional counselor. *Journal of Counseling & Development, 77,* 350–358. doi:10.1002/j.1556-6676.1999.tb02459.x

The Thoughtful Counselor Podcast. Retrieved from https://thethoughtfulcounselor.com

Yalom, I. D. (2002). *The gift of therapy: An open letter to a new generation of therapists and their patients.* New York, NY: HarperCollins Publishers.

REFERENCES

Adler-Milstein, J., Holmgren, A. J., Kralovec, P., Worzala, C., Searcy, T., & Patel, V. (2017). Electronic health record adoption in U.S. hospitals: The emergence of a digital "advanced use" divide. *Journal of the American Medical Association, 24*(6), 1142–1148. doi:10.1093/jamia/ocx080

American Counseling Association. (2014). *2014 ACA code of ethics.* Alexandria, VA: Author.

American Mental Health Counselors Association. (2015). *AMHCA code of ethics.* Alexandria, VA: Author.

American Mental Health Counselors Association. (2017a). *AMHCA standards for the practice of clinical mental health counseling.* Alexandria, VA: Author.

American Mental Health Counselors Association. (2017b). *Facts about clinical mental health counselors.* Retrieved from https://amhca.site-ym.com/page/facts

Babor, T. F., Higgins-Biddle, J. C., Saunders, J. B., & Monteiro, M. G. (2001). *The alcohol use disorders identification test: Guidelines for use in primary care* (2nd ed.). Geneva, Switzerland: World Health Organization.

Beck, A. T., & Steer, R. A. (1993). *Beck Anxiety Inventory manual.* San Antonio, TX: Psychological Corporation.

Beck, A. T., Steer, R. A., & Brown, G. K. (1996). *Manual for Beck Depression Inventory II (BDI-II).* San Antonio, TX: Psychology Corporation.

Council for Accreditation of Counseling and Related Educational Programs. (2016). *2016 CACREP standards.* Retrieved from http://www.cacrep.org/wp-content/uploads/2018/05/2016-Standards-with-Glossary-5.3.2018.pdf

Dougherty, A. M. (2009). *Psychological consultation and collaboration in school and community settings* (5th ed.). Belmont, CA: Brooks/Cole Cengage Learning.

Green, A. E., Albanese, B. J., Shapiro, N. M., & Aarons, G. A. (2014). The roles of individual and organizational factors in burnout among community-mental health service providers. *Psychological Services, 11*(1), 41–49. doi:10.1037/a0035299

Hirschfield, R. M. A., Williams, J. B. W., Spitzer, R. L., Calabrese, J. R., Flynn, L., Keck, P. E., … Zajecka, J. (2000). Development and validation of a screening instrument for bipolar spectrum disorder: The Mood Disorder Questionnaire. *American Journal of Psychiatry, 157,* 1873–1875. doi:10.1176/appi.ajp.157.11.1873

Kim, J. J., Brookman-Frazee, L., Gellatly, R., Stadnick, N., Barnett, M. L., & Lau, A. S. (2018). Predictors of burnout among community therapists in a sustainment phase of a system-driven implementation of multiple evidence-based practices in children's mental health. *Professional Psychology: Research and Practice, 49*(2), 132–141. doi:10.1037/pro0000182

Luther, L., Gearhart, T., Fukul, S., Morse, G., Rollins, A. L., & Salyers, M. P. (2017). Working overtime in community mental health: Associations with clinician burnout and perceived quality of care. *Psychiatric Rehabilitation Journal, 40*(2), 252–259. doi:10/1037/prj0000234

Montgomery, E. C., Kunik, M. E., Wilson, N., Stanley, M. A., & Weiss, B. (2010). Can paraprofessionals deliver cognitive-behavior therapy to treat anxiety and depressive symptoms? *Bulletin of the Menninger Clinic, 74*(1), 45–62. doi:10.1521/bumc.2010.74.1.45

Natwick, J. (2017). Boon or bother? Social media marketing and ethics. *Counseling Today.* Retrieved from https://www.counseling.org/docs/default-source/ethics/ethics-columns/ethics_february-2017--social-media-marketing.pdf?sfvrsn=1225522c_6

Pollak, J., Levy, S., & Breitholtz, T. (1999). Screening for medical and neurodevelopmental disorders for the professional counselor. *Journal of Counseling & Development, 77,* 350–358. doi:10.1002/j.1556-6676.1999.tb02459.x

Posner, K., Brown, G. K., Stanley, B., Brent, D. A., Yershova, K. V., Oquendo, M. A., … Mann, J. J. (2011). The Columbia-Suicide Severity Rating Scale: Initial validity and internal consistency findings from three multisite studies with adolescents and adults. *American Journal of Psychiatry, 168,* 1266–1277. doi:10.1176/appi.ajp.2011.10111704

Prins, A., Ouimette, P., Kimerling, R., Cameron, R. P., Hugelshofer, D. S., Shaw-Hegwer, J., … Sheikh, J. I. (2003). The primary care PTSD screen (PC-PTSD): Development and operating characteristics. *Primary Care Psychiatry, 9,* 9–14. doi:10.1185/135525703125002360

Shook, M. (Producer). (2018, June 20). *Self-care, burnout, and the way forward: One counselor's inspiring story with Jessica Smith* [Audio podcast]. Retrieved from https://thethoughtfulcounselor.com

Skinner, H. A. (1982). *Drug use questionnaire (DAST-10).* Toronto, ON: Centre for Addiction and Mental Health.

Tromski-Klingshirn, D. (2007). Should the clinical supervisor be the administrative supervisor? *The Clinical Supervisor, 25*(1–2), 53–67. doi:10.1300/J001v25n01_05

West, J. D., Hosie, T. W., & Mackey, J. A. (1987). Employment and roles of counselors in mental health agencies. *Journal of Counseling & Development, 66*(3), 135–138. doi:10.1002/j.1556-6676.1987.tb00818.x

CHAPTER 11

CONTEXTS OF CULTURAL AND SYSTEMIC INFLUENCE

CARLOS P. ZALAQUETT | LATOYA HAYNES-THOBY

This chapter addresses system views, integrated care, barriers to treatment, multicultural issues, and the use of multicultural and social justice skills in the provision of clinical mental health counseling. Specific topics include a discussion of systems, holistic care, barriers to healthcare, and culturally competent counselors. The chapter further explores the connections between culturally competent care and the potential role for clinical mental health counselors in ascertaining the systemic need for new agency- and integrated healthcare-based programs. The student is introduced to basic tenets of system worldviews, developing integrated new programs aimed at meeting the clinical mental health needs of diverse and varied clients, and the application of multicultural and social justice skills in clinical mental health counseling. The following Council for Accreditation of Counseling and Related Educational Programs (CACREP) standards are addressed in this chapter:
   CACREP 2016:
      2F1.b, 2F2.c, 2F2.e, 2F2.h, 5C2.j
   CACREP 2009:
      2G1.i, 2G2.a, 2G2.b, 2G2.c, 2G2.d, 2G2.e, 2G5.e

LEARNING OBJECTIVES

After reviewing this chapter, the reader should be able to:

1. Define and present the basic tenets of cultural systems.

2. Describe the systems worldview applied to clinical mental health counseling.

3. Identify the multiple roles of counselors in mental health systems.

4. Outline the rationale for integrated systems of care.

5. Discuss the barriers to mental healthcare, including racism and other types of discrimination.

6. Denote strategies for removing barriers and increasing access to mental healthcare.

7. Stress the importance of acquiring multicultural counseling competencies and implementing cultural adaptations to counseling.

▥ INTRODUCTION TO SYSTEMS OF SOCIOCULTURAL INFLUENCE AND MENTAL HEALTH DISPARITIES

Clinical mental health counselors and their clients are members of various sociocultural systems and subsystems within their societal contexts. These systems and subsystems include, but are not limited to, family, workplace, community, and society. These influential systems, organized along social and cultural values, may be very useful for the client, as they offer care, support, and resources. On the other hand, some of these systems may not be as useful, because they may serve as barriers or obstacles to the client's progress. In fact, some systems may work to advance the majority of its members but may oppress those who are in the minority.

The increasing diversification of the United States (U.S. Census Bureau, 2011), with its significant growth in racial and ethnic minority groups, provides a good example of the sociocultural systems' effect. This significant diversification, which is expected to grow larger over the next 40 years (Vespa, Armstrong, & Medina, 2018), has created persistent disparities in the mental health status and mental healthcare of clients from minority groups (National Institute of Mental Health [NIMH], 2019). Similar disparities have been reported previously for individuals living in poverty and in rural areas. Compared with the majority population, access and quality of care of minority and low income groups are less than optimal (Agency for Healthcare Research and Quality [AHRQ], 2018). Members of racial and ethnic minority groups in the United States are less likely to have access to mental health services, less likely to use community mental health services, more likely to use inpatient hospitalization and emergency departments, and more likely to receive lower quality care (NIMH, 2019).

Majority and minority groups represent the rich diversity tapestry of the United States. Effective clinical mental health counselors value diversity and are fully aware of the persistent disparities observed in mental health. These clinical mental health counselors use a sociocultural approach in their work with their clients. They focus on the individual clients and the sociocultural systems in which the clients are situated. They treat both as an entire entity, as a *whole*, to achieve desired changes. They believe that if change can happen and remain over time, the whole needs to be the focus of treatment (Ivey, Ivey, & Zalaquett, 2018; Ratts, Singh, Nassar-McMillan, Butler, & McCullough, 2015; Zalaquett, Ivey, & Ivey, 2019).

Clinical mental health counselors provide culturally sensitive services. As stated in the American Mental Health Counseling Association *Code of Ethics* (C.1.g), counselors "recognize the important need to be competent in regard to cultural diversity and are sensitive to the diversity of varying populations as well as to changes in cultural expectations and values over time" (2015, p. 15).

This chapter discusses the importance of systems and culture in professional work with clients. Counselors and clients are immersed in a social and cultural context and embedded in multiple systems and subsystems, such as family, workplace, community, and society. Each of these systems significantly influence the client in positive or negative ways. Integrated and culturally sensitive care offers a way to service clients in a holistic and cultural way. Examples of culturally integrated systems of care are reviewed and potential access, barriers, discrimination, and racism are noted. Ways to remove barriers and other limitations are discussed. Use of multicultural and social justice skills in the work with clients completes the chapter.

THE SOCIOCULTURAL SYSTEMS WORLDVIEW

The different systems and subsystems involving clients' lives are embedded in and represent networks of mutually interdependent elements that continually influence one another. To understand a client's situation fully, clinical mental health counselors apply a holistic view to uncover the role and contribution of the multiple components of the client's issues (Zalaquett et al., 2019). One of the systems of which most clients are a part is the family, and this unit demonstrates the importance of considering cultural systems in counseling clients. A family is a network of individuals who interact, support, and influence one another in an ongoing fashion. Sometimes this influence is positive, like in families that support the client's choice of career; sometimes this influence is negative, like in families that oppose the client's career choice. The family relationship may be enhanced in the first case but may be strained in the latter. In both cases, emotions such as love and sense of belonging can be affected, but the effect would be positive in one case and negative in the other.

Because the family members are interconnected, the behavior of each member is shaped by the rest of the family. Positive and negative comments from family members promote growth and change in the family as a whole. When helping clients make a career choice, exploring family members' views of career options may help understand potential support or rejection. Clinical mental health counselors can use this information to assist clients to prepare to respond to family reactions.

Clinical mental health counselors benefit from investigating clients' issues from a systems perspective, because every part of the system is interconnected. A change in any component of a system can create a ripple effect in other parts of the system; those effects, in turn, can affect everything else, including the client. Furthermore, the clients and their contexts are essential for successful counseling change to be sustainable over time.

TIP FROM THE FIELD 11.1

A WORD OF CAUTION ON OVERLOOKING EXTERNAL FACTOR

In spite of the focus on the sociocultural systems view and the emphasis on cultural competence, an important clinical tension affecting counselors and clients still remains. Clinical mental health counselors focus mostly on the client's internal attributes, traits, and characteristics to explain the cause of their mental disorders and stress reactions, and overlook potential systemic influences. Based on such individualistic conceptualization, clinical mental health counselors and students-in-training tend to provide only individual treatments.

Focusing only on the client's internal characteristics places the onus of responsibility for their mental health concerns on the client and discounts the influence of external factors. Blaming the client and overlooking contextual factors may prevent an effective resolution of the client's issues.

Many theories of counseling ascribe the causes of clients' issues to internal or intrapsychic structures or functions (Ratts & Greenleaf, 2018; Zalaquett et al., 2019). Such conceptualizations lead clinical mental health counselors and students-in-training to provide only individual treatments. Moreover, clients also tend to look for individual counseling to address their anxiety, depression, or other mental health concerns. However, each of the clients is always influenced by one or more of the various cultural systems in which they are engaged. An individual also may be influenced by several intersecting systems (Carbado, Crenshaw, Mays, & Tomlinson, 2013). It is important to know and understand those systems, in order to use them to advance client progress. Each of those systems may offer resources for client progress. Some clients may not be aware of the resources available to them, and the clinical mental health counselor's task will be to increase clients' ways to access those resources. Furthermore, some of those systems may impose barriers to client progress. These barriers may have multicultural and social justice aspects, and counselors may need to focus on removing or navigating such barriers as a part of their interventions. Many of the competencies presented in Chapter 9 of this textbook can help counselors achieve this goal at a systems level, using a systems worldview.

■ THE SYSTEMS WORLDVIEW APPLIED TO CLINICAL MENTAL HEALTH COUNSELING

Counselors who really want to understand depression, anxiety, stress, trauma, or any mental disorder need to look at the client and his or her surrounding context using a sociocultural systems or ecological view. Through this holistic view, counselors unveil the effects these constituents have on the client's reported concerns.

Of course, counselors can begin from the analysis of a specific component of a system, that is, the client, but to understand a client's issues fully, they need to use a holistic view. The focus on the interconnectivity and mutual influencing of sociocultural systems is the hallmark of the ecological approach. Ecological models that are applied to human systems offer a specific framework to understand the interconnections between clients and their multiple systems (McMahon, Mason, Daluga-Guenther, & Ruiz, 2014). Models such as Bronfenbrenner's bioecological model of human development (1981), discussed briefly in Chapter 1, provide counselors with a framework to understand the interconnections between humans and their multiple sociocultural contexts (Conyne & Cook, 2004).

Clinical mental health counselors who use a sociocultural system worldview do not reject traditional individual counseling methods. They expand individual counseling by infusing a sociocultural system or ecological worldview. This infusion allows clinical mental health counselors to expand the ways that traditional theories are applied in their work (Cho, Crenshaw, & McCall, 2013). This worldview includes psychosocial assessments and interventions that are applicable across sociocultural systems, including peer groups, families, work environments, institutions, and communities. As a result, clinical mental health counselors are better equipped to conceptualize a client's underlying concerns within the context of multiple potentially oppressive or empowering systems that influence their presenting concerns. Clinical mental health counselors study the complexities of the person–environment relationships in order to understand clients' challenges or concerns and to develop intervention strategies for increasing the positive fit between clients and their environments.

Case Illustration 11.1 demonstrates the application of the bioecological model to client issues. In this case, the focus is on the extended system and how it affects a couple's (the client) marital relationship.

CASE ILLUSTRATION 11.1

EXTERNAL SYSTEM'S EFFECTS ON A MARRIAGE: THE HUSBAND AT HIS JOB

Even though the wife is never physically at the husband's workplace, what happens there influences the wife's life and her relationship with her husband. For example, the husband's job security affects the way the couple relates. If the husband gets a promotion at work, the wife can buy needed household items. If the husband loses his job, the couple could lose the security of their home.

Counselors work to gain an ecological empathy toward understanding the client holistically and from within the client's current environment or ecological niche. Equipped with this information, counselors can offer contextualized forms of help (Conyne & Cook, 2004). A systems-minded counselor would assess the quality of the husband's job to determine how it affects the couple's relationship.

Successful counseling is accomplished by helping clients improve the quality of their lives through interventions directed at both the personal and cultural environmental systems (Cook & Coaston, 2012; Zalaquett et al., 2019). Clinical mental health counselors can offer interventions such as learning new skills, and using available resources to navigate or overcome oppressive systems that have an impact on a client's daily functioning. Furthermore, counselors can encourage advocacy skills by learning to assist their clients in engaging in effective ways to affect their systems and to accomplish their desired changes.

The Multiple Roles of Counselors in Mental Health Systems

Equipped with a systems worldview, mental health counselors can focus on individual client issues, along with the systems in which the client is embedded (Zalaquett et al., 2019). Clinical mental health counselors are further able to support clients to explore, acknowledge, or affirm their experiences through the multiple lenses by which their intersecting identities may be informed. As a result, clinical mental health counselors are able to apply theory in ways that are informed by knowledge of the ways in which systems might intersect for their clients. Using the systems worldview, counselors integrate the client, family, groups, neighborhood, community, cultural identification, intersecting identities, and society into the assessment of the client's presenting concern and the organization of a treatment plan. The treatment plan may include interventions to affect the larger systems surrounding the client. For example, a counselor and a female client may discuss self-advocacy skills to alter the policies used in her workplace, because they limit women's promotion.

Counselor and client work collaboratively to establish treatment goals and to determine one or more modalities of intervention. Intervention modalities include individual, group, and family counseling as well as consultation and advocacy.

▐ INTEGRATED SYSTEMS OF CARE

An integrated system of care represents another application of the system worldview to mental health. Traditional individualistic approaches often have offered fragmented treatments to clients affected with physical illnesses and mental or substance use disorders. This dichotomy represents an old tension in the field, because the lack of a systemic view can produce very negative consequences. For example, clients who are treated by using the traditional model may suffer more, and ultimately die earlier than others, because of untreated and preventable physical illnesses, such as hypertension, diabetes, or obesity. On the other hand, clients affected by physical illnesses may suffer from inadequate physical activity, poor nutrition, substance use, and mental disorders (Substance Abuse and Mental Health Services Administration [SAMHSA], 2018b). The World Health Organization (WHO, 2018) reports that people with severe mental disorders such as bipolar disorder and schizophrenia generally die 10 to 20 years earlier than the general population. The majority of these premature deaths are due to physical health conditions. While these issues are able to be treated by primary medical providers, they often are overlooked, especially for individuals whose identities are outside of the dominant culture, including, but not limited to women, people of color, individuals who are not heterosexual, individuals from lower socioeconomic status groups, and immigrants. In addition to individual client suffering, a client's individual disadvantages cyclically impact larger systems in a myriad of ways, including economic loss.

The lost economic output caused by untreated mental disorders produces damaging consequences worldwide. The result of diminished productivity at work, reduced rates of labor participation, foregone tax contributions, and increased welfare costs amounts to more than 10 billion days of lost work annually; this is equivalent to $1 trillion per year (Chisholm et al., 2016). Box 11.1 reports the prevalence of mental illnesses in the United States.

BOX 11.1   PREVALENCE OF MENTAL ILLNESS IN THE UNITED STATES

Any mental illness (AMI) is defined as a mental, behavioral, or emotional disorder. AMI can vary in impact, ranging from no impairment to mild, moderate, and even severe impairment. The prevalence of AMI is noteworthy:

- In 2016, there were an estimated 44.7 million adults aged 18 or older in the United States with AMI. This number represented 18.3% of all the U.S. adults.

- The prevalence of AMI was higher among women (21.7%) than men (14.5%).

- Young adults aged 18 to 25 years had the highest prevalence of AMI (22.1%) compared to adults aged 26 to 49 years (21.1%) and aged 50 and older (14.5%).

- The prevalence of AMI was highest among the adults reporting two or more races (26.5%), followed by the American Indian/Alaska Native group (22.8%). The prevalence of AMI was lowest among the Asian group (12.1%).

Prevalence of AMI among adolescents (13–18 years old):

- An estimated 49.5% of adolescents had AMI.

- An estimated 22.2% had severe impairment.

SOURCE: National Institute of Mental Health. (2017). Retrieved from https://www.nimh.nih.gov/health/statistics/mental-illness.shtml

Unfortunately, access to comprehensive health services is limited for the majority of people with severe mental disorders in the United States and the world. Historical inequities deny marginalized populations the same access to quality healthcare as majority populations (NIMH, 2019). To help address this inequity, WHO has released evidence-based guidelines on the management of physical conditions in adults with severe mental disorders (see the Resources section at the end of this chapter).

Today, the healthcare systems in the United States and around the world promote the adoption of integrated systems of care. An integrated system of care embraces a holistic view that integrates physical and mental health and uses a systems worldview in the assessment and treatment of clients. These systems have the potential to redress the historical inequalities that have existed in healthcare. Most of these integrated healthcare systems offer a welcoming environment, staff, and services for marginalized clients.

A current trend within the integrated care movement is the integration of mental health counselors into healthcare systems. The integration of counselors into the primary care sector attends to the mental health issues experienced by their regular patients. Several physicians, hospitals, and health insurance systems are combining routine screening of patients for depression, anxiety, and other mental disorders, and offering immediate intervention by mental health professionals. The CODAC system, described in the following section, has several mental health counselors employed in their team of providers.

Combining behavioral healthcare and primary healthcare services creates opportunities to reverse the fate of clients with co-occurring medical and mental health conditions, a concept termed *comorbid conditions*. The integration of clinical mental health counselors in primary care creates a crucial response to the need to address patients experiencing comorbid conditions, using a culturally sensitive approach.

■ CODAC BEHAVIORAL HEALTH SERVICE EXEMPLIFIES A CULTURALLY INTEGRATED CARE

The following example illustrates a successful integration of behavioral healthcare and primary healthcare systems. CODAC Behavioral Health Services is a provider of substance abuse, mental health, and primary care services to more than 12,000 people per year while offering prevention services to another 10,000 members of the Tucson community. But such care was not always the case.

CODAC used a SAMHSA Primary and Behavioral Health Care Integration (PBHCI) grant, received in 2009, to partner with the El Rio Santa Cruz Neighborhood Health Center. Based on their needs assessment, they created a new structure and culture to integrate both organizations. During the first months of the project, they modified their shared building layout to accommodate for the flow of primary and behavioral health services. Monthly meetings of a steering committee followed to produce and implement a plan for the provision of integrated services, which was the ultimate goal of this project.

In addition to the definition of services and steps for implementation, the plan included ways to make the integrated services sustainable. Part of the first steps to accomplish this goal was to underscore that everybody in their shared building was working on the same team. Small group conversations got professionals talking and relating to one another. Weekly team meetings, weekly full-staff meetings, and monthly case review meetings between the health and behavioral teams were used to get everyone involved with a client to discuss that case and care practices. They did this to ensure that every member of the care team would recognize that they are valued and responsible members of the whole team, and not separate providers of a particular client. The traditional and separate delivery system was replaced, de facto, by all providers, and it involved talking about cases together. This was a real demonstration of integrated, holistic care.

The CODAC and El Rio team includes 12 full-time employees, dedicated to the provision of integrated and holistic health services. Nurses, medical assistants, and behavioral health professionals work with a clinical manager and an office specialist to combine their expertise, in the best ways possible, to serve the 1,200 clients enrolled in their system.

Of course, the integrated care system faces some challenges. All agencies need to maintain their respective licenses. Collection and sharing of client records and data need to operate smoothly between both agencies. Continuing education is mandated to ensure that everybody buys into the model and understands that each worker is a part of the whole team. The following three elements are important to ensure the sustainability of the culturally integrated model of care:

1. The right people: All staff, from the front office to the behavioral specialists, need to understand the importance of integrated services and why the agency provides these services.

2. The right training: The organization needs to provide staff with the tools and knowledge to work within an integrated health program.

3. The right culture: An agency-wide culture shift is necessary to make these changes. Traditional treatment views alone can damage integration. All the agency members understand what they are doing, where they are going, and why.

Today, CODAC has 11 service locations and over 450 staff and volunteers, serving more than 15,000 individuals and families a year. A team of experts, including primary care providers, psychiatrists, nurses, medical assistants, mental health counselors, addiction counselors, case managers, and peer support specialists work as one team at each location. They focus on physical and mental health, to give their clients a holistic healthcare service.

TIP FROM THE FIELD 11.2

SAMHSA'S ADVICE TO THE INTEGRATION OF PRIMARY AND BEHAVIORAL HEALTHCARE SYSTEMS

Winners of PBHCI grants, Cobb–Douglas Community Service Boards, GA; The Providence Center, RI; Asian Community Mental Health Services, CA; and Alaska Island Community Services, offer the following tips for making integration work (SAMHSA, 2018a, "Quick tips: 6 keys to integration success," para. 1–7).

- *Hire Peers*: Integrated programs need a peer workforce in both the whole health and the wellness sides of the clinic. There are a lot of reasons an individual might lose hope and not return for treatment. A peer can instill hope, empower clients, and form a connection that supports ongoing access to services.

- *Get Organizational Buy-In:* Integrated care needs top-down buy-in, but it also needs to have bottom-up buy-in. If the front desk staff doesn't know what integrated care is, and a client asks a question about it, there could be confusion. It's important that everyone has a level of buy-in. Also, having a position that's dedicated to overseeing and managing the integrated care process of your organization is critical.

- *Address Cultural and Linguistic Competency:* Organizations need to meet clients where they are, whether that's through being able to communicate with them in a language they understand or through recognizing how their culture impacts their values and actions.

- *Co-locate for Better Communication and Better Care:* Embedding a health clinic within a behavioral health organization or having behavioral health staff work onsite at the health center offers clients a chance to walk in to the first appointment already feeling like they're understood. Co-location helps staff feel supported in managing complicated cases that otherwise might have posed some issues. For instance, a primary care doctor who doesn't know what psychiatric medication a client is on or what issues that might present can quickly consult with the appropriate behavioral health colleagues regarding the potential impact of those medications on the client's health.

- *Implement Health Information Technology:* Sharing data is absolutely critical for outcome management. Implementing shared health IT means updated release forms, behavioral health forms, and electronic health records. Right away that allows both partners to use each other's electronic health records to see anything they need about the client.

- *Make Wellness Fun, Accessible, and Social:* Get clients involved around wellness. Create a wellness advisory board made up of clients or engage clients to advise program development based on their interests and health goals. By ensuring that wellness programs meet the clients where they are—and with regard to their health needs—individuals are more likely to stay engaged and involved in wellness activities. A recent study found that individuals with severe mental illnesses and obesity who exercised in groups and participated in a group nutrition class for an 18-month period were able to lose weight and keep it off. (SAMHSA, 2018a, "Quick tips: 6 keys to integration success," para. 1–7)

BARRIERS TO MENTAL HEALTHCARE

Effective, integrated systems of care have the potential to produce positive benefits to clients, their families, and others in their surrounding and extended social contexts. Unfortunately, barriers that prevent clients from seeking treatment and barriers to having access to care systems still exist (NIMH, 2019). Approximately, 52% to 74% of people with mental disorders do not receive treatment in the United States and Europe each year. Low and middle income groups have limited access to quality care and receive less treatment (Clement et al., 2015; Kessler et al., 2005; Mojtabai et al., 2011; NIMH, 2019). In addition to the access barrier, which is created by the traditional model of services mentioned earlier, a lack of available health centers that are nearby and a lack of affordable insurance remain as obstacles to care.

The challenges inherent in navigating complex healthcare systems create additional obstacles. These obstacles include not knowing where to go for help, mistrust of health and mental healthcare providers, lack of health insurance, not knowing how to complete forms, and not understanding the language used in forms. Clients may get lost in these complex systems. A clinical mental health counselor's role may include helping clients to work with their healthcare systems. Additionally, clients may hold historical knowledge or collective distrust in current service provider models. Clinical mental health counselors working to respond holistically to clients' concerns should explore their intersecting identities in the context of their location within society, with an appreciation for their historical milieu.

Another obstacle to effective mental healthcare is the current tendency of clients to report their mental health concerns to their primary care physician. This tendency is making primary care settings the gateway to the behavioral health system. Unfortunately, primary care physicians and assistants are not always fully trained in diagnosing mental health disorders and providing appropriate treatments. Furthermore, primary care providers who are trained in the diagnosis of mental disorders do not always screen for mental disorders, negative lifestyle habits, or wellness activities.

Primary care systems and providers need support and resources to screen and treat individuals with behavioral and mental health issues. Therefore, integrating mental health, substance abuse, and primary care services represent an effective solution (SAMHSA, 2018b). SAMHSA defines integrated care as "the systematic coordination of general and behavioral healthcare" (SAMHSA, 2018b, "What is integrated care?," para. 3). Integrated systems of care offer a holistic approach to caring for clients. Investing in the current integration of mental health services can generate enormous returns in terms of improving clients' quality of life and well-being, reducing disability and premature death, and reversing historical inequalities of care. The priorities are well known and the needed projects and activities are clear and possible. Clinical mental health counselors have the responsibility to bring these possibilities to completion.

Reasons for Not Seeking Treatment and Client Dropout

In addition to the systemic barriers mentioned earlier, many clients do not seek treatment, and many who receive treatment drop out before completing treatment (Wang et al., 2007). An important step in reducing unmet needs for mental healthcare involves understanding the reasons why individuals with mental disorders either do not seek treatment or drop out of care. Among the reasons that prevent clients from seeking treatment are a fear of being labeled as abnormal, the feeling that seeking help takes too much time or is inconvenient, a lack of certainty about where to go for help, and a perceived lack of treatment effectiveness (Clements et al., 2018; Mojtabai et al., 2011).

Multiple studies have found that stigma is associated with mental disorders and often prevents clients from seeking and adhering to counseling treatment. Clients are afraid that the diagnostic label of a mental disorder would mark them for social rejection or discrimination. Such fear frequently is exacerbated by claims that conflate criminal activity or violence with mental disorders, as sometimes used in legal procedures and often reinforced by popular media (Levers, 2001).

While stigma is important, many studies show that disclosure and confidentiality concerns represent more prominent types of barriers among adults (Clements et al., 2015). Furthermore, a major national population study listed the wish to handle mental health concerns on one's own and the perception of a low need for care as the most important barriers among adults, while stigma and confidentiality were among the most important for adolescents (Mojtabai et al., 2011).

TIP FROM THE FIELD 11.3

BARRIERS FOR SEEKING MENTAL HEALTH TREATMENT

Reported reasons for not seeking treatment at any time in the past 12 months:

I. Perceived need:
    Low perceived need for treatment

II. Structural barriers among those with perceived need:
    Financial
    Lack of health insurance coverage
    Availability
    Transportation
    Inconvenience

III. Attitudinal/evaluative barriers among those with perceived need:
    Wanted to handle on own
    Perceived ineffectiveness of counseling
    Stigma
    Thought it would get better
    Reluctance to face issues
    Problem was not severe
    Unable to find a counselor with whom to feel comfortable
    Lack of knowledge of available counseling

Barriers for seeking mental health assistance among young people included stigma, confidentiality issues, lack of accessibility, self-reliance, low knowledge about mental health services, and fear or stress about the act of help seeking or the source of the help itself (Clements et al., 2015; Mojtabai et al., 2011).

▨ RACISM AND DISCRIMINATION BARRIERS

The persistence of racism over time and its strong association with population patterns of health, well-being, and health inequalities, described at the beginning of this chapter, is one of the greatest public mental health challenges of our time (Bastos, Arnois, & Yin, 2018). Empirical studies have shown, systematically, that multicultural variables such as race/ethnicity, disability status, sexual orientation, and gender underlie health inequities among different social groups.

From a sociocultural systems worldview, the negative health and psychosocial effects of institutionalized (macro-level) and interpersonal (micro-level) racism accumulate over the course of a person's life, as well as over generations. For example, at the micro level, African Americans receive significantly lower quality healthcare than do White Americans, are less likely to undergo coronary artery bypass, are less likely to receive kidney transplants, and suffer longer delays in transfer between healthcare units (Phelan & Link, 2015). At the macro level, the concentration of racial minorities in communities lacking high quality healthcare facilities prevents their access to high quality care (Krieger, 2014). The cumulative effects of racism give rise to disease and treatment inequalities in our societies. These effects are not limited to race or ethnicity but also include other multicultural dimensions, such as age, class, gender, and lifestyle.

REMOVING BARRIERS AND INCREASING ACCESS TO MENTAL HEALTHCARE

Improving the mental health of those affected by mental disorders or psychosocial distress, which are caused by challenging circumstances, is at the top of clinical mental health counselors' goals. To accomplish this goal, clients should be informed of treatment options, their effectiveness, and ways to gain access to those treatments. Removing barriers and facilitating access are essential.

TIP FROM THE FIELD 11.4

WAYS TO INCREASE KNOWLEDGE OF AND ACCESS TO TREATMENT FOR MENTAL ISSUES OR CONCERNS

The following suggestions for action aim to increase knowledge about the importance of seeking treatment for mental issues or concerns, to remove barriers, and to increase access to help:

- Engage in discussions; create plans of action regarding ways to minimize barriers; and create ways to address those barriers on an institutional level.
- Educate clients regarding all types of services available in the community and where to go to receive those services.
- Provide referrals tailored to the client's needs.
- Engage in evidence-based research and publish the findings.
- Provide articles, blogs, video blogs, workshops, and other information for consumers to understand the efficacy of counseling approaches, tools, and techniques.

- Offer a treatment setting and environment that welcomes individuals from diverse cultural backgrounds.
- Promote culturally sensitive practices and procedures.
- Create integrated systems of care, adapted to clients' needs.
- Advocate for policies and regulations that reduce health inequities and facilitate access to mental health treatments.

Empowering people and clients to become active agents in the pursuit of appropriate treatments represent another powerful strategy to confront existing barriers. Consumer guides represent one way to achieve this goal. *Seeking Drug Abuse Treatment: Know What to Ask* (National Institute of Drug Abuse [NIDA], 2018) is an evidence-based guide for people seeking addiction treatment for themselves or loved ones, with questions they should ask potential treatment centers. NIDA's guide exemplifies best ways to educate clients and increase treatment adherence and completion.

First, the guide informs the public of available addiction-related treatments and their effectiveness. This information aims to reduce clients' doubts. Second, the guide helps clients find an appropriate treatment, suitable for them or for another person in need of treatment. Finding such treatment is essential to stop drug use and regain the capacity to engage in productive relationships with family, workplace, and community. Clients who find such treatment are more likely to stay in treatment long enough to achieve their goals. Finding such treatment depends on the nature and severity of the client's addiction and related issues, appropriateness of treatment, availability of additional services, and quality of interaction between the client and the counselor and integrative team providers (NIDA, 2018).

TIP FROM THE FIELD 11.5

NIDA GUIDING QUESTIONS FOR FINDING APPROPRIATE TREATMENTS

To facilitate finding an appropriate treatment, NIDA (2018) suggests asking the following questions:

- Does the program use treatments backed by scientific evidence?
- Does the program tailor treatment to the needs of each client?
- Does the program adapt treatment as the patient's needs change?
- Is the duration of treatment sufficient?
- How does the specific recovery program fit into drug addiction treatment?

In addition to the above NIDA-specified questions, we also recommend that multicultural dimensions of the program be examined for good fit with client needs.

▧ MULTICULTURAL COUNSELING COMPETENCIES

As mentioned earlier in this chapter, the persistence of racism and discrimination represents a significant public mental health challenge (Bastos et al., 2018). Efforts to reduce these barriers are addressed by organizations such as American Mental Health Counselors Association (AMHCA). According to AMHCA standards for the practice of clinical mental health counseling:

> *This work of clinical mental health counselors serves the needs of socially and culturally diverse clients (e.g. age, gender, race/ethnicity, socio-economic status, sexual orientation) across the lifespan (i.e. , children, adolescents and adults including older adults and geriatric populations). (AMHCA, 2017, p. 2)*

Furthermore, Diversity and Advocacy in Clinical Mental Health Counseling (p. 5) represent one of the required areas of training for mental health counselors. In addition, the AMHCA standards offer a nondiscrimination and professional development requirement:

> *Clinical mental health counselors provide services to each client requesting services regardless of lifestyle, origin, race, color, age, handicap, sex, religion, or sexual orientation. They are knowledgeable and sensitive to cultural diversity and the multicultural issues of clients. Counselors have a duty to acquire the knowledge, skills, and resources to assist diverse clients. (p. 12)*

Mental health counselors are expected to develop awareness, knowledge, and skills to work with diverse clients, and engage in actions that result in effective counseling of all clients (Zalaquett et al., 2019).

Privilege and Power

Counseling and therapy are processes of interpersonal influence. Many mental health counselors come from a background of privilege. For example, many counselors are White, from middle or high income families, and raised and educated in affluent communities. They are part of the majority and dominant culture. In Western societies, the majority defines what is important and what is acceptable. This advantage can affect minority groups adversely, creating occasions for inequality, biases, and furthering systems of oppression. When the latter happens, those with majority power have the capability to intensify those differences further or, conversely, to advocate for or participate in actions that are aimed at reducing oppression, removing barriers, and challenging inequalities.

The White racial majority in the United States enjoys what is called White privilege. White privilege is the collection of advantages and benefits that White people receive from a system normed on the experiences, values, and perceptions of their own racial group (McIntosh, 1988; Sue, Sue, Neville, & Smith, 2019). These unearned privileges usually are not available to people of color. White privilege is mostly invisible to those who have it and, therefore, is very difficult to acknowledge. The latter phenomenon has been termed the *invisible veil* (Sue et al., 2019). To elaborate on the concept of the invisible veil a bit, the following represent the first few items in McIntosh's (1988) list of 50 White privileges:

1. I can arrange to be in the company of people of my race most of the time.

2. I can go shopping alone most of the time, pretty well assured that I will not be followed or harassed.

3. I can turn on the television or open to the front page of the paper and see people of my race widely represented.

Racial privilege represents one form of privilege in our society. Other forms of privilege are based on gender, sexual orientation, class, religion, age, ability, and education. For example, males continue to hold a level of privilege over people of the other gender; able-bodied individuals display higher rates of employability than individuals with disabilities; higher social class continues to open access to educational opportunities and participation in politics; and a higher level of education increases salary income, just to name a few existing privileges.

Mental health counselors must consider how their own life experiences are influenced by existing societal privileges. Gaining awareness allows counselors a larger empathic understanding of the relationship between power and privilege. With such self-awareness, many counselors would realize that they are privileged individuals. Furthermore, having access to higher education, a necessary step to receive a master's or doctoral degree in clinical mental health counseling, confers with it a number of privileges. Educational privilege opens doors to a mental health career and opportunities to help others. Mental health counselors also must consider how client experiences are connected to and situated within large and intersecting systems in society. Additionally, counselors need to assess the effect of power and privilege on clients, as well as the effect of their own power and privilege on the counseling relationship with their clients. The purpose of reflecting on the counselor's and client's power and privilege is to recognize that the social relations within society have created conditions in which one or more dimensions of privilege are advantaged over others. Many aspects of everyday life that privileged people take for granted are not even available to people of minority or marginalized groups. Clients from marginalized groups may be suffering from depression or anxiety as a consequence of discrimination and oppression experienced in their school, workplace, neighborhood, and other societal contexts. As important, clients may experience further oppression when privileged counselors fail to understand or devalue the worldview of clients, and attempt to impose their own views or values on the client.

Privileged counselors may think that their views are the norm and come to expect that clients behave as they do. They may believe that what is good for them is good for everybody else, including individuals from different cultural groups. The counselors' responses to clients' concerns may reflect a privileged worldview. The manner in which the counselor conceptualizes the world of the client can have a great influence on how clients think and act in the future. How a counselor responds to the client greatly determines what will happen next. In fact, the counselor's responses may determine whether or not the conversation will continue.

It is possible for any clinical mental health counselors to become effective, culturally intentional counselors. Effective counseling requires the ability to change, grow, and develop with clients. Having faith in humanity and possessing humility on the part of the counselor are two basic ingredients for this process. Multicultural counseling and therapy (MCT) is a theory that recognizes that all counseling theories and methods are born in and exist within a cultural context. MCT has developed a large array of culturally sensitive therapeutic strategies to work with a diverse clientele and advance social justice action. The role of mental health counselors is not just to work with an individual but also with the family *and* extended systems that may be important to the client. A Latinx client who suffers from depression should not be treated just as an isolated person; his or her cultural context, which may be pervaded by racism and sexism that may contribute to that depression, also needs to be addressed. Many clients come to counseling blaming themselves for their conditions. Mental health counselors can liberate these clients from self-blame and encourage them to see their issues in a social context. Furthermore, they can facilitate clients' personal actions in order to improve their situations as well as those of others. The multicultural and social justice framework views the client as a person-in-relation to others and to social and cultural context. Interdependence is basic to culturally sensitive counseling and it is conceptualized as an ethical action.

Identification and rejection of harmful therapeutic treatments has been promoted by Lilienfeld's (2007) publication of psychological treatments that cause harm and Barlow's (2010) publication of negative effects from psychological treatments. Wendt, Gone, and Nagata (2015) highlight the importance of avoiding potentially harmful counseling, and they emphasize the need to include the lack of multicultural counseling among potentially harmful therapeutic interventions. If a counselor's mandate is to do no harm, then monocultural counseling that is applied to culturally diverse clients may violate that mandate. Wendt et al. (2015) provide a compelling argument for the integration of potentially harmful therapy and multicultural counseling discourses. Counseling and therapy can be inherently ethnocentric and, as such, capable of harming minority clients. They assert that studies of harm should be integrated with multicultural and social justice perspectives.

Current descriptions of multiculturalism are inclusive and embrace race, ethnicity, social class, gender, sexual orientation, disability, spirituality, and other cultural dimensions. Multicultural counseling occurs when a counselor and client are from different cultural groups. Sue and Sue (2016) define multiculturalism as "the integration, acceptance, and embracing of cultural differences that include race, gender, sexual orientation, and other sociodemographic identities" (p. 747).

Research on Mental Health Services for Minority Clients

Zalaquett et al. (2019) have offered the following summary of the research on mental health services for cultural minorities.

1. There are important differences in the conceptualization of psychological issues and treatments. The Surgeon General has asserted that culture counts in the understanding of mental disorders (2001). Many minority groups conceptualize psychological difficulties as more organic in nature and believe that mental health treatments can be enhanced by sheer will and the avoidance of morbid thoughts (Jimenez, Bartels, Cardenas, Daliwal, & Alegría, 2012; Sue, 1988). The *Diagnostic and Statistical Manual of Mental Disorders, Fifth Edition* (*DSM-5*) inclusion of the cultural concept of distress (CCD), which refers to the ways cultural groups experience, understand, and communicate suffering, behavioral disorders, or negative thoughts and emotions, demonstrates psychiatrists' recognition of the importance of cultural worldview (American Psychiatric Association [APA], 2013). Understanding cultural differences is important for counseling and therapy. What is a concern for a White client may not be an issue for an Asian American client (Kohrt et al., 2015).

2. Many counselors often hold negative stereotypes toward those who are different from them. Differing worldviews and values associated with multicultural dimensions can introduce both conscious and unconscious biases into a counselor's perception of the client, diagnosis, and treatment options (Sue & Sue, 2016; Zalaquett & Chambers, 2017). Therapists' perceptions of social class and low income clients frequently elicit predictions of poor therapeutic outcome (Kunstman, Plant, & Deska, 2016; Liu, Soleck, Hopps, Dunston, & Pickett, 2004; Smith, 2005, 2013). Likewise, negative attitudes toward older adults and other multicultural groups may make counseling a waste of time, energy, and money (Laganà & Shanks, 2002). Afrocentric versus Eurocentric discussions illustrate how very differently the world is viewed by different cultural groups (Leong et al., 1995; Sue & Sue, 2016). Counselors who view these differences as constructions rather than as "reality" are applying a multicultural understanding and opening ways for understanding, collaboration, and progress.

3. Despite the issues mentioned, research evidence clearly indicates that minority clients can benefit from therapy. Counseling and psychotherapy can help minority clients, if approached from a culturally relevant perspective. Research has confirmed what Griffith and Jones (1978, p. 230) have stated: "Unquestionably, race makes a difference in psychotherapy. Still, this is not to say that the skillful and experienced White therapist cannot effectively treat the Black client. Rather the critical requisite is that the White therapist is sensitive to the unique ways in which … race affects the course of treatment." Treatment outcome studies confirm, for example, that depression therapy helps minority, low income mothers to overcome clinical depression (Cicchetti, Toth, & Handley, 2015; Toth et al., 2015) and that counseling provided by college counseling centers helps minority clients significantly improve on a variety of issues (Lockard, Hayes, Graceffo, & Locke, 2013).

4. The client–therapist matching is complex. The examination of cultural matching represents the intersectionality of multiple social identities and

developmental factors (Umaña-Taylor et al., 2014). Multicultural scholars have exposed cultural differences in privilege and power and have suggested ways to work with those who are ethnically and racially different from Caucasians (Arredondo et al., 1996; Sue & Sue, 2016). Furthermore, many propose moving beyond an "us versus them" dichotomy, to a more inclusive perspective, and suggest looking at cross-cultural misunderstandings as communication break-downs that should trigger coordinated efforts to establish shared understandings (Sametband & Strong, 2013).

It seems likely that cultural identity theory may explain some of the complexities associated with counselor and client racial or ethnic matching. If clients are matched with therapists who have similar cultural awareness (and the therapists are competent), a good result may be expected. A culturally sensitive, White therapist may be equally effective if the client is at a level of cultural identity development that makes seeing a White counselor a viable alternative. "Ethnicity is important, but what is more important is its meaning" (Sue, 1988, p. 307). Multicultural counselors stress the need for "culturally responsive" counseling and therapy, the need for more prevention work on the part of professionals, and the need for more effective health policies, thus making help available to those who presently do not have the choice of seeking counseling assistance.

Cultural Adaptations to Counseling

A meta-analysis of culturally adapted mental health treatments, which are evidence-based treatments (EBTs) systematically modified to make them compatible with clients' culture, meaning, and values, found that culturally adapted mental health therapies were superior to those that do not explicitly incorporate cultural considerations (Smith, Domenech Rodrıguez, & Bernal, 2011). The meta-analysis of 65 studies, involving 8,620 participants, showed an effect size of $d = 5.46$, indicating that treatments specifically adapted for minority clients were more effective with that clientele than traditional treatments. Furthermore, treatments with greater numbers of specific cultural adaptations were more effective.

The authors (Smith et al., 2011) asserted that cultural adaptations should be considered evidence-based practices (EBPs) and recommended the following evidence-based therapeutic adaptations:

- Clients benefit more when counselors and psychotherapists align treatment with clients' cultural backgrounds.
- Counselors and psychotherapists should attend to how client age and acculturation interact with their treatments.
- Counselors and psychotherapists should conduct psychotherapy in the client's preferred language if possible.
- Culturally adapted treatments should address multiple components, as the more components are incorporated into the cultural adaptations, the more effective the treatment is.

- Culturally adapted treatments are much more beneficial when they are specific to clients of a given race than when they are provided to a group of clients with varied races or ethnicities. The more specific to clients' cultural backgrounds, the more effective is the therapy.

- The more culturally focused and specific the treatment, the more effective it will be.

The following guidelines, for adapting therapy to client's cultures, suggest that counselors and psychotherapists should:

- Practice flexibly and respectfully.

- Communicate empathy in a culturally appropriate manner.

- Obtain relevant and effective multicultural competence training.

- Learn about specific cultural norms, study literature about available culture-specific treatment techniques, and consult with expert colleagues.

- Conduct a culturally informed but person-specific functional assessment before implementing treatment.

- Explore client's views of seeking counseling treatment and the nature of the therapeutic relationship.

- Not dismiss traditional treatments, as they may serve as potential resources.

- Review with the client services that may be meaningful within their cultural worldview and context.

- Implement appropriate and specific cultural adaptations.

- Avoid interpreting cultural differences as deficits.

- Identify client's culturally related strengths and resources for use in a client's treatment.

- Remain open to what clients bring to counseling. (Asnaani & Hofmann, 2012; Pedersen, Lonner, Draguns, Trimble, & Scharrón-del Río, 2016; Smith et al., 2011; Sommers-Flanagan, 2015)

In counseling practice, mental health professionals should take cultural context into account at all times, recognize and align with client culture, and apply culturally appropriate skills, assessments, and interventions. Multicultural therapy constitutes not only best practice but also ethical practice. Counselors have developed a large array of culturally sensitive therapeutic strategies to work with a diverse clientele and advance social justice action. The Multicultural Counseling Competencies Revisions Committee of the Association for Multicultural Counseling and Development offers a set of multicultural and social justice counseling competencies (MSJCC; Ratts et al., 2015). These competencies address the complex multicultural dimensions of the counseling relationship, acknowledge the importance of understanding clients within their social contexts, recognize the negative consequences of oppression and discrimination on clients' mental health and well-being, and integrate multicultural and social justice competencies within all counseling modalities—individuals, couples, families, groups, and institutions.

Counselors and clients bring to the counseling relationship their various identities, privileged and marginalized statuses, and cultural values, beliefs, and biases. The MSJCC provide a framework for addressing the various identities of counselors and clients. Furthermore, the MSJCC set the expectation that counselors address issues of power, privilege, and oppression affecting clients; ask counselors to use a culturally contextual/ systemic framework to understand client concerns; and recommend intervening at the individual and systems level (Ratts et al., 2015). Figure 11.1 offers a schema for understanding the various elements of the MSJCC.

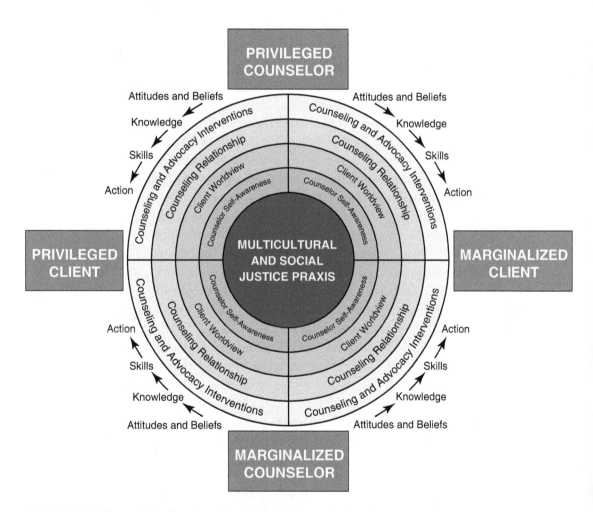

FIGURE 11.1 The multicultural and social justice competencies.

SOURCE: Ratts, M. J., Singh, A. A., Nassar-McMillan, S., Butler, S. K., & McCullough, J. R. (2015). *Multicultural and social justice counseling competencies*. Retrieved from http://www.counseling.org/docs/default-source/competencies/multicultural-and-social-justice-counseling-competencies.pdf?sfvrsn=20

As can be seen in Figure 11.1, the MSJCC present quadrants, domains, and competencies. Four quadrants result from the intersection of two foundational dimensions—privileged/marginalized client and privileged/marginalized counselor:

Quadrant I: Privileged Counselor–Marginalized Client

Quadrant II: Privileged Counselor–Privileged Client

Quadrant III: Marginalized Counselor–Privileged Client

Quadrant IV: Marginalized Counselor–Marginalized Client

For example, an African American, lesbian counselor may experience the counseling relationship with a White, gay physician, consulting for depression, in different ways. She may feel both are interacting from Quadrant II because of their educational backgrounds. She also may feel interacting from Quadrant III due to their racial differences. The MSJCC also include several developmental domains that can help counselors provide effective interventions. These domains are counselor self-awareness, client worldview, counseling relationship, and counseling and advocacy interventions.

Counselor self-awareness is important for identifying cultural identity, values, beliefs, and biases. This awareness may reveal worldviews or biases negatively affecting help that needs to be provided to the client. Learning about the client's cultural identity, values, beliefs, and biases may help counselors to understand clients' worldviews and their effects on the current reasons for consultation. Applying quadrants' frameworks of privileged and marginalized statuses may help to establish a working counseling relationship. Integrating the information gained within these domains may help to determine the best treatment and level of intervention. Interventions may be delivered at various levels of the client's ecological context. Counseling and advocacy interventions may be delivered at the intrapersonal, interpersonal, institutional, communal, societal, or global levels of the world of the client.

The MSJCC recognize the importance for counselors to develop attitudes and beliefs, knowledge, skills, and actions (AKSA) that allow them to work successfully with clients from diverse backgrounds. Awareness of A, attitudes and beliefs, means learning about personal values, beliefs, and biases that the counselor holds about self and clients. K, knowledge, means that the counselors are being informed of their clients' cultural identities and worldviews, and the positive and negative effects of privileged and marginalized statuses. S, skills, ask counselors to learn culturally sensitive techniques and select interventions attuned to the worldview of their clients. A, actions, imply a commitment by counselors to act on their awareness, knowledge, and skills, at the various levels needed by the client. Without action, all of the counselor's awareness, knowledge, and skills will remain inert.

Table 11.1 illustrates the application of the MSJCC (Ratts et al., 2015) to the counseling relationship. The table outlines some of the goals that may be useful to advance effectiveness as a mental health counselor. The goals, related to the counseling relationship, are briefly discussed as follows:

1. *Counselor Attitude and Beliefs.* If counselors are to be empathic with clients of different backgrounds, it is essential that they become self-aware. Furthermore,

TABLE 11.1 Counseling relationship social justice competencies.

1. ATTITUDES AND BELIEFS	2. KNOWLEDGE	3. SKILLS	4. ACTION
■ Acknowledge that the worldviews, values, beliefs, and biases held by privileged and marginalized counselors and clients will positively or negatively influence the counseling relationship.	■ Develop knowledge of the worldviews, values, beliefs, and biases held by privileged and marginalized counselors and clients and its influence on the counseling relationship.	■ Acquire assessment skills to determine how the worldviews, values, beliefs, and biases held by privileged and marginalized counselors and clients influence the counseling relationship.	■ Take action by initiating conversations to determine how the worldviews, values, beliefs, and biases held by privileged and marginalized counselors and clients influence the counseling relationship.

SOURCE: Adapted from Ratts, M. J., Singh, A. A., Nassar-McMillan, S., Butler, S. K., & McCullough, J. R. (2015). *Multicultural and social justice counseling competencies.* Retrieved from http://www.counseling.org/docs/default-source/competencies/multicultural-and-social-justice-counseling-competencies.pdf?sfvrsn=20

privileged and marginalized counselors need to become aware of how their and their clients' worldviews, values, and group status affect the relationship with their clients.

2. *Counselor Knowledge.* Privileged and marginalized counselors work intentionally to acquire knowledge of how the worldviews, values, and experiences with power, privilege, and oppression affect the counseling relationship.

3. *Skills.* Privileged and marginalized counselors learn the skills to discuss observed cultural differences with clients. The goal is to discuss how their worldviews affect their relationship and the best ways to understand one another.

4. *Action.* Both privileged and marginalized counselors act intentionally to increase their understanding of the way they and the client see the world.

■ CONCLUSION

This chapter emphasized the use of sociocultural systems worldview in the clinical mental health counselors work with clients. Contemporary culturally integrated systems of care recognize the importance of combining physical and mental health services in a culturally sensitive manner. Integrated systems of care offer a path to resolving historical inequalities of care, and clinical mental health counselors can—and have the responsibility to—play an active role in these systems. Using a systems of culture approach, clinical mental health counselors can understand how these systems affect clients and have an impact on their issues and concerns. Armed with this lens, clinical mental health counselors can suggest comprehensive evaluations and treatment plans, unveil resources available to clients, and facilitate their use. Furthermore, these professionals can discover barriers to access and instances of racism and discrimination and work collaboratively to remove them. Integrated and culturally sensitive care offers a way to service clients in a holistic and culturally sensitive way. Empowered with multicultural and social justice skills, clinical mental health counselors can help diverse clients to change and to exert changes within the systems with which they interact.

RESOURCES

The CODAC's Model. Retrieved from www.codac.org

Multicultural and Social Justice Counseling Competencies: Practical applications in counseling. Retrieved from https://www.counseling.org/docs/default-source/competencies/multicultural-and-social-justice-counseling-competencies.pdf?sfvrsn=20

National Institute on Drug Abuse. (2018). *Principles of drug addiction treatment: A research-based guide* (3rd ed.). Retrieved from https://www.drugabuse.gov/publications/principles-drug-addiction-treatment-research-based-guide-third-edition/drug-addiction treatment-in-united-states

National Institute of Drug Abuse. (2018). *Seeking Drug Abuse Treatment: Know What to Ask.* Retrieved from https://www.drugabuse.gov/publications/seeking-drug-abuse-treatment/1 -does-program-use-treatments-backed-by-scientific-evidence.

This is an evidence-based guide for people seeking addiction treatment for themselves or loved ones with questions they should ask potential treatment centers. The NIDA website also features videos of firsthand stories on recovery and from leaders in the recovery field.

Thoughts on Recovery from Patients. Retrieved from https://www.drugabuse.gov/nidamed/thoughts-recovery-patients-video

World Health Organization. (2018). *Management of physical health conditions in adults with severe mental disorders. WHO guidelines.* Retrieved from https://www.who.int/mental _health/evidence/guidelines_physical_health_and_severe_mental_disorders/en.

People with severe mental disorders—including severe depression, bipolar disorder, and psychotic disorders such as schizophrenia—generally die 10 to 20 years earlier than the general population. The majority of these premature deaths are due to physical health conditions. Access to comprehensive health services remains out of reach for the majority of people with severe mental disorders. To help address this inequity, WHO has released, for the first time, evidence-based guidelines on the management of physical conditions in adults with severe mental disorders.

REFERENCES

Agency for Healthcare Research and Quality. (2018). *National healthcare quality and disparities report.* Rockville, MD: Author. AHRQ Pub. No. 18-0033-EF.

American Mental Health Counselors Association. (2015). *Code of ethics.* Retrieved from http://www.amhca.org/learn/ethics

American Mental Health Counselors Association. (2017). *AMHCA standards for the practice of clinical mental health counseling.* Retrieved from http://www.amhca.org/learn/standards

American Psychiatric Association. (2013). *Diagnostic and statistical manual of mental disorders* (5th ed.). Washington, DC: Author.

Arredondo, P., Toporek, R., Pack Brown, S., Jones, J., Locke, D. C., Sanchez, J., & Stadler, H. (1996). Operationalization of the multicultural counseling competencies. *Journal of Multicultural Counseling and Development, 24,* 42–78.

Asnaani, A., & Hofmann, S. G. (2012). Collaboration in multicultural therapy: Establishing a strong therapeutic alliance across cultural lines. *Journal of Clinical Psychology, 68,* 187–197. doi:10.1002/jclp.21829

Barlow, D. H. (2010). Negative effects from psychological treatments: A perspective. *American Psychologist, 65,* 13–20. doi:10.1037/a0015643

Bastos, J. L., Harnois, C. E., & Paradies, Y. C. (2018). Health care barriers, racism, and intersectionality in Australia. *Social Science & Medicine, 199,* 209–218. doi:10.1016/j .socscimed.2017.05.010

Bronfenbrenner, U. (1981). *The ecology of human development: Experiments by nature and design.* Cambridge, MA: Harvard University Press.

Carbado, D. W., Crenshaw, K. W., Mays, V. M., & Tomlinson, B. (2013). Intersectionality: Mapping the movements of a theory. *Du Bois Review: Social Science Research on Race, 10*(2), 303–312. doi:10.107/51742058x13000349

Chisholm, D., Sweeny, K., Sheehan, P., Rasmussen, B., Smit, F., Cuijpers, P., & Saxena, S. (2016). Scaling-up treatment of depression and anxiety: A global return on investment analysis. *Lancet Psychiatry, 3,* 415–424. doi:10.1016/S2215-0366(16)30024-4

Cho, S., Crenshaw, K. W., & McCall, L. (2013). Toward a field of intersectionality studies: Theory, applications, and praxis. *Signs: Journal of Women in Culture and Society, 38*(4), 705–810. doi:10.1086/669608.

Cicchetti, D., Toth, S. L., & Handley, E. D. (2015). Genetic moderation of interpersonal psychotherapy efficacy for low-income mothers with major depressive disorder: Implications for differential susceptibility. *Development and Psychopathology, 27,* 19–35. doi:10.1017/S0954579414001278

Clement, S., Schauman, O., Graham, T., Maggioni, F., Evans-Lacko, S., Bezborodovs, N., ... Thornicroft, G. (2015). What is the impact of mental health-related stigma on help-seeking? A systematic review of quantitative and qualitative studies. *Psychological Medicine, 45,* 11–27. doi:10.1017/S0033291714000129

Conyne, R. K., & Cook, E. P. (2004). Understanding persons within environments: An introduction to ecological counseling. In R. K. Conyne & E. P. Cook (Eds.), *Ecological counseling: An innovative approach to conceptualizing person-environment interaction* (pp. 3–36). Alexandria, VA: American Counseling Association.

Cook, E. P., & Coaston, S. C. (2012). Behavior is changeable. In E. P. Cook (Ed.), *Understanding people in context: The ecological perspective in counseling* (pp. 129–160). Alexandria, VA: American Counseling Association.

Griffith, M., & Jones, E. E. (1978). Race and psychotherapy: Changing perspectives. *Current Psychiatric Therapies, 18,* 225–235.

Ivey, A., Ivey, M. B., & Zalaquett, C. (2018). *Intentional interviewing and counseling: Facilitating client development in a multicultural society* (9th ed.). Belmont, CA: Cengage Learning.

Jimenez, D. E., Bartels, S. J., Cardenas, V., Dhaliwal, S. S., & Alegría, M. (2012). Cultural beliefs and mental health treatment preferences of ethnically diverse older adult consumers in primary care. *American Journal of Geriatric Psychiatry, 20*(6), 533–542. doi:10.1097/ JGP.0b013e318227f876

Kessler, R. C., Berglund, P., Demler, O., Jin, R., Merikangas, K. R., & Walters, E. E. (2005). Lifetime prevalence and age-of-onset distributions of *DSM-IV* disorders in the National

Comorbidity Survey Replication. *Archives of General Psychiatry, 62*, 593–602. doi:10.1001/archpsyc.62.6.593

Kohrt, B. A., Jordans, M. J., Rai, S., Shrestha, P., Luitel, N. P., Ramaiya, M. K., ... Patel, V. (2015). Therapist competence in global mental health: Development of the ENhancing Assessment of Common Therapeutic factors (ENACT) rating scale. *Behaviour Research and Therapy, 69*, 11–21. doi:10.1016/j.brat.2015.03.009

Krieger, N. (2014). Discrimination and health inequities. In L. F. Berkman, I. Kawachi, & M. M. Glymour (Eds.), *Social epidemiology* (pp. 63–125). New York, NY: Oxford University Press.

Kunstman, J. W., Plant, E. A., & Deska, J. C. (2016). White ≠ poor: Whites distance, derogate, and deny low-status in group members. *Personality and Social Psychology Bulletin, 42*, 230–243. doi:10.1177/0146167215623270

Laganà, L., & Shanks, S. (2002). Mutual biases underlying the problematic relationship between older adults and mental health providers: Any solution in sight? *International Journal of Aging and Human Development, 55*, 271–295. doi:10.2190/1LTE-F1Q1-V7HG-6BC9

Leong, F. T. L., Wagner, N. S., & Tata, S. P. (1995). Racial and ethnic variations in help-seeking attitudes. In J. G. Ponterotto, J. M. Casas, L. A. Suzuki, & C. M. Alexander (Eds.), *Handbook of multicultural counseling* (pp. 415–438). Thousand Oaks, CA: Sage.

Levers, L. L. (2001). Representations of psychiatric disability in fifty years of Hollywood film: An ethnographic content analysis. *Theory and Science, 2*(2). Retrieved from http://theoryandscience.icaap.org/content/vol002.002/lopezlevers.html

Lilienfeld, S.O. (2007). Psychological treatments that cause harm. *Perspectives on Psychological Science, 2*, 53–70. doi:10.1111/j.1745-6916.2007.00029.x

Liu, W. M., Soleck, G., Hopps, J., Dunston, K., & Pickett, T., Jr. (2004). A new framework to understand social class in counseling: The social class worldview model and modern classism theory. *Journal of Multicultural Counseling and Development, 32*, 95–122. doi:10.1002/j.2161-1912.2004.tb00364.x

Lockard, A. J., Hayes, J. A., Graceffo, J. M., & Locke, B. D. (2013). Effective counseling for racial/ethnic minority clients: Examining changes using a practice research network. *Journal of College Counseling, 16*, 243–257. doi:10.1002/j.2161-1882.2013.00040.x

McIntosh, P. (1988). *White privilege: Unpacking the invisible knapsack*. Retrieve from https://www.racialequitytools.org/resourcefiles/mcintosh.pdf

McMahon, H. G., Mason, E. C. M., Daluga-Guenther, N., & Ruiz, A. (2014). An ecological model of professional school counseling. *Journal of Counseling & Development, 92*, 459–471. doi:10.1002/j.1556-6676.2014.00172.x

Mojtabai, R., Olfson, M., Sampson, N. A., Jin, R., Druss, B., Wang, P. S., ... Kessler, R. C. (2011). Barriers to mental health treatment: Results from the National Comorbidity Survey Replication. *Psychological Medicine, 41*, 1751–1761. doi:10.1017/S0033291710002291

National Institute of Drug Abuse. (2018). *Seeking drug abuse treatment: Know what to ask.* Retrieved from https://www.drugabuse.gov/publications/seeking-drug-abuse-treatment/1-does-program-use-treatments-backed-by-scientific-evidence

National Institute of Mental Health. (2019). *Minority health and mental health disparities program.* Retrieved from https://www.nimh.nih.gov/about/organization/gmh/minority-health-and-mental-health-disparities-program.shtml

Pedersen, P., Lonner, W., Draguns, J., Trimble, J. E., & Sharron-del Rio, M. (Eds.). (2015). *Counseling across cultures* (7th ed.). Los Angeles, CA: Sage.

Phelan, J. C., & Link, B. G. (2015). Is racism a fundamental cause of inequalities in health? *Annual Review of Sociology, 41*, 311–330. doi:10.1146/annurev-soc-073014-112305

Ratts, M. J., & Greenleaf, A. T. (2018). Counselor–advocate–scholar model: Changing the dominant discourse in counseling. *Journal of Multicultural Counseling and Development, 46*, 78–96. doi:10.1002/jmcd.12094

Ratts, M. J., Singh, A. A., Nassar-McMillan, S., Butler, S. K., & McCullough, J. R. (2015). *Multicultural and social justice counseling competencies.* Retrieved from http://www .counseling.org/docs/default-source/competencies/multicultural-and-social-justice -counseling-competencies.pdf?sfvrsn=20

Sametband, I., & Strong, T. (2013). Negotiating cross-cultural misunderstandings in collaborative therapeutic conversations. *International Journal for the Advancement of Counselling, 35,* 88–99. doi:10.1007/s10447-012-9169-1

Smith, L. (2005). Psychotherapy, classism, and the poor: Conspicuous by their absence. *American Psychologist, 60,* 687–696. doi:10.1037/0003-066X.60.7.687

Smith, L. (2013). So close, and yet so far away: social class, social exclusion, and mental health practice. *American Journal of Orthopsychiatry, 83,* 11–16. doi:10.1111/ajop.12008

Smith, T. B., Domenech Rodriguez, M., & Bernal, G. (2011). Culture. *Journal of Clinical Psychology, 67,* 166–175. doi:10.1002/jclp.20757

Sommers-Flanagan, J. (2015). Evidence-based relationship practice: Enhancing counselor competence. *Journal of Mental Health Counseling, 37,* 95–108. doi:10.17744/mehc.37.2 .g13472044600588r

Substance Abuse and Mental Health Services Administration. (2018a). *Integration continues to grow.* Retrieved from https://www.integration.samhsa.gov/about-us/esolutions-newsletter/ september-2013-esolutions

Substance Abuse and Mental Health Services Administration. (2018b). *What is integrated care?* Retrieved from https://www.integration.samhsa.gov/about-us/what-is-integrated-care

Sue, D. W., & Sue, D. (2016). *Counseling the culturally diverse: Theory and practice* (7th ed.). Hoboken, NJ: Wiley.

Sue, D. W., Sue, D., Neville, H. A., & Smith, L. (2019). *Counseling the culturally diverse: Theory and practice* (8th ed.). Hoboken, NJ: Wiley.

Sue, S. (1988). Psychotherapeutic services for ethnic minorities: Two decades of research findings. *American Psychologist, 43*(4), 301–308. doi:10.1037/0003-066X.43.4.301

Toth, S. L., Sturge-Apple, M. L., Rogosch, F. A., & Cicchetti, D. (2015). Mechanisms of change: Testing how preventative interventions impact psychological and physiological stress functioning in mothers in neglectful families. *Development and Psychopathology, 27,* 1661–1674. doi:10.1017/S0954579415001017

Umaña-Taylor, A. J., Quintana, S. M., Lee, R. M., Cross, W. E., Rivas-Drake, D., Schwartz, S. J., ... Study Group on Ethnic and Racial Identity in the 21st Century. (2014). Ethnic and racial identity during adolescence and into young adulthood: An integrated conceptualization. *Child Development, 85,* 21–39. doi:10.1111/cdev.12196

U.S. Census Bureau. (2011). *The Hispanic population: 2010. 2010 census briefs.* Retrieved from https://www.census.gov/prod/cen2010/briefs/c2010br-04.pdf

Vespa, J., Armstrong, D. M., & Medina, L. (2018). *Demographic turning points for the United States: Population projections for 2020 to 2060.* Current Population Reports, P25-1144, U.S. Census Bureau, Washington, DC, 2018.

Wang, P. S., Gruber, M. J., Powers, R. E., Schoenbaum, M., Speier, A. H., Wells, K. B., & Kessler, R. C. (2007). Mental health service use among hurricane Katrina survivors in the eight months after the disaster. *Psychiatric Services (Washington, D.C.), 58*(11), 1403–1411. doi:10.1176/appi.ps.58.11.1403

Weisz, J. R., Weiss, B., Han, S. S., Granger, D. A., & Morton, T. (1995). Effects of psychotherapy with children and adolescents revised: A meta-analysis of treatment outcome studies. *Psychological Bulletin, 117,* 450–468. doi:10.1037/0033-2909.117.3.450

Wendt, D. C., Gone, J. P., & Nagata, D. K. (2015). Potentially harmful therapy and multicultural counseling: Bridging two disciplinary discourses ψ. *The Counseling Psychologist, 43,* 334–358. doi:10.1177/0011000014548280

World Health Organization. (2018). Management of physical health conditions in adults with severe mental disorders. *WHO guidelines*. Retrieved from https://www.who.int/mental _health/evidence/guidelines_physical_health_and_severe_mental_disorders/en

Zalaquett, C. P., & Chambers, A. L. (2017). Introduction to the special issue: Counseling individuals living in poverty. *Journal of Multicultural Counseling and Development, 45*, 152–161. doi:10.1002/jmcd.12071

Zalaquett, C. P., Ivey, A., & Ivey, M. B. (2019). *Essential theories of counseling and psychotherapy: Everyday practice in our diverse world*. San Diego, CA: Cognella Academic Publishing.

CHAPTER 12

ADVOCACY, THIRD-PARTY PAYERS, AND MANAGED CARE

REX STOCKTON | RATANPRIYA SHARMA

This chapter addresses managed care as a major factor in healthcare reimbursement as well as the counselor's role in managed care. The importance of advocacy for the profession is also emphasized. Additionally, the chapter demystifies the issues of payment for counseling services, specifically third-party billing, managed care, medical assistance programs, and other issues therein. The importance of government legislation and public policy with respect to the profession are addressed too.

The following Council for Accreditation of Counseling and Related Educational Programs (CACREP) standards are addressed in this chapter:

CACREP 2016:
2F1.d, 2F1.f, 2F1.g, 5C2.i, 5C2.k, 5C2.m
CACREP 2009:
2G1.g, 2G1.h

LEARNING OBJECTIVES

After reviewing this chapter, the reader should be able to:

1. Understand the concept of managed care.

2. Understand advocacy and why it is important.

3. Understand counselors' roles as advocates and ways to get involved.

4. Identify various types of managed care.

5. Identify issues of payment for counseling services.

6. Identify the importance of government legislation and public policy, with respect to the profession.

7. Understand that advocacy can be for the profession or for clients.

8. Participate in advocacy efforts through writing a supportive letter or other means.

INTRODUCTION

We begin by defining managed care. "Managed care plans are a type of health insurance. They have contracts with healthcare providers and medical facilities to provide care for members at reduced costs. These providers make up the plan's network. How much … care the plan will pay for depends on the network's rules" (U.S. National Library of Medicine, "Summary," 2018).

When the senior author began a limited practice during the 1970s, he was able to practice within this framework, because faculty members at his institution could have a day each week for outside activities. So he joined a practice of physicians who wanted someone to focus on their clients' mental health issues. After seeing a client, all he had to do was bill their insurance. He had the requisite training and thus was eligible for reimbursement for the procedure. This is called an indemnity plan; the insurance company then would pay off whatever the clients' plan would provide, usually the normal charge for seeing a client. Later, it became important to have a license, and because the senior author had a psychologist license, this did not present a problem. All he had to do was list his license when submitting a bill to the insurance company.

Later, as managed care began to take hold, it became important to have a physician's referral in order to see a client. Because the senior author worked with physicians, this was not a problem. However, counselors at that time did not have licensure in Indiana, the state where the senior author resided. For a while, they were able to work for agencies without having to have a license. However, it was clear that licensure was going to be required in the future. So a program of legislative advocacy, which eventually resulted in licensure legislation for mental health counselors in the state of Indiana, was begun. This would not have happened without the strong support of various constituencies, including the state branch of the American Counseling Association (ACA) and the National Board for Certified Counselors (NBCC).

Counselor educators, including the senior author and counseling association representatives, as well as practicing Indiana counselors, found themselves traveling to the state capital to testify before legislative committees. At the same time, similar events were taking place in many states throughout the country. Gradually, through efforts such as these, the laws establishing licensure for master's level counselors took place. It took a good 10 years before every state had license laws for counselors. Without a license, it is now illegal to practice counseling in Indiana, and without legislative advocacy, this never would have happened. (We have more to say about advocacy later in the chapter.)

MANAGED CARE

This section of the chapter aims to shed light on the managed care healthcare system and answer some of these pertinent questions that counseling professionals often come across.

As the name would suggest, managed care plans manage healthcare services. According to American Federation of State, County and Municipal Employees (AFSCME):

> *This means that the plan itself [rather than the clinician] sets guidelines for determining when given surgeries are needed, what tests are appropriate, how long a patient should remain in the hospital...If a push to cut costs takes precedence over clinical considerations, care management programs become a dangerous problem. (AFSCME, para 4, n.d.)*

As an example of mandated guidelines, the senior author recently had the following medical experience. When his prescribed medicine needed to be reauthorized, his doctor renewed his prescription medicine. However, the managed care organization did not accept the doctor's choice and substituted another medication that the doctor had not chosen, albeit, a similar medicine. Although the original medication was ordered by his doctor and known to be effective, the managed care organization still could dictate the change without being required to offer any specific justification.

As far back as 1973, the passage of the Health Maintenance Organization Act provided managed care as a major way to control healthcare costs, which were rising rapidly (Speights, 2015). U.S. healthcare costs continue to increase, rising from 5% of the gross domestic product (GDP) in 1960 to 18.2% in 2018 (Statistica, 2018). Not surprisingly, mechanisms were developed to constrain the costs. As Joshua M. Gross, Director of Group Programs at Florida State University and widely regarded as an expert in group counseling and therapy, noted, the premiums for private employers rose, on average, 15% to 20% per year in the 1970s (J. M. Gross, personal communication, November 27, 2018). Throughout this era, healthcare spending per capita in the private sector accelerated far more rapidly than a Medicare enrollee's cost (Reinhardt, 1998). Thus, it was not surprising that efforts to contain costs became paramount. "Medicaid managed care grew rapidly in the 1990s. In 1991, 2.7 million beneficiaries were enrolled in some form of managed care. By 2004, that number had grown to 27 million, an increase of 900 percent" (National Conference of State Legislatures, "Managed Care in Medicaid," para. 1, 2017). It has been one of the major mechanisms that providers of care such as physicians, counselors, and other licensed healthcare practitioners can provide to a delivery system for managed care. There are a variety of ways in which this can be done, including health maintenance organizations (HMOs), in which the participant chooses a primary care physician and relies on that physician for referrals for services rendered; in this case, the patient also must utilize participating providers. As far back as 1997, Gross (1997) noted that there are various interactions among providers, patients, and the contract relationships of third-party payers. The result is an operating system with all of the components interacting. Prior to treatment, preauthorization is necessary for healthcare providers' services. According to Gross (J. M. Gross, personal communication, November 27, 2018), "Normally, a provider must be a member of a panel of providers and must be referred by physician, who is a primary care provider."

Another variant of the traditional HMO model is a preferred provider organization (PPO). PPOs encourage but do not require that participants choose a primary care provider from within the organization. However, if the participant does not utilize a network clinician, the participant must pay higher deductibles and copayments. Yet another model is the point of service plan (POS). These plans reimburse a set percentage, no matter who renders the service. Alternatively, participants may be in an exclusive provider organization (EPO), where providers have agreed to render their services at a discounted rate, so long as the participant remains in the network of providers (Patient Advocate Foundation, n.d.). Also, in some cases, providers agree to a set capitation fee for all services provided. The provider must estimate carefully the possible usage of services by the client in order to avoid the possibility of losing profit. On the other hand, if the capitation funds are not totally utilized, the provider can keep a percentage of the obligated funds.

There are other alternatives than simply not participating in managed care programs and having clients pay out of pocket for services rendered. One of the few examples of this, and a valid employment opportunity for counselors working in the United States, is at college counseling centers. Ribeiro, Gross, and Turner (2017) have noted the following:

> College counseling centers are a domain of clinical mental health practice that have been quietly training, supervising, and preparing student group therapists for independent licensed practice for more than fifty years. The college counseling center may be one of the last mental health-service delivery environments that is free from payment negotiation, because of the long-standing tradition of those services being paid via overall student health and/or service fees. (Preface, p. 1)

Among other things, this mechanism allows counselors and other mental health professionals to address clients with mental health issues without a referral directly from a physician. It further allows mental health clinicians to work with an organization whose only purpose is to provide for mental health.

Cost Containment

It cannot be overemphasized that the end result of managed care is cost containment through the various mechanisms employed. An approach called "step therapy" illustrates this point. It is a form of cost management that insurers use. In terms of medicine, providers are required to use the lowest dose possible and to start with the fewest drugs before going to the next step if the patient does not improve—or worsens (Burns, 2018). For counselors, it means having the least amount of client hours possible to get positive therapeutic results. While this is an effective cost containment mechanism, it is sometimes the case that more counseling time and medication are necessary than the managed care company is initially willing to permit at the lowest level.

While cost containment has become necessary, it is important to note that there are negatives associated with this approach as well. As an Indiana University master's-level intern commented recently:

> My experience as an intern has given me some inside knowledge. I have learned how little the therapist or company gets paid from the insurance company; it is substantially lower than the office rates. It can also take several months to get paid from the insurance companies, so the therapist may go without pay for that time. (L. Reece, personal communication, November 14, 2018)

We chose this quote because it illustrates a tension with which counselors may have to contend when they deal with managed care. Of course, on the positive side, a check eventually does arrive, and clients can be referred by the managed care organization to counseling providers. Having a flow of clients without having to advertise can be very helpful. However, this does not mean that there are no problems with managed care.

Lack of Access to Healthcare

While it is important to contain costs, the mechanisms may fail to account for individual differences or cultural and racial disparities. Dana (1998) commented about the fact that one third of all patients fits into this population: "Cost first and quality care second in providing mental health services has evolved and been operationalized into generic treatments which can be ranked for accessibility by cost" (p. 3). It can be safely assumed that the same conditions remain today. As Mas (2013) has noted, with the advent of managed care, the consequences for those outside of the system have been compromised. Mas has supported this admonition by stating the following: "Price competition or other forms of financial pressures, undermine the ability of a hospital to cross-subsidize. This imposes a large strain on safety net hospitals, challenging their financial sustainability and their survival" (p. 2). This has resulted in closures of smaller hospitals and safety-net hospitals. It also has resulted in the closing of health services by hospitals that serve an uninsured clientele.

The low payment rates associated with managed care, particularly for Medicaid beneficiaries, can be a problem. Healthcare providers are free not to accept lower payments, which can result in gaps in care or lack of care. At first, Medicaid and Medicare did not participate in managed care strategies. However, since 1982, the states increasingly have placed their Medicaid patients in managed care systems. Often, these have taken the form of capitated contracts conducted by Medicaid Managed Care Organizations (MMCO; Book, 2012). These usually accrue to physicians, who then must contract with a clinician for mental health services.

According to Browning and Browning (1996), there are a variety of issues that create problems and make it easy for managed care organizations to deny payment. These issues extend to the present time. Browning and Browning further state that case managers:

> ... want definitive diagnosis within the first five sessions or sooner. It is important to demonstrate that you demonstrate long-range planning after discharge of your client. In order to be able to receive third party payments, therapists must be degreed and licensed to practice psychotherapy. (p. 24)

Gross (personal communication, November 27, 2018) confirms that the Browning and Browning statements regarding the issues with managed care remain relevant today.

System Growth

Professor Gary Burlingame of Brigham Young University has had a distinguished career. He is widely published and has had many consultancies. Burlingame was a consultant to managed care organizations for two decades. He thus has a 20-year perspective on the topic. He commented that size matters.

> *Managed care organizations vary in size. The largest ones can have up to 70 million partici-pants, and the smaller ones can range from 1 million to 20 million participants. Size matters in that smaller organizations can be more nimble and responsive with a more personal touch. The managed-care field changes, as smaller organizations are sometimes acquired by larger organizations, which can get quite large through the merger-acquisition process. It is import-ant to keep in mind that managed care organizations are motivated by profit. Therefore, it is in their best interest to be able to deny payment for clinical activities that do not appear to be evidence based or medically necessary, which results in a gate keeping effect.*
>
> *On the positive side, the managed care organizations tend to approve payment when there is scientific evidence of the efficacy of the treatment. One of the easiest evidence-based prac-tices for a managed care organization to implement is feedback-informed treatment; thus the development of instruments that can be utilized during the treatment process and afterwards is to provide feedback on the progress of therapy. (G. Burlingame, personal communication, September 21, 2018)*

Treatment Efficacy

As Peter Drucker famously stated, "If you can't measure it, you can't improve it" (as cited in Lavinsky, n.d.). One of the most commonly used outcome measurements in counsel-ing is the OQ-45.2, which is designed to measure a client's progress over the course of therapy and after termination. It has three subscales that target problematic areas as a focus of treatment. These three areas provide a continuum over how the client feels inter-nally, how he or she is handling relationships, specifically with significant others, and how he or she is doing in necessary daily tasks, such as work and school. The OQ-ASC (Assessment for Signal Clients) is also commonly used, and it is specifically intended to improve positive psychotherapy results in clients predicted to respond poorly to treat-ment. The OQ-45.2 TA is used to assess a client's perception of his or her relationship with the counselor. According to Burlingame, "The managed-care organizations are looking for at least average therapeutic success as demonstrated by average clinicians who can demonstrate therapeutic success with their clients. This is most easily done with feedback instrumentation results" (personal communication, September 21, 2018). In Burlingame's view, this has enhanced the practice of psychotherapy and can be regarded as a major plus.

Cost-Effectiveness (or Not)

Interestingly, according to Brantes (2018, p. 1), "There is very little risk taken by insur-ers in the commercial sector." Because most large organizations directly bear the risk of healthcare cost, they typically employ a third-party administrator to handle insurance transactions. However, they still utilize managed care, because it operates as a business, with an emphasis on the bottom line. As referred to earlier in this chapter, certain treat-ment decisions are based upon financial interest rather than being strictly guided by clinical considerations. At the same time, lower level employees are wringing every dollar out of clinical care that they can. "Executives at the top of managed care organizations are paid very high salaries and they live a life style that is very different from the average American" (G. Burlingame, personal communication, September 21, 2018). For example, Mark Bertolini, Aetna's CEO, received $41 million in compensation, "including gains on restricted stock granted from 2013–2015 and stock options he was awarded in 2016" (Lee, 2017). According to *Modern Healthcare* (Livingston, 2018), Anthem President and CEO Gail Boudreaux made roughly $2.2 million last year. Hospitals are not immune to paying their administrators large salaries; for example, according to the University of Pittsburgh Medical Center's 990 schedule for fiscal year 2017, the CEO, Jeffrey Romoff, earned a salary just short of $6 million. Additionally, this compensation afforded him access to a private chef, chauffeur, and a private jet. Furthermore, there are a dozen administrators who work under Romoff, who earned over $1 million each in compensation.

It is obvious that managed care must have extremely high profits in order to pay the levels of salaries and to provide this type of compensations noted. And managed care organizations can be very profitable. For example, United Health had a market capital of $179 billion, with a 5-year annual return of 29.8%. Centene Healthcare had a market capital of $14 billion and had a 5-year annual return of 36.4%. Humana had a $34 billion market with a 5-year annual return of 27.6 (Caplinger, 2017).

Medicare and Medicaid

Traditionally, fee for service, or the indemnity plan payments for services performed, was the primary mode of payment for medical care, including mental health services, until Managed Care entered the scene. In 1965, the Medicare program "recognized pre-paid health care plans as a different kind of entity for which a different kind of payment method was necessary" (Zarabozo, 2000). Counselors so far have not been eligible to provide services for Medicare and Medicaid patients, but Medicare and Medicaid have become prominent sources of healthcare, and by extension, mental healthcare. For this reason, increased legislative advocacy for counselor inclusion in this area has been important.

Legislation that was passed in 1972 and 1973 made it possible for Medicare to adopt managed care provisions. The National Health Insurance Proposals in 1972 resulted from then-President Nixon's recommendations in 1971, in which he commented on how much the federal programs spent (as opposed to private insurance) and presented the idea that Medicaid and Medicare should utilize managed care as well. However, instead of large-scale managed care, Medicaid and Medicare only had demonstration projects. As a part of the Tax Equity and Fiscal Responsibility Act of 1982 (TEFRA), through a contracting program that was authorized by the legislation, it became possible for Medicaid and Medicare to institute large-scale managed care programs. In time, these became the largest segment of managed care. In 1985, there were 480 operating HMOs in the United States and 87 Medicare risk contractors. According to Zarabozo (2000, "TEFRA," para. 5), "By the end of 1987, the number of risk contractors rose to 161 (out of 662 operating HMOs)."

▨ PROFESSIONAL ADVOCACY

This section of the chapter aims to shed some light upon the issue and answer some of the pertinent questions that counseling professionals often come across. Counseling is a demanding profession, and there are many medical, ethical, and financial responsibilities that counselors have toward their patients. The idea of advocating actively for a cause can be intimidating, especially for individuals who are not very vocal. Some counselors may want to get involved in professional advocacy but do not know where to start. Some may be involved but lose motivation when challenging circumstances arise. Some may not be interested in participating, as they are burdened by other responsibilities. Thus, it is very important to understand what advocacy is and how it can be exercised. What does it look like in the role of a counselor? What difference does it make?

What Is Advocacy?

Advocacy involves being an active member of the society and speaking on behalf of oneself, as well as others, when needed. It may involve participating in rallies to oppose a law that supports marginalization or oppression or that is not in favor of the general good of the society. It may include writing letters to government officials regarding policy issues, volunteering at community organizations, being active on social media about issues related to policies and public welfare, and educating people about policy issues. Sometimes, advocacy is as simple as making a phone call to the right person.

Counselor Advocacy

In the case of counselor advocacy, it is important to realize that our field of counseling has benefited greatly from legislation over the last four decades, especially legislation related to counselor licensure. The legislation has made it possible for professionals to receive a license and to have both a legal and professional role to play in enhancing the quality of life for others. This did not happen until legislation made it possible. As an example, a great deal of effort was made in the senior author's home state of Indiana. It took several years of working with legislative committees and building support throughout the state so that the legislators understood there was a groundswell of support for Counselor Licensure before legislation was enacted.

Working collaboratively with others and advocating for desirable change certainly can be an important part of the counselor's role. It is important to identify the problems that need to be addressed, and to have a plan for advocacy that can include writing letters and identifying allies, opponents, relevant decision makers, and important committees. In some cases, speaking on behalf of an issue is important; in other cases, listing others as allies and having a joint effort is the best way to influence legislation. As noted earlier, counselors are not approved as providers for Medicare and Medicaid; this most likely will not change without a great deal of advocacy.

Client Advocacy

In the context of professional counseling, advocacy for clients involves providing resources to empower the client, collaborating with community organizations, participating in rallies to support a cause, and writing to lawmakers on behalf of the client. However, the idea here is not to try to be a savior but, rather, a guide. The aim is to contribute toward creating policies that empower people so that they can be more independent and take better steps to improve their lives.

According to Baruth and Manning (2016), multicultural competence is one of the core aspects of client advocacy. Developing an understanding of different cultures also enables clinicians to understand the flaws in a system and to be aware of how they contribute to the oppression of certain groups of people and perhaps even propagate clinical problems in the society.

As counselors, clinicians, researchers, and educators, it is our responsibility, and a rather important one, to come forward as advocates for the field, for best practices, and for better laws.

Advocacy is a complex issue; however, one of the simplest functions that counselors can perform, as advocates for social justice, is to educate their clients about mental health-related policies and their effect on clients' health and well-being. In order to do this, counselors have to educate themselves first. The best way to become educated regarding current issues in the field is to get involved with professional counseling organizations.

Professional Associations

Counseling organizations provide a reliable resource for remaining current with matters in the field and for networking with other professionals. Counselors are able to gain access to trainings and certifications offered by the professional organizations, to keep abreast of current clinical updates, and to learn about better career prospects. Large associations also provide professional resources, liability insurance, and a variety of discounts to their members. Research even has shown that counselors who have emblems from reputed organizations displayed in their offices are perceived as being more competent by their clients (Heppner & Pew, 1977). We have included six counseling organizations, relevant to the discussion in this chapter, with brief descriptions of their areas of focus, membership benefits, trainings and certifications, the communities they serve, and how actively they advocate for clients and encourage participation by the counselors.

1. *American Counseling Association*

   The ACA is the largest association in the world that represents the field of counseling. Its members get an exposure to a variety of learning experiences through webinars, podcasts, and online courses, making it easier to earn continuing education (CE) credits and access to professional resources such as books, journals, online community, and membership discounts. In addition to this, ACA is a well-represented platform and garners national media attention for advocacy and promoting counseling as a profession. The ACA public policy website at *counseling.org/publicpolicy* is a great resource to learn about legislative issues and advocacy in general.

2. *National Board for Certified Counselors*

   The NBCC is the credentialing body for counselors. It provides information regarding applicable contacts, available licenses, and required examinations in different states within the United States. It has a broad network of certified counselors, which can be a helpful resource for career development.

   The NBCC also is actively involved in governmental affairs and advocacy to help pass measures that support the counseling profession. The NBCC's grassroots network is a good place to start getting involved in advocacy as counselors.

3. *American Mental Health Counselors Association*

   American Mental Health Counselors Association (AMHCA) works exclusively for the mental health counseling profession, promoting career growth in the mental health profession by developing a better understanding of issues related to medical settings, risk prevention, ethical standards, and other issues related to mental health counseling. Members can earn CE credits and accrue benefits related to health and insurance. The AMHCA is working actively to promote Medicare provider recognition for counselors, improve insurance portability, increase professional unification between education and training, and enhance benefits pertaining to many other important professional issues.

4. *American School Counselor Association*

   The American School Counselor Association (ASCA) focuses on supporting school counselors and helping them resolve issues related to academic, career, and social–emotional development of students. Members have access to online journals, archives, free professional liability insurance, and free resources such as sample lesson plans, job descriptions, and checklists. The ASCA also provides professional development opportunities through conferences, webinars, and workshops.

5. *Association for Multicultural Counseling and Development*

   The Association for Multicultural Counseling and Development (AMCD) promotes and defends human and civil rights and encourages cultural diversity and acceptance. It helps members in developing multicultural competencies and promotes career growth through participation in regional and state division activities.

6. *National Association for Alcoholism and Drug Abuse Counselors*

   The National Association for Alcoholism and Drug Abuse Counselors (NAADAC) is a global organization that focuses on addiction prevention, treatment, recovery, and education. NAADAC has a wide network of 100,000 counselors and educators. NAADAC actively advocates in favor of providing affordable care to individuals affected by substance abuse, ensuring that the Affordable Care Act is not repealed and increasing federal funding for addiction prevention, treatment, and research. NAADAC provides several membership benefits that include free CE credits, subscription to its official magazine, webinars, and networking opportunities and certifications.

We discussed the importance of legislative advocacy earlier. When thinking about counselor advocacy, it is important to think of the small ways that we, as counselors, can make a difference in the lives of our clients. It does not have to be big; sometimes, just a phone call is enough. A graduate student from the University of Miami shared her experience in working with clients who learned English as their second language: "I would help them in understanding insurance policies and make necessary calls on their behalf" (personal communication, October 10, 2018). Another final-year graduate student from the University of Miami talks about her experience in working with HIV-positive clients:

> As a counselor working with HIV-positive populations, my responsibility is not limited to simply counseling. I address the fact that my clients are going through other issues that have a cumulative effect on their medication adherence and general health attitude. I make referrals for anyone that needs them. Also, helping them in finding a job or getting them on disability if they qualify goes a long way as prescription and other treatments can take a toll financially. (personal communication, October 28, 2018)

CONCLUSION

The aim of the chapter was to shed light on how the managed care system works as well as the counselor's role in managed care and the importance of advocacy and issues related to payment and reimbursement. This chapter offers a starting point to understand the system, and counselors must continue to seek more resources, join organizations, and build networks with other counselors and change makers to become active members of the professional community. Managed care is an integral part of the healthcare system, and it is imperative for counselors to be able to understand the system in order to navigate it better. Counselors can anticipate the issues that are related to cost and payments and can provide more efficient service to the clients, if they understand how the managed care system operates. Not only understanding the system but being an active participant when it comes to legislation and changing the system for the benefit of clients and counselors themselves are also part of being a responsible counselor.

RESOURCES

American Counseling Association: https://www.counseling.org
American Mental Health Counselors Association: www.amhca.org

American School Counselor Association: www.schoolcounselor.org

Association for Multicultural Counseling and Development: https://multiculturalcounsel ingdevelopment.org

National Association for Alcoholism and Drug Abuse Counselors: https://www.naadac.org

National Board for Certified Counselors: www.nbcc.org

REFERENCES

American Federation of State, County, and Municipal Employees. (n.d.). What is managed care? Retrieved from https://www.afscme.org/news/publications/health-care/managed -care-what-you-dont-know-can-hurt-you/what-is-managed-care

Baruth, L. G., & Manning, M. L. (2016). *Multicultural counseling and psychotherapy: A lifespan approach.* New York, NY: Routledge.

Book, R. (2012, October 18). Benefits and challenges of Medicaid managed care. Retrieved from https://www.forbes.com/sites/aroy/2012/10/18/benefits-and-challenges-of-medicaid -managed-care/#7b27798c720f

Brantes, F. (2018, October 29). An APM that would actually work. Retrieved from https:// www.managedcaremag.com/archives/2018/11/apm-would-actually-work

Browning, C. H., & Browning, B. J. (1996). H*ow to partner with managed care: A "do-it -yourself kit" for building working relationships & getting steady referrals* (Exp. ed.). Oxford, UK: John Wiley & Sons.

Burns, J. (2018, November). There's a better way to do step therapy. Retrieved from https:// www.managedcaremag.com/archives/2018/11/there-s-better-way-do-step-therapy

Caplinger, D. (2017, July 15). What managed care organizations are and how investors can profit from them. Retrieved from https://www.fool.com/investing/2017/07/15/what -managed-care-organizations-are-and-how-invest.aspx

Dana, R. H. (1998). Problems with managed mental health care for multicultural populations. *Psychological Reports, 83*(1), 283–294. doi:10.2466/PR0.83.5.283-294

Gross, J. M. (1997). Promoting group psychotherapy in managed care: Basic economic principles for the clinical practitioner. *International Journal of Group Psychotherapy, 47*(4), 499–507. doi:10.1080/00207284.1997.11490847

Heppner, P. P., & Pew, S. (1977). Effects of diplomas, awards, and counselor sex on perceived expertness. *Journal of Counseling Psychology, 24*(2), 147. doi:10.1037/0022-0167.24.2.147

Lavinsky, D. (n.d.). The two most important quotes in business. Retrieved from https://www .growthink.com/content/two-most-important-quotes-business

Lee, M. (2017, April 11). Aetna CEO Mark Bertolini's compensation surged in 2016. Retrieved from https://www.courant.com/business/hc-aetna-ceo-pay-20170411-story.html

Livingston, S. (2018, March 12). Health insurer CEOs see some significant pay bumps in 2018. Retrieved from https://www.modernhealthcare.com/article/20180312/NEWS/180319975

Mas, N. (2013). Responding to financial pressures. The effect of managed care on hospitals' provision of charity care. *International Journal of Health Care Finance and Economics, 13*(2), 95–114. doi:10.1007/s10754-013-9124-7

National Conference of State legislatures. (2017, July 1). Managed care, market reports and the states. Retrieved from http://www.ncsl.org/research/health/managed-care-and-the -states.aspx

Patient Advocate Foundation. (n.d.). Managed care answer guide. Retrieved from http:// fliphtml5.com/fnpt/yipm

Reinhardt, U. E. (1998). Quality in consumer-driven health systems. *International Journal for Quality in Health Care, 10*(5), 385–394. doi:10.1093/intqhc/10.5.385

Ribeiro, M. D., Gross, J. M., & Turner, M. M. (Eds.). (2017). *The college counselor's guide to group psychotherapy.* New York, NY: Routledge.

Speights, K. (2015, October 6). What is managed care. Retrieved from https://www.fool.com/investing/general/2015/10/06/what-is-managed-care.aspx

Statistica. (2018). U.S. national health expenditure as percent of GDP from 1960 to 2018. Retrieved from https://www.statista.com/statistics/184968/us-health-expenditure-as-percent-of-gdp-since-1960

U.S. National Library of Medicine. (2018). Managed care. Retrieved from https://medlineplus.gov/managedcare.html

Zarabozo, C. (2000, Fall). Milestones in Medicare managed care. Retrieved from https://www.ncbi.nlm.nih.gov/pmc/articles/PMC4194694

SECTION V

CLIENT-CARE AND
SELF-CARE PRACTICES

CHAPTER 13

CLINICAL SUPERVISION AND PROFESSIONAL DEVELOPMENT

DEBRA HYATT-BURKHART

This chapter provides a brief overview of models of clinical supervision. It also offers a brief discussion of best practices, common struggles, and a salutogenic- or wellness-based approach to supervision, emphasizing how the latter complements parallel treatment interventions with consumers. The chapter urges counselor trainees to engage continuing education and continued professional development as a part of their career-pathway planning. The discussion emphasizes the importance of remaining current, concerning clinical counseling issues as an ethical issue that is inherent in being a professional. The following Council for the Accreditation of Counseling and Related Educational Programs (CACREP) standards are addressed in this chapter:
   CACREP 2016:
     2F1.k, 2F1.l, 2F1.m
   CACREP 2009:
     2G1.e

LEARNING OBJECTIVES

After reviewing this chapter, the readers should be able to:

1. Demonstrate an understanding of the purpose, importance, and value of clinical supervision;

2. Demonstrate a basic knowledge of the commonly used models of clinical supervision;

3. Articulate an understanding of a wellness-based and salutogenic-based approach to clinical supervision; and,

4. Demonstrate an understanding of the importance of continuing education and professional development as a part of ethical practice.

▤ INTRODUCTION: DEFINITION OF CLINICAL SUPERVISION

Long before professional counselors embarked upon any kind of professional path, they received supervision. Merriam-Webster.com defines supervision as "a critical watching and directing (as of activities or a course of action)." Parents, teachers, babysitters, coaches, and a whole host of other adults provided these counselors with critical watching and directing beginning on the day that they were born. As children, they were supervised in order to protect them from dangers of which they may have been unaware, to help them learn new ways of behaving, and to develop an understanding of social norms and expectations. As they matured, that watching and directing became more focused, nuanced, and targeted toward areas for growth and the enhancement of existing skills. As they moved into the world of work, a superior or boss at a job provided training, guidance, and an evaluation of their performance at that place of work. In internships and field experiences, on-the-job training and oversight by an experienced practitioner in the field was provided as an integral part of the learning environment. These activities were all types of supervision. Someone who had more knowledge, skills, and competencies helped those counselors to grow and develop in a way that informed them and kept them safe as they learned.

Supervision is an essential component of the ethical practice of counseling. The 2014 American Counseling Association (ACA) *Code of Ethics* contains a number of standards that specifically address the need for ongoing supervision and consultation as a best practice for the field. Counseling supervision is an extension of the types of supervision that commonly are received throughout our early lives, but this supervision is specifically focused on professional counseling-related behaviors. Although readers of this text are likely at the beginning of their educational process and have little practical experience with counseling, having a basic knowledge of the definition, purpose, approaches, and theories of clinical supervision will become highly applicable as they move forward in their careers.

There are two main types of supervision in which professional counselors participate. The first is administrative supervision. Administrative supervision generally refers to the monitoring, mentoring, and oversight counselors may receive regarding their general job functions. Here, the focus is usually upon documentation, paperwork, workplace behaviors, such as timeliness, and other managerial issues that can be found in most employment settings. The second type of supervision for professional counselors is clinical supervision. This supervision is focused upon a counselor's work in the treatment of clients. It is quite common that one supervisor is responsible for providing both types of supervision, which, as I will discuss later, can be a significant tension that can create interesting issues for both the supervisor and supervisee. As clinical supervision is unique to the helping professions, we will focus more on its provision throughout this chapter.

Bernard and Goodyear (2018) have provided one of the most commonly used definitions of clinical counseling. They define supervision as:

> ... an intervention provided by a more senior member of a profession to a more junior colleague or colleagues who typically (but not always) are members of the same profession. This relationship is evaluative and hierarchical, extends over time, and has the

simultaneous purposes of enhancing the professional functioning of the more junior person; monitoring the quality of professional services offered to the clients that she, he, or they see; and serving as a gatekeeper for the particular profession the supervisee seeks to enter. (Bernard & Goodyear, 2018, p. 9)

There are parts of this definition with which I agree, and others to which I prefer a different approach. Supervision is not always provided by a senior member to a junior member. Sometimes, peers of equal tenure provide supervision to one another and, in fact, sometimes the supervisor is actually newer to the profession than the supervisee. Other definitions of clinical supervision provide a clearer delineation of the purpose and desired outcomes without limiting the scope of the relationship. One such definition is that provided by Inskipp and Proctor (2019) who define supervision as:

A working alliance between the supervisor and counsellor in which the counsellor can offer an account or recording of her work; reflect on it; receive feedback and where appropriate, guidance. The object of this alliance is to enable the counsellor to gain in ethical competence, confidence, compassion and creativity in order to give her best possible service to the client. (p. 1)

This definition encompasses many of the components of the Bernard and Goodyear definition but seems more clearly to articulate the tasks involved in supervision and its overall purpose. In particular, the notions that the work is conducted through an alliance between the counselor and supervisor (without specification of the tenure or status of the participants) and that the ultimate goal of supervision is to improve the functioning of the counselor in order to attend best to the client's needs seem to be highlighted.

Purpose of Clinical Supervision Within Ethical Practice

These definitions delineate three important facets of the work of clinical supervision. The primary objective is to protect the client and ensure that the counselor is providing services that, at a minimum, do no harm and, at an aspirational level, are providing the best services possible to the clients. In short, there is a gatekeeping, evaluative function to supervision wherein the supervisor is responsible for ensuring that the supervisee is competent, healthy, and unimpaired relative to the practice of counseling.

The second objective of clinical supervision is to enhance the ethical and practical functioning of the counselor. Supervisors work to assist supervisees to improve their general skills, develop their competencies, and enhance their understanding and implementation of the code of ethics.

Finally, supervisors provide support, encouragement, and guidance to their supervisees. Supervision is a multipurpose endeavor that, when done well, balances the tension between the supervisor being appropriately challenging and thought-provoking and offering the necessary support and reassurance. When provided effectively, supervision can be an important part of counselor self-care. Self-care is an important part of a counselor's efforts to maintain general and mental health. Taking care of one's self and maintaining a healthy emotional approach to the work is also essential for a clinician's ability to provide clients with the best possible services. Supervisors have the ability to help counselors stay well, find benefit from the work, and maintain longevity in the profession.

As mentioned, supervision is a vital component of the ethical practice of counseling. The 2014 ACA *Code of Ethics* contains a number of standards that specifically address the need for ongoing supervision and consultation as a best practice for the field. Standard F.1.a. of the ACA 2014 *Code of Ethics* states that "A primary obligation of counseling supervisors is to monitor the services provided by supervisees. Counseling supervisors monitor client welfare and supervisee performance and professional development" (p. 12). The work of counseling is serious. Counselors are involving themselves in people's lives, relationships, fundamental psychological functioning, and systemic contexts. Having oversight of one's work is crucial to maintaining objectivity. We cannot always know where our blind spots or missteps are, but a supervisor can help us to see them, reflect upon them, and keep our clients safe.

When discussing supervision with my students, I like to use the analogy of golf. I love to play the game, but I am by no means ready for the professional tour. I have bad habits with my form that have developed over time. I know I have these bad habits, because when I hit the ball, it does not always go where I want it to go. Sometimes, it ends up in the woods or in the lake, despite that fact that I was aiming at the hole in the center of the green. When I hit an errant shot, I rarely know what I did wrong, but my playing partners, who can see my swing, do know. They watched me swing the club! They can see that I picked my head up, or lifted my foot, or failed to rotate my hips. From my vantage point, inside my own body, I can't see those things. Their vantage point, or their "super vision," can provide me with critical information that may improve my next shot. Clinical supervision of counseling is much the same. Practitioners are often too close to the treatment of the client to see clearly what is occurring with the process. There may be areas for improvement and areas of strength that, when pointed out, can be changed or enhanced to increase the efficacy of the supervisees' work. A knowledgeable, outside supervisor, who has the benefit of greater objectivity, often can help to expose such issues.

With respect to skill development, standard C.2.d. of the ACA (2014) *Code of Ethics* states "Counselors continually monitor their effectiveness as professionals and take steps to improve when necessary. Counselors take reasonable steps to seek peer supervision to evaluate their efficacy as counselors" (p. 9). It is not just supervisors who are responsible for monitoring our effectiveness; it is our responsibility to seek out supervision. Early in counseling practitioners' careers, some level of clinical supervision is mandated. The CACREP (2015) standards dictate that practicum and internship students receive a minimum of 1.5 hours of group supervision at the university level and 1 hour of individual supervision at their sites. Further, all state licensure boards require that prelicensed counselors work under clinical supervision for 2 or more years, although the number of hours and types of supervision vary widely (ACA, 2016). A review of state requirements reveals that most stipulate a minimum of 100 hours of face-to-face clinical supervision prior to being eligible to obtain a license. Many states permit a blend of distance and in-person oversight, as well as group and individual formats. Just as there is no uniform requirement for counseling licensure in the United States, there is no standardized approach as to the number of hours, type, and approach to prelicensure supervision (Gray & Erickson, 2013). What is clear in the ACA 2016 report is that prelicensed counselors are required to engage in supervised work in order to qualify to earn their license. The implication is that supervision is an essential part of counselor development.

Unfortunately, the requirement for clinical supervision does not generally extend beyond the achievement of licensure. A review of the continuing education requirements for licensed professional counselors across the country contained in the ACA 2016 report cited earlier found no mandate for any ongoing supervised practice. There are requirements for continuing education hours related to training as a supervisor, but there is no reference to any need to continue to receive some level of clinical supervision once a practitioner has obtained a license. This lack of mandate for ongoing supervision may be one reason that not all counseling positions offer clinical supervision as a routine or compulsory part of the job. Often, supervision is conducted at the personal cost of the counselor or through a network of peers who agree to support one another. Regardless of how it occurs, ongoing, post-licensure clinical supervision is an important part of an ethical approach to the work of counseling. As research into the benefits of supervision continues, such practice may be incorporated into continuing education requirements in the future.

Models of Clinical Supervision

Just as there are many theoretical models of counseling, there are many theoretical models that are applied to clinical supervision. Counseling theory provides an organizational framework that helps clinicians to understand their client's development, behavior, and thinking (Kottler & Montgomery, 2010). Further, theory can provide clinicians with insight into the overall direction of treatment and appropriate interventions to use with their clients (Rønnestad & Skovholt, 2013). The same notions apply to grounding the work of clinical supervision into a theoretical orientation or specific model. Supervision theory provides the supervisor with a conceptual framework or mechanism for understanding counselors and their work (Bernard & Goodyear, 2018). As in counseling theory, the models of supervision can be segregated into categories based upon the focus of the models themselves. What follows is a brief discussion of the categories of models of clinical supervision and an overview of common approaches within each category. These models and approaches are provided as an introduction to theories of clinical supervision. As students progress through their program of studies and begin to practice counseling and receive supervision, it will be important for them to develop a deeper understanding of supervisory practices. Students quickly will become consumers of supervision in the fieldwork experiences. Further, it is not uncommon for relatively novice counselors to find themselves in supervisory roles in the field. This basic overview can serve as a springboard toward a more nuanced understanding of supervision.

Developmental Models of Clinical Supervision

As the name implies, developmental models of clinical supervision focus on the stage or level of evolving skills, competencies, confidence, and awareness of the counselor supervisee and the ways in which supervisors accommodate the changing needs of their supervisees. These models subscribe to the notion that as supervisees grow and acquire more advanced competencies, their needs and preferences within the supervisory relationship also shift (Russell-Chapin & Chapin, 2012). As the needs of the supervisee shift, it is the responsibility of supervisors to alter their approach and interventions to meet the new needs of their supervisee. Throughout the process of developmental supervision, it is the job of the supervisor to provide interventions, feedback, and support that are appropriate for the current functioning of the supervisee, while being mindful to challenge the supervisee in order to scaffold higher order thinking (Smith, 2009).

There are many developmental models of supervision that differ slightly in the lens through which development is viewed. Some developmental models take an approach grounded in psychosocial developmental theory (Loganbill, Hardy, & Delworth, 1982; Stoltenberg, 1981), while others adopt a life-span approach (Rønnestad & Skolvholt, 2003). What is consistent among these models is that they identify specific characteristics common to counselors at various stages of growth and that they pinpoint corresponding sets of supervisory tasks and interventions necessary to support supervisees during each state of development. For the purposes of this overview, I present Stoltenberg, McNeil, and Delworth's (1998) Integrated Developmental Model (IDM) of supervision, which is the most widely used of these types of models (Bernard & Goodyear, 2018) and the Rønnestad and Skolvholt (2003) model, which emphasizes the continued development of counselors across the life span.

Integrated Developmental Model

The IDM provides four distinct levels or stages of supervisee development (although the forth level is labeled 3i, which can be confusing). Each level is assessed through the domains of motivation, autonomy, and awareness. Level 1 supervisees are characterized as having limited training and/or experience (perhaps at the beginning of field work). Motivation is generally high, as is the level of anxiety. Level 1 supervisees want to know the "right" way to work with clients. Their autonomy is limited, they depend on the supervisor for positive support, and they prefer little confrontation. Level 1 supervisees have limited awareness. They tend to focus on themselves with minimal insight. They are resistant to evaluation, which may be perceived as critical and discouraging. Supervision at this level tends to be characterized by a great deal of support with directive or prescriptive interventions provided by the supervisor.

Level 2 supervisees have some experience (perhaps being toward the end of their practicum or internship). Their motivation and confidence fluctuate from confused and unsure to very confident. Autonomy also vacillates between dependency and a strong desire for independence. Awareness is more centered on the client instead of the self, but issues with fusion and enmeshment may arise with the growing ability to empathize with the client. Level 2 counselors function much like adolescents commonly behave with their parents. There is a push and pull between needs and wants. A tension exists between the counselors wanting to be independent and autonomous versus wanting to be given direction and told how to do the work correctly. Here, supervisors must balance support and challenge with direction and self-determination as supervisees' needs dictate.

Level 3 supervisees are much more stable in their functioning. These counselors are more experienced and secure in their competencies (new professionals). They tend to have stable motivation that involves realistic assessments of their own functioning. They have developed a sense of their own competencies and skills sets and can thereby function autonomously with confidence. Level 3 supervisee awareness is comprised of a balance between empathetic engagement with the client and attention to self-care and individuation (Falender & Shafrenske, 2004). Level 3 supervisees are approaching a more collaborative and collegial relationship with the supervisors as skill levels between the two tend to be less and less disparate. The supervisory relationship here is less hierarchical and more egalitarian. There is little direct intervention and a more consultative atmosphere to the work.

Finally, Level 3i (integrated) supervisees have begun to integrate skills and competencies across all of the domains involved with client care (Bernard & Goodyear, 2018). Stoltenberg et al. (1998) identified the following eight areas of professional growth in which the supervisee will develop:

1. Interventions skills competence—the confidence to engage in therapeutic interventions;

2. Assessment techniques—understanding and administering assessments;

3. Interpersonal assessment—using the self in conceptualizing client issues;

4. Client conceptualization—being able to understand how the clients' biopsychosocial environment influences their functioning;

5. Individual differences—understanding multicultural influence upon the client;

6. Theoretical orientation—understanding and applying theory;

7. Treatment plans and goals—ability to plan and organize appropriate interventions; and,

8. Professional ethics—integration of professional and personal ethics.

Level 3i supervisees have a motivation toward professional practice that is characterized by autonomy and an accurate assessment of their own strengths and areas for growth. Supervision with Level 3i supervisees is much more consultative and collegial than at lower levels of development. The supervisor is a partner in the ongoing, collaborative development of the supervisee. As part of the ongoing refinement of the IDM model, McNeill, Stoltenberg and Romans (1992) developed the Supervisee Levels Questionnaire—Revised, which can be used by supervisors to assess objectively the developmental level of their supervisees.

The IDM is not without criticism. Ladany, Marotta, and Muse-Burke (2001) conducted a study of 100 supervisees and found that there was no predicted preference for supervisor style or approach based on the trainees' experience, skill with conceptualization, or familiarity with client's presenting symptoms. Their study suggests that developmental models may take too simplistic of an approach to counselor development and should, perhaps, incorporate a more nuanced assessment that focuses less on supervisee experience levels. Further, although IDM has been explored empirically and refined as a result of the research conducted, the model does not contain significant detail regarding specific supervisor interventions and techniques for working with supervisees at each level. There are few explicit details as to how a supervisor can and should intervene in order best to meet the needs of practitioners at each specific stage. Finally, the model also is weighted heavily toward the examination of counselor trainees and students and does not give consideration to the ongoing developmental behaviors of counselors across their life span (Haynes, Corey, & Moulton, 2003). This final criticism leads us to the discussion of the Rønnestad and Skovholt model.

Rønnestad and Skovholt Model

Rønnestad and Skovholt (1993) formulated their model as a result of a longitudinal, qualitative study of 100 counselors who had a range of experience from beginning graduate school through 40 years of practice, with an average of 25 years of experience. Initially, their data led them to identify eight stages of counselor development, 20 themes of development that occur over time, and a general model of development and stagnation. In 2003, Rønnestad and Skovholt presented a more refined approach to their model that contains six "phases" of development and 14 themes. They dropped the use of the term "stage" in favor of the use of the word "phase" because they felt that the word stage indicated a "hierarchical, sequential and invariant ordering of qualitatively different functioning/structures" (Rønnestad & Skovholt, 2003, p. 40). The names of each phase are fairly self-explanatory, but I describe them briefly in the following for clarity. Note that the first three phases correspond quite closely with the first three level of the IDM.

Phase 1: Lay Helper. This phase is characterized by new counselors who are not particularly well trained and rely upon their own experiences to provide support and to give advice. They tend to have issues with becoming enmeshed with their clients.

Phase 2: Beginning Student. This phase is characterized by students early in their professional training. These supervisees are generally anxious, rely upon their supervisors for guidance and direction, and have low self-confidence that they know the "right" approach to their clients. They need significant support and may respond to criticism negatively.

Phase 3: Advanced Student. This phase is characterized by students who are generally finishing their program of studies and fieldwork experiences. These practitioners have more confidence than those in previous phases of development but still require support and encouragement that they are on the right path with their clients. Phase 3 supervisees are generally cautious and do not engage in significant risk taking (Bernard & Goodyear, 2018).

Phase 4: Novice Professional. Spanning across the first few years after graduate school training, novice professionals are engaged in solidifying their own style and approach to counseling independent of the guidance of formal schooling. These supervisees are establishing their own preferences and approach to the work of counseling. They are growing in confidence while developing a more realistic assessment of their own skill sets and strength.

Phase 5: Experienced Professional. In this phase, relatively experienced counselors are engaged in integrating their own core understanding of the work and themselves within the counseling relationships that they form. They are better able to establish working relationships that are characterized by appropriate boundaries that promote quality empathetic engagement without enmeshment. Counselors in this phase have developed an understanding that there really is no "right" answer or approach with any given client, and they are flexible with their style.

Phase 6: Senior Professionals. Characterized by practitioners with more than 20 years of experience, this phase looks in some ways like Erikson's stage of integrity versus despair. Here, counselors have a realistic view of the work. They have developed an individualized, genuine style and are consciously aware of their own importance within the work. This phase may contain themes of loss as mentors may have retired or died.

As mentioned, Rønnestad and Skovholt's (2003) study also produced 14 themes related to counselor development. These themes are:

1.   Professional development involves an increasing higher order integration of the professional self and the personal self.

2.   The focus of functioning shifts dramatically over time from internal to external to internal.

3.   Continuous reflection is a prerequisite for optimal learning and professional development at all levels of experience.

4.   An intense commitment to learn propels the developmental process.

5.   The cognitive map changes: Beginning practitioners rely on external expertise, while seasoned practitioners rely on internal expertise.

6.   Professional development is a long, slow, continuous process that can also be erratic.

7.   Professional development is a lifelong process.

8.   Many beginning practitioners experience much anxiety in their professional work. Over time, anxiety is mastered by most.

9.   Clients serve as a major source of influence and serve as primary teachers.

10.   Personal life influences professional functioning and development throughout the professional life span.

11.   Interpersonal sources of influence propel professional development more than "impersonal" sources of influence.

12.   New members of the field view professional elders and graduate training with strong affective reactions.

13. Extensive experience with suffering contributes to heightened recognition, acceptance, and appreciation of human variability.

14. For the practitioner there is a realignment from self as hero to client as hero.

Supervisors can use this list of themes to help supervisees explore specific areas for growth and development within any of the six phases. These themes help to provide the supervisor with directions upon which to focus supervisee self-reflection, which Rønnestad and Skovholt (2003) assert is an essential part of counselor development.

Theoretic Specific Models of Counselor Supervision

If there is a theoretic orientation to counseling, there is likely a corresponding theory of supervision that goes along with it. Theoretic specific approaches to supervision tend to wax and wane in popularity along with the theories to which they are attached. There are, however, a number of theories that have endured, which I briefly review in the following subsections.

Psychodynamic Supervision

I begin our discussion of the theoretic specific models of supervision with the psychodynamic model because it has its beginnings rooted in classic, Freudian psychodynamics. As expected, this approach examines the transference and countertransference, affective reactions, and defense mechanisms familiar to the practice of psychodynamic-based counseling. In its earliest forms, psychodynamic supervision fell into one of two distinct views. Those in the Budapest School believed that supervision should be a part of the therapist's personal work in analysis. Those in the Viennese School believed that supervision should be a process by which the supervisee was taught about and learned about psychodynamic work and how his or her experience within the work was explained by the theory. In either case, the supervisor, just as the psychoanalyst, is seen as an uninvolved expert who possesses the skills and knowledge to educate and promote the supervisee's development (Frawley-O'Dea & Sarnat, 2001).

Psychodynamic supervision has continued to be developed, refined, and researched. Frawley-O'Dea and Sarnat (2001) sought to modernize psychodynamic theory as it is applied to supervision. They conceptualize the work as occurring in three separate categories: patient-centered, supervisee-centered, and supervisory matrix-centered. Patient-centered revolves around the patient's (or client's) behaviors, symptoms, and presentation, where the supervisor maintains the detached, expert role. Here, the supervisor is very much a teacher engaged in a low conflict, didactic relationship with the supervisee. Supervisee-centered focuses on the counselor's experience of and reactions to the work of counseling while addressing their own anxieties and resistance (Falender & Shafranske, 2004). Finally, the supervisory matrix-centered approach focuses on both the client's and supervisee's issues as needed. There is also an additional layer of examination of the relationship between the supervisee and the supervisor, because this relationship often can mimic that which happens between counselor and client. This phenomenon is called parallel process.

CASE ILLUSTRATION 13.1

AN EXAMPLE OF PARALLEL PROCESS

Take the case of a Sam, a supervisee who is defensive regarding the feedback that the supervisor is providing regarding the treatment of a client. Sam's supervisor has been working with him regarding his tendency to not confront his clients in session. Sam has difficulty accepting this criticism and finds ways to refute or discount the information as being false. He tries to provide his supervisor with examples of when he has been confrontational and prove to his supervisor that her assessment of his abilities is incorrect. Sam's client, Michael, also is demonstrating resistance to the feedback that is being provided during counseling sessions. Sam has been trying to point out that Michael says that he wants to have a closer relationship with his wife, but his actions push her away. In session, Michael attempts to provide Sam with examples of times that he acted in a manner that would bring him closer to his wife. He tried to prove that Sam is incorrect in his observations.

Michael is engaged in denying or rejecting Sam's critical information. Although the topic at hand is not the same, Sam and Michael are both trying to discount the feedback they are receiving and disprove the observations of another.

Parallel process can be a powerful dynamic in the client–counselor–supervisor relationship that can negatively impact progress if it left unaddressed. I will talk more about this process later in this chapter.

Frawley-O'Dea and Sarnat (2001) discussed three dimensions of psychodynamic supervision that can provide a conceptual framework within which to understand the process of supervision. Dimension one is the nature of the supervisor's authority in relationship to the supervisee. Bernard and Goodyear (2018) describe this authority as occurring on a continuum between uninvolved/involved and knowing/unknowing. Dimension two is the focus of the supervisor related to the three categorical approaches described previously. Finally, dimension three refers to the roles and approach that the supervisor may adopt within the supervisory session. Frawley-O'Dea and Sarnat (2001) identify didactic teacher, Socratic questioner, container of supervisees' affective reactions, and counselor, among others (Bernard & Goodyear, 2018).

Person-Centered Supervision

Person-centered supervision is based upon the counseling theory of the same name developed by Carl Rogers. His theory centers upon the belief that people are capable of understanding themselves and their problems and that they can use this understanding to resolve effectively their own issues without direction, guidance, or interpretation of these issues from a counselor (Haynes et al., 2003). Of importance in Roger's theory was the emphasis that he placed upon the characteristics of the counselor and the relationship between counselors and clients in assisting clients to achieve self-actualization and the attainment of their goals. In person-centered counseling, the counselor is not an expert or an authority, but someone who creates a relationship that is characterized by genuineness, caring, respect, acceptance, and understanding that helps clients to feel free to work toward the resolution of their own problems (Corey, 2017).

Person-centered counseling supervision is conducted in much the same manner as counseling. The supervisor is not viewed as an expert or an authority figure but rather acts as a collaborator or partner (Smith, 2009). The relationship between the supervisor and supervisee is the primary facilitator for growth and change on the part of the supervisee. The supervisor's role is to create the environment that helps to free supervisees from being locked into their own preconceived notions of themselves and the work so that they can develop more effective ways of functioning.

Cognitive Behavioral Supervision

Cognitive behavioral supervision (CBS) is based upon the tenets of cognitive behavioral therapy (CBT) first developed by Aaron Beck in the 1960s. He found that people's automatic thoughts, beliefs, and assumptions created distress and disturbance and led them to behave in certain ways. Beck and his colleagues described CBT as follows:

> *The approach consists of highly specific learning experiences designed to teach the patient the following operations: (1) to monitor his negative, automatic thoughts (cognitions); (2) to recognize the connections between cognitions, affect, and behavior; (3) to examine the evidence for and against his distorted automatic thoughts; (4) to substitute more reality-oriented interpretations for these biased cognitions; and (5) to learn to identify and alter the dysfunctional beliefs which predispose him to distort experiences. (Beck, Rush, Shaw, & Emery, 1979, p. 4)*

In CBS, the central purpose is to teach clinicians CBT and enhance their understanding of the use of the theory and to eliminate any misconceptions related to the provision of CBT (Liese & Beck, 1997). The focus is on the supervisor teaching and evaluating the skills and competencies of the supervisee as they relate to the provision of CBT. As the theory has developed, some supervisors have begun to incorporate a focus on the supervisees' own cognitions and beliefs as they influence the supervisees' behavior with clients and perhaps the supervisees' professional identity (Haynes, Corey, & Moulton, 2003). As in CBT, the relationship between the supervisee and supervisor has only minimal importance to the process, which is focused on mastery of CBT skills.

Systemic Supervision

Systemic models of supervision most often are used by those who are engaged in the practice of family therapy. Models such as structural, Bowenian, and strategic family therapy all share a focus upon the interactions, relationships, and systemic dynamics that influence a system's members. As with other theoretically specific models, the supervisory applications of systems theories all vary slightly in accordance with the specific approach, but they have a common understanding of the importance of client, supervisee, and supervisor as in relationship with one another. Further, the biopsychosocial context of all of the members of the system is viewed as an essential component of the functioning of the relationship. Simply put, the client/family has a context and a worldview that are created as a result of their experience within their own context. The counselor/supervisee and the supervisor each has his or her own unique context and worldview. When the counselor/supervisee is in relationship with the client, the counselor must consider the context and worldview of the client in order to be effective. So too must the supervisor take into consideration the context of the supervisee *and* the client. The participants are in relationship with one another (even if the supervisor is in relationship with the client through the supervisee), and each must consider the context of the other in order to promote understanding and communication.

The supervisory process is characterized by oversight of the work from the perspective of the specific model's tenets (e.g., rules, roles, hierarchy in structural family therapy; triangles, differentiation and cut-offs in Bowenian family therapy) and an exploration of the supervisee's experiences as a *part* of the family's system. One of the unique features of systemic supervision is the focus on the isomorphic process systemic therapists believe is inherent to the work. Isomorphism is similar to parallel process, but it is more than simply a replication of patterns of behavior, it is a similarity in structure and form of the relationships. The word itself is from the Greek *isos* meaning equal and *morphe* meaning form or shape. In supervision, isomorphism is the mirroring of the supervisor/supervisee relationship to supervisee/client relationship and perhaps even further to the dynamic relationships of the family (Liddle, 1988). Often, isomorphic relationships create "stuckness" or lack of progress in counseling (Lee, 1997).

CASE ILLUSTRATION 13.2

ISOMORPHISM IN SUPERVISION

Once when I was supervising a team of counselors who were conducting in-home family therapy, the team expressed feeling as if they were making no headway in counseling. They had been working with this particular family for about 7 months and were feeling as if the family had just decided to stop trying. The team talked about the parents' relationship struggle and how, when they first began counseling, they were excited about doing their homework and actively engaged in activities designed to improve their relationship. Now, they often failed to complete tasks, had returned to old patterns of behavior, and seemed as distant from one another as they had at the start of their counseling work. Further, the kids in the family had increased their acting out behaviors leaving mom feeling overwhelmed and unsupported by dad. When we processed this information and the team's feelings about their progress in supervision, it dawned on me that the team had become less productive in supervision. They had been late with paperwork, failed to follow through with suggestions, and seemed to be somewhat overwhelmed by their cases.

Upon further reflection, I came to see that I had been less attentive in supervision and less available to them due to a number of administrative concerns that were pressing and that were negatively impacting my ability to function. When I exposed this isomorphic process in supervision, the team and I were able to re-contract how we wanted our relationship to function. I agreed to return to making the time for supervision a priority and increase my responsiveness to their needs. They in turn agreed that they would be more mindful about how they divided the work between them so that neither of them felt overwhelmed or overburdened. As a team, they presented their thoughts to the parents, who endorsed that they had been feeling stuck, but did desire positive change. In the end, the changes made at multiple levels of the system nudged all of the members to make alterations in their functioning that led to individual and system changes. Awareness of the influence of isomorphism and its power as a disrupter of and tool for change is one of the greatest contributions of systemic supervision to the field (Bernard & Goodyear, 2018).

Integrative Supervision

Not surprisingly, integrative models of supervision are those that incorporate the techniques, theories, and tenets of multiple approaches (Haynes et al., 2003). Sometimes, supervisors practice what often is referred to as technical eclecticism, where the supervisor is merely pulling techniques and activities from various theoretical approaches without grounding them in the theory from which they are borrowed. This notion is akin to technical eclecticism in counseling where, for example, an individual who practices from an existential model may borrow the empty chair exercise from Gestalt therapy. A psychodynamic supervisor might ask the supervisee to look at the contextual experience of the client, or a supervisor who uses the IDM may ask the supervisee to explore the dynamic present in the supervisory relationship. The use of the technique from another theory is a tool that does not alter the theoretic orientation to the work itself.

Theoretically, integrative supervision is the synthesis or fusion of the basic tenets and concepts of multiple theories of supervision (Smith, 2009). Here, the theories themselves are overlaid onto one another. Most supervisors are likely to have a foundational grounding in person-centered supervision but most also lay another theory on top of that. Many supervisors practice a strength-based approach that is grounded in a specific theoretic model, such as psychodynamic or IDM.

Social Role Supervision

According to Holloway (1995), social role models of supervision focus more on what supervisors do during the process and how they organize the supervision than from what theory they practice. The most widely known of these types of models is likely Bernard and Goodyear's (2018) discrimination model.

The discrimination model provides supervisors with an organizational structure within which they can perform the work, understand their role and function, and react flexibly to the needs of their supervisees. The model provides supervisors with a way to conceptualize their roles and their focus during the supervisory session. There are three roles that a supervisor may assume, based upon the presenting needs of the supervisee: teacher, counselor, and consultant. Within these three roles, the supervisor may concentrate on three foci: intervention skills, conceptualization skills, and personalization skill.

The roles that a supervisor may assume are relatively self-explanatory. The teacher role refers to the instruction or sharing of knowledge that supervisors are often tasked with performing. Supervisors teach specific techniques, role play scenarios, instruct, and educate their supervisees on myriad topics. Within the counselor role, the supervisor attends to the more personal experiences of the supervisee. These issues might be related to transference, countertransference, and personal issues that are interfering with the work. Finally, the consultant role is more collegial and cooperative, with the supervisor and supervisee working together to advance the treatment of the client.

The three foci refer to specific areas in which supervisees might need to enhance their skills. Intervention skills relate to what the supervisee is doing with clients during counseling sessions. These skills are generally basic counseling skills, such as attending, reflecting, reframing, and so forth. Conceptualization skills refer to how the supervisee chooses interventions, understands the processes that occur in session, and is able to identify patterns within the context of the session (Bernard & Goodyear, 2018). Finally, personalization skills are the ways in which the person of the counselor enters into the counseling relationship with the client. These skills include the ability to tolerate confrontation, ability to keep one's personal beliefs separate from the counseling process, ability to have respect for clients regardless of their issues, and how the supervisee manages countertransference within the relationship.

These three foci and three roles can be combined into nine different combinations that can be used in situationally specific ways.

CASE ILLUSTRATION 13.3

USING THE TEACHER, COUNSELOR, AND CONSULTANT ROLES IN SUPERVISION

Mary is a counselor who is having difficulty with an adolescent client who refuses to talk during session. She expresses not knowing what other techniques or approaches she can use to get her client to be more verbal. Mary's supervisor, Elaine, provides instruction to Mary regarding specific techniques and approaches that she might take to prompt the client to be more engaged in the therapeutic process. Elaine teaches Mary how to use a few artistic tools, prompted journaling, and homework assignments in and out of session. She explains each of these approaches to Mary and describes how they might increase the client's comfort and thereby his willingness to talk in session.

In the teacher role, Elaine educates Mary related to skills and techniques with which she is unfamiliar. Elaine assumes the role of counselor, while focusing Mary on personalization skills. Here, she addresses Mary's internal experience related to having a client who seems disengaged or resistant to the counseling process. Elaine helps Mary to explore how this client's behavior in session has created some doubt in her abilities and negative feelings toward working with this particular client. Through this experience, Mary is able to see how her own emotional process is having an impact upon her work with the client.

The role and focus of the supervisory session may switch multiple times during a session, often without the supervisor or supervisee being aware of the change. Supervisors may plan from what role they want to intervene on particular foci, or the role and foci may emerge spontaneously with the flow of the supervisory session.

The discrimination model provides a good framework for understanding the process and tasks of supervision. It does not provide any specific theoretical orientation, which allows supervisors to infuse their own approach into the model. It is important to keep in mind that the model is primarily descriptive and does not provide any real direction or tools for specific interventions.

Strength-Based, Salutogenic Approach to Counseling Supervision

The profession of counseling can be differentiated from the other helping professions through an examination of its roots. Counseling was born and developed from the idea that human beings are in a continual state of growth throughout their life spans, that people have the capacity and tendency toward wellness, and that, given the right tools and support, people have the ability to solve their own problems and move toward a growth orientation. This orientation toward growth, wellness, and strength has been the foundation upon which the counseling profession has been built. Over time, pressures such as the advent of managed care organizations, diagnostic requirements, and the need for counselors to provide a justification that their clients are "ill enough" in order to receive third-party payment had moved the field toward a more pathologized or illness-based approach to the work of counseling.

In recent decades, there has been a resurgence of a more positive or strength-based approach to counseling that has, in turn, influenced the field of clinical supervision. As discussed earlier in this chapter, there are parallel and isomorphic processes that occur during clinical supervision. When clinicians are provided with strength-based supervision, they tend to practice counseling from a more strength-based approach. What follows is a discussion of salutogenic supervision, which is one model of a positive or strength-based approach to supervision.

Definition of Salutogenic Approach

Salutogenics (from the Latin *salus* = health and Greek *genesis* = origin) is a term coined by Aaron Antonovsky, who was a medical sociologist who examined what, in spite of the many stressors present in our physical world, keeps people well (Antonovsky, 1979). Antonovsky found that health is more than just the absence of illness. He believed that if individuals were able to attain a significant level of a "sense of coherence," they would be able to withstand stressors and remain well (Antonovsky, 1987). Antonovsky defined sense of coherence as comprised of three components: comprehensibility, manageability, and meaning. If people are able to understand what is happening around them, have the resources and skill sets to withstand the challenges they face, and can find reasons for or a purpose in the act of surmounting the challenges, they have a sense of coherence that likely allows them to be mentally well. Counselors can use this focus on the components of the sense of coherence to promote well-being and successful coping in their work with their clients. So too can this approach be used in supervision.

Salutogenics in Supervision

Often, the practice of supervision is focused on what isn't going well. Supervisors may ask their supervisees where they need help, with whom they are experiencing a feeling of "stuckness," and if there are problems that need to be addressed. These are all important topics that help us meet the ethical mandates of supervision, but they tend to create a negatively focused approach to the work. Salutogenic supervision seeks to find the strengths inherent in the clinician and apply those strengths to expressed areas of need. Instead of asking the clinician where they need help, the salutogenic supervisor asks the supervisee what is going well. There is then the ability to take what is working and use it in areas where the work has been less successful. Instead of exploring what has not been accomplished, there is a focus on what has been achieved and how this momentum can be used as a catalyst for future success. The process is by no means only about what is positive, such that critical feedback or corrective interventions are absent. I already have discussed the importance of the gatekeeping function that supervision plays to the profession. There is a place for confrontation and critical feedback within a salutogenic, strength-based approach; however, this feedback is couched in the ways in which supervisees can use other skills to compensate for their current deficiencies.

Benefits of Salutogenic Supervision

There are many benefits to a strength-based approach to clinical supervision. Supervisees are provided with a place of encouragement where their skills are validated and enhanced. The quality and safety of the supervisory environment can lead to increased willingness to engage in self-reflection that may increase self-awareness. These benefits then extend to the clients who may experience and increase in the quality of services provided to them. Finally, and most importantly, a strength-based approach to supervision can parallel a similar type of intervention with our clients, which returns us to the roots of our profession. Further, there is some suggestion that a strength-based approach to the work has the effect of increasing our clients' experience of growth (Gelso & Woodhouse, 2003; Rashid, 2015). In turn, a salutogenic approach also may reduce the deleterious effects of vicarious exposure to trauma in clinicians and promote vicarious posttraumatic growth as well (Brockhouse, Msetfi, Cohen, & Joseph, 2011; Hyatt-Burkhart & Owens, 2016). Issues related to trauma are detailed in Chapter 4.

Continuing Education and Professional Development

Counselors undergo an extensive training during their master's programs. Those who attend and graduate from a CACREP-accredited program will have completed 60 credit hours of coursework, 100 hours of practicum fieldwork experience, and 600 hours of internship fieldwork experience. Upon graduation and prior to licensure, most states require that these same counselors participate in a minimum of 2 years of clinical work that is supervised by a licensed clinician. After licensure is earned, all states require a certain amount of ongoing continuing education that must be accomplished in order for counselors to maintain their licenses. Most states require between 30 and 50 hours of continuing education or continuing education credits (CECs) between licensure renewals (ACA, 2016). There are states that require education in specific topics, such as ethics, law, and mandated reporting of abuse. In states where supervisors are licensed, there are requirements for continuing education related to supervision.

Why is continuing education so important that states have written it into their regulatory codes for licensure? First, our professional organization tells us that it is. The ACA's 2014 *Code of Ethics* section C.2.f states:

> *Counselors recognize the need for continuing education to acquire and maintain a reasonable level of awareness of current scientific and professional information in their fields of activity. Counselors maintain their competence in the skills they use, are open to new procedures, and remain informed regarding best practices for working with diverse populations. (p. 9)*

In that section of the code, we get a clear definition of the purpose of continuing education. Ongoing education helps us to stay up to date with trends and scientific findings in our field. Research informs our work. Theories, techniques, and approaches are refined through the work of practitioners and scholars, and we need to keep abreast of advances in our field. Further, continuing education helps us to stay sharp related to the skills that we use. We can learn new skills that enhance the practice in which we are already engaging. Continuing education helps counselors to stay connected with the same body of information in which they were immersed during their degree studies but may provide insight and opportunity to develop and hone new and more effective ways of working with clients.

Continuing education can take many forms. Many colleges and universities offer courses specifically designed to meet the needs of graduates who require CECs. Professional organizations, such as the ACA and National Board for Certified Counselors (NBCC) offer CECs for participation in webinars or reading materials in their publications. CECs can be earned by attending professional conferences through state, regional, and national organizations. The plethora of ways through which a counselor can earn

CECs speaks to the field's understanding of the importance of the process of furthering one's professional understanding through ongoing education.

Tensions

There are a number of tensions that arise that are unique to the provision of clinical supervision in counseling. As I mentioned earlier, there is often pressure when the same person is providing administrative supervision and clinical supervision. Administrative supervision frequently is characterized by a push toward compliance with agency policy, billable hour requirements, and general workplace behaviors. Such supervision is generally not strength based but, rather, is focused on employee deficiencies. In contrast, clinical supervision usually is characterized by supportive, growth-oriented interventions in a collaborative environment. A clinical supervisor seeks to establish a trusting relationship in which the supervisee can share struggles and issues without fear of reprimand or retribution. It can be difficult for a supervisor to balance successfully these competing roles.

Another tension that can be present in clinical supervision is the balance between challenging, thought-provoking interventions, with which the supervisee may struggle, and supportive guidance. Further complicating this balance is the supervisee's need for autonomy and independence that must be in balance with the supervisor's assessment of the supervisee's skills and competencies. What results is a push and pull between support and challenge, and independence and direction. When there is a mismatch in perceptions and approaches, supervision may become ineffective or even conflictual.

Likely the greatest tension, with respect to clinical supervision, is the cost–benefit analysis in which agencies engage. The costs of clinical supervision are many. Supervisees and supervisors who are engaged in supervision are not providing billable services, which reduces agency revenue. The very cost to pay someone to conduct supervision can be a deterrent to providing the service. If there is little perceived benefit to providing counselors with clinical supervision, agencies may forego the service completely or only offer what is regulatory required. Such a disregard for supervision is especially common in agencies that are not managed by helping professionals or that operate from a for-profit business model.

CONCLUSION

This chapter has focused on the practice and importance of clinical supervision and continuing education for professional counselors. It has reviewed some of the most common theoretical approaches to supervision and how they may be used. It has also provided a discussion of how a salutogenic or strength-based approach to supervision can be employed to promote an isomorphic positive approach to the work with clients. The chapter has been concluded with a discussion of the ethical mandate and benefits of continuing education for counselors.

RESOURCES

Articles and Publications

Bray, B. (2018, May). Counselor supervision: Reflections and lessons learned. *Counseling Today*. Retrieved from https://ct.counseling.org/2018/05/counselor-supervision-reflections-and-lessons-learned

Center for Credentialing & Education. (n.d.). *Clinical supervision: An overview*. Retrieved from https://www.i-counseling.net/pdfs/clinical_supervision_overview.pdf

Substance Abuse and Mental Health Administration. Clinical supervision and professional development of the substance abuse counselor. Retrieved from https://store.samhsa.gov/system/files/sma14-4435.pdf

Videos

Microtraining Associates (Producer). (2004). *Five approaches to supervision: Developmental, integrated, IPR, Psychodynamic, and microskills*. Available through Alexander Street database at alexanderstreet.com

Sween, E. (2009) *Becoming a therapist; Inside the learning curve*. Psychotherapy.net

University of South Wales, Newport (Producer) (2012). *Making the most of supervision*. Available through Alexander Street database at alexanderstreet.com

Ethical Standards

American Counseling Association. (1990). *Standards for counseling supervisors*. Alexandria, VA: Author.

Links to Helpful Sites

American Counseling Association. Retrieved from http://counseling.org

Center for Credentialing & Education—Approved Clinical Supervisor credential. Retrieved from https://www.cce-global.org/ACS

The Professional Counselor. Retrieved from http://tpcjournal.nbcc.org

REFERENCES

America Counseling Association. (2014). *ACA code of ethics*. Alexandria, VA: Author.

American Counseling Association Center for Counseling Practice, Policy and Research. (2016). *Licensure requirements for professional counselors: A state-by- state report*. Alexandria, VA: Author.

Antonovsky, A. (1979). *Health, stress, and coping*. San Francisco, CA: Jossey-Bass .

Antonovsky, A. (1987). *Unravelling the mystery of health*. San Francisco, CA: Jossey-Bass.

Beck, A. T., Rush, J. A., Shaw, B. F., & Emery, G. (1970). *Cognitive therapy of depression*. New York, NY: Guilford Press.

Bernard, J. M., & Goodyear, R. K. (2018). *Fundamentals of clinical supervision* (6th ed.). Upper Saddle River, NJ: Pearson.

Brockhouse, R., Msetfi, R. M., Cohen, K., & Joseph, S. (2011). Vicarious exposure to trauma and growth in therapists: The moderating effects of sense of coherence, organizational support, and empathy. *Journal of Traumatic Stress, 24* (6), 735–742. doi:10.1002/jts.20704

Corey, G. (2017). *Theory and practice of counseling and psychotherapy* (10th ed.). Belmont, CA: Cengage.

Council for Accreditation of Counseling and Related Educational Programs. (2015). *2016 CACREP standards.* Retrieved from http://www.cacrep.org/wp-content/uploads/2018/05/2016-Standards-with-Glossary-5.3.2018.pdf

Falender, C. A., & Shafranske, E. P. (2004). *Clinical supervision: A competency-based approach.* Washington, DC: American Psychological Association.

Frawley-O'Dea, M. G., & Sarnat, J. E. (2001). *The supervisory relationship: A contemporary psychodynamic approach.* New York, NY: Guilford Press.

Gelso, C. J., & Woodhouse, S. (2003). Toward a positive psychotherapy: Focus on human strength. In W. B. Walsh (Ed.), *Contemporary topics in vocational psychology. Counseling psychology and optimal human functioning* (pp. 171–197). Mahwah, NJ: Lawrence Erlbaum Associates.

Gray, N. D., & Erickson, P. (2013). Standardizing the pre-licensure supervision process: A commentary on advocating for direct observation of skills. *Professional Counselor, 3* (1), 34–39. doi:10.15241/ndg.3.1.34

Haynes, R., Corey, G., & Moulton, P. (2003). *Clinical supervision in the helping professions: A practical guide.* Pacific Grove, CA: Brooks/Cole.

Holloway, E. L. (1995). *Clinical supervision: A system approach.* Thousand Oaks, CA: Sage.

Hyatt-Burkhart, D. G., & Owens, E. W. (2016). Salutogenesis: Using clients' strengths in the treatment of trauma. *Counseling Today.* April.

Inskipp, F., & Proctor, B. (2009). *The art, craft and tasks of counselling supervision part 1: Making the most of supervision.* Twickenham, UK: Cascade Publications.

Kottler, J. A., & Montgomery, M. J. (2010). *Theories of counseling and therapy: An experiential approach.* Thousand Oaks, CA: Sage.

Ladany, N., Marotta, S., & Muse-Burke, J. L. (2001). Counselor experience related to complexity of case conceptualization and supervision preference. *Counselor Education and Supervision, 40* (3), 203–219. doi:10.1002/j.1556-6978.2001.tb01253.x

Lee, R. E. (1997). Seeing and hearing in therapy and supervision: A clinical example of isomorphism. *Journal of Family Psychotherapy, 8* (3), 51–57. doi:10.1300/J085V08N03_04

Liddle, H. A. (1988). Systemic supervision: Conceptual overlays and pragmatic guidelines. In H. A. Liddle, D. C. Breunlin, & R. C. Schwartz (Eds.), *The Guilford family therapy series. Handbook of family therapy training and supervision* (pp. 153–171). New York, NY: Guilford Press.

Liese, B. S., & Beck, J. S. (1997). Cognitive therapy supervision. In C. E. Watkins Jr. (Ed.), *Handbook of psychotherapy supervision* (pp. 114–133). New York, NY: John Wiley and Sons.

Loganbill, C., Hardy, E., & Delworth, U. (1982). Supervision: A conceptual model. *Counseling Psychologist, 10,* 3–42. doi:10.1177/0011000082101002

McNeill, B. W., Stoltenberg, C. D., & Romans, J. S. (1992). The integrated developmental model of supervision: Scale development and validation procedures. *Professional Psychology: Research and Practice, 23*(6), 504.

Rashid, T. (2015). Positive psychotherapy: A strength-based approach. *The Journal of Positive Psychology, 10* (1), 25–40. doi:10.1080/17439760.2014.920411

Rønnestad, M. H., & Skovolt, T. M. (1993). Supervision of beginning and advanced graduate students of counseling and psychotherapy. *Journal of Counseling and Development, 71,* 396–405. doi:10.1002/j.1556-6676.1993.tb02655.x

Rønnestad, M. H., & Skovholt, T. M. (2003). The journey of the counselor and therapist: Research findings and perspectives on professional development. *Journal of Career Development, 30,* 5–44. doi:10.1177/0894845303030001002

Rønnestad, M. H., & Skovholt, T. M. (2013). *The developing practitioner: Growth and stagnation of therapists and counselor.* New York, NY: Taylor & Francis.

Russell-Chapin, L. A., & Chapin, T. J. (2012). *Clinical supervision theory and practice.* Belmont, CA: Books/Cole.

Smith, K. L. (2009). *A brief summary of supervision models.* Retrieved from http://www .marquette.edu/education/grad/documents/Brief-Summary-of-Supervision- Models.pdf

Stoltenberg, C. D. (1981). Approaching supervision from a developmental perspective: The counselor complexity model. *Journal of Counseling Psychology, 28,* 59–65. doi:10.1037/0022 -0167.28.1.59

Stoltenberg, C. D., McNeill, B., & Delworth, U. (1998). *IDM supervision: An integrated Developmental model for supervising counselors and therapists.* San Francisco, CA: Jossey-Bass.

Supervision. (2019). In Merriam-Webster.com. Retrieved from https://www.merriam-webster .com/dictionary/supervision

CHAPTER 14

COUNSELOR SELF-CARE AND PERSONAL DEVELOPMENT

DEBRA HYATT-BURKHART

This chapter addresses issues related to counselor self-care and maintaining a healthy ability to continue with the work of counseling. The issues that are addressed include vicarious responses to trauma (both positive and negative), a biopsychosocial systemic approach to counselor wellness, strategies for engaging in wellness-focused self-evaluation, techniques and tools for stress management, and approaches for maintaining a healthy work/life balance. The following Council for the Accreditation of Counseling and Related Educational Programs (CACREP) standards are addressed in this chapter:
   CACREP 2016:
     2F1.k, 2F1.1
   CACREP 2009:
     2G1.d

LEARNING OBJECTIVES

After reviewing this chapter, the reader should be able to:

1. Demonstrate an understanding of the potential deleterious impacts of the work of counseling (e.g., counter transference, burnout, compassion fatigue, secondary traumatic stress, and vicarious trauma);

2. Demonstrate an understanding of the potential positive effects of the work of psychological helping (e.g., compassion satisfaction and vicarious posttraumatic growth [VPTG]);

3. Demonstrate an understanding of a biopsychosocial, systemic conceptualization of counselor wellness;

4. Identify strategies for effective self-evaluation that may be employed in counselors' assessment of their own wellness; and,

5. Identify potential strategies and tools that may be used to mitigate the potential negative consequences of the work of caring and promote the positive responses and to encourage wellness.

▨ INTRODUCTION

There is an often-cited quote from a popular self-help book regarding the need for mothers to take care of themselves that reads, "Self-care is not selfish or self-indulgent. We cannot nurture others from a dry well. We need to take care of our own needs first, then we can give from our surplus, our abundance" (Louden, 1992, p. 11). Although the text in which this quote appears focused on women and mothers, the sentiment presented is highly apropos to those working in the counseling profession. Counselors must engage in caring for their own needs in order to be able to do the difficult work of the profession. An essential part of the American Counseling Association's (ACA) 20–20 definition of counseling states that counseling is a "professional relationship that empowers diverse individuals" (Kaplan, Tarvydas, & Gladding, 2014). Within this relationship, and likely because of the relational nature of helping work, counselors are asked to draw continually from their own resources, their own "well," as they empower others.

The ACA's *Code of Ethics* (2014) directs that "counselors monitor themselves for signs of impairment from their own physical, mental, or emotional problems" (p. 9). It is counselors' ethical duty to examine their own wellness and to take steps to promote their health, for we must replenish and sustain our own "well" in order to be able to help others. The dangers of impairment place both the counselor and the client at risk. Impaired or unwell counselors may cause themselves harm (e.g., occupational impacts, family relationship disruption, psychosomatic illness, and psychological distress), may result in the provision of ineffective interventions to the clients at best, and may cause damage or injury to the clients (e.g., exacerbate symptoms, retraumatize, and violate practice standards) at worst.

The continued empathetic engagement and pull on a counselor's internal reserves has been well documented to have potentially negative emotional consequences for the overall well-being and mental health of professional helpers. Empathic engagement refers to the process of counselors feeling, on some level, what their clients are feeling. As part of the work of counseling, clinicians connect with or open themselves up to the emotional experiences of their clients. There is a long history of the exploration of the myriad ways that empathetic engagement can have a negative impact on helping professionals. The Freudian notion of countertransference, Jackson and Maslach's (1982) work-related burnout, Figley's (1995) compassion fatigue, Stamm's (1995) secondary traumatic stress, and Pearlman and Saakvitne's (1995) vicarious trauma are all constructs that detail how the work of helping has the potential to be a significant drain upon on a counselor's internal reserves and psychological well-being.

There is also a growing realization of the potential positive consequences of empathetic engagement as a result of the work of counseling, which has brought a new focus within the research literature. Scholars have begun to explore the constructs of compassion satisfaction (Figley, 1995), VPTG (Tedeschi & Calhoun, 1996), and vicarious resilience (VR; Hernandez, Gangsei, & Engstrom, 2007), which are constructs that center upon describing the emotional benefits that may be derived from our work with our clients. In contrast to the deleterious effects, these positive experiences may be a part of how counselors stay well in the midst of the difficult work that we do. Rather than creating wear on a counselor's internal emotional capital, this benefit finding (i.e., the ability to see the positive effects or consequences) can be an essential part of how helpers remain healthy while they are engaged in psychological helping relationships.

The profession of counseling has begun to focus on the notion of counselor health, wellness, and well-being as a necessary component for stamina and competence in the work. There are a number of tasks in which counselors must engage as they seek to maintain wellness within their work. First, counselors must be aware of the importance of their own wellness as it relates to their personal and professional success. One of the reasons that we have given this topic an entire chapter within this text is to highlight the importance of counselor well-being and to help our readers to develop an understanding of this crucial counselor characteristic. Second, counselors must develop an ability to monitor themselves effectively regarding their emotional wellness and fitness for the work. Monitoring and assessment are essential to maintaining wellness. If we are not engaged in constantly examining our own emotional status within the work, we may find that the persistent pressures of the job have had a creeping, cumulative effect that, while we were not looking, has become impairing. Finally, it is vital that counselors have a personal knowledge of practical ways that they can maintain, replenish, and recharge their own internal resources. Such knowledge, when combined with awareness and assessment, can mitigate the deleterious effects of the work and sustain counselors as they continue to perform the task of psychological helping.

This chapter provides an in-depth discussion of the aforementioned possible benefits and costs of empathetic engagement and practical approaches to self-assessment and appraisal of one's wellness and fitness for the work. Further, I delineate strategies that counselors can employ to enhance their wellness and work/life balance. It is important to note that none of the conditions contained in this chapter are foregone conclusions of engaging in the work of counseling. Some clinicians experience them, some clinicians do not. What is important is that all counselors are aware of the potential for both disturbance and benefit and of how these conditions can influence counselor wellness, and thereby effectiveness, with their clients.

POTENTIAL STRAINS OF THE WORK OF COUNSELING

Countertransference

Early on in the development of his understanding of psychoanalytic theory and the work of psychological intervention, Sigmund Freud (1910) began to discuss "Gengenübertrgung" or countertransference. In his 1910 work, "The Future Prospects of

Psycho-Analytic Therapy," he discusses the notion that analysts may experience personal emotional strain as a result of their work with patients. In an anthology of his reflections, Carl Jung is noted to have cautioned that countertransference may cause the analyst and the patient to "both fall into the same dark hole of unconsciousness" (Jacobi, 1986, p. 140). Initially discussed as an unconscious response to a patient's experience of transference with the analyst, countertransference came to be defined broadly as the totality of a clinician's internal (both conscious and unconscious) emotional responses to a client (Hayes et al., 1998). An integral part of the psychoanalytic approach to the work of psychological helping, countertransference most often is looked upon as a naturally occurring phenomenon that either can hinder the work or be harnessed by the clinician in the furtherance of treatment. There are entire books that are devoted to the exploration of the psychoanalytic notion of countertransference. An in-depth discussion of this concept is well beyond the scope of this single book chapter. Suffice it to say, the construct is complex, nuanced, and still being researched today. Scholars continue to explore how counselors who work in specific fields, such as trauma (Pearlman & Saakvitne, 1995), with children (Schowalter, 1986), with people who experience personality disorders (Volkan, 2018), and end-of-life care (Katz, 2016), are influenced by countertransference. Additionally, research has been conducted on how a counselor's personal characteristics may contribute to positive and negative experiences of countertransference (Cain, 2000; Rosenberger & Hayes, 2002). What is of import here is that we recognize that Freud's early understanding and awareness that the work of analysis had the potential to have an emotional impact upon the person of the analyst is foundational to our current understanding of the potential effect of the work of helping. It is his thinking on countertransference that began our exploration into additional constructs such as burnout.

Burnout

There are a number of terms that are commonly used to describe the potential negative results of empathetic engagement. Terms such as burnout, compassion fatigue, and secondary traumatic stress often are used interchangeably, but there are subtle and important distinctions between the constructs that we will attempt to delineate in this chapter. The first among these constructs is burnout. The term "burnout" is a common expression that frequently is used when people talk about jobs, tasks, or activities in which they are engaged. With some regularity, we hear phrases like "I'm burned out on binge watching Netflix" and "Work has me so burned out on customer service that I think I might quit." Burnout has come to be understood as a weariness that sets in after overdoing a task, or when something that one does repetitively loses its appeal or is fraught with unsatisfactory characteristics, such as poor management. To put it simply, burnout is the result of the daily hassle of the work world. Burnout seems to be a construct with which popular culture is familiar, but it has specific meaning when we explore the continuum of potential negative emotional experiences of the work of helping. Burnout, as first proposed by Freudenberger (1974), described the effects of ongoing, long-term occupational stress on clinic workers. He discussed "staff burnout" in terms of a professional exhaustion that is not necessarily found in the popular understanding of the term. In our example, there is not usually a professional component to binge watching a show on Netflix. In further explorations of this professional definition of burnout, Maslach and Jackson (1981) clarified the term as a stress reaction that results from a combination of an individual's personal characteristics, the general conditions of the work environment, and exposure to the struggles of others. The general daily pressures of a job (e.g., paperwork, administrative pressures, work culture, pay scale, and commute time), combine with a clinician's personal sensitivities and the specifics of the work to create negative physical and emotional symptoms. Further, burnout also may have a component that is a result of the interconnectedness of the subjective experiences of the individual counselor and the work environment (Collings & Murray, 1996).

There is a suite of typical reactions that may occur in an individual who is experiencing burnout. Jackson and Maslach (1982) found that workers might experience physical symptoms of fatigue, body aches and pains, stomach or intestinal distress, and headaches. He further delineated emotional symptoms of frustrations, anger, cynicism, callousness, apathy, and feelings of being overwhelmed as common among those who were suffering from burnout. There is scholarly evidence to suggest that individuals can experience work-related burnout in many professions. Studies have explored management (Ginsburg, 1974), athletics (Smith, 1986), teaching (Farber, 1991; Hakanen, Bakker, & Schaufeli, 2006), and students (Schaufeli, Maritinez, Pinto, Slanova, & Bakker, 2002), among others. However, far more research has been conducted regarding professions, such as counseling, that require empathetic engagement. As the basic conceptual framework of burnout is predicated upon a provider/consumer relationship being present in the work (Marek, Schaufeli, & Maslach, 2017), the volume of research related to burnout in counselors seems appropriate. In short, helping professions seem to provide greater opportunity for individuals to experience psychological fatigue as a result of their work. In the continuum of potential negative consequences of the work of counseling, burnout is at the lower end of the scale due to its apparent limited disruption of the personal life of the clinician. Generally, individuals who exhibit classic burnout with their jobs are not experiencing significant spillover into their personal lives, which can result in some of the other constructs that are discussed in subsequent sections of this chapter.

Of note, practitioners are often reluctant to acknowledge or endorse that they may be experiencing negative disturbance as a result of their work (Corey, Corey, & Callanan, 2011; Kottler, 2017). Counselors often seem to believe that experiencing any negative effects from the work demonstrates weakness. The notion of being adversely affected by the work seems to imply that the counselor has failed to practice the very self-care that we often encourage our clients to engage in. In order to avoid the unpleasant experience of admitting "failure," clinicians may engage in denial or ignore their symptoms, which can lead to impairment in treatment provision (Everall & Paulson, 2004). In a self-report survey of more than 500 practicing counselors, Lawson (2007) found that none of them endorsed that they were functioning in the impaired range of stress as measured by the Professional Quality of Life (ProQOL) scale (Stamm, 2005). Yet, when these same practitioners were asked to rate the levels of stress of their peers, they endorsed that over 4%

were practicing at stress levels that likely indicated impairment. Such disparity between self-report and reporting on others seems to support the notion that disturbance and impairment related to the very difficult job of ongoing empathetic engagement is viewed as something to conceal from others. However, as stated earlier in this chapter, counselors have an ethical mandate to engage in ongoing self-evaluation of emotional fitness for the work.

There are several tools available that counselors can access to measure their level of burnout. The most widely used instrument is the Maslach Burnout Inventory (MBI), first developed by Maslach and Jackson in 1981. The MBI is a 22-item inventory that measures the affective dimension of burnout within three subscales. The first subscale explores emotional exhaustion or feelings of being overwhelmed or emotionally over-extended and fatigued by one's work. The depersonalization subscale measures the level of detachment or feeling of ambivalence to one's clients or those receiving interventions of some sort as provided by the helping professional. The final subscale is related to personal accomplishment or feeling of success, achievement, and satisfaction in the work. Individuals who take the MBI review statements such as "I feel emotionally drained from my work" and "In my opinion, I am good at my job" and rank them related to frequency of occurrence of having that feeling (Maslach, Jackson, & Leiter, 1996). The rating scale ranges from experiencing a few times a year or less, through every day. There is a nominal cost to use the MBI. Resources regarding further information regarding burnout and how to access the MBI are provided at the end of this chapter.

Another newer instrument for the assessment of burnout is the Copenhagen Burnout Inventory (CBI), developed by Kristensen, Borritz, Villadsen, and Christensen (2005). Their scale was designed to be more culturally broad, to be less helping-profession specific, and to provide a generic scale that could be used by all people regardless of occupation (Kristensen et al., 2005). The CBI also has three subscales, but they are designed to measure personal burnout, work-related burnout, and client-related burnout. The instrument does not make a distinction between emotional and physical fatigue but attempts to capture the overall picture of the broad definition of burnout as physical and psychological fatigue and exhaustion related to person, work, and client (or colleague, student, consumer, etc.). In the CBI, 16 questions such as "How often are you physically exhausted?," "Do you feel that every working hour is tiring for you?," and "Do you find it hard to work with clients?" are rated on a 4-point Likert scale ranging from always, to a very high degree, to never. Available in a variety of translations, the CBI has been used in a number of different helping professions. It is readily available on-line and is free to access.

Research has been conducted in an attempt to uncover what factors place counselors at risk for the development of burnout. There appears to be little evidence to support that demographic variables, such as age, gender, specific role or job, and education level, play any major role in the development of burnout. It does seem that helpers, who themselves have a significant personal history of traumatic exposure, are more prone to having negative vicarious experiences related to their work exposure (Emery, Wade, & McLean, 2009). There are a few other characteristics that seem to create an increased risk for the development of burnout. An inability to leave work issues at work (Killian, 2008), a need for therapeutic control (Deutsch, 1984), rigid and perfectionist expectations of progress (Pearlman & Saakvitne, 1995), poor tolerance of client emotional distress (Farber, 1983), and the experience level of the clinician (Ruysschaert, 2009) all seem to elevate the possibility of counselor burnout.

Compassion Fatigue

As investigation into the vicarious experiences of psychological helping advanced, new concepts emerged to help to explain the reactions that may be seen in counselors. In the early 1980s, Charles Figley began to look at what he termed "the cost of caring." He found that the task of empathizing with and providing emotional support to people who had experienced trauma placed a unique psychological strain upon the helper (Figley, 1995). He labeled this condition compassion fatigue and defined it as "the natural consequent behaviors and emotions resulting from knowing about a traumatizing event experienced by a significant other and the stress resulting from helping or wanting to help a traumatized or suffering person" (Figley, 1995, p. 7).

Like burnout, compassion fatigue can affect how counselors function in their jobs and in their personal lives. Professionally, counselors can become desensitized to the concerns of their clients, becoming less empathetic and colder with a decreased ability to connect with them. These characteristics of empathy and connection are central to the work of counseling, and without them, the relational aspect that is so vital to the work may be seriously impaired or lost. There also may be a diminishment in the quality of the counselor's work related to task-oriented errors, lapses in judgment, and mistakes in documentation or other work-related functions. Further, counselors who are experiencing compassion fatigue may exhibit symptoms of anxiety and depression that may have implications for their personal lives (Mathieu, 2012).

There are several specific measures that can be used to assess a clinician's level of compassion fatigue. The most frequently used instrument is the Compassion Fatigue Self-Test (CFST), which was developed by Figley in 1995. This tool is a 40-item questionnaire that has two subscales, which assess levels of compassion fatigue and burnout. Items are evaluated according to how frequently a clinician experiences certain situations or characteristics from 1—rarely/never to 5—very often. Sample items from the CFST include "I am preoccupied with more than one client and their family," "I force myself to avoid certain thoughts or feeling that remind me of a frightening experience," and "I feel little compassion toward most of my coworkers." The CFST can be found online at no cost. This instrument has been revised several times and now includes subscales to assess positive constructs such as compassion satisfaction. We will look at the revised version later in this chapter.

The Compassion Fatigue Scale—Rev (Gentry, Baranowsky, & Dunning, 2002) is a revised version of the original CFST that contains 30 items, and the Compassion Fatigue Short Scale (Adams, Figley, & Boscarino, 2002) contains 13 items that are designed to pinpoint the level of distress present due to vicarious exposure to a client's trauma (client trauma is discussed in detail in Chapter 5. Items such as "I am losing sleep over a client's traumatic experiences" and "I have frequently felt weak, tired or rundown as a result of my work as a caregiver" are directly focused upon the internal emotional disturbance that can be a consequence of the work of counseling.

As with burnout, there has been interest in examining what counselor characteristics may create a propensity for compassion fatigue and those that act as protective factors. It appears that beginning or novice counselors, or a practitioner who primarily works with a clientele whose issues are trauma focused, create increased risk for compassion fatigue (Harrison & Westwood, 2009).

Secondary Traumatic Stress

Secondary traumatic stress (STS) is yet another construct that describes the potential adverse reaction that a counselor may have to the work of empathetic engagement. This condition encompasses elements of burnout and compassion fatigue, such as exhaustion, feeling jaded, anxiety, and disillusionment with the work, but it also involves symptoms that look like posttraumatic stress disorder (PTSD) as experienced by people who experience trauma directly. STS is generally a fairly sudden reaction to hearing or learning about the trauma of others that results in a set of specific observable reactions that mirror PTSD in clients. Symptoms, such as re-experiencing the client's trauma, hyperarousal and hypervigilance, avoiding reminders of the trauma, and numbing in response to the exposure, among others, are all possible reactions a counselor may experience (Jenkins & Baird, 2002). In some cases, the symptoms can be of a severity that meets the diagnostic criteria for PTSD itself. In his 2007 study of the prevalence of STS among social workers, Bride (2007) found that 15.2% of the professionals whom he studied, who worked with trauma-exposed individuals, met core criteria for a diagnosis of PTSD. According to the National Center for PTSD, this prevalence rate is significantly higher than that expected in the general population, where PTSD rates fall at about 7% to 8%.

The instruments that have been designed to measure STS are also numerous. The ProQOL was developed by revising the aforementioned CFST to include measures of compassion satisfaction, burnout, and STS. This instrument is currently in its fifth edition (Stamm, 2005) and is similar in its approach to the CFST in that it provides individuals with a series of statements that they may endorse or deny, to varying degrees. This instrument is available online, is free, and open for use. The STS scales (Bride, Robinson, Yegidis, & Figley, 2004), the Secondary Trauma Questionnaire (Motta, Kefer, Hetz, & Hafeez, 1999), and the Questionnaire for Secondary Traumatization (FST; Weitkamp, Daniels, & Klasen, 2014) are all self-report instruments designed to expose levels of STS in helping professionals.

Vicarious Trauma

The last construct related to possible negative reactions to the work of counseling is vicarious trauma (VT). VT is similar to the conditions delineated earlier in this chapter in that it results from secondary or vicarious exposure to the trauma of others. Individuals who are experiencing VT may have similar symptoms as those who are experiencing burnout, compassion fatigue, or STS, but VT is theoretically centered on the inner experience of the helper. First developed by McCann and Pearlman in 1990, the construct is based on Constructivist Self-Development Theory (CSDT). CSDT is centered upon the notion that people construct or build their own reality or understanding of the work around them through the development of mental frameworks or cognitive schemas (Pearlman & Saakvitne, 1995). These schemas include people's beliefs, assumptions, and expectations regarding the world and other people within it.

Pearlman and Saakvitne (1995) define VT as "a process through which the therapist's inner experience is negatively transformed through empathic engagement with a client's trauma material" (p. 31). McCann and Pearlman (1995) assert that this negative transformation can result in permanent changes to a counselor's cognitive schemas and world view. They identified seven basic psychological needs that may be disrupted including intimacy (connecting with others), power and control, trust, esteem (feeling valued or of value), safety, and frame of reference (making sense out of why things happen; Dunkley & Whelan, 2006). These shifts are more than merely symptoms; they are fundamental changes in the way in which persons view and comprehend the world around them.

The primary measure for VT is the Trauma and Attachment Belief Scale (TABS; Pearlman, MacIan, Johnson, & Mas, 1992). This tool is designed to measure changes in the cognitive schemas mentioned previously. With self-report questions targeted to assess the changes in perceptions, the tool was specifically created to try and distinguish VT from the other negative vicarious constructs.

There is considerable debate as to whether or not the disturbances that we have described are actually separate conditions, or if they are all integrally intertwined parts of the experience of helping. Some studies even have suggested that the impact of VT on counselors is inconsequential or negligible (Kadambi & Ennis, 2004; Sabin-Farrell & Turpin, 2003). Regardless, it is important for professional counselors to have an understanding of the potential for deleterious effects from the work so that they may monitor themselves for any disturbance that may arise. As we mentioned before, counselor wellness, which is an ethical mandate, is not only important for the counselors themselves but plays a significant part in the quality of service delivery.

▓ POTENTIAL BENEFITS OF THE WORK OF COUNSELING

The personal psychological implications for counselors as a result of their work are by no means all negative. Human beings are remarkably resilient and hardy individuals when it comes to withstanding psychological stressors. We see this as we look at the prevalence rates of the majority of mental health disorders in the *Diagnostic and Statistical Manual of Mental Disorders* (American Psychiatric Association [APA], 2013), the handbook that clinicians use to guide their process of diagnosis with clients. The prevalence rates for the majority of the disorders indicate that less than 5% of the population meet the criteria for any given diagnosis (APA, 2013). The good news is that wellness and heath are generally normative. Within the last few decades we have seen a growing body of evidence that suggests that although clinicians may experience negative symptoms as a result of their work, they also may find benefit in and even psychologically grow from vicariously experiencing the distress of others.

We know that counselors can be distressed by hearing the stories of the disturbing experiences of their clients. Our client's suffering can find ways to infiltrate our own psyches. The previous part of this chapter delineated many of the ways that vicarious exposure can be disruptive to counselors. But clients do not only suffer from their traumatic experiences and life stressors. They often find ways to make sense of, bounce back from, and indeed grow as a result of their life's struggles. There is a significant amount of research that supports the notion that people can and do find benefit from hardship. It is likely that we all know someone who has been changed positively through adversity. We may know people who have been diagnosed with a serious illness and survived. These people likely experienced fundamental changes in the way that they viewed their life, and they acted differently as a result. They may have adopted a "life is too short" mentality that spurred them to become more adventurous, or developed a greater appreciation for relationships with those whom they loved and, as a result, spent more time with family than before. Counselors who work with such people are privileged to experience these positive changes vicariously just as we experience our clients' traumas. It only makes sense that if counselors can be disturbed by their clients' disturbances, then we can experience positive changes as a result of witnessing the same. Research indicates that these positive experiences are often found in conjunction with the deleterious effects detailed earlier in this chapter. Often, the disturbance that a counselor experiences when confronted with their client's distress or trauma is the very catalyst for the counselor's own growth. The following sections of this chapter describe several of the constructs in this new frontier of vicarious benefit finding.

Compassion Satisfaction

Compassion satisfaction (CS) is, according to Stamm (2005), the pleasure that may be gained as a result of being good at one's job. It may be derived from feeling like one is making a contribution to the field or society as a whole. Whereas CF is a drain upon the proverbial well of the counselors' resources, CS is the positive feeling about one's self and the work that seems to replenish that well of resources. In short, compassion satisfaction is the sense of a job well done and a person being helped. Stamm (2010) suggests that CS may result in the development of greater self-knowledge, confidence, and a stronger sense of self within the clinician.

There are a number of self-report measures that are designed to assess clinicians' negative and positive reactions to the work of helping. In the late 1990s, Dr. Beth Hundall Stamm expanded upon the work that Dr. Charles Figley had done regarding the assessment of compassion fatigue by developing the ProQOL This scale is now the primary tool that is used by the helping professions to measure CS (Stamm, 2010). The ProQOL, which is now in its fifth edition, has three separate scales that measure compassion satisfaction, burnout, and STS. The CS subscale contains questions such as "I feel invigorated after working with those I help" and "I like my work as a helper" are rated on a five point

Likert scale from 1 = never to 5 = very often. The instrument is very easy to use and access. There is a comprehensive manual available for download that explains the tool, reliability and validity, implementation, and appropriate use of the scale. Links to gain access to the manual are provided in the resource section of this chapter.

Vicarious Resilience

Resilience is defined as the ability to resume an original shape or recover quickly from illness, difficulties, misfortune, or change. When we discuss psychological resilience, we are referencing people's ability to sustain or to return to healthy levels of functioning after some sort of painful or traumatic experience (Bonanno, 2004; Hernandez et al., 2007). There has been significant research that has examined this construct in populations such as survivors of the 9/11 attacks (Bonanno, Galea, Bucciarelli, & Vlahov, 2006), military personnel (Pietrazak, Johnson, Goldstein, Malley, & Soutwick, 2009), and disadvantaged youth (Harvey & Delfabbro, 2004), among others. As we have come to a greater understanding of the concept of psychological resilience itself, we have begun to explore VR in helpers. First described by Hernandez et al. (2007) as "a unique and positive effect that transforms therapists in response to client trauma survivors" (p. 237), VR addresses how counselors bearing witness to and indirectly experiencing how their clients have overcome adversity promotes positive changes in the counselors themselves. In much the same way as vicarious trauma has been found to alter negatively the fundamental schemas related to how counselors view their world, VR seems to alter positively similar schema. Hernandez, Engstrom, and Gangsei (2010) delineated seven specific areas in which clinicians found positive changes in their own beliefs, behaviors, and feelings as a result of their empathetic engagement. The areas included (a) thoughts regarding people's ability to heal, (b) validation of the benefit of therapy, (c) finding hope, (d) re-evaluating one's own problems, (e) increased comprehension and validation of the role of spirituality in healing, (f) finding the value in community healing, and (g) becoming more engaged in publicly discussing the impact of trauma. These shifts speak to the benefit finding that may occur within counselors themselves.

The Vicarious Resilience Scale (VRS) (Killian, Kernandez, Engstrom, & Gangsei, 2017) is a self-report instrument designed to assess counselors' levels of VR. This instrument has been developed to measure similar areas as detailed in the preceding. The VRS looks at: (a) changes in life goals and perspective (e.g., life direction, priorities, connection with others), (b) client inspired hope (increased recognition of clients' capacities and resources for healing and recovery, and being inspired by these capacities), (c) increased recognition of clients' spirituality as a therapeutic resource, (d) increased self-awareness and self-care practice, (e) increased consciousness about power and privilege relative to clients' social location, (f) increased capacity for resilience and resourcefulness, and (g) increased capacity to remain present during clients' trauma narratives (Killian et al., 2017). These categories of change describe long-term, life-altering shifts in functioning and understanding that are representative of the experience of many counselors. If a sample of practicing clinicians were asked to discuss a client who inspired or changed them for the better, most would have trouble narrowing their stories down to just one.

CASE ILLUSTRATION 14.1

SHEILA'S STORY: AN INSPIRATIONAL CLIENT

Sheila was a client who had been subjected to extensive domestic violence. She had been systematically tortured by her spouse over a period of years. Sheila was physically, emotionally, and mentally abused in ways that were unimaginable to her counselor. Eventually, Sheila's spouse had tried to kill her. Sheila came for counseling in order to get help with her anxiety, and her counselor was awestruck. Sheila was experiencing panic attacks and persistent sleep disturbance related to her trauma, but she had been holding a job, living independently, and volunteering at a women's shelter. She had begun to date and was finding that experience gratifying, although challenging. What was so inspiring to her counselor was the determination that Sheila had to reclaim her life. She was not going to be defined by that one singular set of experiences in her life and was going to make the most of what she now perceived was the gift of independence and freedom. Over time, her anxiety was under better control and she felt ready to forge ahead without counseling. It may be that she left her counselor with as much as she claimed to have gained from their relationship.

I have had clients who have affected me in much this same way. I have listened to stories of trauma and abuse that found me struggling to wrap my own mind around how the people who lived these stories had moved beyond surviving to thriving. When I was a relatively young counselor, I was fortunate that my life experience had not exposed me to the realities of violence, trauma, and abuse beyond what I had seen on television, in the movies, or had read about in books and learned through my training. So often, clients like Sheila came in for sessions with a voracious enthusiasm for life, despite their traumatic experiences, that was contagious. As a result of these clients, I began to examine my own struggles in comparison to theirs, and mine seemed minimal. I was motivated to strive for excellence, as well as peace and contentment, through watching them do the same. Witnessing these clients' journeys has changed me in some very specific ways over the course of my career. I find that these changes are explained well by the construct of VPTG.

Vicarious Posttraumatic Growth

VPTG is essentially secondhand posttraumatic growth (PTG). First conceptualized by psychologists Richard Tedeschi and Lawrence Calhoun in the 1990s, PTG refers to positive changes that may result from a person's life struggle or with a traumatic experience (Tedeschi & Calhoun, 2004). The construct of PTG bears explanation here as the vicarious experience is simply parallel to that of those who directly experience a significant life stressor or trauma. Tedeschi and Calhoun identified five domains in which growth tends to occur that are detailed in the following sections.

The first domain is a sense of new possibilities or opportunities that may not have been present for individuals prior to their experience. The individual in Case Illustration 14.1 likely never would have imagined herself in a helping role with others, but there she was, volunteering at the shelter and considering going to school to become a counselor herself. She endorsed that it was her survivorship that spurred this change in how she viewed the possibilities for her life.

The second domain of PTG is an increased sense of the importance of and change in the nature of relationships with others. People may find that they now recognize relationships with family as more important than many other things in their lives. They may have an increased capacity or desire for intimacy with others. Further, individuals may find that they have an increased ability to engage empathically with others who have experienced pain.

The third domain is an increased sense of one's own strength and capacity to tolerate and withstand adversity. Individuals may have a sense that their past experiences are a demonstration that they are able to handle much more pain and distress than they previously believed themselves able to do. While she was in counseling, the client in Case Illustration 14.1 lost her job as a result of downsizing at her company. This event left her financially vulnerable and scrambling to find another job. She discussed this event in highly relative terms. She stated that "This is a big deal and I am really concerned about getting another job, but I have had someone trying to kill me. I think that I can take a simple lay off in stride."

The fourth domain of PTG is a greater appreciation for life in general. This domain may involve a change in perception about the general value of life or a feeling that one has been given a second chance that should not be wasted. Often, behavioral changes such as working less and spending more time with family or having a more laissez-faire attitude toward life stressors are characteristic changes within this domain (Calhoun & Tedeschi, 2018). The client in Case Illustration 14.1 really had what only can be described as an example of "life is too short to worry about unimportant things when there are so many big things that matter" approach to life. She placed value on kindness, altruism, people, and experiences rather than worrying about what people thought about her or what possessions she owned. This value system was quite contrary to her former life where there was an emphasis on things, achievement, status, and affluence.

The final domain of PTG is an increase in spirituality. Not necessarily an increase in religiosity (although this may occur), this domain refers to a strengthening or deepening of an individual's spiritual life. There may be an increased sense of faith or an opening to questions of a spiritual nature or as a means to make sense of an individual's experience (Lindstrom, Cann, Calhoun, & Tedeschi, 2013). The client in Case Illustration 14.1 had never been a particularly religious or spiritual person. She had not attended a church or been raised to subscribe to any one religious affiliation. In her healing, she found a spiritual or more metaphysical meaning in her trauma. She came to believe that there was a higher purpose for and meaning of her experience that involved her helping and caring for others. Although I believe she still was ambivalent regarding the existence of God, she did adopt a more spiritual outlook regarding the interconnectedness of human experience and life's purpose.

Studies have been done regarding the potential for VPTG on a number of professions. There have been examinations of mental health workers who work with multiply traumatized children (Hyatt-Burkhart, 2014), psychotherapists (Arnold, Calhoun, Tedeschi, & Cann, 2005), funeral directors (Linley & Joseph, 2005), nurses and rehabilitation teams (Shiri, Wexler, & Kreitler, 2010), and language interpreters working with asylum seeking refugees (Splevins, Cohen, Joseph, Murray, & Bowley, 2010). The primary measure of VPTG is the Posttraumatic Growth Inventory (PTGI). This 21-question self-report measure is designed to assess directly the changes that an individual experiences within the previously delineated five domains. Questions such as "I have a greater feeling of self-reliance," "I know better that I can handle difficulties," and "I can better appreciate each day" are rated on a 6-point Likert scale from 0 = I did not experience this change as a result of my crisis to 5 = I experienced this change to a very great degree as a result of my crisis (Tedeschi & Cahoun, 1996). The PTGI has been validated as a measure of vicarious responses to traumatic exposure as well. By changing the scale to indicate that the change that has occurred is a result of a helping relationship, the instrument has proven to be an effective tool in the assessment of VPTG.

It is important to note that not all people who experience a major life stressor become disturbed by it or struggle with it. It is not a given that counselors will experience deleterious psychological consequences as a result of their work. It is equally true that not all people who experience struggle will thrive after it or grow from it. There are counselors who will not experience psychological growth as a result of their work with people who have grown as a result of their trauma. In fact, there is controversy regarding whether or not PTG and benefit finding in the aftermath of struggle is real or just part of how people cope with and make sense of their experiences (McFarland & Alvaro, 2000). Further exploration needs to be done to clarify these constructs and delineate their relevance to clients and practitioners alike.

Wellness Conceptualized

Now that we have presented a comprehensive overview of the potential negative and positive effects of the work of counseling, we can move into a discussion of how clinicians can behave in ways that keep them well. By definition, wellness can be conceptualized as "a way of life oriented toward optimal health and well-being, in which body, mind, and spirit are integrated" (Myers, Sweeney, & Witmer, 2000, p. 252). This definition is consistent with a biopsychosocial conceptualization of wellness, which we endorse. We extend the components of wellness to include an additional focus that incorporates the interactions between a counselor and the various layers of their systemic experiences. As with Bronfenbrenner's (1979) ecological systems theory, our approach to wellness incorporates the interaction between individuals and their environment as well as the holistic mind–body–spirit interaction found in a biopsychosocial interpretation. Counselors experience a bidirectional impact with many different systems. Individual characteristics of gender, age, years of experience, personal history of traumatic exposure, race, and ethnicity have all been found to play a role in counselors' unique approaches to maintaining wellness along with risks for diminishment in wellness (Lawson, 2007). Of further influence are the micro systemic components of family, work, and peers. As we expand outward, a counselors' exosystem, which comprises factors such as the community in which they live, societal position, and job status, add an additional layer of contribution to overall wellness. The final tier of influence is the macrosystemic component of facets such as social norms, socioeconomic status, income, and spirituality that are a force within an overall composite of wellness. These facets function in a bidirectional manner, where counselors have both influence upon and are influenced by their unique set of components. These components have a potentially protective effect and also may provide a significant source of stress for the individual. An effective self-evaluation of wellness should include an exploration of how these systemic influences are interacting within the individual's unique context. It is impossible to separate counselors' work from their personal lives and vice versa. The notion of being able to leave work at work and leave home at home is somewhat of a fallacy. Counselors continually must strive to maintain awareness of how they are being influenced, by all of the many systems within which they function, and then take steps to ameliorate any deficiency or stressors that may be occurring.

Wellness is generally normative. It is, however, an easier task to act in ways that help us to remain healthy rather than to have to remediate disturbance. Arguably the most important task related to maintaining counselor wellness is for counselors to engage continually in reflective practice so as to maintain a sense of awareness of their functioning (Lawson & Myers, 2011).

■ METHODS OF EVALUATION OF COUNSELOR WELLNESS

In recent decades there has been a great deal of focus on wellness as an integral part of counselor effectiveness. Entire volumes have been written on specific methods of assessment and evaluation, some of which we already have detailed in this chapter. With the advent of the Internet, access to myriad instruments that explore a wide variety of aspects and models of wellness are available with a few clicks at the keyboard. We provide links to many of the more popular and reliable tools in the Resources section of this chapter and will cover a few of them here.

First, it is important to discuss easily identifiable signs and symptoms that one's health is less than optimal. Every counselor will have his or her own set of "tells" or clues that something is amiss. Symptoms such as an increase in irritability, forgetfulness, distractibility, and lack of attention to detail may be indications of a problem. My personal warning sign is a disturbance in my sleep. In times of stress, I find that I have difficulty falling asleep and sleeping soundly, and I often have work-related dreams. My family might endorse that I also become a little grumpy. Counselors can engage in reflective processes, such as journaling, supervision, and self-assessment, to discover their own initial indicators.

At times, the indicators of stress may be more severe, especially if the initial warning signs have been missed or ignored. Skovholt (2001) found chronic fatigue, anxiety, depression, frequent headaches, and emotional exhaustion to be common signs of insufficient self-care by counselors. If left untreated or unaddressed, such symptoms may progress to be significantly impairing to a counselor's work and overall functioning. Further, a lack of attention to symptoms related to the distress created by the work may lead to one of the deleterious conditions detailed earlier in the chapter and, at worst, a diagnosable disorder.

At times, it can be useful to employ a more standardized approach to self-assessment of wellness. Instruments such as the MBI, ProQOL, and PTGI can have an important place in a counselor's approach to healthy functioning. Another tool that specifically targets the assessment of wellness is the Wellness Evaluation of Lifestyle Inventory (WEL; Myers & Sweeny, 2005). The WEL is based on Sweeney and Witmer's (1991) Wheel of Wellness model. In this model, wellness is conceptualized as a wheel that has spirituality at its center and spokes that radiate out that represent the life tasks of establishing cultural identity, sense of worth, sense of control, realistic beliefs, emotions awareness and coping, sense of humor, nutrition, exercise, self-care, stress management, and gender identity (Witmer, Sweeney, & Myers, 1998). The outer rims of the wheel hold systemic forces that interact dynamically with the life tasks delineated herein (Myers, Sweeny, & Witmer, 2000). The innermost rim of the wheel contains work, leisure, love, and friendship, while the outermost rim comprises items such as family, community, media, and education. Just as with Bronfenbrenner's (1979) model, these interrelated components of an individual's life are all found to have a significant impact on overall health and wellness. When there is a change in functioning in one area of the wheel, there is a likely change in another. This model can be used as an informal method of assessment. Myers et al. (2000) suggest rating one's self on a scale of 1 to 10 (1 being the lowest to 10 being the highest level of functioning) for overall wellness on each dimension represented on the wheel. They further suggest a second rating, using the same scale that evaluates the individual's desired level of functioning on each domain. Allowing for individual differences in value of the domains of the wheel promotes self-determination and provides a bit more clarity regarding areas that may require change. Once the domains have been evaluated, counselors then can reflect upon and examine their responses in order to find patterns and themes, which may have emerged from the exercise of rating each component, and then base changes and interventions upon those. Myers, Sweeney, Witmer, and Hattie (1998) first developed the WEL as a more formalized approach to assessment. The most recent version (WEL-S) includes 120 items scored on a 5-point Likert-type scale (1 = strongly agree to 5 = strongly disagree). Scores are "simple sums of responses divided by the total points possible: thus, scores represent percent of total wellness" (Myers, Leucht, & Sweeny, 2004, p. 3).

The Five Factor Wellness Inventory (FF-WEL; Myers & Sweeny, 2005) is a more recent adaptation of the WEL that focuses on the specific factors of the creative self, coping self, social self, essential self, and physical self. This 73-item self-report measure is designed also to incorporate the dimensions addressed in the original WEL. Items such as "I like myself in spite of my imperfections" and "I am an active person" are rated on a 4-point Likert scale where 1 = strongly disagree to 5 = strongly agree (Sweeney & Myers, 2003). This instrument purports to provide users with an evaluation that helps them to make choices for healthier living through an exploration of the balance between and interrelated functioning of the various domains addressed in the assessment.

Awareness of the need for wellness, self-reflective practice, and ongoing evaluative behaviors are an integral part of maintaining counselor wellness. It is important for counselors to know their own "normal" and to be able to identify if their status begins to change. The following two sections discuss strategies for maintaining counselor health.

Staying Well

The best strategy for maintaining wellness is to engage in preventive behaviors. As stated earlier, it is much easier to stay well than to remediate or treat impairment. We've already set the foundation for staying well through the discussion of how counselors can be aware of the pitfalls and benefits of practice, engage in self-assessment, and use formal instruments for ongoing evaluation of their level of functioning. Behaviorally, there are many other tasks in which counselors can engage that may serve to keep them well in their work. These tasks can be specific work behaviors as well as those that counselors may undertake in their personal lives.

Within the realm of work behaviors, clinical supervision is one of the most effective mechanisms to promote, maintain, and reinforce wellness. More than just a place to discuss approaches to client treatment and administrative issues, clinical supervision can be used to help counselors explore their own internal reactions and responses to their work with clients (Venart, Vassis, & Pticher-Heft, 2007). Supervision also has been shown to be a positive component in countering the negative effects of the work of counseling (Pearlman, 1995). Whether the supervision occurs one-on-one, in a group format, or in a peer consultation model, a positive and supportive supervisory outlet can be vital to helping counselors discuss and process the parts of the work that are most difficult. In this textbook, we devote an entire chapter to the process of supervision due to its important role in the profession of counseling (see Chapter 13, Clinical Supervision and Professional Development).

Clinicians can benefit from adopting healthy thought patterns around the work they do and the work environment itself. Setting boundaries around work hours and availability is a key component to stress reduction (Young & Lambie, 2007). Using vacation time, sticking to one's expected number of hours per week, and minimizing office conflict involvement are all ways to reduce work stress. Addressed below in the section on tensions, finding a balance between work and life, setting limits around working time, and actively disengaging from the work are often difficult to do, given the pressures of the job and the fact that we are dealing with real people who have real problems. Choosing not to answer emails after hours, not taking paperwork or other tasks home to complete, and not being "on-call" 24/7 for our clients are all ways to behave purposefully to attempt to achieve balance. Certainly there are times when clinicians must take an on-call rotation or work extra or late hours to ensure client safety and appropriate standards of care. Such events are a necessary component of the work. Problems can arise when a clinician becomes overly responsible for the work of the client and has difficulty disengaging from the work.

One of the ways that counselors may set boundaries cognitively is to place the onus for client progress with the client. Thinking realistically about one's abilities and being aware that "one's role is not to 'cure' or 'save' clients, but to facilitate a positive change at this particularly difficult time in clients' lives" (Osborn, 2004, p. 322) can help to reduce feelings of responsibility that often compel counselors to over-function. When counselors place the responsibility for change with their clients, the burden of positive change can be reduced substantially. It is also important for clinicians to view their clients' struggles with the therapeutic process with patience and understanding.

I often have worked with counselors who become frustrated with client "resistance" to the process. Often, this so-called resistance serves a protective function for the client. Perhaps the work is too painful. Maybe there is a mismatch between client and counselor perception on what issues are most pertinent to the work, or maybe there is not a sufficient client/counselor relationship established in order for the client to trust the clinician to help. Reframing a counselor's negative perceptions of clients can be a valuable tool in maintaining satisfaction with the work and promoting wellness. In his 2007 survey, Lawson delineated (a) maintaining a sense of humor, (b) spending time with partner/family, (c) maintaining a balance between professional and personal lives, (d) maintaining self-awareness, and (e) maintaining a sense of control over work responsibilities as the top strategies that counselors reported as effective in promoting wellness. These five strategies are primarily cognitive patterns, but there are actual behaviors in which counselors can engage that also contribute to overall well-being.

The wellness-oriented behaviors in which counselors can engage are nearly unlimited and depend on what each individual finds of value. Venart, Vassos, and Pitcher-Heft (2007) discuss the aspects of physical, cognitive, and relational tasks that can enhance counselor wellness, which provide a framework in which to organize possible counselor behaviors. The following discussion is by no means exhaustive but provides some concrete examples that illustrate what types of activities may enrich each domain.

Physical wellness is essential to mental wellness. Engaging in exercise and physical activity can be an effective tool in stress reduction. From simply taking a short walk during a break in the work day to embarking on a long-term physical fitness plan, exercise is a key component in the mind–body connection. There is evidence to suggest that exercise can reduce depression and anxiety (Stathopoulou, Powers, Berry, Smits, & Otto, 2006) and improve overall mental health and quality of life (Penedo & Dahn, 2005). Beyond exercise, eating well, maintaining healthy sleep patterns, minimizing the use of alcohol and nicotine, and engaging in preventive health maintenance and the treatment of chronic illness all are part of a positive physical health routine. Dancing, yoga, aerobics, hiking, biking, kayaking, jogging, sailing, and skiing—whatever activity a person finds enjoyable can be a contributing factor to overall wellness.

The cognitive domain encompasses the way we think about things. We have already discussed how the ways in which we view ourselves and our clients in the work can have an effect on well-being. In a more general sense, how we view the world and ourselves in it also can play a role. People who think in black-and-white terms may struggle to keep well in the work (Venart et al., 2007). If there is only one right way, one path to appropriate, and no shades of gray, counselors may struggle with the world view of their clients, the policies and procedures of their place of employment, even the behaviors of those around them, and allow themselves to become disturbed by them. Similarly, catastrophic thinking and thinking in absolutes may lead to counselor distress. Skovholt (2001) suggests that counselors who are able to recognize small successes and incremental changes experience greater sustainability in the work. The mindset of the counselor has an impact on wellness.

Finally, engaging in relationships that support wellness in one's work and in one's personal life are associated with better overall wellness (Sheldon, Elliot, Kim, & Kasser, 2001). Engaging in time with close friends and family can have a protective or mitigating effect on the stressors created by the work environment. Although Lawson (2007) found that counselors did not find discussing work stressors with their friends and family particularly helpful, they did endorse their personal relationships as an important part of their well-being. It is valuable to consider that counselors spend their days engaging in relationships that are comprised of "one-way caring" (Skovholt, 2001). These relationships are not emotionally reciprocal. Finding mutuality in personal relationships is important. These relationships provide a sounding board, an avenue for genuine feedback, emotional support, and caring that sustain counselors in their work as well.

No discussion of possible strategies to maintain counselor wellness would be complete without mentioning the benefits of personal counseling. Counseling is not just for clients, but for counselors as well. When we engage in personal counseling, we place the focus on our own needs and experiences. We also role model the value of counseling for our clients and colleagues.

In summary, there are no limits on the types of activities that can help counselors reduce stress and remain well. Listening to music, spending time outdoors, painting, pottery, cooking, knitting, and so forth all can be wellness-inducing activities when they are behaviors that an individual finds comforting, stimulating, relaxing, or any number of types of potential benefit. In my supervisions I ask "what do you groove on?" meaning what sparks your interest and gets you energized? I love to fish. I don't really care if I catch anything, but I enjoy being in nature, the physical behavior of casting and reeling in my line, and being quiet and alone with my thoughts. I find that it centers me and brings me a feeling of calmness, even in the most stressful times. Each counselor must find her or his own groove and act upon it. The work of counseling is hard and rewarding. Attending to our own wellness is not only ethical and part of best practice, but it can serve to protect us from the adverse effects of the work and help us to keep our own wells brim full.

Tensions

There are a number of tensions that present themselves when we look at the positive and negative effects of the work, counselor self-care, and wellness. The greatest challenge may be setting personal boundaries. Most people choose the field of counseling because they want to help people. It can be difficult to maintain an appropriate sense of who is responsible for change in a counseling relationship when the counselor is someone inherently invested in helping. Finding the balance of doing with instead of doing for can be a challenge for some counselors.

Another challenge is the reality of the pressures of the job. There are demands to maintain a high caseload, complete extensive documentation for insurance companies, and hit targeted productivity standards that may burdensome but part of the fiscal reality of the agency. It is often difficult to function within the parameters of the job and find ways to establish limits. It is not always possible to limit the work week to 40 hours, but being a strong advocate for one's self with one's supervisors around issues of wellness is essential.

CONCLUSION

This chapter provided an overview of the possible effects that the work of counseling may have upon counselors themselves. It has long been recognized that exposure to the distressing experiences and feelings of others can cause similar distress in those who listen and provide intervention. We also recognize that counselors can derive benefit and grow from the work that they do with their clients. Finding approaches to the work of counseling that enhance the potential for growth while minimizing distress is a significant part of maintaining a successful counseling practice. An essential part of such an approach is counselor wellness.

Counselors have an ethical duty to monitor themselves and their colleagues for fitness for the work. Wellness is an essential element of fitness. Counselors must be emotionally, physically, and spiritually sound in order to provide appropriate care to their clients. Finding ways to maintain and refill one's own reservoir of internal resources is a crucial element in sustaining a counselor's ability to safely and effectively work with clients.

Counseling is often emotionally difficult work. We hear terrible stories of human suffering and tragedy, but we also hear amazing tales of resilience, joy, and success. Through a conscious effort to engage in self-evaluation and practice good self-care, counselors can mitigate the negative effects of the work and enhance their ability to continue to engage in the process of helping in ways that benefit their clients and themselves.

RESOURCES

Video Links

Compassion Fatigue
https://www.youtube.com/watch?v=ZsaorjIo1Yc
https://www.youtube.com/watch?v=uOzDGrcvmus

Assessment Tools

Post Traumatic Growth Inventory (Tedeschi & Calhoun, 1996)
https://www.emdrhap.org/content/wp-content/uploads/2014/07/VIII-B_Post-Traumatic
-Growth-Inventory.pdf
Professional Quality of Life Instrument (ProQOL)

https://proqol.org
Maslach Burnout Inventory
https://www.mindgarden.com/117-maslach-burnout-inventory
America Counseling Association Taskforce on Counselor Wellness and Impairment
http://www.creating-joy.com/taskforce/tf_wellness_strategies.htm

Books

Corey, G., Muratori, M., Austin, J. T., & Austin, J. A. (2018). *Counselor self-care.* Alexandria, VA: American Counseling Association.

Figley, C. R. (2013). *Compassion fatigue: Coping with secondary traumatic stress disorder in those who treat the traumatized.* New York, NY: Routledge.

Jung, C. G., Adler, G., & Hull, R. F. C. (2014). *Collected works of C. G. Jung, Volume 18: The symbolic life: Miscellaneous writings.* Princeton, NJ: Princeton University Press.

Myers, J. E., & Sweeney, T. J. (2005). *Counseling for wellness: Theory, research, and practice.* Alexandria, VA: American Counseling Association.

Quitangon, G., & Evces, M. R. (Eds.). (2015). *Vicarious trauma and disaster mental health: Understanding risks and promoting resilience.* New York, NY: Routledge.

Rothschild, B. (2006). *Help for the helper: The psychophysiology of compassion fatigue and vicarious trauma.* New York, NY: W.W. Norton & Co.

Trotter-Mathison, M., & Skovholt, T. (2014). *The resilient practitioner: Burnout prevention and self-care strategies for counselors, therapists, teachers, and health professionals.* New York, NY: Routledge.

REFERENCES

Adams, R. E., Boscarino, J. A., & Figley, C. R. (2006). Compassion fatigue and psychological distress among social workers: A validation study. *American Journal of Orthopsychiatry, 76* (1), 103–108. doi:10.1037/0002-9432.76.1.103

American Counseling Association. (2014). *ACA code of ethics.* Alexandria, VA: Author.

The American heritage dictionary of the English language (5th ed.). (2019). Boston, MA: Houghton Mifflin.

American Psychiatric Association. (2013). *Diagnostic and statistical manual of mental disorders* (5th ed.). Washington, DC: Author.

Arnold, D., Calhoun, L. G., Tedeschi, R., & Cann, A. (2005). Vicarious posttraumatic growth in psychotherapy. *The Journal of Humanistic Psychology, 45* (2), 239. doi:10.1177/0022167 805274729

Bonanno, G. A. (2004). Loss, trauma, and human resilience: Have we underestimated the human capacity to thrive after extremely aversive events? *American Psychologist, 59* (1), 20. doi:10.1037/0003-066X.59.1.20

Bonanno, G. A., Galea, S., Bucciarelli, A., & Vlahov, D. (2006). Psychological resilience after disaster: New York City in the aftermath of the September 11th terrorist attack. *Psychological Science, 17* (3), 181–186. doi:10.1111/j.1467-9280.2006.01682.x

Bride, B. E. (2007). Prevalence of secondary traumatic stress among social workers. *Social Work, 52* (1), 63–70. doi:10.1093/sw/52.1.63

Bride, B. E., Robinson, M. M., Yegidis, B. L., & Figley, C. R. (2004). Development and validation of the Secondary Traumatic Stress Scale. *Research on Social Work Practice, 14* (1), 27–35. doi:10.1177/1049731503254106

Bronfenbrenner, U. (1979). *The ecology of human development.* Boston, MA: Harvard University Press.

Cain, N. R. (2000). Psychotherapists with personal histories of psychiatric hospitalization: Countertransference in wounded healers. *Psychiatric Rehabilitation Journal, 24* (1), 22. doi:10.1037/h0095127

Collings, J. A., & Murray, P. J. (1996). Predictors of stress amongst social workers: An empirical study. *The British Journal of Social Work, 26* (3), 375–387. doi:10.1093/oxfordjournals.bjsw.a011101

Corey, G., Corey, M. S., & Callanan, P. (2011). *Issues and ethics in the helping professions* (8th ed.) Pacific Grove, CA: Brooks Cole.

Deutsch, C. J. (1984). Self-reported sources of stress among psychotherapists. *Professional Psychology: Research and Practice, 15*, 833–845. doi:10.1037/0735-7028.15.6.833

Dunkley, J., & Whelan, T. A. (2006). Vicarious traumatisation: Current status and future directions. *British Journal of Guidance & Counselling, 34* (1), 107–116. doi:10.1080/03069880500483166

Emery, S., Wade, T. D., & McLean, S. (2009). Associations among therapist beliefs, personal resources and burnout in clinical psychologists. *Behaviour Change, 26* (2), 83–96. doi:10.1375/bech.26.2.83

Everall, R., & Paulson, B. (2004). Burnout and secondary traumatic stress: Impact on ethical behaviour. *Canadian Journal of Counselling, 38* (1), 25.

Farber, B. (1983). *Stress and burnout in the human service professions.* New York, NY: Pergamon Press.

Farber, B. A. (1991). *Crisis in education: Stress and burnout in the American teacher.* San Francisco, CA: Jossey-Bass.

Figley, C. R. (1995). Compassion fatigue and secondary traumatic stress: An overview. In C. R. Figley (Ed.), *Compassion fatigue: Coping with secondary traumatic stress disorder in those who treat the traumatized* (pp. 1–20). New York, NY: Routledge and Taylor & Francis.

Freud, S. (1910). The future prospects of psychoanalytic therapy. In J. Strachey (Ed.), *The standard edition of the complete psychological work of Sigmund Freud* (Vol. I, pp. 139–151). London, UK: Hogarth Press.

Freudenberger, H. J. (1974). Staff burn-out. *Journal of Social Issues, 30* (1), 159–165. doi:10.1111/j.1540-4560.1974.tb00706.x

Gentry, J. E., Baranowsky, A. B., & Dunning, K. (2002). ARP: The accelerated recovery program (ARP) for compassion fatigue. In C. Figley (Ed.), *Treating compassion fatigue* (pp. 123–137). New York, NY: Brunner-Routledge.

Ginsburg, S. G. (1974). The problem of the burned out executive. *Personnel Journal, 53*, 598–600.

Hakanen, J. J., Bakker, A. B., & Schaufeli, W. B. (2006). Burnout and work engagement among teachers. *Journal of School Psychology, 43* (6), 495–513. doi:10.1016/j.jsp.2005.11.001

Harrison, R. L., & Westwood, M. J. (2009). Preventing vicarious traumatization of mental health therapists: Identifying protective practices. *Psychotherapy: Theory, Research, Practice, Training, 46* (2), 203–219. doi:10.1037/a0016081

Harvey, J., & Delfabbro, P. H. (2004). Psychological resilience in disadvantaged youth: A critical overview. *Australian Psychologist, 39* (1), 3–13. doi:10.1080/00050060410001660281

Hayes, J. A., McCracken, J. E., McClanahan, M. K., Hill, C. E., Harp, J. S., & Carozzoni, P. (1998). Therapist perspectives on countertransference: Qualitative data in search of a theory. *Journal of Counseling Psychology, 45* (4), 468. doi:10.1037/0022-0167.45.4.468

Hernández, P., Engstrom, D., & Gangsei, D. (2010). Exploring the impact of trauma on therapists: Vicarious resilience and related concepts in training. *Journal of Systemic Therapies, 29*(1), 67–83. doi:10.1521/jsyt.2010.29.1.67

Hernandez, P., Gangsei, D., & Engstrom, D. (2007). Vicarious resilience: A new concept in work with those who survive trauma. *Family Process, 46* (2), 229–241.

Hyatt-Burkhart, D. (2014). The experience of vicarious posttraumatic growth in mental health workers. *Journal of Loss and Trauma: International Perspectives on Stress & Coping, 19* (5), 452–461. doi:10.1080/15325024.2013.797268

Jackson, S. E., & Maslach, C. (1982). After-effects of job-related stress: Families as victims. *Journal of Organizational Behavior, 3* (1), 63–77. doi:10.1002/job.4030030106

Jacobi, J. (1986). *Psychological reflections: an anthology of Jung's writings 1905-1961.* New York, NY: Taylor & Francis.

Jenkins, S. R., & Baird, S. (2002). Secondary traumatic stress and vicarious trauma: A validational study. *Journal of Traumatic Stress, 15* (5), 423–432. doi:10.1023/A:1020193526843

Kadambi, M. A., & Ennis, L. (2004). Reconsidering vicarious trauma: A review of the literature and its limitations. *Journal of Trauma Practice, 3* (2), 1–21.

Kaplan, D. M., Tarvydas, V. M., & Gladding, S. T. (2014). 20/20: A vision for the future of counseling: The new consensus definition of counseling. *Journal of Counseling & Development, 92* (3), 366–372.

Katz, R. S., & Johnson, T. A. (Eds.). (2016). *When professionals weep: Emotional and countertransference responses in palliative and end-of-life care.* New York, NY: Routledge.

Killian, K., Hernandez-Wolfe, P., Engstrom, D., & Gangsei, D. (2017). Development of the Vicarious Resilience Scale (VRS): A measure of positive effects of working with trauma survivors. *Psychological Trauma: Theory, Research, Practice, and Policy, 9* (1), 23. doi:10.1037/tra0000199

Killian, K. D. (2008). Helping till it hurts? A multimethod study of compassion fatigue, burnout, and self-care in clinicians working with trauma survivors. *Traumatology, 14* (2), 32–44. doi:10.1177/1534765608319083

Kristensen, T. S., Borritz, M., Villadsen, E., & Christensen, K. B. (2005). The Copenhagen Burnout Inventory: A new tool for the assessment of burnout. *Work & Stress, 19* (3), 192–207. doi:10.1080/02678370500297720

Kottler, J. A. (2017). *On being a therapist* (5th ed.). Oxford, UK: Oxford University Press.

Lawson, G. (2007). Counselor wellness and impairment: A national survey. *Journal of Humanistic Counseling, Education and Development, 46* (1), 20–34. doi:10.1002/j.2161-1939.2007.tb00023.x

Lawson, G., & Myers, J. E. (2011). Wellness, professional quality of life, and career-sustaining behaviors: What keeps us well? *Journal of Counseling and Development, 89* (2), 163–171. Retrieved from https://search-proquest-com.authenticate.library.duq.edu/docview/85839 0611?accountid=10610

Lindstrom, C. M., Cann, A., Calhoun, L. G., & Tedeschi, R. G. (2013). The relationship of core belief challenge, rumination, disclosure, and sociocultural elements to posttraumatic growth. *Psychological Trauma, 5* (1), 150–155. doi:10.1037/a0022030

Linley, P. A., & Joseph, S. (2005). The human capacity for growth through adversity. *American Psychologist, 60*(3), 262–264. doi:10.1037/0003-066X.60.3.262b

Louden, J. (1992). *The woman's comfort book: A self-nurturing guide for restoring balance in your life.* New York, NY: Harper Collins.

Marek, T., Schaufeli, W. B., & Maslach, C. (2017). *Professional burnout: Recent developments in theory and research.* New York, NY: Routledge and Taylor & Francis.

Maslach, C., & Jackson, S. E. (1981). The measurement of burnout. *Journal of Occupational Behavior, 2* (2), 99–113. doi:10.1002/job.4030020205

Maslach, C., Jackson, S. E., & Leiter, M. P. (1996). *MBI: Maslach burnout inventory.* Sunnyvale, CA: CPP, Incorporated.

Mathieu, F. (2012). *The compassion fatigue workbook: Creative tools for transforming compassion fatigue and vicarious traumatization.* New York, NY: Routledge and Taylor & Francis.

McCann, I. L., & Pearlman, L. A. (1990). Vicarious traumatization: A framework for understanding the psychological effects of working with victims. *Journal of Traumatic Stress, 3*(1), 131–149. doi:10.1007/BF00975140

McFarland, C., & Alvaro, C. (2000). The impact of motivation on temporal comparisons: Coping with traumatic events by perceiving personal growth. *Journal of Personality and Social Psychology, 79*, 327–343. doi:10.1037/0022-3514.79.3.327

Motta, R. W., Kefer J. M., Hertz, M. D., & Hafeez, S. (1999). Initial evaluation of the Secondary Trauma Questionnaire. *Psychological Reports, 85*, 997–1002. doi:10.2466/pr0.1999.85.3.997

Myers, J. E., Luecht, R. M., & Sweeney, T. J. (2004). The factor structure of wellness: Reexamining theoretical and empirical models underlying the Wellness Evaluation of Lifestyle (WEL) and the Five-Factor WEL. *Measurement and Evaluation in Counseling and Development, 36* (4), 194–208.

Myers, J. E., & Sweeney, T. J. (2005). *Counseling for wellness: Theory, research, and practice.* Alexandria, VA: American Counseling Association.

Myers, J. E., Sweeney, T. J., & Witmer, J. M. (2000). The wheel of wellness counseling for wellness: A holistic model for treatment planning. *Journal of Counseling and Development, 78*, 251–266. doi:10.1002/j.1556-6676.2000.tb01906.x

Osborn, C. J. (2004). Seven salutary suggestions for counselor stamina. *Journal of Counseling & Development, 82*(3), 319–328. doi:10.1002/j.1556-6678.2004.tb00317.x

Pearlman, L. A. (1995). Self-care for trauma therapists: Ameliorating vicarious traumatization. In B. H. Stamm (Ed.), *Secondary traumatic stress* (pp. 51–64). Lutherville, MD: Sidran Press.

Pearlman, L. A. (2003). *Trauma and attachment belief scale.* Los Angeles, CA: Western Psychological Services.

Pearlman, L. A., & McCann, I. L. (1995). Vicarious traumatization: An empirical study of the effects of trauma work on trauma therapists. *Professional Psychology: Research and Practice, 26*, 558–565. doi:10.1037/0735-7028.26.6.558

Pearlman, L. A., & Saakvitne, K. W. (1995). *Trauma and the therapist: Countertransference and vicarious traumatization in psychotherapy with incest survivors.* New York, NY: W.W. Norton & Co.

Penedo, F. J., & Dahn, J. R. (2005). Exercise and well-being: A review of mental and physical health benefits associated with physical activity. *Current Opinion in Psychiatry, 18* (2), 189–193. doi:10.1097/00001504-200503000-00013

Pietrzak, R. H., Johnson, D. C., Goldstein, M. B., Malley, J. C., & Southwick, S. M. (2009). Psychological resilience and postdeployment social support protect against traumatic stress and depressive symptoms in soldiers returning from Operations Enduring Freedom and Iraqi Freedom. *Depression and Anxiety, 26* (8), 745–751. doi:10.1002/da.20558

Rosenberger, E. W., & Hayes, J. A. (2002). Origins, consequences, and management of countertransference: A case study. *Journal of Counseling Psychology, 49* (2), 221. doi:10.1037/0022-0167.49.2.221

Ruysschaert, N. (2009). (Self) hypnosis in the prevention of burnout and compassion fatigue for caregivers: Theory and induction. *Contemporary Hypnosis, 26* (3), 159–172. doi:10.1002/ch.382

Sabin-Farrell, R., & Turpin, G. (2003). Vicarious traumatization: Implications for the mental health of health workers. *Clinical Psychology Review, 23* (3), 449–480. doi:10.1016/S0272-7358(03)00030-8

Schaufeli, W. B., Martinez, I. M., Pinto, A. M., Salanova, M., & Bakker, A. B. (2002). Burnout and engagement in university students: A cross-national study. *Journal of Cross-Cultural Psychology, 33* (5), 464–481. doi:10.1177/0022022102033005003

Schowalter, J. E. (1986). Countertransference in work with children: Review of a neglected concept. *Journal of the American Academy of Child Psychiatry, 25* (1), 40–45. doi:10.1016/S0002-7138(09)60597-5

Sheldon, K., Elliot, A., Kim, Y., & Kasser, T. (2001). What is satisfying about satisfying events? Testing 10 candidates psychological needs. *Journal of Personality and Social Psychology, 80* (2), 325–339. doi:10.1037/0022-3514.80.2.325

Shiri, S., Wexler, I. D., & Kreitler, S. (2010). Cognitive orientation is predictive of posttraumatic growth after secondary exposure to trauma. *Traumatology, 16* (1), 42–48. doi:10.1177/1534765609348243

Skovholt, T. M. (2001). *The resilient practitioner: Burnout prevention and self-care strategies for counselors, therapists, teachers, and health professionals.* Needham Heights, MA: Allyn & Bacon.

Smith, R. E. (1986). Toward a cognitive-affective model of athletic burnout. *Journal of Sport Psychology, 8*(1), 36–50.

Splevins, K. A., Cohen, K., Joseph, S., Murray, C., & Bowley, J. (2010). Vicarious posttraumatic growth among interpreters. *Qualitative Health Research, 20* (12), 1705–1716. doi:10.1177/1049732310377457

Stamm, B. H. (1995). *Secondary traumatic stress: Self-care issues for clinicians, researchers & educators.* Baltimore, MD: The Sidran Press.

Stamm, B. H. (2005). *The ProQOL manual: The professional quality of life scale: Compassion satisfaction, burnout & compassion fatigue/secondary trauma scales.* Baltimore, MD: Sidran Press.

Stamm, B. H. (2009). *ProQOL concise manual* (2nd ed.). Retrieved from https://proqol.org/uploads/ProQOL_Concise_2ndEd_12-2010.pdf

Stamm, B. H. (2010). *The concise ProQOL manual* (2nd ed.). Pocatello, ID: ProQOL.org. Retrieved from proqol.org/uploads/ProQOL_Concise_2ndEd_12-2010.pdf

Stathopoulou, G., Powers, M. B., Berry, A. C., Smits, J. A., & Otto, M. W. (2006). Exercise interventions for mental health: A quantitative and qualitative review. *Clinical Psychology: Science and Practice, 13* (2), 179–193. doi:10.1111/j.1468-2850.2006.00021.x

Sweeney, T. J., & Myers, J. E. (2003). *The indivisible self: An evidence-based model of wellness.* Greensboro, NC: Authors.

Sweeney, T. J., & Witmer, J. M. (1991). Beyond social interest: Striving toward optimal health and wellness. *Individual Psychology, 47,* 527–554.

Tedeschi, R., Shakespeare-Finch, J., Taku, K., & Calhoun, L. (2018). *Posttraumatic growth: Theory, research, and applications.* New York, NY: Routledge.

Tedeschi, R. G., & Calhoun, L. G. (1996). The posttraumatic growth inventory: Measuring the positive legacy of trauma. *Journal of Traumatic Stress, 9,* 455–471. doi:10.1002/jts .2490090305

Tedeschi, R. G., & Calhoun, L. G. (2004). *Posttraumatic growth: Conceptual foundation and empirical evidence.* Mahwah, NJ: Lawrence Erlbaum Associates.

Venart, E., Vassos, S., & Pitcher-Heft, H. (2007). What individual counselors can do to sustain wellness. *The Journal of Humanistic Counseling, Education, and Development, 46* (1), 50–65. doi:10.1002/j.2161-1939.2007.tb00025.x

Volkan, V. D. (2018). Countertransference reactions commonly present in the treatment of patients with borderline personality organization. In A. Alexandris & G. Vaslamatzis (Eds.), *Countertransference* (pp. 147–163). New York, NY: Routledge and Taylor & Francis.

Weitkamp, K., Daniels, J. K., & Klasen, F. (2014). Psychometric properties of the Questionnaire for Secondary Traumatization. *European Journal of Psychotraumatology, 5* (1), 21875. doi:10.3402/ejpt.v5.21875

Witmer, J. M., Sweeney, T. J., & Myers, J. E. (1998). *The wheel of wellness.* Greensboro, NC: Authors.

Young, M. E., & Lambie, G. W. (2007). Wellness in school and mental health systems: Organizational influences. *The Journal of Humanistic Counseling, Education and Development, 46*(1), 98–113. doi:10.1002/j.2161-1939.2007.tb00028.x

CHAPTER 15

NEW FRONTIERS FOR CLINICAL MENTAL HEALTH COUNSELORS

DEBRA HYATT-BURKHART | LISA LOPEZ LEVERS

This final chapter summarizes pertinent issues discussed throughout the text, especially reinforcing the multiple emphases on systems-of-care, ecological, salutogenic, social justice, and diversity approaches. In addition, the chapter identifies new frontiers for counselor practice, such as new opportunities for counselors within the Veterans Administration (VA) and TRICARE system, in hospital settings, in hospice programs and assisted living environments, in other community settings, in school-based programs, in college counseling centers, and in sports counseling. The chapter also addresses the influence of technology upon the counseling profession, discussing Internet-based services, such as virtual counseling, and telecounseling. The chapter provides a discussion of the ethical, legal, and practice concerns related to this developing branch of counseling. The following Council for the Accreditation of Counseling and Related Educational Programs (CACREP) standards are addressed in this chapter:
CACREP 2016:
2F1.b, 2F1.d, 2F1.e, 2F1.f, 2F1.g, 2F1.j, 2F2.a, 2F5.e, 2F8.a

LEARNING OBJECTIVES

After reviewing this chapter, the reader should be able to:

1. Identify issues important for the development of the field of clinical mental health counseling,

2. Recognize new areas in which clinical mental health counseling opportunities are expanding, and

3. Understand the importance of advocacy to the continued growth of the profession and the promotion of the most relevant wellness and diversity approaches to practice.

INTRODUCTION

Throughout this textbook, readers have been provided with an overview of the history of the development of counseling as a distinct profession, the roles and functions of clinical mental health counselors, the arenas in which clinical mental health counselors typically work, and a variety of contemporary issues that clinical mental health counselors and the field are facing. Through the lens of a strength-based, bioecological perspective, the text has incorporated a salutogenic or wellness orientation, thus reinforcing the current trend to reinvigorate essential elements of the profession's original wellness roots. This chapter provides a brief summary of the topics identified in previous chapters that are important to the field of counseling as it moves forward into new frontiers in the 21st century. We also discuss new opportunities and venues in which clinical mental health counselors are practicing and contributing. A discussion of the American Counseling Association (ACA) special interest networks is provided so that readers can gain a sense of how professional organizations are supporting the growth of these opportunities. We conclude the chapter with a focus on critical professional issues, such as licensure portability and Medicare reimbursement, underscoring the importance of the profession's continued and sustained advocacy efforts.

NEW FRONTIERS FOR THE PROFESSION

The authors of the various chapters of this book have infused discussions of what comes next for the profession and have identified some horizons toward which we need to strive. Organically, without a prompt from us as editors, an important theme has emerged from their efforts. In almost every chapter of this text, there is a call for professional advocacy. As the counseling profession continues to strengthen its identity and role within the larger mental health field, it is clear that we need to engage in the self-promotion of our profession's values and tenets. The chapter authors have identified the need for professional counselors to push toward a model that values integrated systems of care and systemic approaches to treatment. Through this mechanism, professional advocacy naturally reinforces client advocacy, and, in fact, has the potential to open new avenues for pursuing client advocacy in even more robust modes. In this way, the authors have urged community engagement and involvement, both for the profession and for our clients, particularly as social systems can provide much needed support for those who are in all types of psychosocial and emotional recovery. The potential for the field of professional counseling to have a role in the reduction of the stigma associated with mental health issues, to play an integral part in increasing social compassion, and to create pathways toward social change has been highlighted in each chapter and through the important research that the authors have cited. Advocacy for the profession and for our clients is essential as we move forward together.

NEW FRONTIERS IN SERVICE PROVISION

The field of counseling is not static and the venues in which counselors are employed continue to evolve over time. Counseling is a young profession that continues to advance as it matures. Many of the advancements that have occurred within the field have been due to legislative initiatives like the Mental Health Parity and Addiction Equity (MHPAE) Act of 2008 and the Patient Protection and Affordable Care Act (PPACA) of 2013. These Acts codified that medical insurances cover the treatment of mental health and substance use disorders on par with physical health services, increased affordable access to mental health services and expanded the arenas in which such services are provided. Counselors have enjoyed an increasing ability to be credentialed by third-party payer insurance companies and are now participating in managed care organizations as well (Goldman, McCulloch, & Sturm, 1998). Counselors are no longer relegated to working only in private practice, schools, and community clinics. As the profession continues to carve out its own identity, the venues in which services are provided offer many new frontiers to professional counselors, in general, and to clinical mental health counselors, in particular.

Veteran's Administration and TRICARE

Until the passage of the Veterans Benefits, Health Care, and Information Technology Act of 2006, professional counselors were not recognized or hired as mental health providers within the VA health system. A result of the lobbying and advocacy efforts of the ACA and the National Board for Certified Counselors (NBCC) among others, the 2006 legislation added licensed professional mental health counselors and marriage and family therapists to the roster of approved providers of counseling services within the VA system. Although this inclusion was a major victory for the profession, the VA continued primarily to hire social workers for open mental health positions. Further, the VA did not include counselors in their Health Professionals Trainee Program, one of their main recruitment vectors (NBCC, 2019). The pace of hiring counselors was slow, at best. In April of 2014, the U.S. House Appropriations VA subcommittee approved the Military Construction and Veterans Affairs Appropriations bill that contained language encouraging the training of mental health professionals regarding the unique needs of veterans. In April of 2015, the VA began to include mental health counselors into their trainee program. The path to parity within the VA system has been winding. There have been numerous bills, in both the U.S. House and the Senate, which were designed to increase the number of counselors employed by the VA but that have failed to be enacted. On December 16, 2016 President Obama signed H.R. 6416 (114th), the Jeff Miller and Richard Blumenthal Veterans Health Care and Benefits Improvement Act of 2016, which provided further clarification of the role of counselors as important players in the mental healthcare that is provided through the VA system. This Act also recognized the professional skills and competencies of individuals who hold doctoral degrees in counselor education as integral members of the VA treatment approach. It is important to note that the VA released qualification standards for counselors on September 28, 2010 that specify that mental health counselors must have a master's degree from a CACREP-accredited institution and must be able to secure state licensure within 2 years of their hire date.

Beginning on August 18, 2014, the U.S. Department of Defense enacted a final rule that permitted mental health counselors to become TRICARE Certified Mental Health

Counselors (TCMHC; Federal Register, 2014). TRICARE is the healthcare insurance program that is provided to uniformed service members, the U.S. armed forces military personnel, military retirees, and their families. In short, it is the healthcare program provided to individuals employed by the U.S.Department of Defense. Prior to this rule, counselors were excluded from being credentialed, and, therefore, from being compensated for treatment provided to individuals covered by TRICARE insurance. As with the VA, the TRICARE system requires that counselors hold a master's degree in clinical mental health or a mental health counseling degree from a CACREP-accredited program in order to attain this credential.

Services to Older Adults

According to the U.S. Census Bureau's 2017 Nation Population Projections, by the year 2030 one in every five adults will be of retirement age (U.S. Census Bureau, 2017). Prevalence rates of substance use problems and behavioral health disorders in adults over the age of 65 range from 14% to 20% (Moye et al., 2018). In 2017, those 85 years of age or older had the second highest rate of suicide, by age cohort, in the United States (American Foundation for Suicide Prevention, n.d.). Further, up to 17% of adults over 65 have an alcohol abuse problem (Office of Alcoholism and Substance Abuse Services, n.d.). These prevalence rates demonstrate that as the baby boomers age, there will be an increasing need for mental health services for older adults. Clinical mental health counselors will be in demand to provide intervention to this growing population.

There are myriad issues that this new generation of older Americans will face that may contribute to their burgeoning need for mental health intervention. Financial stressors are likely to be a major concern. Social security benefits are inadequate to maintain most people's quality of life, and many people are not sufficiently prepared for the cost of living in retirement. Sporadic work histories, frequent job changes, intermittent contributions to investment plans, resources already spent to care for their own aging parents, and the disappearance of pension plans may leave older Americans working later in life (Dixon, Richer, & Rollins, 2003). Career and job issues will remain a focus for this population. People in this age demographic also are likely to have issues related to the loss of a spouse and friends, the development of physical disabilities, and changes in identity and self-esteem levels due to the loss of careers and vocations (Myers & Harper, 2014). Older adults also may face issues related to a loss of autonomy if they become unable to live independently and must leave their own homes to secure the support that they need. Although the period of older adulthood presents many challenges and life transitions, mental healthcare has historically not been a predominant focus for this population

It is interesting to note that, at a mere 3%, older adults have the lowest usage rate for mental health services of any age group (ACA, 2011). One hypothesis regarding such low rates of service use is that providers of geriatric care have focused on the physiological component of aging as the primary marker of healthy functioning (Martinson & Berridge, 2015). A move toward a more strength-based, wellness-oriented approach to aging that rejects the deficit-based assumptions of a strictly biomedical model can further amplify a multifaceted view for treatment interventions with older populations

(McMahon & Fleury, 2012). By using a bioecological, strength-based orientation, professional counselors can move beyond addressing only physical concerns and integrate other domains, such as social, recreational, spiritual, and vocational affairs, into a systemically focused treatment, which is more likely to produce positive results (Fullen, 2016).

Opportunities for clinical mental health counselors to work with the aging population are expanding as rapidly as new and innovative approaches to the experience of growing old are being developed. Counselors are providing home-based services to older adults in much the same way that services are provided to children and families. In-home counseling that is delivered through an integrated team consisting of case managers, physicians, occupational and physical therapists, and others, has proven to be successful in improving outcomes and reducing the cost of care (Kunik et al., 2017). Clinical mental health counselors now are working in arenas that traditionally have been staffed by social workers. Nursing and personal care homes, transitional living facilities, and continuing care retirement communities, where people have access to all levels of care from independent living through skilled nursing care, are all venues in which counselors may find employment. Many counselor education programs now have specialized gerontology tracks or programs to help prepare clinical mental health counselors for the needs of this increasing demographic.

Although it is not always a service that is provided to the aging population, hospice care is another niche in which clinical mental health counselors are being employed. Hospice provides medical care, emotional support, and pain management to those with terminal illnesses (Ghesquiere, 2018). They also provide bereavement services to family members and loved ones after the death of the patient. In the past, these services were provided by nurses and social workers, but there has been a recent increase in the number of clinical mental health counselors providing these services. Clinical mental health counselors can be highly qualified to provide end-of-life interventions and grief counseling. The focus on life-span development in counselor training programs prepares clinicians to identify, address, and support patients and families through this journey. Although most people who use hospice services return to their pre-experience functioning, approximately 11% go on to develop mental health disorders such as depression or complicated grief reactions (Ghesquiere et al., 2015). Clinical mental health counselors are generally trained to perform the assessments necessary to identify such reactions and to intervene appropriately. There are many available continuing education opportunities that provide clinical mental health counselors with the necessary specialized training in grief counseling to enable them to work effectively with this population.

Community Settings and Diversity and Social Justice Arenas

According to the *Occupational Outlook Handbook* (U.S. Department of Labor, 2019), the job outlook for substance abuse, behavioral disorder, and mental health counselors is expected to grow much more rapidly than the average for other occupations. With an anticipated growth of 23% between 2016 and 2026, by implication, it is reasonable to expect to see expanded opportunities for clinical mental health counselors in a variety of community settings. The U.S. Department of Labor states the following: "Employment growth is expected as people continue to seek addiction and mental health counseling" (U.S. Department of Labor, 2019, "Job outlook", para. 1).

As professional counseling, in general, and the field of clinical mental health counseling (CMHC), specifically, have gained increased recognition and greater status, clinical mental health counselors have continued to move into newer areas of clinical and administrative supervision as well as program development. In increasingly greater numbers, counselors have been instrumental in designing, initiating, supervising, and maintaining new programs across service delivery sectors. For example, the demand for innovative community programming exists for needed services in some of the following areas: the current and devastating substance abuse and opioid crisis (Bradley University, n.d.); specialized community-based services for immigrants and refugees (Levers, Biggs, & Strickler, 2015; Levers & Mancilla, 2013; Mpofu, Levers, Mpofu, Tanui, & Hossain, 2015); integrating mental health services in legal and correctional settings with forensic counseling (Best Counseling Degrees, 2019); and the reconceptualization of all community-based resources as integrating a much-needed trauma-informed perspective across all service delivery systems (Levers, 2012).

One aspect of the need for innovative community-based program development involves the arena of diversity and social justice. Counselor Education Programs long have offered courses on multicultural counseling issues; just as an example, the second author of this chapter took such a course in 1975 as a part of her master's degree in counseling. While Counselor Education Programs have been "talking the talk" for decades, the pre-service preparation has yet, consistently and reliably, to "walk the walk." The *invisible veil* (Sue, Sue, Neville, & Smith, 2019), a concept that was discussed in Chapter 11, has continued to exist in the form of White privilege in many Counselor Education Programs. Some amount of criticism has appeared in the literature concerning this lack of authentic focus on diversity issues (e.g., Akkurt, Carter, & Saint-Jean, 2013; Ratts, Singh, Butler, Nassar-McMillan, & McCullough, 2016; Sue, Arredondo, & McDavis, 1992; Sue et al., 2019). The call for multicultural counseling-specific competencies was raised in the early 1990s (Sue et al., 1992), and scaffolding upon these original competencies, the more recent *Multicultural and Social Justice Counseling Competencies* were proposed and endorsed by the profession (Ratts et al., 2016).

A strong need exists for integrating multicultural and social justice competencies across all dimensions of the professional counseling field (Ratts et al., 2016). While the authentic implementation of these competencies opens many unique pathways for addressing real needs in communities across the nation, there are also opportunities for CMHC students, post-graduation, to enhance their multicultural and social justice skills in practice. They then may offer culturally relevant supervision to newer CMHC students in field placements—perhaps even students from their alma maters, thus contributing to culturally stronger Counselor Education Programs and a feel-good sense of "paying it forward," in terms of promoting a more robust diversity and social justice ethos in the professional counseling arena.

Clinical mental health counselors who graduate from Counselor Education Programs have the opportunity to initiate culturally relevant and culturally sensitive programming in any variety of community agencies and community-based services. Many social justice challenges continue to affect the mental and behavioral health of the populace, particularly persons experiencing all types of discrimination, persons living in poverty, persons living with disabilities, and persons who have experienced trauma or disasters. The issue of historical trauma links the culturally sensitive needs of historically disenfranchised peoples with the effects of transgenerational trauma, as with African Americans, Native American Indians, and Jewish Americans whose families survived the Holocaust (DeGruy, 2005; Substance Abuse and Mental Health Services Administration [SAMHSA], 2018). The need to initiate trauma-informed care across service sectors constitutes a relatively new dimension for CMHC practice, and, as an extension of addressing trauma, cutting edge research in neuroscience is identifying new treatment modalities for mental health practice. Additionally, some counselors are moving into the forensic counseling area, in which they may combine counseling and legal issues or work with human trafficking. Many challenges remain in community mental health settings that require new and innovative approaches and programming, and clinical mental health counselors are uniquely positioned to recognize methods for addressing these challenges in meaningful ways.

School-Based Counseling

School counseling has a decades-long history of a lack of clarity as to the professional roles and purpose associated with the work (Astramovich, Hoskins, Gutierrez, & Bartlett, 2013; Lambie & Williamson, 2004). Originally conceptualized as vocational counseling during the American Industrial Revolution, the field was designed to help schools to prepare their students for better employment (Dollarhide & Saginak, 2017). Over time, the needs of schools changed, and school counselors became tasked with the responsibilities of standardized testing, course scheduling, conflict resolution, and crisis management (Anderson, 2002). In 2003, the American School Counselors Association (ASCA, 2003) introduced the ASCA National Model in an attempt to define the role and purpose of school counselors clearly. This model delineated the role of school counselors as falling into three domains: academic, career, and social/emotional functioning. According to the ASCA National Model (2012), the goal of school counselors is to promote student success and well-being (Chandler et al., 2018).

As the landscape of education shifted, due to reports such as George W. Bush's *2003 New Freedom Commission on Mental Health*, which recommended that school mental health programs be improved and expanded, the function of school counselors with respect to mental health treatment also has evolved. The Commission's report recognized that the number of children who could benefit from mental health services is increasing and that their issues are becoming more severe. They recommended that there be a concerted effort to promote intervention within school settings in an acknowledgment that poor mental health functioning can be an impediment to academic success. Focusing on these mental health needs within the school setting has many ancillary benefits. This approach can help to reduce barriers to access, because all children are required to attend school where the service is provided. In-school services also can assist to normalize help seeking, reduce stigma, and provide a more systemically focused intervention that occurs within the unique context of the child (Stephan, Weist, Kataoka, Adelsheim, & Mills, 2007). There are caveats to the purported benefits of school-based services. Schools may not have the staffing, expertise, or perceived mission to provide focused mental health treatment. Often, school counselors provide initial interventions but refer students to practitioners in the community for ongoing treatment. Such referrals may be due to district policy, lack of resources, or an unwillingness of the system to accept responsibility for the mental healthcare of its students. As a result, children often fail to continue with treatment or encounter various barriers that interfere with service provision.

Over time, the needs of children and adolescents and the difficulties with schools assuming the responsibility for mental health treatment, has led to the development of school- and community-based partnerships. These partnerships are implemented in a variety of ways. Some partnerships are constructed with community providers having offices from which they provide services that are housed directly within the schools. Counselors offer services to students in much the same manner as they would in a traditional outpatient setting. Referrals may come from students themselves, from teachers, or from parents. Partnerships also may be structured by having a community agency's counselors placed within special-needs classrooms. These counselors are charged with attending to the mental health or social and emotional needs of the students within that class. The counselors may facilitate groups, provide individual counseling, and even do family work, depending on the needs of the students and the structure of the specific program. School mental health partnerships also may be structured through the establishment of treatment teams that include nurses, social workers, and physicians (Paternite, 2005). In this type of arrangement, the team coordinates the services that a student may need through collaborative assessment and intervention. Services may include individual counseling, in-home services, and advocacy.

As school and community mental health partnerships become more common, opportunities for clinical mental health counselors to work within schools are increasing. It is no longer necessary to be a certified school counselor or a teacher in order to provide intervention within the school setting. As ASCA continues to work to define the identity of school counselors, it is likely that creative approaches to school and community agency partnerships will continue to evolve as well.

College Counseling

College counseling centers were first developed in the late 1940s, when servicemen returning home from World War II began to take advantage of the GI Bill and matriculate into universities in large numbers. These first centers primarily focused on assisting veterans with their transition into the academic realm and helping them to plan for their education through vocational counseling and testing (Prince, 2015). As time progressed, those in the general student body began to avail themselves of these services. With the growing popularity of the self-help movement of the 1960s, college counseling centers began to provide interventions designed to address psychological distress. Within the past few decades, there has been an increase in the severity of issues with which college and university counseling centers are faced. It is no longer expected that the majority of clients will present with academic-related stress, homesickness, and personal relationship issues, such as a romantic breakup, or roommate conflicts. The number of students who are seeking help at university counseling centers is on the rise, and these centers are seeing the full gamut of psychological disorders (Watkins, Hunt, & Eisenberg, 2012).

In the past, services in college counseling centers typically have been provided by psychologists (Gallagher, 2013). This trend seems to be waning, as more university counseling centers are redesigning their student services into a more integrated model of care. As a result, we find health centers, student services, and counseling centers working in collaboration with one another in order to promote the general well-being of students (Prince, 2015). This integration of services, combined with a solidification of counselors as integral and important members of the helping professions, has begun to increase the number of clinical mental health counselors employed within such settings.

Although it is not necessary to have a degree specifically in college counseling in order to be employed by a university counseling center, CACREP does accredit programs that are designed for individuals who wish to specialize as college counselors and work in higher education settings. As of this writing, there are 27 fully accredited student affairs and college counseling programs across the United States (CACREP, 2018). Clinical mental health counselors without these specialty degrees increasingly are being employed as full-time staff members of college and university counseling centers, career centers, and within student services. Individuals with doctoral degrees in counselor education and supervision are finding success with securing positions in such centers as well.

One current trend among universities may hold currency for clinical mental health counselors who are employed by university counseling centers. Universities recently have revisited the principle of in loco parentis (Lee, 2011; Patel, 2019), which entails the philosophy of the university acting "in the place of the parent." While this concept played a reasonable role in the 19th and early 20th century university environments, legal challenges in the 1960s saw its demise, and students were enabled to exercise their rights with increasing independence. However, the pendulum has swung so far in the other direction, for example, with irresponsible fraternity- and sorority-associated hazing deaths, that universities once again are moving in the direction of in loco parentis. As this philosophy is reconstructed, parsed in more contemporary terms, it is likely that clinical mental health counselors who are working at university counseling centers will play a role in tempering students' rights with developmental and psychosocial dilemmas.

Sports Counseling

Another area of growing opportunity for clinical mental health counselors is the field of sports counseling. As early as the 1920s, there were professionals within the field of psychology who were focusing on bringing the principles of psychology to bear upon the performance of athletes (Miller & Wooten, 1995). In 1985, the Association for the

Advancement of Applied Sport Psychology (AAASP) was founded as a means to punctuate this distinct branch of psychology. During the 1980s, sports counseling competencies were developed by the Association for Counselor Education and Supervision as a part of their Counselors of Tomorrow Interest Network (Nejedlo, Arrendondo, & Benjamin, 1985). Throughout the following decades, this specialty area remained of interest but did not seem to expand in any substantive way. Recently there has been renewed interest in establishing counseling for athletes as a major component in the field of professional counseling. This interest may be driven by the fact that nearly half of all 6 to 12 year olds in the United States are participating in team sports (Hebard & Lamberson, 2017). Increased participation rates translate to increased need.

Not simply designed to enhance the physical performance of athletes, as had been the focus in the past, this new push for sports counseling calls for a broader emphasis on emotional well-being as an essential part of functioning. The National Athletic Training Association (NATA) and the National Collegiate Athletics Association (NCAA) have both taken steps to prioritize the mental health concerns of athletes (Hebard & Lamerson, 2017). Sports counseling specialties are now being offered as part of CMHC degrees in a number of institutions. Some college counseling centers are partnering with their college's sports programs to provide services to athletes, given their unique pressures. Issues such as eating disorders (Currie & Morse, 2005), overtraining (Raglin & Wilson, 2000), and the demands of balancing academics with athletics are all part and parcel of sports counseling. Combined with increasing rates of depression, anxiety, and other major mental health disorders, these unique systemic pressures may make athletes particularly vulnerable to mental health distress. For those who are interested in this area, the ACA offers a *Sports Counseling Interest Network* (initiated by the second author of this chapter), which is described in the following section of this chapter.

Summary of New Frontiers for Clinical Mental Health Counselors

As the field of counseling continues to hone its identity and secure its place in the realm of helping professions, broader opportunities for the employment of clinical mental health counselors are likely to continue to develop. The burgeoning fields of neurocounseling, business counseling, and a whole host of new and developing evidence-based practices continues to expand the options available to clinical mental health counselors. Counselors can use their requirements for continuing education as a mechanism to expand their skills and competencies within these new frontiers.

ACA INTEREST NETWORKS AS INDICATORS OF EMERGING FRONTIERS

In addition to the various specialty areas of professional counseling, which have been discussed throughout this textbook, the ACA also offers a variety of special-issue *Interest Networks (INs)*. These networks are open to all ACA members. Information about the INs can be found on ACA's website; the specific site for the INs can be found in the Resources section at the end of this chapter.

We believe that the topical areas of the INs represent some of the most cutting-edge aspects of our profession. For this reason, we are including the information from the ACA website (ACA, 2019, "Interest networks", para. 4–26) here.

ACA Ethics Interest Network

Members that may want to join: The purpose of an ACA Ethics Interest Network is to connect professional counselors, counselor educators, graduate students and other professionals with an interest in professional counseling ethics. These professionals are found in many settings where professional counselors work, and also include colleagues in closely related areas (i.e., state licensure boards, division and branch ethics committees, and professional publications pertaining to ethics.)

ACA Interest Network for Integrated Care

Members that may want to join: The purpose of the ACA Interest Network for Integrated Care is to collaborate and share information regarding best practices in preparing to work in an integrated care setting. This interest network is relevant to professional counselors, counselor educators, new professionals, as well as graduate students.

ACA Interest Network for Professional Counselors in Schools

Members that may want to join: The network provides networking and collaboration opportunities for licensed professional counselors (LPCs) currently working in school settings or those who may be interested in working as a counselor in schools; counselors in guidance programs who want to focus their identities as professional counselors; and counselor educators and supervisors who are interested in advocating for and researching new models for the delivery of mental health counseling services to children and adolescents in school settings.

ACA International Counseling Interest Network

Members who may want to join: The purpose of an ACA International Counseling Interest Network is to address the present day counseling needs created by globalization in this very interconnected world. It is hoped that this newly created interest network will provide much needed guidance, leadership, and resources to focus on international counseling, global diversity, human rights issues, and alternative approaches to counseling and internationally focused research. Moreover, this interest network will provide much needed collaborative opportunities for the counselors to engage in joint efforts to enhance the quality of life throughout the world. This Interest Network will facilitate the newly emerging international identity of the counselors and help them advance from diversity to international diversity, from justice to international justice, and national advocacy to international advocacy.

Animal Assisted Therapy in Mental Health Interest Network

Members that may want to join: The network promotes knowledge, research, and practice of animal assisted therapy (AAT) in the mental health field.

Children's Counseling Interest Network

Members that may want to join: Anyone interested in children's issues and promoting children.

Counseling and Technology Interest Network

Members that may want to join: Our mission is to enhance the quality of life in society by promoting the development of professional counselors and advancing the counseling profession by supporting new and innovative technologies across the spectrum of practice. Doing so will enable professional counselors to keep pace with the digital revolution and the associated realities of the 21st century.

Distance Learning in Counseling Education

Members who may want to join: Any ACA member who is interested in discussing the pedagogy of teaching in an online environment to discuss specific and unique challenges in delivering counseling curriculum through distance learning, share various approaches to incorporate technology in the learning process, and potentially collaborate to develop research for outcome-based research on distance learning in counseling.

Forensic Counseling Interest Network

Members that may want to join: This interest network will advance the contributions of all counselors whose work intersects with understanding of human behavior and laws, legal processes and legal systems. The interest network shall also serve to inform the counseling and legal communities, as well as the public, of current research, educational and service activities in the field of counseling and the law. The impact of professional counseling in this domain may influence policy, program development, mediation, advocacy and arbitration, as well as teaching and research.

Grief and Bereavement Interest Network

Members that may want to join: All counselors would do well to have training in grief and bereavement or just simply to know that the interest network is there to have a source for referrals.

Historical Issues in Counseling Network

Members that may want to join: Members of this Interest Network are interested in the significant people, trends and issues of our profession's history.

Interest Network for Advances in Therapeutic Humor

Members that may want to join: This network was designed to help counselors realize the value of humor in the therapeutic setting and how to appropriately use humor: Humor helps to establish rapport but requires strict boundaries in knowing what kind of humor to use, when to use it, how to use it, and with which clients it is appropriate. Humor may include something as simple as a magic trick, a simple statement, the use of a printed cartoon, or humorous body language.

Intimate Partner Violence Interest Network

Members that may want to join: This interest network is designed to connect counselors, students, counselor educators, and other helping professionals with an interest in counseling intimate partner violence (IPV) survivors, research, advocacy, cultural competency, and best practice models.

Multiracial/Multiethnic Counseling Concerns Interest Network

Members that may want to join: This interest network has broad application to the work of professional counselors in all settings, working with all ages and developmental stages. The issues and concerns of this population cut across all aspects of the profession; hence, counselors affiliated with all entities and divisions of ACA can find application to their work.

Network for Jewish Interests

Members that may want to join: Individuals interested in Jewish issues in the counseling profession, through advocacy, research or identification with Judaism, may find a home in this interest network.

Neurocounseling Interest Network

Members that may want to join: The purpose of the network will be to connect interested counselors throughout the organization who are actively using neuroscience and neurocounseling in their current counseling work.

Sexual Wellness in Counseling

Members that may want to join: This interest network will provide an opportunity to establish a professional network for accessing a wealth of resources related to providing sexuality counseling interventions to diverse populations, as well as encouraging research and training in sexual wellness.

Sports Counseling Interest Network

Members that may want to join: This interest network would be a good match for those counselors who want to make a career out of this area, as well as those who want to make sports counseling one aspect of their career. For example, advisers for athletes are those whose responsibilities include academic advising, life skills development, performance enhancement, and psychosocial development at both the collegiate and high school levels. Professional counselors may hold positions as academic advisers for athletes, may be in private practice for clinical and mental health issues, or may hold full-time positions within professional sporting organizations, colleges/universities, school settings, or community agencies.

Traumatology Interest Network

The Traumatology Interest Network is any professional counselor, counselor educator, or graduate student who is interested in traumatology and trauma therapy, or [those] who are already providing counseling services to trauma- or disaster-affected people, schools, and communities. The Interest Network is helpful to Counselor Educators seeking to incorporate trauma-relevant CACREP standards into their programs. Those who are interested in Disaster Mental Health are also ideal members of this community, along with those interested in any of a growing number of subspecialties, including the neuroscience of trauma, posttraumatic growth, traumatic stress as a public health issue, creating safe and secure schools, refugee trauma, social justice and trauma, and multicultural aspects of trauma care.

Veterans Interest Network

Members who may want to join: Any ACA member interested in counseling-related issues of service members and/or their families. We are comprised of veterans, military family members, current/previous/retired troops from all military branches, and nonmilitary members who work with service members. Our veterans function as advisors and educators on military-specific matters. All members are offered opportunities to get actively involved through advocacy, education, outreach, support, and liaison efforts to advance mental healthcare services for troops and families.

Wellness Interest Network

Members that may want to join: Counselors work from a preventive, developmental, wellness-oriented perspective. It is the philosophy underlying all that we do. In particular, counselors wanting to find other counseling practice or research might use the network to share ideas and projects.

Women's Interest Network

Members that may want to join: Women and anyone interested in women's issues and promoting women.

NEW FRONTIERS IN COUNSELING TECHNOLOGY

No discussion of new frontiers in counseling could be complete without an examination of the influence of changing technology upon the field. Gone are the days when the use of technology-assisted counseling meant that sessions would be conducted over the telephone. We have entered a technological era in which telepsychiatry, video conferencing, and Internet-based counseling are common. Services such as Talkspace and Betterhelp are offering counseling interventions that are provided by licensed counselors via text messaging, audio and video messaging, and text-based chat rooms. These services allow clients to communicate with their counselor at any time that they wish. Clients can expect that their counselor will respond to messages several times per day and be available to schedule more extended text, video, and phone conferences as needed. Assessment apps for evaluating the behavioral and mental health services that may be needed by clients also are on the horizon (Price et al., 2014).

These technology-based approaches to counseling do not replace traditional face-to-face counseling. All of the currently available platforms outline that people who are experiencing serious or acute issues, suicidal thoughts, or who need assistance with medication management are not appropriate candidates for their service. Technology-based counseling can be used for specific applications and situations. Individuals who live in rural areas where there is a lack of access to mental healthcare, those who travel a great deal, or people who experience limited mobility may all benefit from technology-based services. In addition, there is a growing comfort and familiarity with forming relationships online, especially among young people. Establishing a counseling relationship of this type may seem familiar and routine to many individuals. This normalcy, combined with ease of access and a sense of anonymity, makes technology-based counseling a viable option as we move into the 21st century.

There are some ethical concerns that arise, which are related to the use of technology-based counseling. It is imperative that counselors have demonstrated skills and competencies with the technology that they are using and that they can ensure that the types of technology that they are using are not beyond the capability of the client (Elleven & Allen, 2004). Problems with the technology interface are also of concern. Dropped phone calls, disrupted Internet service, and computer problems may interrupt counseling services. Counselors need to be able to compensate for these difficulties by ensuring that other means of communication are available in order to protect their clients in the best ways possible (Riemer-Reiss, 2000).

Other ethical concerns are more related to relational or practice aspects of the work of counseling. It is much more difficult to ensure that an intervention is appropriate for a client when a counselor is unable to observe and pick up verbal cues from that client. Facial expressions, body language, hygiene, eye contact, and tone of voice all provide a counselor with important information regarding a client's emotional state and functioning that is unavailable to them via text. This lack of nonverbal information also can lead to miscommunication and misinterpretation, as counselors usually rely upon these types of observation for a significant part of assessment of both the client and the efficacy of the process (Harris & Birnbaum, 2015). A quality diagnosis includes an observation of a client's physical functioning, social interactions, speech patterns, and much more that cannot be discerned over text or accurately over video chat. There are serious questions regarding the ethical nature of attempting to do so.

The use of technology may initiate confusion and misinterpretation that can interfere with effective assessment and intervention. Most people have experienced a situation in which they have sent a text message to another individual and the meaning of that text was taken to be something that was not intended. We all know that "tone" is nearly impossible to discern from text alone. That is why emoji were developed. The same is true in text-based counseling services. Both counselors and clients may ascribe meaning to a message that was not intended. It is much harder for the parties to know that they were misinterpreted than if they were sitting in a room talking. The counselor may not know that a message was received incorrectly by a client. The relationship may be damaged by this misinterpretation, and the counselor may not even be aware of the circumstance. Further, a counselor may misinterpret the messages from a client. The counselor may take a text more seriously than intended or may minimize a message. Both of these circumstances could have serious consequences. The fact is that social cues that humans give to one another in person generally are not discernible over technology. Special care needs to be taken to ensure that communication is both clearly provided and interpreted.

There are further concerns with the type and frequency of contact in technology-based counseling. Most services encourage clients to communicate when they wish, but the counselor's response may not be immediate. Unless client and counselor are engaged in a synchronous chat, there may be a delay in response that could raise client anxiety (Richards & Vigano, 2013). Further, the illusion of constant access may give clients the false sense that the counselor is available for emergency or crisis intervention, even though most sites specifically state that such services are not a part of the program. Well-defined guidelines, which are clearly communicated to clients about the frequency of contact and the type of services that are provided, become an imperative with technology-based counseling services.

Other ethical concerns are related to specific legal and ethical mandates of the profession. A counselor's ethical and sometimes legal duty to warn others of danger and to protect clients from harming themselves or others can become quite challenging when services are delivered from a distance (Mallen, Vogel, & Rochlen, 2005). Knowing the client well enough, with some sense of predictability, should be a standard part of the practice of informed consent. The informed consent process is not always as clear-cut with technology-based services. These services afford clients an anonymity that presents both benefits and challenges. Anonymity may encourage greater access to mental health services, because people may feel that there is less chance that they will be stigmatized for their treatment as no one, not even the counselor, will know the client's identity. Clients also may be more honest and open with their counselor because of this feeling of anonymity. The challenge is that clients can choose not to be truthful about their whereabouts, identity, age, and the severity of their disturbance. Without a face-to-face intervention, a counselor may have no idea that the information a client has provided is inaccurate, thereby potentially endangering the client, others, and even the counselor (Kraus, 2004).

CASE ILLUSTRATION 15.1

AN ETHICAL DILEMMA OF TECHNOLOGY-BASED COUNSELING

Patrick is an Licensed Professional Counselor (LPC) who is employed on a part-time basis with a technology-based counseling service. He has committed to respond to his clients no less than two times per day via text messaging. Patrick has been providing this service for about a month and is enjoying the work. He has not found the interventions to be too burdensome, so he decides to take on some new clients.

Patrick is an LPC in Georgia, and the provider only gives clinicians clients from the state in which they are licensed. In Georgia, the age of consent for mental health treatment is 18. Patrick takes on a new client whose intake and consent-to-treatment documents indicate they he is over that age of 18 and is exercising his right to consent for treatment as an adult. Over time, based on the situations and issues about which the client is texting, it becomes apparent to Patrick that the client is in his early high school years. Patrick checks the documents he has been provided and finds no information that would indicate that his client was held back or delayed in his educational progress, such that he simply would be older than the typical high school freshman or sophomore. Patrick is now faced with the ethical issue of having engaged in the treatment of a minor without parental consent, which is also a violation of Georgia law.

Situations such as that in this case are not unique to technology-based services, but the challenges faced are complicated by a lack of face-to-face contact in which visual cues can assist with prevention. In person, Patrick may have been tipped off to his client's age by his appearance. The client may not have been able to drive himself to his appointments, which may have provided another clue to his age. Patrick also may have been more apt to connect his client's affect and cognitive content with his age if they were from the same community and had a shared context.

Other ethical concerns become nuanced when providing technology-based treatment. Counselors must be aware of maintaining client confidentiality, engaging in adequate record keeping, and following the same ethical mandates that one would in traditional, face-to-face counseling. These mandates can become complicated by the use of technology-based formats. Ensuring that servers and storage are Health Information Portability and Accountability Act compliant, having the capacity to encrypt communication, and making sure that the computer or phone upon which one communicates are password protected and secure are all the responsibility of the individual counselor, even if he or she is providing services through an organization. As with all developing fields, care needs to be taken to ensure that ethical codes, regulations, and counselor training keep pace with that of the growth of the use of technology. There is little doubt that the trend toward technology-based services will continue to expand as we move forward in the 21st century.

▨ NEW FRONTIERS FOR ADVOCACY

As mentioned previously in this chapter, the bifurcated issues of professional advocacy and client advocacy emerged as major themes presented and endorsed by most of the authors of the chapters in this textbook. In this final section of discussion, concerning new professional frontiers for clinical mental health counselors, we emphasize the absolute importance of continued advocacy in the areas of Medicare reimbursement and licensure portability.

Medicare Reimbursement

One of the most significant barriers for clinical mental health counselors, and a frontier which needs to be crossed, is the lack of LPCs' ability to be reimbursed through Medicare. Medicare is the federal health insurance program that covers over 51 million Americans age 65 or older and approximately 8.6 million persons with disabilities (U.S. Center for Medicare & Medicaid Services Fast Facts, 2019). The program covers mental health services that are provided by clinical social workers, mental health clinical nurse specialists, and psychologists but does not currently recognize LPCs, despite their similar educational requirements, training, ethical and practice standards, and acceptance in many other behavioral and mental healthcare venues. Mental health treatment is an important part of any healthcare plan. This unsubstantiated limitation on who can provide treatment is a problem for counselors, but even more so for those who rely on Medicare for their health coverage needs. By restricting providers of mental health services, beneficiaries of Medicare are not afforded the same access to counseling services as those with private insurance. This clearly and readily becomes a social justice issue regarding access and equity.

Professional organizations like the ACA, the AMHCA, and NBCC have been engaged in lobbying efforts, for quite some time, to spur the federal government to enact legislation that would change the Medicare reimbursement rules. As the country's flagship healthcare program, it is essential that professional counselors be included in Medicare, so as to have parity with other mental health professions. There have been a number of bills that have been introduced into both the House and Senate in recent years, but none has been successful. Two bills that were both introduced in 2017 currently sit in committee. In the Senate, the Seniors Mental Health Access Improvement Act, S. 1879 was introduced by Senator John Barrasso (R-WY) and Debbie Stabenow (D-MI). This bill was referred to the Senate Finance Committee on 09/27/2017. In the House of Representatives, the Mental Health Access Improvement Act, H.R. 3032 was introduced by Representative John Katko (R-NY) and Mike Thompson (D-CA). This bill was referred to the House Subcommittee on Health on 07/05/2017. Both bills would allow LPCs to receive Medicare reimbursement for mental health services. Professional counseling organizations have continued to pursue this important legislative initiative, but it is also important for CMHCs to engage in this process by keeping abreast of developments regarding these issues and by contacting their Congressional representatives to express the importance of such legislation for professional counselors and those whom they serve.

Licensure Portability

Perhaps the single most important task for the future of the field of professional counseling is that of licensure portability. In 1976, Virginia was the first state to license professional counselors, thereby setting practice and educational standards. On October 11, 2009 California became the final state to achieve counselor licensure by passing California Senate Bill 788 (Shallcross, 2009). The success of this legislation meant that master's-level mental health counselors now could be licensed in all United States jurisdictions. Nationwide licensure has helped the profession advance in many ways, but the lack of standardization in licensure requirements continues to be a barrier to those in the field. Social work and psychology have both endorsed national standards that specify educational expectations and that detail the scope of practice for their license holders that are consistent across the country (Lawson, Trepal, Lee, & Kress, 2017). Counseling has adopted no such set of standards, which places limits upon counselors in transferring licensure from one state to another. Of further concern is that by not having standard requirements for education and supervised practice, it remains more difficult to present arguments to address and support the issues related to Medicare reimbursement, as discussed above. The federal government's position seems to be, in part, that it cannot recognize the qualifications of LPCs to provide services under Medicare, if the profession itself cannot say, unequivocally, what those qualifications are.

A number of organizations currently are working to advance the cause of uniformity of licensure standards and license portability for counseling. The NBCC, the American Mental Health Counselors Association (AMHCA), and the ACA all have concentrated advocacy efforts designed to advance this cause. Currently, these entities are focusing on the CACREP accreditation process as a mechanism to ensure the standardization of educational preparation of counselors and to create uniformity in state requirements (Lawson et al., 2017). In the past decade, Ohio, Kentucky, and North Carolina have changed their laws to require that independent practitioners must be graduates of a CACREP accredited program in order to obtain licensure. There has been a great deal of discussion about and resistance to using CACREP accreditation and the requirement that licensees be graduates of CACREP-accredited programs in order to attain licensure. Arguments have been made that this restriction places an undue burden on institutions of higher education, due to the associated costs of accreditation, faculty ratios, and the costs of ongoing accreditation efforts. Some assert that requiring graduation from schools accredited by a single body threatens the sustainability of the profession itself (Brady-Amoon, 2012; Hansen, 2012).

CACREP's status as the flagship accrediting body for professional counseling programs has not gone without challenge. In 2011, the Masters in Psychology and Counseling

Accreditation Council (MPCAC) announced its intent to begin to offer an alternative to CACREP (mpcacaccreditation.org, n.d., history). The MPCAC was inaugurated in advocacy for counseling psychology programs. One part of the contentiousness was that while CACREP accredits counseling and *related programs*, the American Psychological Association only accredits psychology programs; the promotion of the MPCAC seemed to emerge in response to CACREP strengthening its advocacy for the professional counseling field. To date, there are only 22 mental health and school counseling programs that have been accredited by this body (O'Connor & Bartoli, 2018) in contrast to 859 CACREP accredited programs (CACREP, 2018). As previously mentioned, CACREP accreditation is a mandated requirement of some state counselor licensure laws, whereas no state requires the MPCAC for licensure. The MPCAC stresses that it wishes to promote the range of counseling and psychological services that may be housed in various disciplines and to provide an accreditation option for master's degrees in psychology and counseling psychology, which are not accredited by the American Psychological Association (mpcacaccreditation.org, n.d., history). However, this assertion comes long after professional counseling and psychology have been established as separate-but-equal fields of practice. Quite importantly, MPCAC has not been recognized by the Commission on Higher Education Accreditation (CHEA), whereas CACREP and the American Psychological Association are recognized members of CHEA. This is an important consideration for students understanding the importance of graduating from an accredited program; it is also a consideration that is germane to the identity of being a professional counselor. It is this broader scope of accreditation against which those who favor the use of the CACREP standards must continue to push. Although using the requirement of graduation from a CACREP accredited program and the use of the CACREP standards as evidence that programs have prepared their graduates adequately and comprehensively for the profession appears to be somewhat controversial for some in the wider mental health profession, it is no different from the process that is endorse by psychology and social work. Graduation from an American Psychological Association accredited institution is a requirement for licensure as a psychologist (Danish & Smyer, 1981); likewise, graduation from a Council on Social Work Education (CSWE) accredited institution is generally required for master's-level social workers to apply for and maintain their state clinical licenses and national certifications (CSWE, 2019). In line with the movement to standardize the competencies of the field, starting January 1, 2022, NBCC (2014) will require a master's degree or higher from a CACREP-accredited counseling program in order to obtain their credential. Continued advocacy for CACREP's ongoing efforts to maintain the highest preservice educational standards for the profession of counseling is essential to the health of our profession.

CONCLUSION

The field of counseling is quite young in comparison to its helping profession counterparts. In the relatively short time that professional counseling has been a recognized discipline, it has grown and changed substantially. Since its roots in vocation and career guidance to its current status as an accepted provider of diagnostic, treatment, and integrated mental health interventions, counseling has solidified its place in the arena of behavioral and mental healthcare. Work remains to be done in further delineating our identity and forging a path into service provision in the 21st century, with all that this might entail. With our professional organizations and the advocacy efforts of our practitioners and educators, the future holds great promise for the further development of professional counseling as an important part of the field of mental health and wellness.

RESOURCES

American Counseling Association. Retrieved from www.counseling.org

American Counseling Association. (2019). *ACA interest networks.* Retrieved from https://www.counseling.org/aca-community/aca-connect/interest-networks

Betterhelp. Retrieved from www.betterhelp.com

Council for Accreditation of Counseling & Related Education Programs. Retrieved from www.cacrep.org

National Board for Certified Counselors. Retrieved from http://nbcc.org

Ratts, M. J., Singh, A. A., Nassar-McMillan, S., Butler, S. K., & McCullough, J. R. (2015). Multicultural and social justice counseling competencies. Retrieved from https://www.counseling.org/docs/default-source/competencies/multicultural-and-social-justice-counseling-competencies.pdf?sfvrsn=20

Talkspace. Retrieved from www.talkspace.com

REFERENCES

Akkurt, M. N., Carter, J., & Saint-Jean, F. (2013). What is wrong with multicultural training in America? *International Academic Conference on Social Sciences: Conference Proceedings* (No. 42, pp. 154–157). Retrieved from http://socscienceconf.com/admin/editor/uploads/files/IACSS%202013%20Proceedings%20Book.pdf

American Counseling Association. (2011). *The effectiveness of and need for professional counseling services.* Alexandria, VA: Author.

American Counseling Association. (2019). *ACA interest networks.* Retrieved from https://www.counseling.org/aca-community/aca-connect/interest-networks

American Foundation for Suicide Prevention. (2019). Retrieved from https://afsp.org

American School Counselor Association. (2003). *The ASCA National Model: A framework for school counseling programs.* Alexandria, VA: Author.

American School Counselor Association. (2012). *The ASCA National Model: A framework for school counseling programs* (3rd ed.). Alexandria, VA: Author.

Anderson, K. (2002). A response to common themes in school counseling. *Professional School Counseling, 5* (5), 315–322.

Astramovich, R., Hoskins, W., Gutierrez, A., & Bartlett, K. (2013). Identifying role diffusion in school counseling. *The Professional Counselor, 3,* 175–184. doi:10.15241/rla.3.3.175

Best Counseling Degrees. (2019). *What is forensic counseling?* Retrieved from https://www.bestcounselingdegrees.net/faq/what-is-forensic-counseling/

Bradley University. (n.d.). *How professional counselors can help address the opioid crisis.* Retrieved from https://onlinedegrees.bradley.edu/blog/how-professional-counselors-can-help-address-the-opioid-crisis/

Brady-Amoon, P. (2012). Further extending the humanistic vision for the future of counseling: A response to Hansen. *The Journal of Humanistic Counseling, 51,* 184–196. doi:10.1002/j.2161-1939.2012.00018.x

Chandler, J. W., Burnham, J. J., Riechel, M. E. K., Dahir, C. A., Stone, C. B., Oliver, D. F., ... Bledsoe, K. G. (2018). Assessing the counseling and non-counseling roles of school counselors. *Journal of School Counseling, 16* (7), n7.

Council for Accreditation of Counseling and Related Educational Programs. (2018). *CACREP 2017 annual report.* Retrieved from https://www.cacrep.org/about-cacrep/publications/cacrep-annual-reports/

Council on Social Work Education. (2019). *Social work education at a glance.* Retrieved from https://www.cswe.org/Students/Prepare-for-Your-Career/Social-Work-At-A-Glance

Currie, A., & Morse, E. D. (2005). Eating disorders in athletes: Managing the risks. *Clinical Sports Medicine, 24*, 871–883. doi:10.1016/j.csm.2005.05.005

Danish, S. J., & Smyer, M. A. (1981). Unintended consequences of requiring a license to help. *American Psychologist, 36* (1), 13. doi:10.1037/0003-066X.36.1.13

DeGruy, J. (2005). *Post traumatic slave syndrome: America's legacy of enduring injury and healing.* Milwaukie, OR: Uptone Press.

Dixon, C. G., Richard, M., & Rollins, C. W. (2003). Contemporary issues facing aging Americans: Implications for rehabilitation and mental health counseling. *Journal of Rehabilitation, 69* (2), 5.

Dollarhide, C. T., & Saginak, K. A. (2017). *Comprehensive school counseling programs: K-12 delivery systems in action* (3rd ed.). Boston, MA: Pearson.

Elleven, R., & Allen, J. (2004). Applying technology to online counseling: Suggestions for the beginning e-therapist. *Journal of Instructional Psychology, 31* (3), 223–227.

Fullen, M. C. (2016). Counseling for wellness with older adults. *Adultspan Journal, 15* (2), 109–123.

Gallagher, R. P. (2013). National survey of counseling 2012. Project Report. The International Association of Counseling Services (IACS). Retrieved from http://d-scholarship.pitt.edu/id/eprint/28175

Ghesquiere, A. R. (2018). Hospice services and grief support groups. In *Clinical handbook of bereavement and grief reactions* (pp. 241–258). New York, NY: Humana Press.

Ghesquiere, A. R., Aldridge, M. D., Johnson-Hürzeler, R., Kaplan, D., Bruce, M. L., & Bradley, E. (2015). Hospice services for complicated grief and depression: Results from a national survey. *Journal of the American Geriatrics Society, 63* (10), 2173–2180. doi:10.1111/jgs.13656

Goldman, W., McCulloch, J., & Sturm, R. (1998). Costs and use of mental health services before and after managed care: Six years of data show that managed behavioral health care has reduced mental health care costs for one large employer. *Health Affairs, 17* (2), 40–52. doi:10.1377/hlthaff.17.2.40

Hansen, J. T. (2012). Extending the humanistic vision: Toward a humanities foundation for the counseling profession. *The Journal of Humanistic Counseling, 51*, 133–144. doi:10.1002/j.2161-1939.2012.00011.x

Harris, B., & Birnbaum, R. (2015). Ethical and legal implications on the use of technology in counselling. *Clinical Social Work Journal, 43* (2), 133–141. doi:10.1007/s10615-014-0515-0

Hebard, S. P., & Lamberson, K. A. (2017). Enhancing the sport counseling specialty: A call for a unified identity. *Professional Counselor, 7* (4), 375–384.

Kraus, R. (2004). Ethical and legal considerations for providers of mental health services online. In R. Kraus, J. Zack, & G. Stricker (Eds.), *Online counseling: A handbook for mental health professionals* (pp. 123–144). San Diego, CA: Academic Press.

Kunik, M. E., Mills, W. L., Amspoker, A. B., Cully, J. A., Kraus-Schuman, C., Stanley, M., & Wilson, N. L. (2017). Expanding the geriatric mental health workforce through utilization of non-licensed providers. *Aging & Mental Health, 21* (9), 954–960. doi:10.1080/13607863.2016.1186150

Lambie, G. W., & Williamson, L. L. (2004). The challenge to change from guidance counseling to professional school counseling: A historical proposition. *Professional School Counseling, 8* (2), 124–131.

Lawson, G., Trepal, H. C., Lee, R. W., & Kress, V. (2017). Advocating for educational standards in counselor licensure laws. *Counselor Education and Supervision, 56*(3), 162–176.

Lee, P. (2011). The curious life of *in loco parentis* at American universities. *Higher Education in Review, 8,* 65–90. Retrieved from https://scholar.harvard.edu/files/philip_lee/files/vol8lee.pdf

Levers, L. L. (2012). Introduction to understanding trauma. In L. L. Levers (Ed.), *Counseling survivors of trauma: Theories and interventions.* New York, NY: Springer Publishing Company.

Levers, L. L., Biggs, B-A., & Strickler, A. (2015). International implications for addressing immigrant and refugee health issues. In E. Mpofu (Ed.), *Community-oriented health services: Practices across disciplines* (pp. 271–292). New York, NY: Springer Publishing Company.

Levers, L. L., & Mancilla, R. (2013). Educating the children of undocumented immigrant parents: The impact of trauma on citizen children's development. In F. E. McCarthy, M. H. Vickers, & E. Brown (Eds.), *International advances in education: Global initiatives for equity and social justice, Volume 6: Migrants and refugees: Equitable education for displaced populations* (pp. 51–72). Charlotte, NC: Information Age Publishing.

Mallen, M. J., Vogel, D. L., & Rochlen, A. B. (2005). The practical aspects of online counseling: Ethics, training, technology, and competency. *The Counseling Psychologist, 33* (6), 776–818. doi:10.1177/0011000005278625

Martinson, M., & Berridge, C. (2015). Successful aging and its discontents: A systematic review of the social gerontology literature. *The Gerontologist, 55,* 58–69. doi:10.1093/geront/gnu037

McMahon, S., & Fleury, J. (2012). Wellness in older adults: A concept analysis. *Nursing Forum, 47,* 39–51. doi:10.1111/j.1744-6198.2011.00254.x.

Mental Health Parity and Addiction Equity Act, Pub. L. 110-343, 122 Stat. 3765, amending 29 U.S.C. 1185a, § 712 (ERISA); 42 U.S.C. 300gg–5, § 2705 (Public Health Service Act); and I.R.C. § 9812 (Internal Revenue Code). (2008). Retrieved from https://www.medicare.gov/what-medicare-covers/your-medicare-coverage-choices/whats-medicare

Miller, G. M., & Wooten Jr., H. R. (1995). Sports counseling: A new counseling specialty area. *Journal of Counseling & Development, 74* (2), 172–173. doi:10.1002/j.1556-6676.1995.tb01845.x

Moye, J., Karel, M. J., Stamm, K. E., Qualls, S. H., Segal, D. L., Tazeau, Y. N., & DiGilio, D. A. (2018). Workforce analysis of psychological practice with older adults: Growing crisis requires urgent action. *Training and Education in Professional Psychology, 13* (1), 46–55. doi:10.1037/tep0000206

Mpofu, E., Levers, L. L., Mpofu, K., Tanui, P., & Hossain, Z. S. (2015). Family assessments in rehabilitation service provision. In M. Millington & I. Marini (Eds.), *Families in rehabilitation counseling: A community-based rehabilitation approach* (pp. 251–266). New York, NY: Springer Publishing Company.

Myers, J. E., & Harper, M. C. (2004). Evidence-based effective practices with older adults. *Journal of Counseling & Development, 82,* 207–219. doi:10.1002/j.1556-6678.2004.tb00304.x

National Board for Certified Counselors. (2014). *Important Announcement: Upcoming change to NBCC educational requirements.* Greensboro, NC: Author. Retrieved from htttps://nbcc.org/Assets/EducationalStandards.pdf

National Board for Certified Counselors. (2019). *Veterans affairs.* Retrieved from http://www.nbcc.org/GovtAffairs/Veterans

Nejedlo, R. J., Arredondo, P. M., & Benjamin, L. (1985). *Imagine: A visionary model for the counselors of tomorrow*. Counselors of Tomorrow Interest Network, Association for Counselor Education and Supervision.

O'Connor, P., & Bartoli, E. (2018). *MPCAC Annual report July 2017–June 2018*. Retrieved from http://mpcacaccreditation.org/wp-content/uploads/2018/07/MPCAC-Annual-report -2017-18.pdf

Office of Alcoholism and Substance Abuse Services. (n.d.). *FYI: Elderly alcohol and substance abuse*. Retrieved from https://www.oasas.ny.gov/admed/fyi/fyiindepth-elderly.cfm

Patel, V. (2019, February 18). The New "In Loco Parentis." *Chronical of Higher Education*. Retrieved from https://www.chronicle.com/interactives/Trend19-InLoco-Main?cid=at&utm_source=at &utm_medium=en&elqTrackId=bcfeceb76b6842daad93c15734c0d607&elq=cec9c056e551 4cd0bd9c83490dbd699d&elqaid=22287&elqat=1&elqCampaignId=10969

Paternite, C. E. (2005). School-based mental health programs and services: Overview and introduction to the special issue. *Journal of Abnormal Child Psychology, 33* (6), 657. doi:10.1007/s10802-005-7645-3

Patient Protection and Affordable Care Act; HHS Notice of Benefit and Payment Parameters for 2012, 78 Fed. Reg. 15410. (2013, March 11). (to be codified at 45 C.F.R. pts. 153, 155, 156, 157, & 158).

President's New Freedom Commission on Mental Health. (2003). *Achieving the Promise: Transforming Mental Health Care in America. Final Report for the President's New Freedom Commission on Mental Health (SMA Publication No. 03-3832)*. Rockville, MD: Author.

Price, M., Yuen, E. K., Goetter, E. M., Herbert, J. D., Forman, E. M., Acierno, R., & Ruggiero, K. J. (2014). mHealth: A mechanism to deliver more accessible, more effective mental health care. *Clinical Psychology & Psychotherapy, 21* (5), 427–436. doi:10.1002/cpp.1855

Prince, J. P. (2015). University student counseling and mental health in the United States: Trends and challenges. *Mental Health & Prevention, 3* (1–2), 5–10.

Raglin, J. S., & Wilson, G. S. (2000). Overtraining in athletes. In Y. Hanin (Ed.), *Emotions in sport* (pp. 191–207). Champaign, IL: Human Kinetics.

Ratts, M. J., Singh, A. A., Butler, S. K., Nassar-McMillan, S., & McCullough, J. R. (2016, January 27). Multicultural and social justice counseling competencies: Practical applications in counseling. *Counseling Today*. Retrieved from https://ct.counseling.org/tag/ multiculturalism-diversity/

Richards, D., & Vigano, N. (2013). Online counseling: A narrative and critical review of the literature. *Journal of Clinical Psychology, 69* (9), 994–1011. doi:10.1002/jclp.21974

Riemer-Reiss, M. L. (2000). Utilizing distance technology for mental health counseling. *Journal of Mental Health Counseling, 22* (3), 189–203.

Shallcross, L. (2009, December). Counseling profession reaches the big 5-0. *Counseling Today*.

Stephan, S. H., Weist, M., Kataoka, S., Adelsheim, S., & Mills, C. (2007). Transformation of children's mental health services: The role of school mental health. *Psychiatric Services, 58* (10), 1330–1338. doi:10.1176/ps.2007.58.10.1330

Substance Abuse and Mental Health Services Administration. (2018). *Behavioral Health Services for American Indians and Alaska Natives: For Behavioral Health Service Providers, Administrators, and Supervisors: TIP 61*. Retrieved from https://store.samhsa.gov/system/ files/tip_61_aian_full_document_020419_0.pdf

Sue, D. W., Arredondo, P., & McDavis, R. J. (1992). Multicultural counseling competencies and standards: A call to the profession. *Journal of Counseling & Development, 70,* 477–486.

Sue, D. W., Sue, D., Neville, H. A., & Smith, L. (2019). *Counseling the culturally diverse: Theory and practice* (8th ed.). Hoboken, NJ: Wiley.

TRICARE Certified Mental Health Counselors. Federal Register, Department of Defense (79)137. (2014, July 17, Thursday).

U.S. Census Bureau. (2017). *National population projection datasets*. Retrieved from https://www.census.gov/data/datasets/2017/demo/popproj/2017-popproj.html

U.S. Centers for Medicare & Medicaid Services. (2019). *Medicare.gov*. Retrieved from https://www.cms.gov/fastfacts/

U.S. Department of Labor, Bureau of Labor Statistics. (2019). *Occupational outlook handbook*. Retrieved from http://www.bls.gov/ooh

Watkins, D. C., Hunt, J. B., & Eisenberg, D. (2012). Increased demand for mental health services on college campuses: Perspectives from administrators. *Qualitative Social Work, 11* (3), 319–337. doi:10.1177/1473325011401468

INDEX

school, 27–28. *See also* school counselors

scope of practice of. *See* scope of practice of counselors

wellness, 283, 289, 295–300. *See also* wellness

countertransference, 33, 155, 268, 273, 282, 283–284

CPTSD. *See* complex posttraumatic stress disorder

CRANIUM care model, 132–133

CRC. *See* Certified Rehabilitation Counselor

CRCC. *See* Commission on Rehabilitation Counselor Certification

credentials/credentialing, 16, 18, 19, 23, 24, 26, 27, 35, 153, 164–165, 168, 169, 252

crisis
  counseling, 16, 74, 93–95
  definitions, 93–94
  intervention models for counseling, 94–95
  management, 60, 94, 313
  types, 93

CS. *See* compassion satisfaction

CFST. *See* Compassion Fatigue Self-Test

CSI. *See* Chi Sigma Iota

cultural and systemic influences, 215–238
  access to mental healthcare, increase of, 227–228
  barriers to mental healthcare, 224–227
  CODAC system, 222–223
  integrated systems of care, 220–222
  mental health disparities due to, 216–217, 221, 226–227
  multicultural counseling competencies, 229–237. *See also* multicultural counseling
  racism and discrimination, 226–227
  sociocultural systems worldview, 217–218
  systems worldview, 218–222

cultural competence, 17, 218
  multi-, 234, 251

cultural concept of distress (CCD), 232

cultural humility, 8, 17

CVW. *See* community virtual ward

DAP. *See* data, assessment, and plan

data, assessment, and plan (DAP), 148

diagnoses/diagnosis, 81–86, 131
  clinical tensions, 84–85. *See also* clinical tensions

the DSM system of, 81–84
  dual, 71–72

Diagnostic and Statistical Manual of Mental Disorders (DSM), 9, 72, 81–85, 110, 289
  cultural concept of distress, 232
  disorders list in *DSM V*, 81–82
  limitations of the system, 82–83
  strengths of the system, 82
  trauma-related diagnoses, 104–105

disasters, 95–98
  climate change, 96
  definition, 95
  preparedness to adaptation, 96–98
  types, 96

diversity, cultural
  client, 16, 20, 28, 127, 173, 216–217, 229, 231, 234, 236, 238, 319
  sensitivity of counselors to, 18, 20, 28, 81, 173, 191, 195, 206, 216–217, 229, 232–233

documentation. *See* record keeping and documentation

DSM. *See* Diagnostic and Statistical Manual of Mental Disorders

EBPs. *See* evidence-based practices

EHR. *See* electronic health records

ElderLynk community outreach model, 132, 133

electronic health records (EHR), 144, 155, 156, 208, 211

electronic medical records (EMR). *See* electronic health records

empathetic engagement, 265, 267, 282–283, 284, 285, 286, 288, 291

ethical decision-making, 19, 151, 164, 169–171, 174–176, 178–180
  model, 174–175, 178–179, 180

ethical dilemmas, 11, 19, 151, 170–171, 173–180, 323
  conflict between ethical principles, 173–174, 176
  ethical stance, 172, 175
  legal stance, 172, 175
  moral stance, 171, 176, 177
  resolution of conflicts, 176–178
  role of consultation in, 175–179
  stakeholder perspectives in, 174

CPSIA information can be obtained
at www.ICGtesting.com
Printed in the USA
BVHW092147081222
653779BV00004B/14